Legends of the Dispossessed

Anthony Nugent

To ~~Eoin Colla~~

with compliments

Anthony Nugent

© **2009 Anthony Nugent**

ISBN: 978-1-907107-05-4

A CIP catalogue for this book is available from the National Library.

This book was published in cooperation with
Choice Publishing & Book Services Ltd, Drogheda, Co Louth, Ireland
Tel: 041 9841551 Email: info@choicepublishing.ie
www.choicepublishing.ie

Legends of the Dispossessed

A compendium of legends, poems, songs, official documents, observations and diaries, which highlight the social effects and cultural history of that period, in Ireland, which can best be described as the Penal Times.

Abstract

What effect, if any, did the dispossession of the native Irish, and subsequent English settlement in Ireland have on the folklore of Ireland? This work is devoted to the legends, traditional narratives, poems, ballads, and recitations concerning the people and events of that turbulent period in Irish history from the English Reformation in 1527 to the passing of the Catholic Emancipation Act in1829. It is framed against a background of official documents, private letters of individuals involved at high levels of government and diaries belonging to soldiers and chaplains who were participants and observers to the events recorded.

Some of these narratives are best exemplified in written sources which are indebted to a greater or lesser extent, to oral tradition current at the time of writing.

There are a number of versions of stories collected directly from oral sources in the Irish Folklore Collection Archive of the Department of Irish Folklore, University College Dublin. I have consulted the relevant manuscript sources in the Archive, and have transcribed, translated, or edited the narratives for the purpose of this work. I have endeavored to contain this work within chapters in chronological order but some individuals and events overshadow one another.

Acknowledgements

I wish to thank the founders of Saor-Ollscoil na hÉireann, whose vision and dedication to the concept of a free university, made it possible for me to engage in the study, which was necessary, before this work could begin, and to all the tutors for their help and advice over many years.
Special thanks to Father John J. Ó'Ríordáin for his invaluable advice .
Special thanks to Professor Patricia Lysaght, and to all the tutors and staff at the Department of Irish Folklore U.C.D.
Special thanks to Professor Dathaí O'hÓgáin for his wisdom and wit, and for permission to use material from his encyclopaedia of The Irish Folk Tradition <u>Myth, Legend & Romance.</u>
In particular I wish to thank my daughter Laoise, for the cover design and without whose help and computer skills this work would not have seen paper.
To Dermot McCabe for his time and expertise in proof-reading the manuscript.
To my wife, Esther, for her patience and encouragement.
The the staff at the National Library in Kildare Street.
To the staff at the Irish Traditional - Music Archives in Merrion Square.
To the staff at The Dublin City Council Library at Cabra Cross
To the staff at the County Library Wexford
To the manager of Dublin Castle for permission to use Penal Cross

This book is dedicated to the memory of my father Patrick Nugent, and my mother Bridget Nugent. May they rest in peace.

Contents

List of Illustrations

Introduction

The Henrician Reformation

Giraldus Combrensis informs us in 1189, that the English Pope, Adrian IV issued his bull, *Laudabiliter,* granting the Lordship of Ireland to Henry II of England.

"Adrian, bishop, servant of the servants of God, to our well-beloved son in Christ the illustrious king of the English, greeting and apostolic benediction, whereas then, well-beloved son in Christ, you have expressed to us your desire to enter the island of Ireland in order to subject its people to law and root out from them the weeds of vice, and your willingness to pay annual tribute to the blessed Peter of one penny from every house, and to maintain the rights of the churches of that land whole and inviolate: we therefore... do hereby declare our will and pleasure that, with a view to enlarging the boundries of the Church, restraining the downward course of vice, correcting evil customs and planting virtue, and for the increase of Christian religion, you shall enter the island and execute whatsoever may tend to the honour of God and the welfare of the land; and also the people of the land shall receive you with honour and revere you as their lord..."[1]

Following the Simnel conspiracy in 1488. The Pope commanded the ecclesiastical authorities in Ireland to give allegiance to Henry VII[2].

In the year 1517 Martin Luther, a Catholic monk, nailed 95 theses or grievances, to the door of the Cathedral of Wittenberg, in Germany. They protested against multiple abuses within the church and argued for reform, thereby causing the beginning of a movement, which became known as the Reformation. Some of the abuses which Martin Luther attacked were revenue generating exercises, for example the sale of indulgences, and the sale of the sacraments. He also protested against the role of the priest as intermediary between God and man. He held that all individuals can have, and should have direct access to God. Those who agreed with him became known as Protestants, and the movement as a whole became known as the Protestant Reformation. In the year 1521 King Henry VIII of England wrote his Defence of the Seven Sacraments *[Assertio Septem Sacramentorum]*. This work defended the position that the Pope is appointed by God as head of the Church, and that it is his office, as such, to give final judgment about the meaning of Scripture. In recognition of this work Pope Leo X conferred

---

[1] From Expugnatio Hibernica, The Conquest of Ireland by Giraldus Combrensis 1189
[2] May 5 1487 Lambert Simnel who claimed to be the Earl of Warwick with 2000 Merceneries lands in Ireland, , crowned King Edward V1 in Christchurch Cathedral Dublin on May 24. Edward V1's Yorkist army lands near Furness and is defeated by Henry V11 at Stoke on June 16.

on Henry the title of Defender of the Faith, a title still used by the English Monarch.

This, Protestant Reformation, had little if any direct impact in Ireland. In 1527 Henry VIII of England sought a divorce from his first wife, Catherine of Aragon, so that he might marry Anne Boleyn. Henry was convinced that Anne Boleyn would produce the male heir he desired. For more than three years he constantly petitioned Pope Clement VII to grant him an annulment, but to no avail. Finally, in desperation, with Anne Boleyn pregnant, in 1533, he declared himself head of the church in England. In 1536 the Irish Parliament enacted the Act of Supremacy which conferred upon Henry VIII of England the title of supreme head on earth of the whole Church of Ireland. In 1530 there was little likelihood that Ireland would become a Protestant country. Unlike Lollardy in England there was no native tradition of heresy. Lutheranism had not gained a foothold, like it had, at the universities in England during the 1520's. There was little direct trading between the Netherlands and Ireland, so the avenue by which some aspects of Protestantism were brought to England by merchants and traders, was not open. There was no tradition of anticlericalism in Ireland. There was no pamphlet war between the ecclesiastical authorities and those proposing reform of the Catholic Church. The political-cultural divide which existed in Ireland at that time created many problems for the enforcing of Tudor ecclesiastical legislation.

For example in order to impose religious reform in Gaelic Ireland, they would first have to secure political conquest by force of arms. In the month of May 1536 The Irish Parliament enacted the Act of Supremacy which conferred upon Henry VIII of England the title of supreme head on earth of the whole Church of Ireland. There was general acceptance of Henry as supreme head of the Church of Ireland among the Anglo-Irish, who saw it as part of a political development which would help to civilize the Gaelic Irish. It is worth noting that this programme of reformation was confined to the area of the Pale. Outside the Pale, the friars in particular preached against these reforms. One report from O'Donnell's country claimed that the lower clergy "preach daily that every man ought, for the salvation of his soul, fight and make war' against the king and that all who died in the attempt would go straight to heaven". In the autumn of 1538, Thomas Cromwell sent to Ireland a version of the New Injunctions. This required the clergy to preach the gospel quarterly, to discourage superstitious practices, such as," wanderings to pilgrimages, offerings.... to feigned relics or images, and vain repetition of prayer over beads".
In may 1539, the English Parliament passed the Act of the Six Articles. These six articles reasserted the orthodoxy of the State Church against Lutheran influences by affirming, transubstantiation, communion under

one species, private masses, auricular confession, clerical celibacy, and the religious vows of chastity, poverty and obedience. In 1542 Henry VIII was proclaimed King of Ireland. This had the effect of removing any legal or quasi-legal connection between the Crown of England and Rome concerning the government of Ireland, which existed under the Lordship of Ireland which owed its legality to a Papal bull. Coupled with the policy of surrender and re-grant, which was devised by Henry and his ministers to separate the Gaelic chiefs from their ancient customs, laws, language, the legal system under which they held their power, the way was set for the conquest of Gaelic Ireland.

Silken Thomas (Lord Offaly) Tenth Earl of Kildare 1513-1537

When Gerald *(Gearóid Óg)* ninth Earl of Kildare answered a summons to London in 1534 he left his son Thomas, Lord Offaly, behind as his deputy. When Kildare was refused permission to return to Ireland, Thomas, fearing for his fathers safety, went into rebellion. He was in possession of information written by Skeffington's secretary, that, he and his five uncles were to be arrested and conveyed to London and there executed. On June 11 1534, before the Irish Council, in the Chapter House of St Mary's Abbey, Silken Thomas resigned the Sword of State in public defiance of Henry VIII. He issued a proclamation that all Englishmen should leave the Lordship of Ireland at once on pain of death. He denounced Henry VIII as a heretic and demanded that all should give oaths of allegiance to the Pope and to himself also.

When news of the rebellion reached England, Henry VIII had Kildare arrested and imprisoned in the Tower of London on June 29th, where he died on September 30th. At this stage the rebellion was widespread and Thomas had the support of the majority of Irish chieftains with the exception of the O'Donnell. The rebels had control of the Pale and the only opposition to them came from the Butlers. In October Skeffington landed with an army of 2300 men and including the latest in field ordnance. During the winter of 1534-35 Thomas supporters drifted away. In the spring of 1535 when ground conditions were suitable Skeffington attacked the fortress at Maynooth.

With the fall of Maynooth the rebellion collapsed and on August 24th of the same year Thomas surrendered (on condition of life and limb). He was incarcerated in the Tower of London for a period of one year and four months when, on the 3rd of February 1537, he and his five uncles were brought to Tyburn and executed.

The Chapter House of St Mary's Abbey Dublin

Our Lady of Dublin

This unique survival from medieval Dublin can be seen today in the Carmelite Church, Whitefriar Street Dublin. It is possibly one of the most interesting and historical of all the statues in Dublin. This life-size model of Our Lady and the Child Jesus, carved from oak, is believed to date from the fifteenth century and although the name of the sculptor is unknown, its gothic style suggests a German origin.

It is believed that the statue was originally commissioned for St Mary's Abbey which was founded in 1156 and was suppressed during the Henrician Reformation in 1544.

It is said that the statue was originally adorned with a silver crown, which was removed and used for the coronation of Lambert Simnel (as King Edward V1), in Christchurch Cathedral on May 24th 1487. In 1544 St Mary's Abbey was suppressed by Henry VIII of England and granted to the Earl of Ormonde, who, is said to have used it as a stable. According to tradition it was ordered that the statue be destroyed and the back of the statue was burned before it was rescued and taken to an inn where it was placed face downwards and the hollowed out back used as a drinking trough for animals. The back of the statue would have been hollowed out prior to carving. During the early period of the Penal Laws the whereabouts of the statue was unknown, but it is reputed to have been seen in the old church of St Michan's Parish, Mary's Lane in 1749, where it stood at the Epistle side of the High Altar. The present Parish Church of St Michans was built in 1817 and the statue seems to have vanished during its construction.

Tradition holds that the Prior of Whitefriars Street the Reverend Dr John Spratt, while walking down Capel Street spotted the statue in the window of a pawn-shop. He bought it and brought it to Whitefriar Street where it is today.

There is an other tradition that the Rev Spratt while walking down Capel Street on another occasion spotted the silver crown which used to adorn the statue, in the window of an antique dealers shop and that he immediately purchased it.

The Carmelite Church in Whitefriar Street, Dublin was opened on the 11th of November 1827 and the statue was placed on the Epistle side of the Altar. In 1915 the Shrine to Our Lady of Dublin was formally erected in the church and the statue was placed in a prominent position above the Altar of Our Lady of Dublin. Here after centuries of abuse and degradation this beautiful work of art has at last found a suitable home and has been a source of spiritual inspiration for many Dubliners.[3]

---

[3] Pamphlet by the late Eamon Chandler, available at Whitefriat St.

Altar to Our Lady of Dublin, Whitefriar Street Church

Fr. David Wolfe

Fr. David Wolfe, a Jesuit from the City of Limerick, was appointed Papal Legate for Ireland in the year 1560. He was a prisoner in Dublin Castle from 1567 until 1572 when he made good his escape and fled to Europe. In 1574 he went to Spain to intercede with the King of Spain for armed intervention into Ireland as part of the Counter Reformation. This is the same (david woolf) mentioned in the Drury Document of 1577. The following is an extract taken from his work *Description of Ireland* which was written in 1574 while he was in Spain.

"The third part of Munster is called Thomond, and its lord up to our time is called O'Brien... In times past he was always king of all Munster and often monarch of the whole island. Not wishing to allow such a renowned name to continue in that country, Henry VIII, about the year 1540, called over to England him who was then O'Brien, and made him lay aside the name and called him earl of Thomond. Today the lord of that country is Cornelius O'Brien, earl of Thomond, and he has a few lords in his country who obey him, but there are other nobles of the same nation who make continual war on him and they are; Baron Inchiquin, the two MacNamaras who are great lords and the two MacMahons also great lords. There are O'Loughlin, O'Grady, O'Connor Corcomroe, Lord Donald O'Brien, and many other noble knights and gentlemen of Spanish descent, who have not the title of lord although they have large territories, castles, and towns, but the majority of these do not obey the earl, because he takes the side of the English and they do the opposite. In Thomond there is no city, or even seaports, although the earl holds many beautiful castles near the river Shannon, where ships may have safe anchor in any storm, but there is no commerce with these castles or towns. In Thomond are many mines of metal and silver, and so indeed in the whole island in abundance, the earl Cornelius worked them with much profit, but the English do not allow him to work them any longer, and he was exiled from his country by Lady Elizabeth in the year 1571 but was afterwards received back into the Queen's favour through the intercession of the King of France, although he is none too secure in his dominion or safe from the wickedness and perfidy of Lady Elizabeth.[4]"

Sir William Drury

Sir William Drury, was appointed Lord President of Munster on June 20th 1576. On June 26th he was issued with a royal commission as Lord President to execute martial law in the counties of Tipperary, Limerick, Cork and Kerry, and in all cities and corporate towns, and to punish by death or otherwise any persons found to be felons, rebels, enemies or notorious evil-doers. This was part of the programme for the Elizabethan conquest of Ireland. In a letter to the Privy Council dated March 24th 1577 Waterford he recounts, "His service against the O Mores. Justice betwixt the gentlemen of the borders next Ormond. Sir William O Carrol's pledges. The people in general like justice, and her majesty's revenue are much increased thereby. Limerick Castle re-edified, Castlemange, which is a principle place, and other castles kept by Drury. Englishmen appointed sherrifs in Desmond and Thomond. Drury has executed 400, for many of whose lives he might have had large sums had he been unjust. The Earl of Desmonds commendation. James FitzMaurice having put to sea with David Wolf to come to Ireland, took an English ship and sent the men to the Inquisition, where they were executed, French preparations at Brest, Nantes and St Malo".[5]

---

[4] Ronan Myles. V, <u>The Reformation in Ireland under Elizabeth</u> (Dublin 1930 p 484)
[5] Calendar of State Papers Ireland-Elizabeth 1574 -1585 Vol IX N.L.I. RR941

April 14 Dungarvin.

President Drury to Walsyngham.

"The intelligence from France is worthy of consideration, incloses Intelligence. The French King is at Blois, where he will remain for four months, pacifying the troubles. James FitzMaurice has gone to the Pope to get his benediction and aid; after his return he will, with a host of French soldiers under M de la Roche, M Daukin and his brother, invade Munster. James will visit the Kings of Spain and Portugal who will give him of their treasures. David Wolf will be sent to the Indies. The spiritual benefices of Munster are all granted by the Pope to James's men. Letters brought from Wexford to James. Two priests from Rome with letters from James will sail presently for Wexford. Plot for the Turk to invade Germany; The French King to persecute the French Protestants and James FitzMaurice to invade Ireland simultaneously".[6]

"A new President, William Drury by name was appointed over the two provinces of Munster this year; and Thomond was separated from Connaught and joined to Munster. The same president made a circuit of the great towns of Munster to establish laws and regulations for the extirpation of thieves and rebels, and put the Barrot to death, and also two noble and valiant young constables of the descendants of Mulmurry, the son of Donough, son of Turlough [MacSweeny], the son of Murrough, son of Mulmurry,and the son of Donough, son of Turlough. From thence [i.e. from Barrot's country] he proceeded to Limerick, where he hanged several of the gentlemen and common people of the O'Briens, and many others besides."[7]

Tobernalt

Holy Well and Mass-Rock

Take the Lough Gill road out of Sligo Town and you will pass Cleaveragh (the place of the basket makers). *Cliabh* -small basket. It was here that sally was grown (salix-willow) for the purpose of basket weaving. This is the Sally Gardens made famous by William Butler Yeats in his poem,

Down by the Salley Gardens

Down by the salley gardens my love and I did meet;
She passed the salley gardens with little snow white feet.
She bid me take love easy, as the leaves grow on the tree;
But I, being young and foolish, with her would not agree.

---

[6] Calendar of State Papers Ireland – Elizabeth Vol LVIII 1577 April - July
[7] Annals of The Kingdom of Ireland 1577 (Annals of The Four Masters)

In a field by the river my love and I did stand,
And on my leaning shoulder she laid her snow-white hand.
She bid me take life easy, as the grass grows on the weirs;
But I was young and foolish, and now am full of tears.

It is said that Yeats was inspired to write this poem when he heard a broadsheet ballad seller singing 'Ye Rambling Boys of Pleasure' at a fair in Ballysadare.

"Down in yon flowery garden where me and my true love did meet
I took her in my arms and to her I gave kisses sweet
She bade me take love easy just as the leaves fall from yon tree
But I being young and foolish with my true love could not agree."

Continue on this road with the lake to the left and you will come upon the Holy Well of Tobernalt on the right hand side of the road. Some say that Tobernalt *(Tobar-an-Ailt)* means the Well of the Cliff, whilst others claim it means, *(Tobar-na-nGealt)* The Well of the Lunatics because people came here to be cured of madness.

I met a man doing the rounds at the well who claimed to have been cured of blindness at the well when he was thirteen years of age. Lady Wilde relates the following story in her book, <u>Ancient Legends Mystic Charms and Superstitions of Ireland,</u>

The Grilled Trout

"In Sligo there is a well called *Tober-na-alt,* beautifully shadowed by trees, the branches of which are thickly hung with all sorts of votive offerings from those who have been cured by the water; and miracle men attended, who professed to heal disease by charms prayers, and incantations".

"A man who had been born blind once recited his experience there."Oh Christians, look at me! I was blind from my birth and saw no light till I came to the blessed well; now I see the water and the speckled trout down at the bottom, with the white cross on his back, Glory be to God for the cure". And when the people heard that he could see the speckled trout, of course they all believed in the miracle. For a tradition exists that a sacred trout has lived there from time immemorial, placed in the well by the saint who first sanctified the water. Now there was an adventurous man who desired much to get possession of this trout, and he watched it till at last he caught it asleep. Then he carried it off and put it on the gridiron. The trout bore the grilling of one side very patiently; but when the man tried to turn it on the fire, the trout suddenly jumped up and made off as hard as it could back to the well, where it still lives, and can be seen at times by those who have done proper penance and paid their dues to the priest, with one side all streaked and marked brown by the bars of the gridiron, which can never be effaced".

In front of the well there is an altar built up from stones and approximately 120 cm x 90cm by 100cm in height. This is the Mass-Rock which was used during the time of the Penal Laws. Here the people would congregate at the break of dawn, with look-outs keeping vigil from the top of Carn Hill. The priest would appear from among the crowd, celebrate mass, dispense the sacraments and then vanish into the crowd.

The site at Tobernalt now contains a grotto to our lady of Lourdes, a representation of the Crucifixion, and the Stations of the Cross. To the right of the altar is a brass plaque bearing the inscription,

"Pilgrim walk softly this is holy ground.
It has been made holy by the feet of generations.
Who came here to worship God.
To hear mass.
To honour our Lady.
To pray for their needs and for peace.
Here are memories of a poor persecuted people.
They braved death to come.
They walked barefoot through the woods.
To worship in secret.
There are memories of hunted priests.
Offering mass in this hallowed place.
At the risk of their lives.
They have handed us a torch.
Let us keep that torch alight.
Will their suffering and sacrifices.
Be in vain.

The holy well and Mass-Rock, enshrined within a grove of green and scented plants, to this day draws a constant stream of people here, to pray and reflect upon their lives. The people of Sligo gather each year at Tobernalt to celebrate Garland Sunday, which is held on the last Sunday in July.

Tobernalt – Holy Well and Mass-Rock

James Fitzmaurice Fitzgerald

James Fitzmaurice Fitzgerald, was the cousin of the Earl of Desmond. During the imprisonment of the Earl in the Tower of London, he was elected Captain of the Geraldines. By 1569 he was in open rebellion. He condemned Queen Elizabeth I as a heretic who was trying to force the Irish, "To forsake the Catholic faith by God unto his church given." At a meeting of rebel leaders it was decided to seek aid from Spain, and offer the crown of Ireland to Phillip II. Maurice Mac Gabhan, the Catholic Archbishop of Cashel, led a delegation to Spain, where they were granted an audience with the king. They condemned, Henry VIII, Edward VI1, and Elizabeth I as schismatics and offered the Irish crown to "Any Catholic and valiant prince" that Phillip would nominate. This unqualified denunciation of Elizabeth's regal authority, which was supposedly signed by four Archbishops, eight Bishops, and thirteen nobles is unique in that it gave the rebellion the character of a religious war supported by the Catholic Church. James Fitzmaurice fled to France in 1573 seeking aid, when this was not forthcoming he moved to Spain where we find him in 1577. Two years later

11

in1579 he returned with a small invasion force, consisting of one ship and three fishing vessels and a force consisting of eighty Spaniards some Italians, a number of Irish and English expatriates. Along with them was Nicholas Saunders who was the Papal Legate, also a brother of Cardinal Allen. He issued a proclamation calling on all Irishmen to forget their quarrels, and take up arms under the papal standard, to fight a just war against Elizabeth. Shortly afterwards James Fitzmaurice was killed in a skirmish with the Burkes, and his force was dispersed around the province.

Dún an Óir

A sequel to the Fitzmaurice rebellion, was the departure on August 28 1580 of a fleet of six ships, from Santander, carrying between 700 and 800, Spanish , Italian, and Irish troops under the command of Sebastino de San Guiseppe, their course set for the Dingle peninsula in support of the Desmond rebellion They arrived at Smerwick harbour in September that same year, and proceeded to re-fortify, *Dún an Óir [Castel del Orro }* = The Golden Castle, a small promontory fort on the west side of the harbour. Before they could complete this work, they were besieged by a government force, under the command of Lord Grey, who was joined on land, by a force under the command of the Earl of Ormond. The harbour was blockaded by Admiral Winter and his fleet. The siege only lasted three days, despite the fact that the fort had provisions enough to last six months, and enough arms and ammunition for four thousand men. On Novenber 5th, the fort was blockaded by sea by Admiral Winter's fleet, and two days later, it was invested by land by Lord Grey and the Earl of Ormond.

Don Bernadino de Mendoza, the Spanish Ambassador to London, wrote to King Phillip II on December 11, "After firing a few shots they dismantled one of the cannons in the Fort, and the besieged at once hoisted a white flag to parley. Notwithstanding that they made not the slightest resistance and did not fire a shot, the Viceroy delayed parleying with them, in the fear that it might be a stratagem to keep him in check until Desmond arrived and attacked him in the rear; since it was impossible for any soldier to believe that there could be so few brave men in the Fort, which they had been strengthening for two months, as to surrender without striking a blow. On being told that, 'they came by orders of the Pope', Grey said he could not treat them as soldiers but simply as thieves. Notwithstanding this, they surrendered on condition of their lives being spared. Twelve of the leaders came out, and were told to order their men to lay down their arms. When this was done the Viceroy sent a company of his men to take possession of the Fort on the 10th; and they slaughtered 507 men who were in it and some pregnant women. Besides which they hanged 17 Irish and

Englishmen, among whom, was an Irishman named Plunkett, a priest and an English servant of Dr Saunders."

In the Fort were found 200 corselets and arquebusses and other weapons sufficient to arm 4,000 men, besides great stores of victuals and munitions enough to last for months, in addition to money. Saunders describes Sebastion de San Giuseppe as being, "A most vile and wicked man" being "avaricious and luxurious and effeminate and arrogant".

Memorial stone at the location of Gort-na-Gearadh.

The garrison of about 600 surrendered on October 10 and all but twenty were massacred on the same day. According to local tradition the victims of the massacre were be-headed in a nearby field known as *Gort na Gearadh* = The Field of the Cutting, which lies 500 metres to the south of the fort, local tradition also holds that, the bodies which were subsequently washed up from the sea were interred at Teampall Bán in Caherquin townland. It is said that the executions were carried out under orders from Captain Walter Raleigh, this is disputed by some historians.

Sir Walter Raleigh

According to the Acts of the Privy Council for 11 July 1580, "Walter Raleigh, gentleman, by the appointment of the Lord Grey is to have charge of one hundred of those men presently levied within the City of London to be transported for her Majesty's service into Ireland."

The following anecdote is told about Walter Raleigh on his march from Cork to Smerwick. It had come to his notice that soon after the English left an encampment the Irish kernes would come to glean whatever was left behind.One day he decided to lay an ambush after they had moved camp. When the Kernes arrived they were all rounded up. One of the prisoners was carrying a large bundle of withies on his back. Raleigh asked him what they were for. "To hang up the English churls with", the man answered. "Is it so?" Raleigh replied. "Well, they shall now serve for an Irish Kerne". He then arranged for the man to be hanged with his own withies.

After the surrender of Dún-an-Óir the prisoners were stripped of their armour and weapons and were herded back into the fort. The fort was searched and a number of Irish women were dragged out along with the priests, Plunkett and Walsh and a friar named Moore. Gallows were erected and the women were hanged despite their pleas of pregnancy.The priests were taken into Smerwick village, where their arms and legs were smashed on an anvil by the local blacksmith. They were then put in a shed for two days without food or water, and afterwards brought to the gallows where they were hanged, drawn and quartered.

Two hundred soldiers under the command of Captains Mackworth and Raleigh were sent into the fort to slaughter the prisoners under the system known as "hewing and punching" that is, slashing at the neck followed by a stab in the belly. The corpses were then stripped and thrown onto the beach below.

It is claimed that Sir Walter Raleigh introduced the potatoe to Ireland.

> They say Sir Walter Raleigh
> So it's generally agreed
> Implanted in our valleys fair
> The first prolific seed.
> There sprang from out the fertile soil
> At least that's what we're told
> With eager care and earnest toil
> A crop a hundred-fold

Shane the Proud

When Conn Bachach O'Neill – Conn the Lame- surrendered up the O'Neill title to the English, and accepted the English title, Baron of Dungannon, his son Shane went into rebellion. On the death of his father, he slew his half-brother, the next Baron, and was inaugurated The O'Neill. He was known to his people as Shane the Proud. Queen Elizabeth and her Lord Deputies tried all forms of diplomacy, deceit, armed aggression, even poison to bring him under the control of the Crown. On one occasion, Sussex, the Lord Deputy, sent a force to capture Armagh and left a garrison there.They were returning to Dublin with their booty when Shane and his followers fell upon them and recaptured the booty. The Lord Deputy wished to make terms, to which Shane replied that he would make no terms until the garrison was removed from Armagh. The Lord Deputy led a great army into Ulster in pursuit of O'Neill, who vanished into the forests and mountains. The Queen invited Shane to London. He accepted her invitation, and arrived in London with a retinue of Galloglass – *Gall- Oglach-* Foreign Warriors. These were handpicked men of great stature, who wore shirts of mail, trousers to the knee and leather leggings. They were armed with swords by their sides and carried great battleaxes. They wore their hair in the Gaelic style, long at the sides and cut short in front of the eyes. Elizabeth received Shane with great honour and bestowed many gifts on him. She recognised him as Chief of the O'Neills. Shane paid homage to her as Queen and swore his allegiance. Furthermore he promised to drive Sorley Buidhe McDonnell, and his Scots out of Antrim.

True to his word, he made war on Sorley Buidhe in Antrim and in 1565 he defeated, captured and imprisoned him. For the next two years he ruled without hindrance or interference from Dublin or London, thinking himself safe as friend of the Queen. The Lord Deputy, Sussex, wrote to him offering the hand of his sister in marriage. He later sent him a gift of wine. Shane and his household drank of the wine, and were lucky to escape death as the wine had been poisoned. This was a wake-up call for Shane He promptly went into rebellion and defeated the English at the battle of the Red Coats, (so named because it was the first time the red-coats had been seen in battle). During an incursion into Tirconnell, O'Neill was surprised by O'Donnell near Letterkenny and his army was decimated. He freed Sorley Beg McDonnell in an attempt to secure a force of galloglass, while he was being entertained by the McDonnells he was cut down and his head sent to Dublin where it remained on a spike for the next four years.

Shane's Head

Is it thus, O Shane the haughty! Shane the valiant! That we meet –
Have my eyes been lit by Heaven but to guide me to defeat?

15

Have I no chief, or you no clan, to give us both defence?
Or must I, too, be statued here with cold eloquence?
Thy ghastly head grins scorn upon old Dublin's Castle – tower.

From the poem 'Shane's Head' by John Savage

Brian of the Ramparts O'Rourke.

In the latter part of the sixteenth century, the strongest chief in the west of Ireland, was The O'Rourke [*Brian na Múrtha*] = Brian of the Ramparts, Chief of Leitrim. He is described as being a tall and remarkably handsome man. It is said that his most distinguishing characteristic was pride. Sir Henry Sydney wrote of him. "he was the proudest man with whom I had to do in my time". Sir Nicholas Malby remarked of him, that he was, "The proudest man who walks upon this earth today"[8].

By the time Richard Bingham came into Connaught, O'Rourke had been involved in several rebellions, and had been victorious in them all. When Sir John Perrott, became Viceroy, O'Rourke made his submission to him. In doing so he recognised Perrott [illegitimate son to Henry VIII] as his lawful superior. Perrott then prevailed upon him to set aside his claim to be Chief of Leitrim, with all its privileges, under the surrender and re-grant programme which had been devised by Henry VIII and his ministers to gain control of the territories of the Irish chiefs. As a consequence of this action he became a great landlord. He retained a great portion of Leitrim in his own hands, and received fixed rents from the proprietors of the rest. After the departure of Perrott, O'Rourke had to contend with Richard Bingham, who despised him and indeed this feeling seemed to have been mutual. In the aftermath of the Spanish Armada disaster in 1588, he gave shelter and sustenance to some shipwrecked Spanish Sailors. The authorities demanded their surrender, O'Rourke refused to comply with this demand, citing the rites of hospitality and personal honour. Bingham immediately gathered a force together and set out to surprise him in his castle on the shores of Lough Gill. Bingham's force was spotted and his surprise attack came to nothing. O'Rourke's eldest son was at that time studying at Oxford University. He sent his trusted confidant Charles Trevor secretly to Oxford to arrange and oversee his safe return. They returned home by way of Scotland and Ulster and, with his son, Brian Óg safe from English hands Brian of the Ramparts once more turned to rebellion. He sent word to all the 'wood-kerne', and gave them licence to plunder and pillage within the confines of Bingham's Presidency. In reply to a letter from Perrott, he stated that he would be under the government of no man save the Viceroy. The

---

[8] O'Grady Standish The Bog of Stars and other Stories and Sketches of Elizabethan Ireland

government sent commissioners to negotiate with him, judges and bishops, but to no avail. He considered himself a prince with no superiors except the Queen and her deputy, the Viceroy. Eventually Bingham brought the Leitrim rebellion under control. O'Rourke fled to Ulster to seek aid from his allay The MacSweeney, foster father to Red Hugh O'Donnell. From Ulster he made his way to Scotland, in search of aid, he was arrested by James VI of Scotland and sent as a prisoner to London. In London he was brought before the Court of Queens Bench, to be tried before a jury on the charge of High Treason. When the indictment was read and translated for him [he spoke only Latin and Gaelic], he refused to plead except on four conditions, which, are as follows,

(1) The assistance of an advocate.
(2)The affidavits forwarded out of Ireland to be put in my hands.
(3) The presence, and examination in court of the persons who swore the affidavits.
(4) The Queen in person to preside as judge at my trial.
It was also charged against him that he had dragged the Queens portrait at the heels of his war- horse, and that he stood by and approved while his men thrust their battleaxes through it.There was no evidence to prove this allegation. The Chief Justice informed him that if he continued with his refusal to plead, he would be obliged to consider the charge proved, and sentence him to death."You will do as you please", replied O'Rourke. The Chief Justice sentenced him to death, and so in the year 1589 he was executed at Tyburn. It is said that at the time of his execution, Miler Magrath, the notorious Archbishop of Cashel offered to administer the last rites.Brian O'Rourkes last words are said to be, "I think thou art a Franciscan who has broken thy vows". He was succeeded by his son Brian of the Battleaxes, who repaired to the Iron Mountains *Sliabh an Iarann* and from there he waged war on Bingham,

O'Ruairc's Request

You ask me what defence is mine? Here! 'midst your armed bands!
  You only mock the prisoner who is helpless in your hands.
  What would defence avail of me though good it be and true,
  Here! In the heart of London town, with judges such as you?

  You gravely talk about my "crime" ! I own no crime at all;
  The deeds you blame I'd do again should such a chance befall.
  You say I've helped the foreign foes to war against the Queen-
Well, challenged so, I'll proudly show what has my helping been.

On that wild day when near our coast the stately ships of Spain.

17

Caught in a fierce and sudden storm, for safety sought in vain;
When wrenched and torn' midst mountain waves some foundered in the
deep,
And others broke on sunken reefs and headlands rough and steep-

I heard the cry that off my land where breakers rise and roar
The sailors from a wrecking ship were striving for the shore.
I hurried to the frightful scene, my generous people, too,
Men, women, even children, came, some kindly deed to do.

We saw them clutching spars and planks that soon were washed away,
Saw others bleeding on the rocks, low moaning where they lay;
Some cast ashore and back again dragged by the refluent wave,
Whom one grip from a friendly hand would have sufficed to save.
We rushed into the raging surf, watched every chance, and when
They rose and rolled within our reach we grasped the drowning men.

We took them to our hearths and homes and bade them there remain
Till they might leave with hope to reach their native land again..
This is the "treason" you have charged! Well, treason let it be,
One word of sorrow for such fault you'll never hear from me.
I'll only say although you hate my race, and creed, and name,
Were your folk in that dreadful plight I would have done the same.

Oh ! you would bring me to your Queen, low at her feet to kneel,
Crave mercy from her stony heart, and urge some mean appeal!
I answer, No! My knees will bend and prayers of mine arise
To but one Queen, the Queen of heaven, high throned above the skies.

And now you ask my dying wish? My last and sole request
Is that the scaffold built for me be fronted to the West.
Of my dear country far away, one glimpse I cannot see,
Wherever, and however high, you raise my gallows tree;
Yet would I wish my last fond look should seek that distant shore,
So, turn my face to Ireland. Sirs, of you I ask no more.(T.D.Sullivan)

Extract from the Annals of the Four Masters
*"O'Rourke, i.e. Brian-na-Murtha the son of Brian, son of Owen, was
banished, as stated before, into the Tuatha in Tirconnell, where he remained
upwards of a year with MacSweeny (Owen Oge). After that he entered into
Scotland, in hopes of obtaining protection, or assistance from the King of
Scotland. A party of the Queens people [however] took him prisoner and
carried him into England and into London, where he remained for some time
in prison".*

Aodh Rua O'Domhnail

It is claimed that Saint Colm Cille was of the O'Donnell clan and because of this relationship they carried his psalter [the Cathach-the battler] into battle with them.

The Incarceration of Red Hugh O'Donnell (1587-1592)

In the summer of 1587, Red Hugh O'Donnell, in the company of Mac Sweeney of the Battleaxes (his foster father) and O'Gallagher of Bally-shannon made a pilgrimage to the Carmelite monastery near Rathmullan. This monastery situated on the western shore of Lough Swilly, was most popular at that time in Tyrconnell. While they were thus engaged, an English merchant ship negotiated Dunaff Head, passed Dunree Head and dropped anchor opposite Rathmullan. (O.S.I. Discovery Series map no 2 grid ref 276 274) The captain of this merchant ship invited all and sundry aboard his vessel, to sample his cargo of fine Spanish wines, with the intention of selling the same cargo. Word of his hospitality and generosity soon spread until he was the talk of Fanad.The young Red Hugh and his companions soon heard of this merchant and his Spanish wines and paid the ship a visit. On board they were made to feel most welcome and treated with great honour and deference by their host. They were wined and dined and entertained most liberally by their host. However when it came time to disembark they found that they had been disarmed and were secure under hatch and the ship was preparing to leave under cover of darkness. The next morning they found themselves being taken South along the Eastern coastline of Ireland and did not stop until they arrived under the walls of Dublin Castle. Prisoners of Perrott's, in the Birmingham Tower, Dublin Castle.

The Bermingham Tower Dublin Castle.
The green in the foreground of the picture is the site of the ancient Black Pool from which Dublin gets its name = *Dubh Linn*

Here Red Hugh was to languish for more than three years, confined to the Bermingham Tower. One dark night with the driving sleet helping to obscure them from the view of the sentries, they made good their escape from Dublin Castle and headed in the direction of the Wicklow Mountains where they could be sure of help. They crossed Three Rock Mountain and were headed in the direction of Glencree[9]. At this point, young Hugh O'Donnell, weakened after more than three years deprivation in prison, was unable to continue his journey. He urged his friends to continue without him and to send help back for him if they reached freedom. Hugh remained in the care of a trusted servant who had been involved in his escape. This servant reached the house of Felim O, Tuathal, who was known to them as a friend. The hills were full of soldiers searching for the fugitives and O'Tuathal unable to bring the youth to safety, and perceiving that he would perish due to the elements, made a grand show of giving him up to the authorities, who promptly returned him to prison in Dublin Castle. On Christmass Day 25th of December 1592, Hugh O'Donnell, Henry O'Neill, and Art O'Neill, (sons of Shane O'Neill) effected their escape from Dublin Castle. (It is said that the Lord Deputy, Fitzwilliam had taken a bribe from the Great O'Neill) The escape is described in The Annals as follows[10],

"One evening he and his companions, Henry and Art, the sons of O'Neill (John), before they had been brought into the refection house, took an advantage of the keepers and knocked off their fetters. They afterwards went to the privy-house, having with them a very long rope, by the loops of which they let themselves down through the privy-house until they reached the deep trench that was around the castle.They climbed the outer side, until they were on the margin of the trench. A certain faithful youth, who was in the habit of visiting them, and to whom they had communicated their secret, came to them at this time and guided them. They then proceeded through the streets of the city, mixing with the people; and no one took more notice of them than of anyone else, for they did not delay at that time to become acquainted with the people of the town; and the gates of the city were wide open. They afterwards proceeded by every intricate and difficult place until they arrived upon the surface of the Red Mountain over which Hugh had passed in his former escape. The darkness of the night, and the hurry of their flight (from dread of pursuit) separated the eldest of them from the rest, namely Henry O'Neill. Hugh was the greenest of them with respect to years, but not with respect to prowess. They were grieved at the separation of Henry from them; but however, they proceeded onwards, their servants guiding them along. That night was snowing so that it was not easy for them to walk, for they were without [sufficient] clothes or

---

[9] O.S.I. Discovery Series Map No 50 181 232
[10] Annals of the Four Masters volume 5

coverings having left their outer garments behind them in the privy-house, through which they had escaped. Art was more exausted by this rapid journey than Hugh, for he had been a long time in captivity, and had become very corpulent from long confinement in the prison. It was not so with Hugh; he had not yet passed the age of boyhood and had not [yet] done growing and increasing at this period, and his pace and motion were quick and rapid. When he perceived Art had become feeble, and that his step was becoming inactive and slow. He requested him to place an arm on his own shoulder, and the other upon the servant. In this manner they proceeded on their way until they had crossed the Red Mountain, after which they were weary and fatigued, and unable to help Art on any further; and as they were not able to take him with them, they stopped to rest under the shelter of a high rocky precipice which lay before them. On halting here they sent the servant to bring news to Glenmalure, where dwelt Fiagh, the son of Hugh [O'Byrne], who was then at war with the English. This is a secure and impregnable valley and many prisoners who escaped from Dublin were wont to resort to that valley for they considered themselves secure there until they could return to their own country. When the servant came into the presence of Fiagh, he delivered his message and how he had left the youths who had escaped from the city, and (stated) that they would not be overtaken alive unless he sent them relief instantly. Fiagh immediately ordered some of his servants of trust, (those in whom he had most confidence), to go to them, taking with them a man to carry food and another to carry ale and beer. This was accordingly done and they arrived at the place where the men were. Alas! Unhappy and miserable was their condition on their arrival. Their bodies were covered over with white-bordered shrouds of hailstones freezing around them on every side, and their light clothes and fine threaded shirts too, adhered to their skin and their large shoes and leather thongs to their shins and feet; so that covered as they were with the snow, it did not appear to the men who had arrived that they were human beings at all, for they found no life in their members, but just as if they were dead. They were raised by them from their bed, and they requested of them to take some of the meat and drink; but this they were not able to avail themselves of, for every drink they took they rejected again on the instant; so that Art at length died and was buried in that place, as to Hugh, after some time he retained the beer and after drinking it his energies were restored, except for the use of his two feet, for they were dead members, without feeling, swollen and blistered by the frost and snow. The men carried him to the valley which we have mentioned and he was placed in a sequestered house, in a solitary part of a dense wood, where he remained under care until a messenger came privately from his brother -in-law the Earl O'Neill to enquire after him."

Art O'Neill Memorial Plaque

The plaque above marks the spot in the Wicklow Mountains where Art O'Neill died in 1592. O.S.I. Discovery Series Map no 56 grid no 038994

Translation [A.Nugent]
In this place according to the folklore of the people
Art O'Neill expired
As he and Red Hugh O'Donnell
Were on the way from Dublin Castle to Glenmalure in the year 1592
Pro fide et Patria
In the year 1992 the Walkers Club of Ireland placed this slab here
In replacement of a slab that was here from 1932

O'Byrne immediately sent word to Hugh O'Neill, who sent one of his men, Turlough Buidhe O'Hagan, to bring the young chief home to Ulster. In 1593 a spy reported to the English that a prophesy was current that, "When two Hughs succeed each other as O'Donnells the last shall be a monarch of Ireland and banish all foreign conquerors.[11]" Aodh Rua, after his dramatic

---

[11] O hOgain Daithi Dr <u>Myth Legend & Romance</u> (Prentice Hall Press New York London

escape from Dublin Castle, had succeeded his father as the O'Donnell and was thus identified as fulfilling the prophesy. His biographer Lughaidh Ó'Cléirigh said he was, "A chosen one whom the prophets had foretold long before his birth.

Red Hugh O'Donnell's raid into Connaught 1595

As recorded by Phillip O'Sullivan Beare:-

"1595, O'Donnell, remembering the cruelty with which the English had thrown women, old men and children from the bridge at Enniskillen, with all his forces invaded Connaught, which Richard Bingham was holding oppressed under heretical tyranny. In his raids extending far and wide he destroyed the English colonists and settlers, put them to flight, and slew them, sparing no male between fifteen and sixty years old who was unable to speak Irish.He burnt the village of Longford in Annaly, which Browne, an English heretic, had taken from O'Farrell. He then returned to Tyrconnell laden with the spoils of the Protestants. After this invasion of Connaught, not a single farmer, settler or Englishman remained, except those who were defended by the walls of castles and fortified towns, for those who had not been destroyed by fire and sword, despoiled of their goods, left for England, heaping curses on those who had brought them into Ireland."

He was present with his followers at the Battle of the Yellow Ford in 1598. His friend and biographer Lughaidh Ó'Cléirigh asked the name of the ford and on being told, (Beal-an-atha-buidhe) he exclaimed! That St Bercan had prophesised a terrible conflict to be fought at a yellow ford, of which the Irish would be the victors. This was one of the greatest battles of Irish history, a pitched battle, fought between two armies of equal strength and although the Irish were victorious, the English were not lacking in bravery or endurance."

Red Hugh O'Donnell's raid into Thomond, 1600

As written by *Lughaidh Ó'Cléirigh*, whose brother, *Duibhgheann*, was killed during the assault on Clare Castle. *Lughaidh Ó' Cléirigh's* book was one of the sources used in the compilation of the Annals of the Four Masters. "His troops were gathered together by O'Domhnaill in the month of June precisely, and they crossed the Saimer, a stream rich in salmon, the Drowes, the Dubh, and the Sligeach, until they came to Ballymote, where the men of Connacht awaited him. After a while he marched with his forces by Corann, through *Magh Aoi Findbendaigh*, through *Clann Chonnmhaigh*, through the territory of Maine, son of *Eochaidh*, and through the plain of Clanrickard without fight or conflict, without wounding or being meddled with during that time. He made a halt in western Clanrickard in *Oireacht*

Réamoinn on the evening of Saturday, and this was the Saturday before St John's day, which was on the following Tuesday. Warning and report went before him to Thomond, but they thought *O'Domhnaill* would not leave the place where he had stopped until Monday morning. This was not what he did at all, but he rose before the early dawn of the morning of Sunday, and after hearing mass himself and the chiefs who were with him, he marched with his troops by *Oireacht Réamoinn, by the mountain of Echtge,* daughter of Urscothach, son of Tinne, to *Cenél Aodha* to *Cenél Dúnghaile* and by upper Glancullen, until he reached the Fergus westwards before mid-day on Sunday, so that they made a halt on the north-western side of Clonroad and Ennis. Ennis was burned and preyed entirely and made bare by the army all but the monastery, for *O'Domhnaill* ordered protection and kindliness to be given to it in honour of the Lord. There it happened to the earl of Thomond, Donncha, son of Conor, lord of Thomond, to be with a small force of not more than two hundred in number at Clonroad, a short distance to the west of Ennis, at the same time that *O'Domhnaill* and his armies came into the country. When he heard the murmur of the great army and the shouts of the soldiers and the noise of the heavy troops and the loud report of the quick-firing from bright, sharp-sighted guns throughout his territory all about him, and the bright, wide-spread conflagrations which extended in every quarter and on every border all round, which he could not defend or protect, what he did was to march with a small body of troops secretly by the bank of the Fergus due west as securely as he could till he came to Clare. That town was one of his fortresses, and it was strong, impregnable, even if he had not the force he had defending it.

As for *O'Domnaill,* when he had reached Ennis, he sent skirmishers to cover the surrounding country. Far and wide, violently, aggressively, these quick active courageous bodies of men separated from each other, for they traversed and plundered before night *Craig Uí Chiordhubháin,* in the lower part of the territory in the cantred of Islands, to *Cathair Murcha* in west *Corco Baiscinn,*to the gate of *Cill Muire,* and *Cathair Ruis* and the plain of Uí Bracáin, to the gate of *Baile Eóin Gabhainn* in Corcomrua, and Boith Néill in *Cenél Fermaic.* There was many a 'time of plenty' For gentlemen, noblemen, and lords of territories with prey and cattle and every sort of spoil, in the hands of a company of four or five of *O'Domhnaill's* people under the shelter of bush or thicket, rock or wood in Thomond that night, for they had to stay wherever the darkness of nightfall overtook them.

O'Domhnaill encamped that night on the bank of the Fergus to the west of Clonroad. This was a famous castle and princely lodgings for him who was chief of the country. The army arose (on Monday exactly) calmly and firmly from their tents and huts and proceeded to march by the road diagonally across Thomond in a north-easterly direction straight through the east of Uí Cormaic and the plain of Cenél Fermaic and the speckled-hilled Boirenn, till

they came at sunset to the monastery of Corcomrua and to Carcair na gCléireach. Those of the forces who were unoccupied throughout the day were traversing and patrolling the lands around, so that they did not leave a habitation or dwelling worth talking about unburnt or undestroyed that day. The troops arose at dawn on Tuesday. They set out with their spoils and preys towards Carcair, and though their march was severe and their pace slow, owing to the enormous amount of cattle and plunder, they left the cleft stone passes of white Boirenn behind. When they came to the dwellings of the smooth plain of Maree, they rested at Cnoc an Ghearráin, between Cill Colgáin and Galway. They divided the spoil between them after that, so that each body had its share of the enemy's cattle, flocks, and booty, and they proceeded the next day to guide and drive their portion of the prey along the roads of the ancient province of Sreng, son of Sengan. The journey they made on that day was not long, for they were tired after the great toil in coming through the narrow mouthed roads of Boirenn, neither had they eaten or slept in comfort the night before, for they had thought the earl of Thomond would come with all his forces in pursuit of them and on their track to attack them, on the winding defiles through which they were marching, though he did not come at all. They made their camp in the neighbourhood that night, since they had banished their fear. They made neither huts nor buildings, owing to the heat of the summer weather, but they lighted bright, flaming fires, and their attendants and servers, their cooks and houseboys, their ostlers and their soldiers fell to butchering and killing, slaughtering and chopping the bones of the enemy's cattle to prepare their dinner for their chiefs and their nobles, till they consumed their feast and slept soundly, as they had cast aside their fear.[12]"
Following the defeat of the Irish at Kinsale, the Irish leaders met in council at Innishannon, on the river Bandon, where it was decided that Red Hugh O'Donnell should go to Spain and report to Phillip 111. There, at the age of twenty eight, he died the following year and was buried with full honours in the Cathedral of St Francis, Valladolid. It is believed that he was poisoned by an agent sent to Spain by Carew, with the approval of Mountjoy.

---

[12] *Ó'Cléirigh Lughaidh Beatha Aodh Rua O'Domhnaill,* (Annals of the Four Masters)

Donegal Castle 2006

The tower house to the right of picture was built by the O'Donnells in 1505, after the Flight of The Earls in 1607 it was occupied by Sir Basil Brooke who extended it to the left by adding the gables and windows and turning the first floor into a banqueting hall.

O'Donnell Abu.

Proudly the notes of the trumpet are sounding,
Loudly the war cries arise on the gale;
Fleetly the steed of Lough Swilly is bounding
To join the thick squadrons in Saimer's green vale;
On every mountaineer,
Strangers to fight and fear,
Rush to the standard of dauntless Red Hugh!
Bonnacht and gallowglass
Throng from each mountain pass,
On for old Erin, O'Donnell Aboo!

Princely O'Neill to our aid is advancing
With many a chieftain and warrior clan;
A thousand proud steeds in his vanguard are prancing
Neath borderers brave from the banks of the Bann;
Many a heart shall quail
Under its coat of mail,
Deeply the merciless foeman shall rue,
When on his ear shall ring,
Borne on the breeze's wing,
Tyr Connel's dread war cry; O'Donnell Aboo!

Wildly o'er Desmond the war-wolf is howling,
Fearless the eagle sweeps over the plain;
The fox in the streets of the city is prowling,
All who would scare them are banished or slain.
Grasp, every stalwart hand,
Hackbut and battle-brand,
Pay them all back the deep debt so long due;
Norris and Clifford well
Can of TyrConnell tell,
Onward to glory, O'Donnell Aboo!

Sacred the cause that Clann Connell's defending;
The altars we kneel at, the homes of our sires.
Ruthless the ruin the foe is extending,
Midnight is red with the plunderer's fires.
On with O'Donnell then,
Fight the good fight again,
Son's of Tyr Connell, all valient and true;
Make the false Saxon feel
Erin's avenging steel!

Strike for your country, O'Donnell Aboo!

This 19th century ballad was written by Michael Joseph McCann

Grace O'Malley – *Gráine Ní Mháille*– Gránia Uaile. Gráine Mhaol.c1530-1603

Grace O'Malley, was the daughter of Dubhdara O'Malley (Black Oak), chief of the O'Malleys, who from ancient times have been chiefs of the *Umhalls* that is the country that surrounds Clew Bay and according to the Book of Rights are tributary kings to the provincial kings of Connaught. During the thirteenth century they were driven from a large portion of their ancestral territories by the Burkes and the Butlers. During her lifetime they retained twenty townlands in Borrishole, and held more of it as tenants to the Earl of Ormonde. The O'Malley Barony of Murrisk included the ocean islands Clare Island, Inisturk, Caher, Inisboffin, and Inisark.
Tradition holds that Gráinne was fostered on Clare Island, which belonged to her family. It was here that she acquired her love of ships and the sea. Family Motto *"Terra Marique Potens"* which means -Power on Land and Sea.

Legend describing how she became known as Gráinne Mhaol

It is said that as a child she begged to be taken on one of her fathers ships which was setting out on a journry to Spain. She was advised by her mother that the life of a sailor was not suitable for a young lady. She withdrew from the company and returned later with her hair cut short, upon which her family named her Gráinne Mhaol – Grace-the-Bald. However it is more than likely that this name owes its origin to the title *Gráinne Umhall* – Grace of the Umhalls, following are some examples of English mispronunciation and misspelling of her name taken from official records.
"Grany omayle, Grany O'Maly, Grany O'Malley, Grany Imallye, Granny Nye Male Grany O'Mayle, Granie ny Maille, Grane ne Male, Grana O'Malley, Grainy O'Maly, Granee O'Maillie, Grany ni Maly, Grany ny Mallye.
In a report from the President of Munster, Sir William Drury to the Privy Council March 1577 (1578 New Style), she is described as, "Grany omayle a woman that hathe impudently passed the parts of womanhode ben a great spoiler and chefe commander and director of theefes and murtherers at the sea tospoille this province having been apprehended by the Erle of desmonde the laste yere his L. hathe now sent her to Lymnick where she remayneth in safe keeping"[13].

---

[13] Sir William Drury, Letter to The Privy Council 1577

History records that Gráinne was married twice. Her first husband was *Dónal-na Chogaidh* (Donal of the Battles) O'Flaherty, of Bunowen, in the Barony of Ballinahinch. He was a direct descendant of Hugh Mór O'Flaherty and was the acknowledged heir to the chieftainship of the western O'Flahertys. This marriage united the two ruling families of Murrisk and Ballinahinch and gave them control over the western sea. She had two sons by Dónal, Owen and Morogh. Her eldest son Owen, fell foul to the intrigues of the Bingham brothers Sir Richard and Captain John, his downfall was brought about in the following manner, 'during the rebellion of the Burkes and the Joyces of McWilliams county, Sir Richard Bingham advised Owen to withdraw to a safe island. At that time Sir Richard's brother, Captain John Bingham, led an armed force against the Joyces. On failing to engage with their quarry, they came to the mainland, close to the island, and called to Owen for provisions. Owen came with a number of boats and ferried the soldiers over to the island, where he provided them with food and drink and shelter. That very night Owen and eighteen of his followers were set upon by their guests and taken into custody. The next day the soldiers took from the island, 4,000 cattle, 5,00 horses and 1,000 sheep and brought them, along with the prisoners, to Ballinahinch. That night Captain John Bingham caused the eighteen followers of Owen O'Flaherty to be hanged. The next night a false alarm was raised, and Owen, who was bound hand and foot in the tent of Captain Grene O'Molloy was stabbed to death, and so with the murder of the eldest son of Gránia Uaile, closes another bloody chapter of Bingham's doings in Ireland. After the death of her first husband, Dónal O'Flaherty, Gráine married Richard Burke (Richard an Iarann) Richard in Iron, So called because he wore a coat of chain-mail. Richard's mother was an O'Flaherty, so Gráine maintained contact with the family of her first husband. As a consequence of her second marriage she became mistress of Carrigahowley castle.

Deputy Sydney made a knight of Richard Burke, to the delight of Gráine, who became Lady Burke, although there is no record of her using that title. One story tells how she gave birth to a son by her second marriage while on board ship. A Turkish corsair attacked the ship that same day, and word of this was passed to Gráinne by her men. She jumped from the bed cursing and swearing, and went up on deck carrying two blunderbusses. She began to caper about on the deck of the ship to attract the attention of the Turks. When she gained their attention she emptied both guns on them. Thus encouraging her crew to redouble their efforts and defeat the Turks[14]. After her marriage to Richard-an-Iarainn Grace went to live at Carrickahowley Castle.

Rockfleet Castle is actually a four story tower house, located on an inlet of Clew bay it offers its inhabitants a commanding view of the bay. This was

---

[14] OhOgain Daithi Dr <u>Myths Legends & Romance</u> (Prentice Hall Press1991

the scene of an affray between Grace and the English authorities. She had become so active in harassing ships which were on route to Galway, that Sir Edward Fitton who was the President of Connaught at that time, sent a force against her under the command of Captain William Martin on the 8th of March 1574. This force laid siege to Rockfleet Castle entrapping Grace within its walls. On the 26th of March Grace turned defeat into victory by attacking the English fleet and forcing them to beat a hasty retreat to avoid capture. This encounter with the English was to enhance her reputation as a leader among her people.

Kildownet Castle, Achill, overlooking Achill Sound.

Another tower house which was inhabited by Gráinne, she is credited with building the nearby church which is dedicated to St Dabhenet, whose Well is situated on the nearby fore-shore. The following song, which was written by Patrick Pearse uses her name as a symbol for Ireland.

Oró, Sé Do Bheata 'Bhaile

1

Sé do bheatha! A bhean ba leanmhar!
B'é ár gcreach tú bheith í ngéibhinn,
Do dhuiche bhrea í seilbh meirleach
'S tú díolta leis na Gallaibh.

Curfá

Oró! Sé do bheatha 'bhaile!
Oró! Sé do bheatha bhaile!
Oró! Sé do bheatha 'bhaile-
Anois ar theacht an tSamhraidh.

2

Tá Gráinne Mhaol ag teacht thar sáile,
Óglaigh armtha lei mar gharda;
Gaeil íad féin 's ní Gaill no Spáinnigh,
'S cuirfid ruaig ar Ghallaibh.

3

A bhuí le Rí na bhfeart go bhfeiceam,
Muna mbeam beo 'na dhiadh ach seachtain,
Gráinne Mhaol agus mile gaiscíoch
Ag fogairt fáin ar Ghallaibh.

Translation (A. Nugent)

1

Oro and Hail! At Home
Hail, O woman who was sorrowful
We were desolate while you were imprisoned.
Your lovely country in the hands of villains
And you, sold to the foreigner.

Chorus

Oro, and Hail at Home,
Oro and Hail at Home,
Oro and Hail at Home,
Now at the coming of Summer.

2

Grainne Mhaol is coming over the sea,
With a guard of armed soldiers,
They are Irish, and not Foreign or Spanish
And they will rout the foreigners.

3

Thank's to The King of Power, that I am seeing
If I only live for a week after,
Grainne Mhaol and a thousand champions
Giving notice of ruin to the foreigner.

The Howth Legend

This legend recalls that Gráinne landed at Howth, which was the principle port for Dublin at that time. She paid a visit to Howth Castle expecting to be received with hospitality. However she found the castle gates locked and she was refused entry as the lord was at dinner and would not be disturbed. Gráinne was furious at this treatment and stormed back to her ship, taking the young heir to Howth with her on her journey back to Clew Bay.The Lord of Howth immediately set out for the west, and on reaching Clew Bay he pleaded with Gráinne for the return of his son and heir. Gráinne returned the boy and the only ransom she demanded was that Howth Castle would never again be closed to anyone seeking hospitality, and that an extra plate would always be set at the dinner table.

The Dark Lady of Doona.

According to this legend Gráinne and some of her followers were making a pilgrimage at the holy well on Clare Island on St Brigid's Day, when they heard that a foreign vessel had foundered near Achill. Gráinne had her galley's launched despite the stormy conditions, in search of survivors. They found one survivor, a young man, Gráinne brought him back to Clare Island, where she nursed him back to health and fell in love with him in the process. One legend tells that he was of Nordic origin, yet another legend, names him as Hugh de Lacy. Whatever his name or origin their love affair was cut short by the murder of the young man, by the MacMahons of Ballycroy whilst hunting deer on Achill. Shortly after this episode the MacMahons were making a pilgrimage to the holy Island of Cahir. Gráinne attacked their boats, cutting off their retreat, she then went ashore and killed those responsible for the murder of her lover. She then set sail for Doona Castle in Blacksod Bay where she evicted the MacMahons and installed her own followers there, thus gaining for herself the title, "The Dark Lady of Doona ". There is a stone plaque on the wall of the Abbey on Clare Island , inside the chancel and adjacent to the tomb of the O'Malleys. The stone which is undated is inscribed with, a rearing stallion above a war-helmet crossed by horizontal bars. There is a wild boar trippant in the centre, with three bows with arrows affixed, aiming at the boar .At the left hand base is the inscription of a galley. Beneath that are inscribed the latin words *Terra Mariq Potens and below in larger capitals* the name O'Maille. There is a tasselled curtain to both left and right of this slab.

The O'Malley tomb in the chancel of the Abbey on Clare Island.
Which local tradition believes to be the last resting place of Gráinne Mhaol

The Legend of Hermits Rock

Hermits Rock is a tiny island in Clew Bay on which lived a holy hermit. While pursuing a local chieftain whose clan she had defeated, Gráinne laid siege to the little church where he had sought sanctuary with the intentions of starving him into submission. With the help of the hermit the chieftain dug a tunnel out to the nearby cliff face from where he made good his escape. The hermit broke his vow of silence to castigate Gráinne for trying to harm one who had received the sanctuary of the church.

Her Visit to Queen Elizabeth 1.

In July 1593 Gráinne wrote her first petition to Queen Elizabeth 1. Written in English and addressed, "To the Queens Most Excellent Majesty", Gráinne in the most humble of tones exonerates herself from forty years of plundering, cattle raiding and piracy, pleading that circumstances compelled her to do so in defence of her property and people.

Early in September1593, in reply to her letter to Queen Elizabeth, Gráinne received a summons to present herself before her Majesty at Greenwich Castle.History records no details of what took place at this meeting of two powerful strong willed women. Legend tells us that Gráinne wore a green chieftain's cloak over a yellow bodice and petticoat, and that she was barefoot. The Queen would have worn an elaborate gown ornamented with embroidery and encrusted with precious stones. Legend relates that during the audience one of the Queen's ladies-in-waiting, seeing that Gráinne was in need of a handkerchief, handed her one made from cambric and lace. When she was finished with it Gráinne threw it into the fire. Elizabeth informed her that she should have put it into her pocket. Gráinne replied that in Ireland they would not think of putting such a soiled article in one's pocket. Whatever transpired at the meeting, Gráinne must have made a good impression on Elizabeth because on the 6th of September 1593 she wrote to Sir Richard Bingham the following letter.

"Where our Treazurer of England, by his letters in July last, did inform you of the being here of three several persons of that our Province of Connaught under your charge, that is, of Sir Morogh O'Flaherty, Knight, Grany ne Maly and Roobuck French, requiring to understand your opinion of every of them concerning their suits; we perceive by your late letters of answer what your opinion is of them, and their causes of complaint or of suit, whereof you have given them no just cause. But where Grany ne Maly hath made humble suit to us for our favour towards her sons, Morogh O'Flaherty and Tibbot Burk, and to her brother Donell O'Piper (na Piopa), that they might be at liberty, we perceive by your letters that her eldest son, Morogh O'Flaherty is no trouble but is a principle man of his country, and as a dutiful subject has served us when his mother, being then accompanied with a number of disorderly persons, did with her 'gallyes' spoil him; and therefore by you favoured, and so we wish you to continue. But the second son, Tibbot Burk, one that hath been brought up civilly with your brother and can speak English, is by you justly detained because he hath been accused to have written a letter to Bryan O'Rork, the late traitors son, though it cannot be fully proved but is by him utterly denied; and for her brother Donald, he hath been imprisoned 7 months past, being charged to have been in company of certain that killed some soldiers in a ward. But for those two you think they may be both dismissed upon bonds for their good behaviour, wherewith we are content, so as the old woman may understand we yield thereto in regard of her humble suit; so she is hereof informed and departeth with great thankfulness and with many more earnest promises that she will, as long as she lives continue a dutiful subject, yea, and will employ all her power to offend and prosecute any offender against us. And further, for the pity to be had of this aged woman, having not by the custom of the Irish any title to any livelihood or position or portion of her two husband's lands, now being a widow; and yet her sons enjoying their father's lands, we require you to deal with her sons in our name to yield to her some maintainance for her living the rest of her old years, which you may with persuasion assure them that we shall theirin allow of them; and you also shall with your favour in all their good causes protect them to live in peace to enjoy their livelihoods. And this we do write in her favour as she showeth herself dutiful, although she hath in former times lived out of order, as being charged by our Treasurer with evil usage of her son that served us dutifully. She hath confessed the same with assured promises by oath to continue most dutiful, with offer, after her aforesaid manner, that she will fight in our quarrel with all the world"[15].

Brian Óg (of the Battle-Axes) O'Rourk.

Brian Óg of the Battle-Axes, succeeded his father, Brian of the Ramparts, as chieftain of the O'Rourkes.The Lord of Leitrim. He installed himself in *Sliabh an Iarann*=Iron Mountain Co. Leitrim. From where, he waged a relentless war on Sir Richard Bingham. He had many victories and won back his fathers territories from the English. It is said that it was his war with Bingham which precipitated the Nine Years War. According to the Annals of the four Masters in 1593,
"A warlike dissension arose in the month of May in this year between Sir Goerge Bingham of Ballymote and Brian-na-Samhthach ie Brian Oge. The cause of this dissension was that part of the Queens rent had not been received out of Breifny on that festival. Brian O'Rourke asserting that all the rents not paid were those demanded for lands that were waste, and that he [Bingham] ought not to demand rents for wastelands until they should be inhabited.Sir George sent soldiers into Breifny to take a prey in lieu of rent; and the soldiers seized on O'Rourke's own milch cows. Brian went to demand a restoration of them but this he did not at all receive. He then returned home and sent for mercenaries and hireling troops to Tyrone, Tirconnell and Fermanagh; and after they had come to him (he set out and) he made no delay by day or by night until he arrived at Ballymote. On his arrival in the neighbourhood of the town, he dispersed marauding parties through the two cantreds of the MacDonaghs, namely, Corann, Tirerrill; and there was not much of that country which he did not plunder on the excursion. He also burned on that day thirteen villages on every side of Ballymote." He fought with Eoghan Roe O'Donnell at the Battle of the Curlew Mountains, where he was wounded twice. Among the enemy dead, was Sir Conyers Clifford, President of Connaught. Brian had his body decapitated and his head sent to Eoghan Roe as a trophy of war which was a custom of that time.

---

[15] Calender of State papers vol clxxii p 184

Fiach MacHugh O'Byrne

Fiach MacHugh was chief of the O'Byrne clan of County Wicklow, famous for his deeds of bravery. He was instrumental in the escape of Eoghan Roe O'Donnell from Dublin Castle in December of 1592 and his safe return to Ulster. In January 1595 the Chief Justiciary of Ireland, Sir William Russell, marched to *Baile-na-Cuirre,* in Glenmalure, in County Wicklow, to capture or defeat Fiach the son of Hugh O'Byrne. "Upon their arrival in the neighbourhood of the castle, but before they had passed through the gate of the rampart that surrounded it, the sound of a drum was accidently heard from the soldiers who were going to the castle. Fiagh with his people took the alarm; and he rose up suddenly and sent a party of his people to defend the gate; and he sent all his people, men, boys and women out through the postern-doors of the castle, and he himself followed them, and conveyed them all in safety to the wilds and recesses where he considered them safe."[16]

Fifteen days after this incident a band of men led by Fiach's son raided the settlement of Crumlin burnt the castle and took away the lead roof.In 1597 the Annals of The Four masters reports, "Fiagh, son of Hugh, son of John O'Byrne from Glenmalure was slain in the first month of summer in this year, having, been treacherously betrayed by his relative at the bidding of the Chief Justiciary of Ireland Sir William Russell."

His defeat of the English army under the command of Lord Grey in 1580 is celebrated in the following ballad.

The Marching Song of Fiach MacHugh.

1

Lift MacCahir Óg, your face,
Brooding o'er the old disgrace
That black Fitzwilliam stormed your place
And sent you to the fern!
Grey said victory was sure-
Soon the fire brand he'd secure
Until he met at Glenmalure
Fiach MacHugh O'Byrne!
Chorus
Curse and swear, Lord Kildare!
Fiach will do what Fiach will dare-
Now Fitzwilliam, have a care;
Fallen is your star low!
Up with halberd, out with sword!
On we go; for, by the Lord!

---

[16] Annals of The Four Masters 1595

Fiach MacHugh has given the word;
"Follow me up to Carlow".

2

See the swords of Glen Imayle
Flashing o'er the English Pale!
See all the children of the Gael!
Beneath O'Byrne's banners!
Rooster of fighting stock,
Would you let a Saxon cock
Crow out upon an Irish rock?
Fly up and teach him manners!

3

From Tassagart to Clonmore
Flows a stream of Saxon gore
Och, great is Rory Óg O'Moore
At sending loons to Hades!
White is sick, and Lane is fled!
Now for black Fitzwilliam's head-
We'll send it over dripping red
To Liza and her ladies!

P.J.McCall

"Rory Ogue, son of Rory, son of Conall O'More; fell by the hand of Brian Mac Gilla Patrick, and that Rory was the chief spoiler and insurgent of the men of Ireland in his time, and no one was disposed to fire a shot against the Crown for a long time after that",[17]

Gleann Maoilughra 1580 A.D.

Le linn an obair do bheith ar siudhal sa Mhumhain do thosnuigh éirghe-amach eile í gCo. Chille Manntáin. Is é Viscount Baltinglass a bhí í gceannas air.Caitiliceach dob ea é agus níor thaithnigh leis mar a bhí na Sasanaigh ag cur na gCaitiliceach fé chois.Do chabhruigh Fiach Mac Aodha Ó'Broin leis agus do Bhriseadar araon cath mór ar na Sasanaigh í nGleann Maoilúghra, Chille Manntáin sa bhliain 1580.[18]

Translation A Nugent

As well as the events in Munster a rebellion took place in Co. Wicklow. Lead by Viscount Baltinglas, a Catholic, who disagreed with the treatment of

---

[17] Annals of the Four Masters
[18] O'Siochfhradha M. M.A. <u>Stair-Sheanchas Eireann 1935</u>

fellow Catholics by the English.He was aided by Fiach MacHugh O'Broin and they defeated the English in one great battle in 1580.

Stone commemorating Fiach's victory in 1580

Translation from Irish (A.Nugent)

The Glen
Where Fiach Mac Hugh O'Byrne
Broke the Foreigners in battle
IN 1580 A.D.

The Great O'Neill, Hugh O'Neill, Aodh Rua O'Neill
Eoghan Roe O'Neill 1550 – 1616

Hugh O'Neill was the grandson of the first Earl of Tyrone and the son of the first Baron of Dungannon. His father had been killed by Shane O'Neill in 1558 and his brother the second Baron of Dungannon had been killed by Turlough Luineach O'Neill. He was fostered by the O'Hagans and the O'Quinns in the early part of his life. He lived in England from the age of nine until his eighteenth year as the *protégé* of Queen Elizabeth, under the guidance of Sydney, who at that time was Lord President of Wales, at Ludlow Castle in Shropshire and at Penhurst in Kent, and with Leicester at Holkham in Norfolk He returned to Ireland as Baron of Dungannon in 1568. His main rival at that time was Turlough Luineach O'Neill and his next rivals were the sons of Sean the Proud. His first wife was the daughter of Sir Brian MacPhelim O'Neill but this marriage was dissolved by the time he was twenty four. He had assisted Essex who was responsible for the death of Sir Brian and all his followers. His second marriage was to Siobhán O'Donnell, daughter of Hugh Dubh O'Donnell, He put his second wife aside in 79-80 to live with a daughter of Turlough Luineach O'Neill, but she was still his wife at the time of her death in 1591. A short time after the death of his second wife he eloped with Mabel Bagenal the daughter of his greatest enemy. In May 1587 in recognition of fifteen years service to the Crown and his help in putting down the Desmond rebellion, he was made Earl of Tyrone with letters Patent drawn up under the Great Seal of England. In February 1589 one of the sons of Sean [the Proud], Hugh Gaveloch O'Neill [Fettered Hugh], so named because his mother bore him in prison, reported to an English Officer Captain Nicholas Merriman, that the Earl of Tyrone was plotting with the King of Spain. In November of the same year Captain Merriman reported that Tyrone was plotting with Angus MacDonnell and that MacDonnell had been a guest at Dungannon Castle. On leaving he had presented plaids to some of O'Neill's men and, that O'Neill had made a present of seven of his best horses to Angus MacDonnell. Because of these allegations O'Neill requested permission to visit London to defend himself before the Queen in person. Maguire captured Hugh Gaveloch in a raid and handed him over to O'Neill who promptly had him executed, It is said that he executed him personally, by hanging him from a thorn tree.The Earl of Tyrone went to London in March 1590, but the Queen refused to see him. He was put under house arrest in the home of Sir Henry Wallop and ordered to appear before the Privy Council, where he requested that consideration be given to the place where this fact was done and to the person-a notable murderer, and to the ancient form of government in Ulster, where there is neither, magistrate, judge, sheriff, nor course of the laws of this realm; but certain customs by which both O'Neill [Turlough Luineach] and he and others of our sort do govern our followers; neither have we been at any time restrained from execution of evildoers, nor of such as be invaders of our country, or professed enemies to the same

O'Neill goes to War.

In February 1595 O'Neill defeated Bagenal at Clontibred. The news of this victory soon spread around Ireland and awakened the people. In Connaught George Bingham was murdered. O'Neill was inaugurated the O'Neill in the ancient manner. In the spring of 1596, after the death of Mabel Bagenal, he married his fourth wife Catherine Magennis. In May 1596 he received despatches from King Phillip of Spain through the visit of Captain Alonso Cobos. At dinner which was attended by Red Hugh O'Donnell, O'Kane, O'Hagan, O'Rourke, Maguire, MacWilliam Burke, he sought aid from Spain in the form of an expedition of 6,000 men and arms and money for ten thousand more. During this period he imported large amounts of, gunpowder, lead, muskets, culivers, morians, swords and daggers. He also strengthened his contacts with other clans such as, O'Connor, O'Reily, MacDermot, O'Flaherty, Magennis, O'Hanlon, M'Connell, O'Kelly, O'Byrne, Kavanagh, O'Moore. In December of 1597 in a parley with the Earl of Ormonde he demanded, Liberty of Conscience, Full Pardon, complete restoration of all his Titles and Patents, the return of his pledges, the restoration to his followers of all their ancient lands. The withdrawal of every garrison, and that Tyrone itself be made a County Palatine. In 1598 Ormonde became Lieutenant- General, and Sir Henry Bagenal was in command of the army. On the tenth of August of the same year Sir Henry Bagenal left the city of Armagh at the head of an English Army. As they were making their way through the winding hills and woods of Grange, a deadly volley of lead swept through their ranks, thus began the battle known as the battle of the Yellow Ford.Volley, after volley, poured into the English ranks. Sir Henry Bagenal himself lead the first division of his army and drove the Irish marksmen from their positions. They pursued them up to the Irish entrenchments, but O'Neill had prepared pits which were covered over with wattles and grass in front of these entrenchments, and many of the English perished in these pits. The main body of O'Neill's army fell upon the English, while his cavalry charged in from the flanks.The rout was complete.Sir Henry Bagenal was among the 3000 Englishmen killed that day. At the Yellow Ford O'Neill had proven himself to be a General to be reckoned with and that an Irish army, trained and equipped properly, was a match for any other army.

The Battle of Kinsale

In January 1601 Spain decided to send 6,000 troops to Ireland. By the month of August, 43 companies consisting of 4,432 troops in total were assembled at Lisbon, from where they set sail for Ireland under the command of Don Juan del Aquila.This fleet landed at Kinsale in county Cork on September 21 1601 minus four ships containing over 600 troops which had become detached in a storm. By October only 2,500 of the Spanish soldiers were fit for action. In December a further 600 Spaniards with fresh supplies of food, arms and equipment were landed to the west of Kinsale but by then del Aquila was under siege at Kinsale. On October 23rd O'Donnell set out for Kinsale, with an army of 2500 men. One week later O'Neill set out at the head of an army of 3500. Upon his arrival at Kinsale O'Neill perceived that the English, who were besieging the Spanish, were themselves suffering from hunger and disease he therefore decided to besiege the besiegers. However Don Juan Del Aquila beseeched O'Neill to attack the English without further delay. At a council of war held at the Irish camp it was decided to attack, despite the opposition of O'Neill. On the night of January 2nd the Irish army left their camp in three divisions, the first division was led by Tyrrell, the centre was led by O'Neill, while O'Donnell took up the rear. It was a dark stormy night and the guides lost their way. What should have taken a few hours took all night. At dawn O'Neill found himself facing an English army ready for battle with cavalry mounted. The English attacked immediately, O'Donnell had not arrived, and when he did it was too late the centre had already collapsed with 1200 dead. And so within an hour O'Neill's reputation was ruined, his moral influence ended. Red Hugh O'Neill spent the next number of years hiding and fighting in the hills of Colraine and the lakes of Fermanagh until in February of 1603 the dying queen agreed to his pardon. When Sir Arthur Chichester became Lord Deputy in 1605 He made life intolerable for O'Neill. He beset him with spies, and had his house searched for priests. In the autumn of 1605 a spy informed Chichester that Maguire and Rory O'Donnell were plotting along with Henry O'Neill (Red Hugh's son) to invade Ulster from abroad. Finally in 1607 Henry O'Neill sent a ship to take him to Europe. On Friday September 14th 1607 O'Neill and Rory O'Donnell and their families and relatives and followers left Ireland for Europe in a flight which became known as the The Flight of the Earls.

Conquering O'Neill

Fierce is the flame of the vengeance of Erin
When roused by the blast of the battle to shine;
Fierce is the flash of her broad sword uprearing
To strike for her rights and her altars divine.

Haste snatch the spear and shield,
Rush to the battlefield,
The Saxon is come from the towers of the Pale;
Sons of the vale and glen,
Children of mighty men,
Swell the dread war- note of conquering O'Neill!

Lightly the Red Hand of terror is streaming,
Like a fire-cloud of death on the hills of Tyrone,
Brightly the spears of Clan Connell are gleaming,
Like Swilly's blue waves in the beam of the sun.
Hark, the wild battle cry,
Rings through the sounding sky,
Valley and mountain are blazing with steel;
Eagles and forest deer
Flee from the heights with fear,
Scared at the war shout of conquering O'Neill!

O'Donnell descends from his fathers dark mountains,
He comes, noble prince, to the strife of the Gael;
He comes like the rush of his own stormy fountains,
Sweeping impetuous over moorland and dale.
On to the Yellow Ford
Chiefs of the flashing sword,
Drive the proud *Sasenach* back to the Pale!
Fierce to the scene of blood,
Wild as a mountain flood,
Charge the stout warriors of conquering O'Neill

Our war shouts shall ring and our musket peal rattle,
Our swords shall not rest from the hot, weary toil;
Our plains shall be drenched with the red showers of battle,
Till the Godless invaders are swept from our soil.
Pikeman and musketeer,
Kern and bold cavalier!
The wolves and the ravens are scenting their meal;
Carve to them red and fresh,
Plenty of Saxon flesh,
Follow your princely chief-conquering O'Neill
Onward O'Neill, with thy Red Hand of glory,
Thy sword lighteth thousands to conquest and fame;
The annals of Eire are emblazed with the story,
Her valleys are filled with the praise of thy name.
On with the Bloody Hand!

Shake the dread battle-brand!
Woe to the spoilers of green Inisfail;
Lo! Their red ranks appear-
Up! every gun and spear-
Charge, charge, O'Donnell and conquering O'Neill!

Michael Hogan. The Bard of Thomond.

A Report by Sir Toby Caulfield to Dublin 1613

The following is a report made by Sir Toby Caulfield to the Dublin authorities on information he had received from Teag Modder McGlone. "Says (ie.McGlone) that on the 11th October 1613, Turlough McCroyden, a Franciscan Friar preached a sermon in the woods called Lisselby Roodan within the barony of Loughensolyn in the county of Londonderry where assembled to hear him, he thinks 1,000 people, whereof examinant was one. All the priests of these parts were there to the number of 14. He prayed long, exhorting them to reform their wicked lives, talking to them of drunkenness, whoredom and lack of devotion and zeal; he willed them to take heed that they were not tempted for fear, or desire of gain to go to the English service, telling them that those were devils words which the English ministers spake, and all should be damned that heard them. He willed them to stand on their keeping and go into plain rebellion rather than go to the English service, and to suffer death by hanging, drawing and quartering sooner than submit themselves to their damnable doctrine. He told them that the Pope had sent him unto them, and that his Holiness had a great care both for their souls and bodies and that every year the Pope would send unto them holy men and that they should not despair nor be dismayed; though for a time God punished them by suffering their lands to be given to strangers and heretics, it was a punishment for their sins, and he bade them fast and pray and be of good comfort, for it should not be long before they were restored to their former prosperitie. He says he lay with the abbot of Armagh four days at the house of Owen Og O Haggan where he said mass every day, but only preached once. The examinant was there all the while many people resorted not to him there because he lay there in a secret manner, neither had he any gifts presented to him there, but great cheer after the Irish manner. He wears English apparel over his friars weeds, and a rapier by his side. He is about thirty years old or better, a native of Tyrone within three miles of Dungannon. There are two other friars who are his consorts and were sent by the Pope to preach to the people of Ulster. One is Hugh McKale, born in Evagh or Lecale who keeps in Evagh or Monaghan, and Henry O Mellan born in Tyrone, who is now in Tredaghe or Dundalk."

43

Dubhaltach Mac Firbisigh
Dudley Mac Firbis

Dubhaltach Mac Firbisigh, was born about 1585 in Lecain Co Sligo. At a young age he went to live at the School of Law and History, which at that time was run by the Mac Eagans of Lecain, in Ormond, modern day Tipperary. From there he went to study at the legal and literary school run by the O'Davorans in the Burren of County Clare, in the year 1595, under the guidance of Daniel O'Davoren, where his subjects included Greek and Latin. From then there is no information on *Mac Firbisigh* until he surfaces in Galway in the year 1645. Here he made the acquaintance of Roderick O'Flaherty, author of *Ogygia,* and Dr John Lynch author of *Cambrensis Eversus*, to both of whom he became tutor. It was at this time that he commenced his work on Irish genealogies, which he did not finish until 1650 at the College of St Nicholas. Eugene O'Curry has this to say about this work.

"This book is perhaps, the greatest national genealogical compilation in the world, and when we remember his great age at the time of its completion, and that he neither received nor expected reward from anyone, that he wrote this book (as he himself says), simply for the enlightenment of his countrymen, the honour of his country, and the glory of God, we cannot but feel admiration for his enthusiasm and piety, and veneration for the man who determined to close his life by bequeathing this precious legacy to his native land"[19].

When Galway surrendered to the Cromwellian forces in 1652, *Mac Firbisigh* lost one of his sponsors. Despite the adverse conditions he continued with the task of transcribing ancient manuscripts which were rapidly decaying. In 1655 he was employed by Sir James Ware to collect and translate material from the Irish annals, to be included in his Ecclesiastical History of Ireland.Upon the death of his sponsor Sir James Ware, *Dubhaltach, left Dublin and returned to* Sligo where he met a sudden and violent death in the year 1670, as narrated in the following passage by Professor Eugene O'Curry,

"Mac Firbis was at that time under the ban of the penal laws, and consequently, a marked and almost defenceless man in the eyes of the law, while the friends of the murderer enjoyed the full protection of the constitution. He must have been then past his eightieth year, and he was, it is believed, on his way to Dublin, probably to visit Robert, the son of Sir James Ware. He took up his lodgings for the night in the village of Dunflin, in his native county. While sitting and resting himself in a little room of the shop, a young gentleman of the Crofton family came in, and began to take some liberties with a young woman who had care of the shop. She, to check

---

[19] O'Curry Eugene. <u>Manuscript Materials of Irish History 1861</u> N.L.I.

his freedom, told him that he would be seen by the old gentleman in the next room; upon which in a sudden rage, he snatched up a knife from the counter, rushed furiously into the room, and plunged it into the heart of Mac Firbis. Thus it was that, at the hand of a wanton assassin, this great scholar closed his long career- the last of the regularly educated and the most accomplished master of the history, antiquities, and laws and language of ancient Erin"[20].

Queen Elizabeth 1

Elizabeth Tudor succeeded her sister, Mary Tudor, to the throne of England on November 28 1558. She inherited a divided kingdom, an empty Treasury and a mountain of debt. Born of the union of Henry VIII and Anne Boleyn, during the lifetime of Henry's first wife, she had been bastardised and disinherited by her own father. The Catholic nobility of Europe denounced her as a heretic, a bastard, and a usurper and claimed that Mary Queen of Scots was the rightful heir to the throne of England. She was excommunicated by Pope Pius Quintus in 1569. One of the longest serving monarchs on the throne of England, Elizabeth is remembered by the English with pride and affectionately known as Good Queen Bess. In Ireland however, she is remembered with hatred and hostility because of her continued imposition of Reformation policies which had been aban-doned by her predecessor. The devastation and slaughter carried out by her armies is still remembered in the folklore of the people. In folklore she is portrayed as both treacherous and promiscuous as the following legend relates, "Brian 'na Múrtha' O'Ruairc, chieftain of the O'Rouaircs of Breifne, was invited by Queen Elizabeth 1 of England to come to London to swear fealty to her. On seeing that he was a handsome man she arranged that he be accommodated in a lavish apartment in her palace. Whilst staying in this apartment he was visited in his bedroom by an unknown lady. One night he noticed by the moonlight that the lady was wearing a beautiful ring. On the following day he noticed the same ring on the Queen's finger and let her know that he recognised it. On the following night an assassin was sent to his room to kill him".

Another legend tells how Elizabeth had a different man brought to her bed chamber every night and under cover of darkness would remove a button from his jacket in order to identify him the following morning and have him executed .However an Irishman outwitted her, by removing a button from the jacket of all her soldiers while they slept. The next day she was unable to identify the man who had slept with her the night before.

---

[20] O'Curry Eugene. <u>Manuscript Materials of Irish History 1861 N.L.I</u>

Three of her protegé's, Essex, Francis Drake, and Walter Raleigh, are remembered in Irish folk tradition as being associated with the massacres at Mullaghmast, Rathlin Island and Smerwick.

Dublin Martyrs

Margaret Ball

Housewife, mother, widow, Mayoress of Dublin. Born circa 1515 at Screen, Co Meath. Gave refuge to priests in her home, Arrested during the celebration of Mass. Died in prison 1584. Declared blessed on September 1992.

Francis Taylor

Merchant and Alderman of Dublin. Born 1550 at Swords Co Dublin, elected Mayor of Dublin 1595. Imprisoned for seven years without charge or trial. Died in prison 30th January 1621.

The bronze memorial at the front of the Pro-Cathedral, Dublin .
It commemorates the martyrdom of Margaret Ball and Francis Taylor.

Conor O'Devany O.F.M. Bishop of Down and Connor.
Patrick O'Loughran O.F.M. priest, Dublin 1st February 1612
Peter O'Higgins O.P. priest, Dublin 1624

Place names of Dublin by The O'Rahilly published in An Claidheamh Soluis 1915.

According to the O'Rahilly the ancient Gaelic name for Dolphin's Barn is *Carnan Cloch*= the little heap of stones. During the Penal Days Mass used to be celebrated in the barn of a Mr Dolphin in this area, hence the name Dolphin's Barn.
(Ordnance Survey Letters Dublin)

Letter to the High Sheriff of the City of Dublin

Whereas we are informed that Charles Dempsey (parish priest of St Brides) and several other popish priests are now confined to New Gate and be under the rule of transportation. These are therefore to direct and require you to cause the said Charles Dempsey and the other convict popish priests now in your custody to be delivered to such merchant owners or Masters of shipps lying within the harbour of Dublin as are or shall be outward bound for any place or port not within either of the kingdoms of Great Britain or Ireland in order to their transportation such merchant owner or master having entered into a recognisance of the penalty of fifty pounds for each of the said priests before the Lord Mayor of the City of Dublin with condition that such merchant owner or master shall transport said priests into some place not within this kingdom or Great Britain.

26 March 1713   J Dawson
To the High Sheriff of the City of Dublin[21]

Seathrún Céitín 1580- 1650
Geoffrey Keating

Seathrún Céitín was born near Cahir Co. Tipperary in 1580, his early education may have been at the MacCraith school of Seanchas at Burges not far from his probable home at Moorestown Castle in the parish of Inishlounaght. He studied for the secular Priesthood in France, and was connected to the universities of Reims and Bordoux. In a list published in the year 1619 by Derby MacCarthy an entry reads,
"P.Geofroy Ketting, docteur en Theologie Vatterford."

---

[21] William P Burke Rev <u>The Irish Priests in the Penal Times</u> N Harvey & Waterford 1914.

He returned to the Diocese of Lismore and Waterford in 1610, where he built a reputation as a fearless preacher. A plaque erected in 1644 over the west doorway of a chapel known as *Cílín Chiaráin in the Parish of Tubbrid bears testimony* to this.

Orate pro animabus Parochi Eugenii Duhy de Tubrud,
Et Divinitatus Doctoris Galfridi Keating hujus Sacelli
Fundatorum; nec non et pro omnibus aliis tam Sacerdotibus
Quam laicis quorum corpora in eodem jacent sacello. Anno Domini
1644
Translation
Pray for the souls of the Priest Eugenius Duhy, Vicar of Tybrud
And of Jeffry Keating. D.D. Founders of this chapel, and also for
All others, both priest and laity, whose bodies lay in the same chapel
In the year of the Lord 1644[22]

The plaque above the west doorway of Cílín Chiaran Tiobraid.

---

[22] Keatings General History of Ireland 1865 I.R 94101 K 5 Dermod O'Connor, Esq
Dublin, James Duffy Wellington Quay 1865

To find this chapel go to Cahir in County Tipperrary take the road to Clogheen go through the crossroads at Kilcomman till you come upon the sign for Tubbrid.
Map no 74 Discovery Series grid ref 034 182

An early work in prose *Eochair-Sgiath an Aifrinn* an explanatory defence of the mass is written as a counter Reformation piece. This was followed by *Trí Bior-Ghaoithe an Bháis* - The Three Sharp Shafts of Death, a meditation on sin and death.

His best known work, written in 1634- *Foras Feasa ar Éirinn* a narrative history of Ireland, is said to have been written in a cave in the Glen of Aherlow, where he was in hiding, as a consequence of a sermon he delivered which offended a member of the Butler family. Elinor Laffan, the wife of Squire Moclar, imagining that a sermon delivered by Doctor Keating was directed against her, invoked the aid of the President of Munster, who immediately put the Penal Laws into effect, the result being; "orders were immediately issued for horse and foot to go in quest of our preacher, as obnoxious to the laws provided against seminary priests etc and a great reward to any who would apprehend him[23]"

I was unable to locate the cave in the Glen of Aherlow. A Mr Denis Lonergan informed me that he had heard the old folk say it was in the vicinity of Kilmoyler on the Cahir to Limerick road and that it was close to a river.

A report drawn up in 1613 containing "the names of sundrie priests and friars within some dioces and counties of Ireland, that you may see what numbers of priests were come over, and whether yt were not tyme to look to their seducinge of the subjects". Goeffry Keating is believed to have been the Parish Priest of Cappaquin and a silver chalice is still in the church bearing the inscription **"Dominus Galfridus Keatinge Sacerd. Sacre Theologiae Doctor me fieri fecit, 23 February 1634"**.

The following is a letter from an ecclesiastic from the Province of Leinster to Father Luke Wadding in Rome.
"Ye 7th Feb 1630

"One Father Keating laboreth much, as I hear say is compiling Irish notes towards a history of Ireland. Ye man is very studious, and yet I fear if his worke ever come to light, it will need an amendment of ill warranted narrations. He could help you to many curiosities, of which you can make a better use than himself. I have no interest in the man, for I never saw him, for he dwelleth in Mounster"

---

[23] Clanrickards Memoirs, Prifoa, London 1722

Sheathrúin Céitinn's love of the Irish language is expressed in the following poem.

1

Milis an teanga an Ghaedhealg
Guth gan chabhair choigcríche
Glór gear-chaoin glé glinn gasta
Suairc séimhidhe sult-blasta

2

Gidh Eabhra teanga is seanda,
Gidh Laidean is léigheanta,
Uatha uirchi níor frithlinn
Fuaim nó focail do chomaoinn[24]

Translation

1

The Irish is a language completely sweet
In aid of which no foreign e'er did meet
A copious, free, keen, and extending voice
And mellifluent, brief; for mirth most choice

2

Although the Hebrew language be the first,
And that for learning Latin be the best
Yet, still, from them, the Irish ne'er was found
One word to borrow, to make its proper sound.

Oral tradition holds that he was murdered in the Church of St Nicholas formerly called Teampuill na Pláighe by Cromwellian soldiers on the 10th of May 1650[25]

Another epitaph to Keating
In one urn in Tybrid, hid from mortal eye
A, poet, prophet and a priest doth lie;
All these, and more than in one man would be
Cocentered were in famous Geoffry.

The Island Prisons of Inish Mór and Inishbofin

In the year 1653, all Roman Catholic priests were proclaimed to be guilty of high treason. It was a felony to shelter, aid, or abet one. It is estimated that at least one thousand were deported from Ireland. However many priests remained and some of those who had gone abroad earlier returned to

---

[24] Dánta Amhráin is Caointe, Sheathrúin Céitinn, Eoin Cathmhaolach Mac Giolla Eáin
Connradh na Gaedhilge Baile Átha Cliath 1900
[25] Waterford Archaeological Journal April 1895

minister to their flocks. With a bounty of five pounds on their heads, they were hunted down without mercy, captured and imprisoned and sold into slavery on the sugar plantations in the West Indies International pressure was brought to bear on the English government, which caused them to re-examine this action. As a result in the month of February 1657, the government decided that the Islands of Inish Mór and Inishbofin were to be used as prison camps for the many priests who were being held in different gaols around the country. At first, fifty priests were transported to these islands, and in the year 1659 a further thirty-six were incarcerated there. At various times public funds were made available for the building of "cabins and the prisons for the said Popish priests". Their plight was desperate, accounts record that they were starving, being forced to live on herbs and water.

With the collapse of the Commonwealth and the restoration of King Charles II to the throne of England in 1660 the condition of the Irish clergy began to improve. It was not until 1662 however, that those clergy who were imprisoned on Inish Mór and Inishbofin were released; it is said that this was done in deference to the new Queen of England, who was a Catholic. Father Brian Conny O.F.M. died on Inishbofin after the others had been released.

Treasury Warrant 1657

" To Col Tho,s, Sadlier, Goverer of Galway, the sum of £100 upon account to be by him issued as he shall conceive meet for the maintainance of such Popish priests as are or shall be confined in the island of Buffin, after the allowance of sixpence per diem each. And for building of cabins, and other necessary accommodation for them.
    Dated 3rd July 1657"[26]

> "They bribed the flock, they bribed the son
> To sell the priest, to sell the sire
> Their dogs were taught alike to run
> Upon the scent of wolf and friar"
> Thomas Davis

---

[26] Treasury Warrants p 352

Dedication of The Annals of the Four Masters

"I invoke the Almighty God, that he may pour down every blessing, corporal and spiritual, on Ferrall O'Gara, Tiern (Lord) of Moy Gara and Culavinne, one of the two knights elected to represent the county of Sligo in the Parliament held in Dublin, this present year 1634".

" It is self evident, wherever nobility and honour flourish, that nothing is more glorious or more worthy of praise than to revive the knowledge of ancient authors and of the illustrious personages and nobles of former times, so that succeeding generations might cherish the memory of their ancestors".

"I, Michael O'Clerigh, a poor brother of the Order of Saint Francis, have come before you, O noble Farrell O'Gara, knowing what grief and sorrow it was to you (for the glory of God and the honour of Ireland) that the race of the gael had passed under a cloud of darkness, and that no memorial remains of our saints and virgins, our bishops, abbots, and church dignitaries, our kings and princes, lords, chieftains and men of learning. I explained to you that I thought I could get the assistance of the chroniclers whom I most esteemed to compile a book of annals, in which the aforesaid matters might be put on record; and that, should they not be written down now, they would not again be discovered to be put on record until the end of the world.[27]"

"On 22nd of January 1630, this work was undertaken in the convent of Dunagall, and was finished in the same convent on the 10th of August 1636"

"I am thine most affectionately "

"Brother Michael O'Clery"

Compiled by

Brother Michael O'Clery, Maurice O'Maolconary, the son of Torna,
Fergus Maolconary, son of Lochlan, of the Countie of Roscommon,
Cucogry O'Clery from Donegal, Cucogry O'Duigenan from Leitrim,
Conary O'Clery from Donegal.

Books used in the compilation of the Annals of the Four Masters.

The Annals of Clonmacnoise.
The Annals of the Island of Saints on the lake of Rive
The Annals of Senat Mac Magnus on the lake of Erne (now called the Ulster Annals)
The Annals of the Maolconarys
The annals of Kilronan compiled by the O'Duigenans

---

[27] Annals of The Kingdom of Ireland by the four masters N.L.I. ir 941 a5

The Annals of Lacan compiled by the MacFirbisses.

The Annals of Clonmacnoise and those of the Island of Saints come down no further than 1227. The second part of this work commences with the year 1208.
The Book of the O'Duigenans from 900 to 1563
The Book of Maolin Mac Bruodin from 1588 to 1603
The Book of Lughad O'Clery from 1586 to 1602

"In front of these evidences we find the dedication of the whole work to Fergal O'Gara Lord of Moy O'Gara and Coolavin in the County of Sligo. The chieftain under whose patronage, and for whose use, the Annals are compiled."

Teige-an-tSleibhe (i.e. Teige of the Mountains) O'Clery, who was the chief compiler of the Annals of the Four Masters, was born about 1575 in the parish of Kilbarron, near Ballyshannon in County Donegal. He was the fourth son of Donough O'Clery, who was the grandson of Tuathal O'Clery head of the Tirconnell branch of the family, who died in 1512. On joining the Franciscan Order in Louvain, he changed his name from Teige to Michael, which was customary at that time. He remained a lay brother and with the consent and support of the Order he continued to practice the hereditary profession of historian. Soon after joining the Order of St Francis at Louvain he was sent back to Ireland, by the Guardian of the Irish convent there, Hugh Ward, to collect and copy old Irish Manuscripts. During the next fifteen years he visited the most distinguished scholars and antiquaries of the time. He transcribed from ancient manuscripts, many lives of saints, several genealogies, and Martyrologies, all of which he transmitted to Hugh Ward in Louvain. Hugh Ward, however died on November 8th 1635, and these works were passed on to the Rev John Colgan, Jubilate lecturer of Theology at Louvain.

On December 8th 1641, an act was passed in Parliament to the effect that the Catholic religion should never be tolerated in Ireland, and in order to carry this act into execution, the Lords Justice issued the following order to the commanders of the Irish forces.

"It is resolved, that it is fit his Lordship do endeavour, with his Majesty's forces, to slay and destroy all the said rebels, and their adherents and relievers, by all the ways and means he may; and burn, destroy, spoil, waste, consume, and demolish all the places, towns and houses where the said rebels are or have been relieved and harboured, and all the hay and corn there, and kill and destroy all the men there inhabiting able to bear arms."

Brian Boy Magee

I am Brian Boy Magee
My father was Eoghan Bán
I was wakened from happy dreams
By the shouts of my startled clan;
And I saw through the leaping glare
That marked where our homestead stood,
My mother swing by her hair
And my brothers lie in their blood.

In the creepy cold of the night
The pitiless wolves came down
Red troops from that Castle grim
Guarding Knockfergus Town,
And they hacked and lashed and hewed
With musket rope and sword,
Till my murdered kin lay thick
In pools by the Slaughter ford.

I fought by my fathers side
And when we were fighting sore
We saw a line of their steel
With our shrieking women before
The red-coats drove them on
To the verge of the Gobbins grey
Hurried them- God, the sight
As the sea foamed up for its prey.

O tall were the Gobbin cliffs
And sharp were the rocks, my woe
And tender the limbs that met
Such terrible death below,
Mother and babe and maid
They clutched at the empty air
With eyeballs widened in fright
In that hour of despair
Sleep soft in your heaving bed,
O little fair love of my heart!
The bitter oaths I have sworn
Shall be of my life a part,
And for every piteous prayer
You prayed on your way to die
May I hear an enemy plead
While I laugh and deny.

In the dawn that was gold and red
Ay, red as the blood soaked stream,
I crept to the perilous brink
Dear Christ, was the night a dream?
In all the Island of Gloom
I only had life that day
Death covered the green hill-sides
And tossed in the Bay.

I have vowed by the pride of my sires
By my mother's wandering ghost
By my kinfolk's shattered bones
Hurled on the cruel coast
By the sweet dead face of my love
And the wound in her gentle breast
To follow that murderous band
A sleuth- hound who knows no rest.

I shall go to Phelim O'Neill
With my sorrowed tale, and crave
A blue- bright band of Spain,
In the ranks of the soldiers brave
And God grant me the strength to wield
That shining avenger well
When the Gael shall sweep his foe
Through the yawning gates of Hell.

I am Brian Boy Magee!
And my creed is a creed of hate;
Love, Peace I have cast aside
But , Vengeance, Vengeance I wait!
Till I pay back the four-fold debt
For the horrors I witnessed there
When my brothers moaned in their blood,
And my mother swung by her hair.

This poem written by Ethna Carbery (1866-1902) remembers the slaughter
of the Magee clan, at the Gobbin Cliffs on Island Magee, in 1641, by the
Redcoats.

Cín Lae Uí Mheallháin.
Friar O Meallan Journal.

Cín Lae Uí Mheallháin is an account of the progress of the Confederate war from the outbreak of rebellion in 1641 until February 1647. It was written, in Irish, by the Franciscan, Tarlach Ó Mealláin, and reflects the Ulster Catholic view of events.

History of the manuscript

Dr William Reeves (1815-92) borrowed the manuscript from Viscount O Neill so that it could be accurately copied, by the scholar Eugene O Curry and his transcript (M.S 23H7) can be seen in the Royal Irish Academy. The original was clandestinely removed from the R.I.A, and its whereabouts were unknown till it reappeared in the second decade of the last century. It is now in the Boole Library of University College, Cork. Reeves made a copy of O'Curry's work, now preserved in Trinity College, Dublin, to which he added the English translation made by Robert MacAdam.
Robert MacAdam, 'Friar O' Meallan's Narrative of the Wars of 1641' in R.M Young (ed) , *Historical notices of Old Belfast pp200-47*.A note on p. 247 of above indicates that a copy was in the Grainger collection in Belfast Free Library (now Belfast Central Library), but a careful search failed to produce the copy. A further copy was in the possession of Rev J O'Laverty, M.R.I.A, but its present location is also unknown. Fr Laurence P. Murray used both the R.I.A, and T.C.D, copies when he published the *Cín Lae,* with an English translation, in the County Louth Archaeological Journal. Laurence P. Murray (ed) 'An Irish diary of the confederate wars' in County Louth Archaeological Journal 1923 to 1930. Where he described MacAdams work as a fairly good English translation. Made directly from the original but noted that, "O' Curry was faithful enough in regard to words, but he transcribed hurriedly, and our impression is that he expanded contractions in accordance with his own ideas of what the missing portion of the word should have been, and he is very careless in reproducing accents, aspirations and eclipses.
The original manuscript was discovered in the Library of Cork University in 1930 (*Lsgr Ó M urchada 111= MS 111of the Ó Murchada Collection).* Soon after this discovery an excellent redaction was made by Professor Tadhg Ó Donnchada (Torna) and published in Analecta Hibernica no.3 (1931)

The Author

Friar Ó Mealláin was one of the Franciscan community who, were expelled from their friary in Armagh, at the end of the sixteenth century, and were forced to seek refuge in the remote areas of South Tyrone. He was a member of a small group who sought the protection of the Ó' Neill Clan of Cashlan. There they built a small friary near the southern shore of a small lake which is now known as Friary Lough.

On June 14th 1643 Eoghan Rua Ó Neill spent the night as guest of the friars. Shortly after his departure the next morning, the Scots burnt the friary. Tradition holds that in such dangerous times the friars took shelter in nearby Carrycastle, where they said mass in a secluded ravine.

Ó Mealláin who was chaplain to Sir Phelim O'Neill was a member of an ecclesiastical family, who were hereditary keepers of the Bell of St Patrick (*Clog na hUachta*). They were a sept of the *Cinéal Eoghan* and ruled an area known as *An Mheallánacht* which encompassed an area of Tyrone and Derry between Slieve Gullion and Lough Neagh.

Translation

Page 1

On the eve of the feast (*oidhche Féil*) of Saint John Capistranus the lords of Ulster planned to seize in one night, unknown to the English and Scots, all their walled towns, castles and bawns. The date chosen was the 22nd of October, Friday to be precise, and the last day of the moon. First, to attack Dublin there went there from Ulster the lord of Enniskillen, Conor Maguire, son of Brian, son of Conor, Hugh Óg MacMahon, son of Brian, son of Hugh Óg, son of Hugh, son of Séan Buí, and Rory O More of Upper Orior; also a party from Meath, from other parts of Leinster and from Munster, etc. Eoghan Connolly, however, made known their plan.

The gates of Dublin were closed, the bells of the City were rung, houses ransacked, and the lord of Enniskillen and young MacMahon captured. The others made good their escape.

Sir Feilim O'Neill, son of Tarlach, son of Henry Óg, son of Sean, son of Conn, son of Henry, son of Eoghan etc, was appointed General in Ulster. Charlemont (*Serlimont*) was captured, its governor Lord Caulfield and all his subordinates (*agus a roibh ann ó sin síos*) made prisoner. Randal MacDonnell, son of Feardorcha, son of Eoin etc, and Pádraig Modhartha O'Donnelly captured Dungannon, took its Captain Perkins and made all his men prisoner. The great fort of Mountjoy was captured by Captain Tarlach Gruama O'Quinn and all its soldiers made prisoners. Lord Caulfields stronghold in Ballydonnelly fell to Pádraig Modartha O'Donnelly, and the manor house of Moneymore, Sir John Clotworty's town, fell to the Commander Cormac O'Hagan (*Guibberneoir*). Mister Whistler's stronghold, Salterstown castle in Killeter was taken by Feilim Gruama O'Neill, son of Niall, son of Feilim Balbh.

Page 2
1641, October

The garrison of Liscallaghan was captured by the men of Keirigeir under the command of Conn O'Neill son of Art, son of Dónal, son of Séan na Mallacht, and the English wardens who occupied it were taken.

23 [Saturday]

The strongly fortified garrison of Tandragee in Orior was captured by Pádraig Óg O' Hanlon who was himself killed the same day. Newry and its great castle were Captured by Conn Magennis son of the lord of Iveagh. The town of Dundalk was captured by Lieutenant- General Brian O'Neil of the Fews, son of Hugh Buí, son of Tarlach, son of Enrí na Garthan, aided by the men of the Fews (*Sliocht Aodh (a)* .

24 [Sunday]

On Sunday Desertmartin and the Manor house of Magherafelt were captured by the Commander Cormac O'Hagan.

26 [Tuesday]

Armagh was captured by General Sir Feilim. Many English had secured themselves in the cathedral there. They had made ample provisions and the means of defending themselves but they accepted the generous quarter offered them.

November

A hosting organised by Sir Feilim marched to Bellaghy. A messenger sent by Sir Feilim to Mister Conway demanding the surrender of the town was met with refusal.

The town was then burnt to the ground and all its haggards, after which Mister Conway accepted quarter and was given safe conduct across the Bann to Masserene. The Manor house of Bellaghy, Sir William Nugents place, and the manor house of Magherafelt were all burnt the same day.

Page 3
1642

To return to the governor. As they crossed the Bann they found that one of their captains, William Taffe, had fallen some distance behind. As he was approaching Movanagher, a foraging party of eleven hundred was on its way from Colereine to Killyquinn to plunder the route. It happened that Séamus (MacDonnell), son of Alastar Carach, Séamus (MacDonnell, son of Colla, and the two sons of Colla Ciotach (MacDonnell) were already encamped at Killyquinn and they sent a message to William Taafe to remain in a wooded glen (*fuireach I ngleann coilleadh*) by the Bann till the Scots approached.

When they saw them drawing near they were to unfurl their banner and beat their drum. This was done and the MacDonnells attacked in full strength; the English allowed them to come in full flight behind them *(do leigeadur na Sasanaigh I raon madhma iad tar a n-ais)* and they were none the better for it. Nine hundred and forty-eight of their numberwere killed at Bendooragh.

To return to governor Tarlach O'Neill, son of Tarlach, son of Henry Óg.

He proceeded to Maserene where two of his captains, Séan O'Hagan, son of Henry, son of Rory Buí, and Captain O Hara, were killed. They left the town and set fire to the corn crops and homesteads of all the Scots and English from there to Larne.

To return to the General. He ordered many of captains to advance with him to Drogheda and ordered a fat beast, a meadar of butter, and four silver shillings to be levied on each ballyboe from Glasdrummond to Tullaghoge.

4 February [Friday]

The General left Charlemont for Armagh and before leaving that city hanged and beheaded six men for the death of Lord Caulfield, thence to Newry and Dundalk and to Beaulieu (Bethelin) where he had his camp. He sent four captains over the Boyne (ós Boinn). These were Niall Óg O'Neill, son of Niall, son of Tarlach, son of Conn Bacach, Pádraig Modartha O'Donnelly, Feilim an Chogaidh O'Neill, and Tarlach Gruama O'Quinn. The English came from the town (*as an gcathraigh)* with a cannon mounted on a cart flanked by the troops (*turpaidhe)*. The Irish swiftly attacked, killed forty of the enemy with a loss of six men. As [the rest] retreated, Captain Niall O'Neill caught them against a stone wall that was near them. His men closed the gate behind them. They [the English?] brought up the cannon to break down the gate but the gun cart broke as they got close to it and they were a long time repairing it (*da corugbadh)*. Night came upon them, they buried the dead in the soft ground and returned to the town. The Irish recrossed the Boyne to Beauilieu, the camp of Sir Phelim, the General.

5 March 1642 [Saturday]

Having learned from their spies that the General would be in the camp of the MacMahons and MacKennas at mid-day on 5 March, the enemy sent a troop of cavalry and a hundred infantry against the MacMahon camp. Although these were resisted for some time, Art Rua MacMahon son of Padraig, son of Art Maol, was wounded and captured, and his brother Rory and many others of our men were killed. That was the day of Tullyallen.

6 March the first Sunday of Lent.

Sermons were preached in Armagh by the Guardian Paul O'Neill, in the church of Carnteel by Fr Henry Ó'Mealláin, in Clonfeacle by Fr Éamon Rua

MacCawell (*Mac Cathmhaoil*) and in the manor house of Dungannon by Fr Joannes A Santo Patritio.

There was a portion of the loft collapsed under the weight of the congregation; several were killed and others had bones broken.

Acting on orders received, Colonel Tarlach O'Neill, son of Art Óg, son of Tarlach Luinach, proceeded to Tir Chonaill where he unfurled seven banners by the banks of the River Finn. On the opposite side was a party of Scots with ten banners unfurled. The O'Donnells (*Conallaigh*) had Sir Ralph Gore and a large company surrounded in Magherbeg. The Scots were on their way to relieve Sir Ralph. The sons of Art Óg (*clan Airt Oig*) and the O'Neills of west Tyrone (*sliocht Airt*) moved after them.

Page 5
March 1642
26 [Saturday]

General O'Neill brought three big guns from Drogheda to Dundalk. Present were his own company and those of Alastar Hovenden and Hugh Buí, son of Calvagh [O'Donnell]. Lord Moore and Sir Henry Tichburne, with eleven standard bearers and three troops of cavalry, attacked them (*Tanic orra*) on the Saturday preceeding Passion Sunday. They approached Warrens Gate on the south dide. They were twice forced to withdraw from the town, several of them being laid low on the greens

(*agus iad da leagadh'na ndrongaibh ar fad na faithchí*) The Irish- those who wore buff coats- attemped to scale the walls. They fired a field gun at them and the gate was broken down. Here they come! They filled the town. More than three hundred of the English, having been killed, the General and his people withdrew with a loss of only four men and six wounded. This was the day the General's piper (*fer ciuil a' Gen*), Thomas Sgimes, was killed in Dundalk.

As regards the General. A great hosting of men marched with him to Dundalk. With him were the Lieutenant General of armaments who had received his training in the army of King Phillip (*fuair [a] thogbhail súas í n-arm in ríogh pilip*) and by Colonel Tarlach O'Neill, son of Henry, son of Tarlach, son of Henry, son of Feilim Rua. They pitched camp beside Dundalk where they lost Tobias Quinn, one of their best cavalry- men (*marcach maith dia muintir*).

The General sent letters to Colonel Tarlach O'Neill, to Sliocht Airt, to the sons of Seán Óg O'Neill and to Art O'Neill, son of Conn, son of Seán, with instructions to await him at the Finn with their very best men (*maillí [re] na dtoighestal airm*).

He sent an emissary from Tullahoge to order the army at Farsetmona (*Fersad Mhonaidh*) to meet him at Kilcronaghan to be reviewed. He spent the night of 20 April at the house of Commander Cormac O'Hagan in Moneymore, and the following night in Calmore in the house of a good

Catholic gentleman named Crosby ['trosbi' in M.S] who was given safe conduct by the general to Coleraine. Among the party who were presented for review in the parish of Kilcronaghan.

Page 6

Were the following Captains from Tullahoge; Feilim Modartha O'Hagan, Seán O'Hagan, son of Cormac; Seán O'Hagan, son of Eoghan; Nial O'Quinn; Hugh O'Hagan, son of Tadhg; Pádraig Ó Mealláin, son of Rory Ballach; Rory Murre O'Devlin; Feilim Gruama O'Neill; Cormac O'Neill of Outleckan, Donal O'Neill, son of Cú Uladh, son of Seán; Art Óg O'Hagan, son of Donal, son of Hugh; Brian O'Neill, son of Feardorcha, son of [Brian] Carrach; Art son of Hugh, son of Seán *ón iair [ón Arrachtra?]*, and William Taffe. A thousand of these were detailed to guard the country between there and Derry, Limavady, *Ard a' Choillin* [Artikelly?] and Coleraine and to keep watch on the boats of Lough Neagh and Clannaboy. Meanwhile the General with a troop of horse proceeded to Strabane where resided the widowed lady of the earl of Abercorn's son.

They attacked the Scots that day and the son of Rory Galda O'Neill was killed. The General took the lady to his home in Charlemont and left her wardens, the Divin family, in Strabane with Seán MacNamee in charge of them. Three days later the Scots of Lifford crossed to Strabane, the wardens fled but all were killed except those who made good their escape by their fleetness of foot. The Scots then entered the manor house and, had they remained within and closed the doors, they were in no danger as they had powder and shot, pikes and swords, food and drink.To return to the General; he sent Patrick Hamill, a friar of the Order of St Francis with a company of horsemen to accompany the lady to Sir George Hamilton in Munster. Because of a five year vow she had made, she declined an offer of marriage from the General whose own wife, the daughter of the Lord of Iveagh, had died the previous autumn.

1 May [Sunday]

Edward Monroe and four thousand men from Scotland came ashore in Trian Conghail and burnt and plundered the Irish till they reached Newry. The castle of Newry, which had an ample supply of food, arms and uniforms (*eide),* was surrendered to Munroe by Hugh Magennis, son of Dónal Óg, son of Éamon, the captain of the town. Monroe left five hundred men to garrison the town and the remaining three and a half thousand were ordered back to ravage Trian Conghail. A monk of the Order of St Bernard and a priest, Rory O'Sheil, were hanged and their bodies thrown over the bridge at Newry to be carried out to sea by the receding tide. Edward Monroe sent an emissary to Randal Óg [MacDonnell], the earl of Antrim, who invited him to Dunluce. The outcome of the invitation was that the earl was arrested and the town taken. Monroe garrisoned the town and the earl remained a prisoner.

Page 7
1642
The General sent Paul O'Neill to Galway to purchase powder and after an absence of forty days, he returned with a quantity of that commodity. Armagh was burnt; the cathedral, its belfry, its bells, its organs, its glass windows, the whole city of lime-washed houses together with all the books of divinity, logic and philosophy which were in the study of the English quarter. It was as a result of very warm weather and an easterly wind that the cathedral caught fire. Loughgall was burnt together with Tandragee, *Uí Nialláin* and *Uí Breasáil* Toaghy was also burnt, as were Maydown and Port Mor. The General issued a call to arms for an attack on Colonel Monroe, at Tandragee and about two thousand responded.

21 [Saturday]
A troop of cavalry came from Dundalk and pillaged the Fews and the area around *Sliabh Fuaid*. Tarlach O'Neill, son of Art Óg, son of Tarlach MacHenry, deprived them of their spoils and killed their captain and fourteen of his men. On the following day a troop of cavalry and a large company of infantry with some draught horses laden with provisions came from Dundalk to place a garrison in Glasdrummond castle. Seán O'Neill, who was in the castle at the time, set the upper story ablaze and he and his company withdrew to the bog. When the assailants saw the castle on fire they returned to Dundalk.

23 [Monday]
Dónal Geimhleach, the son of Ó Catháin, came from Spain and reached the General's quarters in Charlemont on the Sunday.

27 [Friday]
The Masserene Scots crossed Lough Neagh. Captain O'Hagan attacked them and, after four were killed and six wounded, they returned across the lough.

Page 8
May 1642
So huge a force of Scots arrived from Scotland to Trian Conghail that all the Irish, including the countess of Antrim, Sir James [MacDonnell] son of Alastar Carrach, Séamus [MacDonnell], son of Colla,

29

Séamus [MacDonnell], son of Godfrey, son of Henry, and the sons of Colla Ciotach [MacDonnell] fled from that place across the Bann.

31

as did the Lady Iveagh, Sorcha O'Neill, and the family of Lord Iveagh Macartan.

9 June [Thursday, the Feast of Corpus Cristi]

The General marched on the Scots of Tir Chonaill Thry hadn't been long in Tir Éanna when they came near them [the Scots] erected a breastwork that very night and, having placed two thousand musketeers within, they remained peaceful and quiet during the night. The Irish, by contrast, were talkative and perturbed. Early next morning each side charged the other. In the thick of the ensuing battle men were shot and men fell. The Scots decided to fall back to the safety of the breastwork. The Irish suffered heavy fire from them and their ranks of pike began to break. The General and O'Catháin fought steadfastly against the enemy who likewise began to break.The General urged his men to greater effort, saying that the Scots were in flight, but his call was in vain for they did not return. Among the many killed in the engagement were Captains Sean Buí O'Donnelly, Felim Modartha O'Hagan and Felim Gruama O'Neill. Alastar [MacDonnell, son of Colla Ciotach, was wounded. Losses were many. Above one hundred and forty, both blind and lame were killed. A Franciscan preacher named Friar Ludovic MacNamee from Armagh and a Fr Maurice MacCroddan were also killed. A crippled man called Niall O'Neill who had a wooden leg(*bacach coisi croinn),* struck with his big staff at a rider who was about to kill him, unhorsed and killed the rider, and took his horse and weapon.

14 July [Thursday]

Lord Conway, Lord Blaney, young Lord Caulfield and Lord Hamilton arrived with a large army and pitched camp close to Armagh from where they foraged the surrounding area. They sent a large company of cavalry for Lady Caulfield to the house of Laurance Netherville in Minterburn. They burnt Dromorragh, the residence of Sir Felim, together with his plate. Kinnard was burnt on the Sunday, to be precise.

Page 9
July

This great army proceeded to Dunavalley and encamped there. The General left Niall O'Neill in charge of Chalemont and, accompanied by Colonel Conn Óg O'Neill, son of Conn, son of Niall, son of Brian Faghartach, and O'Catháin, he went to Brantry to the house of the friars of Armagh. In spite of the guard on the ford at Port Mór, the English crossed and killed two horsemen of Tarlach Gruama O'Quinn, namely Naos and Pádraig Óg O'Quinn, the sons of Pádraig Mac Feilim Rua.

(July) 21 [Thursday]

Captain Richard Codan was placed in the garrison of Dungannon and, on the orders of the General, the town and surrounding area as well as the manor house of Balleydonnelly were burnt by Randal MacDonnell.Lord Conway and those lords [Blaney, young Caulfield and Hamilton] sent two emissaries to the captain of Charlemont to request the surrender of that town with the promise that he would be awarded the earldom of Tyrone."I will not surrender", was the reply.

After a four day assault on the place [Charlemont], these lords and their great army surrounded Dungannon. The wardens of the town, Nicholas O'Mackin, Pádraig MacManus, Laurence O'Cullen and the others, surrendered [the town] together with the prisoners who were held fettered there. They handed Captain Codan over to Lord Conway who had him and his son hanged, along with a friar of the Order of St Dominic. After placing their own garrison of a troop of horse and some infantry in Dungannon and, hoping to reduce Charlemont in similar fashion, they returned there.

They besieged the place for three full days and nights but to no avail. Raising the siege, they killed old men, women and children, took away the herds of Hugh Buí [O'Donnell], son of Calbhach. They arrested the good priest and skilful preacher and choirist, Seamus O'Fallagan, and Hugh O'Quinn. Their lives would have been spared had they renounced their religion. Instead they were tortured and gibbeted (*Do riagbadg iad*). Letters of Eoghan O'Neill, son of Art, son of Feardorcha, to the effect that he had landed at Doe Castle, invited the Ulster General to meet him there. Three thousand responded to the invitation on 18 July.

Page 10
18 [Monday]

While our forces were absent in Tir Chonaill, the garrisons of Dungannon and Mountjoy plundered the Orritor area (*fon Arachtra*). They took more than three hundred cows and Pádraig Gruama O'Quinn was killed as were three veteran warriors, Feilim Balbh O'Muldoon and the brothers, Tarlach Dubh and Conor O'Gibbon.

31 [Sunday]

From the borders of Brantry at Knockacloy they took over one hundred and forty cows, as well as horses and their harness (*capaill fona mailingthibh*), sheep goats and other spoils (*fadbbhacha*).

4 Aug [Thursday]

The Scots and English mustered from Trian Conghail to Uí Nialláin to join with the Dungannon and Mountjoy garrisons (*i n-oirisgarasdon Dun G is Muinseói*) and crossed the Blackwater (*tar Dubhaill*). They plundered Cloncan and the following day returned to Dungannon with the spoils.

6 [Saturday]

Together they left Dungannon by night and proceeded to Largie Truagh, Clossagh, by the foothills of Slieve Beagh to Glendavagh. There happened to be parties [of Irish] in the woods and there was much slaughter and butchery on both sides. They brought the spoils to Dungannon that day and had eight [dead] troopers with them in sacks.

The same party proceeded to Mountjoy and having camped for some time by the edge of a wood, they were informed of booty to be had in the area around Slieve Gallion.

In taking it they killed (?) and his brother Conor Óg. Twelve of their troopers raided out towards Kilcronaghan and Maghera. The Ulstermen pursued them and not a man of them returned. They were either killed or drowned in the Bann.

12 [Friday, the Feast of Saint Clare]

An army of four thousand returned from Mountjoy to Dungannon. Getting word of booty in the house of Brian Hughes (*ag Brian Ó'hAodha*), *a priest of Glenkeen,* in the Minterburn area, they seized it and arrested Eamon O' Finn, another priest. One trooper rode back towards two young men of the creaght. They took up stones and pelted him with them. They unhorsed him, killed him on the spot and made off with his horse and gear. All that great plunder, seized in the places I have mentioned, they brought to Trian Conghail on the Feast day of Saint Clare.

13 [Saturday]

The General and Eoghan Rua with the O'Reillys, MacMahons, Maguire's people (*Manchaigh*) and the septs of Tyrone (*Eoghanaigh*), returned with a fresh supply of munitions and, as they approached, the English withdrew. The honourable, illustrious and steadfast general (Eoghan Rua) had arrived with a company of soldiers at Doe Castle having sailed by the northern sea with only one ship commanded by the daring Captain Antoni, the Fleming.

Page 11
August 1642
16 [Tuesday]

General Lelslie and Lord Aughinbreck arrived from Scotland and were met in Trian Chonghail by Colonel Munroe. Their combined force of eight thousand men marched to Colraine and on to Farsetmona where they were confronted by a large force under Dónal Geimhleach Ó'Catháin. The Scots having lost one hundred and fifty men, were forced to flee to the woods and the Irish suffered no losses. The people of the Barony of Loughinisholin and the Ó'Catháins (*Cathanaigh*) proceeded to Branter Truagh and Slieve Beagh. The General and Eoghan O'Neill were in Charlemont when they received word of [enemy] forces approaching. Accordingly, the General went to *Sliabh na Maol* where he mustered one thousand men and Eoghan O'Neill went into *Uí Nialláin* where he mustered two thousand.

22 [Monday]
The great Scottish army arrived in Dungannon and discharged a continuous volley of shots, the mighty noise of which I myself heard. They made camp that night at the island of Currin. They were close to Armagh;

24 [Wednesday, the feast of Saint Bartholomew]
and on the feast of Saint Bartholomew they marched to Newry. The General pursued them part of the way.

28 [Sunday]
On the feast of Saint Hieronimus Aug, the General sent five Captains to invest Dungannon and they took from it more than a hundred cows. Trenches were made around the castle and a tunnel excavated underneath it. Captain Jones surrendered on condition that he would be allowed his weapons, and given safe conduct (*adhlacadh*) to Mountjoy. These conditions were agreed to. The General placed Captain Padraig Modartha O'Donnelly in charge of Dungannon and, with him Captains Tarlach O'Neill, son of Art Óg, Tarlach O'Neill, son of Séan Óg, Randal MacDonnell and Nial Óg O'Neill.Art O'Neill, son of Hugh Buí, made a raid into Ballymascanlan, seized sixty cows (*deich mba agus da fhichit deug bó*) out of their enclosure and, fighting hard all the way, drove them through the gate out of the town.

Page 12
August 1642
29 [Monday]
This day was chosen for a general assembly of the Ulster nobles. The General and Eoghan together with all the Clanna Néill met in Clones with clan representatives of the O'Reillys, O'Cath, ains, MacRorys, O'Donnells (Síol nDalaigh), MacMahons, Maguires and the MacDonnells under Sir James MacDonnell, son of Alastar Carrach.
The purpose of the assembly was to appoint a [new] General. Sir Feilim relinquished that title in favour of his older kinsman Eoghan. Eoghan was appointed General of the Ulster forces and Sir Feilim their President.

8 Sept [Thursday]

Some soldiers were sent out with Lieutenant Colonel Séan Óg O'Neill, son of Séan, son of Brian Laighneach. A party of the enemy came in search of fuel. Sixteen of them were killed,and a further twelve the following day.Ó Catháin paid twenty- five pounds, towards the purchase of clothing, to Gillaspic and Randal MacDonnell, the two sons of Colla Ciotach, and quartered them on the Ó Catháin creaghts with free billeting (*agus coinnmbeadh ar'na croidheachtaibh Cathanach go tógbhail buannachta dhóibh*) Ó Catháin followed the General. The sons of Colla completed the muster of their people and ordered the soldiers to take with them the cows, horses, household effects, sheep, goats and even the personal belongings (*gona bhfadhbacha*) of every family on which they were quartered. This was done and they brought the plunder to Colraine where they erected strong enclosures for its protection. The General placed a thousand men to protect the Bann against the enemy of whom there was a large number in Trian Conghail.

3 Oct

The earl of Ormond came with four thousand men and laid siege to Carrickmacross. Captain Fox and the wardens escaped. The following day the foreigners (*na goill)* Came to the manor house and hanged Lady Evelyn, the wife of Art Óg, son of Brian na mBarróg, and daughter of Eiver MacMahon, son of Cú Uladh.

Page 13
(Oct. 17, 1642) [Monday]

Pope Urban VIII sent arms for five hundred men to Ireland Sir Feilim went to get Ulster's share of these arms. He married the daughter of Thomas Preston and received as dowry arms for five hundred horsemen, two hundred muskets and three thousand pounds.The Irishmen (*fir Eirionn*) decided to establish a parliament and council in Kilkenny.

23 November. [Wednesday]

The General attended the Kilkenny parliament.

13 Dec. [Tuesday]

The Enniskillen garrison was taking plunder when they were set upon by the Maguires. Three of our captives- Denis Carrach MacCabe, Séamus [MacDonnell son of Godfrey, son of Henry, and Captain MacCabe- were killed, together with other ranks not accounted for here.

6 January 1643 [Friday]

The General, accompanied by Sir Feilim, returned from the Council of Kilkenny to Charlemont. The plunderer (*in creachadoir*), Rory O'Haran, brought a great hosting from Derry including the son of Sir Thomas Phillips and the people of the Castles.

27 April [Thursday]
In Ballinascreen they met Niall O'Neill the priest of Cappagh (*Ceapach Mhe Cuarta*). From there they proceeded to Lissan where the iron foundry of Tantagilta was burnt by them. They seized a stud of horses from Niall Óg O' Quinn together with his pigs, sheep and about twenty guns. Sean O' Hagan and his people were pillaged.
Rory Ballach Ó Mealláin was captured and Cookstown was burnt.

27 April
The Colraine soldiers came to Rallagh and attacked Cormac O'Neill, son of Feilim Óg, plundered his district and killed his followers, the MacWilliams (*clan Uilliam*).
From there they proceeded to Loughinisholin and to Moneymore where the two hosts were close to each other. They collected a great deal of spoil and the creaghts, after many of them were stripped (*tar eis moran do lomadh*), fled to Dungannon.
The foreigners (*in gall*) returned to Loughinisholin. They sent (their prisoner) Rory Ballach Ó'Mealláin to demand the surrender of the island from Sean O'Hagan, son of Eoghan, son of Eamon Óg, but O'Hagan refused, they fired three cannon shots and then withdrew to their own homes rich in spoil.

27 April
In spite of the efforts of the Irish, the garrison of Mountjoy on Thursday, to be precise, sallied forth with a one thousand-man reinforcement from Mass-erene. They seized thirty cows from Feilim an Chogaidh O'Neill.

28 [Friday]
The following day they raided Cloncan from the same boats and took spoil. The General's men pursued them, killed over sixty of them, retrieved the spoil and took a large quantity of arms. Of the Generals side, eight soldiers of the regiment of Art O'Neill, son of Cormac, son of Tarlach Breasalach were killed. With the return of Sir Feilim the besieging was doubled so that nobody was allowed out and the [Masserene] party was obliged to return empty-handed in the same boats.

Page 14
May 1643
4 May [Thursday]
An army of three thousand men, led by Sir Robert Stewart, came from Tir Chonaill, Plundered the Clossagh and proceeded into Truagh. Five of their horsemen broke from their main line and went to Largie. Sir Feilim and

O'Cathāin happened to be here (abbos) with a hundred horse and as many foot. Donal Geimhleach Ó'Cathāin went out on a reconnaissance of the enemy and found the five horsemen nearby. He gave spur to his horse as he was between the two forces (mar bhí idir in dá shluaigh) But his mount fell. As her head was underneath her body he was unable to raise her before he was taken prisoner; his troops made good their escape by the speed of their horses. Sir Feilim, saying that he would not let Ó'Cathāin be taken from him, immediately followed. A Scotsman, however put a bullet through the head of Ó'Cathāin who fell lifeless to the ground. They took his horse and his arms with them. Sir Feilim found the body and had it buried in Armagh. Elswhere the enemy came to Ballymakenny and after taking the town and a large supply of valuables, they returned.They hanged the priest Henry MacIlmurray in his own parish of Drumragh on Sunday to be precise.

12 May. [Friday]
Robert Munroe, with four thousand men, arrived at Tandragee and began burning houses in Uí Niallāin. The Generals company, both horse and foot, came upon them at the time. A cavalry lieutenant, two captains and several infantrymen were killed.
Night fell upon them and the creaghts of upper Clannaboy, Iveagh and county Armagh fled to Brantry, Oriel, etc. However, the Scots were not without plunder. Three corn- mills were burnt by then. Sir Feilim sent a party to Annasamry to take away what arms were in the Generals house and about three hours later the enemy arrived and burnt Annasamry. A large company of them proceeded to Clancan and plundered it. Sir Feilim sent Colonel Thomas Sanford and three hundred men to intercept them. The plunder was taken from them and about two hundred of them were killed. They were encamped for three days at Tandragee and returned with a large supply of wheat, meal and corn.The plunderer, Rory O'Haran, arrived and brought large forces of Scots troops from the Castles and, with the son of Thomas Phillips of Limavady proceeded to Orritor (don Fharachtra). They plundered Art and Tuathal O'Neill, the sons of Hugh Mac Seain, as well as Alastar Rua MacDonnell?, the people of Desertcreat and a number of others. More than two thousand took part in the onslaught,
They killed Fr Eoghan Modartha O'Crilly, a priest in the parish of Maghera, and his brother Conor Óg and a number of others. Sir Feilim with thirteen standards and many horsemen, pursued them but failed to catch up with them. On the same day Pádraig Modartha O'Loughran was buried in Donaghmore.

Wednesday, 24 May.
Lords Conway, Chichester, Blaney, Hamilton and Montgomery arrived with more than five thousand infantry and five troops of horse. The creaghts

fled. The General detailed two of his men to guard them and they captured two of the enemy riders.

The General exchanged one of these for [the captured] Rory Ballach Ó'Meallán. Because they did not like [encounters] with the Tyrone septs (*mur nar thaitin Eoghanaigh leo*) these lords moved into Oriel where they camped in Monaghan and sent their men out to collect plunder. Lord Moore and the foreigners (*na goill*) took much plunder and the method of dividing the spoils was that the English and the Scots (*na hAlbonaigh*), alternately, would take a full field of cattle. The Scots, however, began packing the cows into their own fields, a practice that displeased the English.

28 [Sunday]

Colonel Robert Munroe came from Trian Conghail to Armagh and thence to Benburb. They killed an old physician named Maurice O'Haughey and several others. Thomas Sanford, one of Sir Feilim's colonels, happened upon them and fought a running battle with them from Benburb to Charle-mont. They camped at Moy and fire directed at them from a cannon, dislodged them. From Moy they proceeded to Moneymore by way of Killyman and Mountjoy. Henry O'Hagan, son of Rory Buí, was plundered by them and many throughout the Killeter area were killed by them.

31 [Wednesday]

The General of the Ulster army and the President, Sir Feilim, held council at Mullintor in the Minterburn area and resolved not to quit the country on any account. It was also resolved that whoever should steal a cow or horse, steed or gelding, sheep or goat or the value of any of these, would have a like amount confiscated from him, if he were a man of means; or hanged if he were a man of no means. Furthermore, any found guilty of drinking from churns or of causing any other damage would be beaten with staves till their backs were broken. Many other fine decisions were made.

There are people in the country, O'Catháins, O'Devlins, O'Haras (*muintir Ara*), the people of Iveagh, all of Clannboy and the Route [reduced to] eating horses and steeds; The end of spring; stealing; carrying off cats; dogs; eating humans [corpses?]; rotten leather (*leathar carbaidh*); and undressed leather (leathar fo na aol).

Page 16
June 1643

Sir Feilim accompanied by the Guardian of the Armagh Franciscans, Paul O'Neill and Captain Tarlach Gruama O'Quinn went in a horse carriage for the arms sent to Ireland by the King of Spain. On Friday Robert Stewart came from Inishowen with four thousand men and plundered the Clossagh. Beforehand, on 9 June, General Eoghan O'Neill had ordered the creaghts to go to County Longford and they were already on their way.

13 [Tuesday, the feast of Saint Anthony of Padua]

On the feast of Saint Anthony of Padua the enemy came to Clones so suddenly that neither the General or any of his party noticed them until they were within two miles of them. The generals regiment, flanked by four troops of cavalry, met them, sounded the alarm and Sir Feilim's regiment under the command of Lieutenant Colonel Seán O'Neill advanced to meet them. The action was exceedingly bitter on both sides and the enemy pressed heavily on us. Colonel Conn Óg O'Neill, son of Conn son of Niall, son of Brian Faghartach was killed as were Captains Niall O'Neill, son of Niall, son of Tarlach, son of Conn Bacach, Eiver O'Neill, son of Cú Uladh, son of Feardorcha,

Brian O'Devlin, a good and valiant soldier, and Cú Uladh Mulholland (*Maolchalluinn*),[Hugh MacMahon], son of Art Óg, son of Art, son of The Baron, Colonel of the MacMahons of Oriel, was captured and [the MacMahons] took flight.

Sean O'Neill, Sir Feilim's lieutenant colonel, was captured, as was Captain Art O'Neill, son of Hugh Buí, son of Tarlach, son of Henry. We all fled from that terrible onslaught and the poor creaghts were left behind. The enemy took what they wished from them (*rugadar leo a dtoil fein díobh*) and the rest were scattered north, south, east, and west. Cormac O'Hagan, son of Eoghan, was killed alas! Alas! A sorry business! And Sir Feilim in Kilkenny at that time. Some of us fled to Breifne and others to Counties Armagh, Tyrone and Louth. The General returned to Truagh and having spent the second night in Brantry in the Friary of *Gort Tamhlacht na Muc*, left the place early in the morning.

15 [Thursday]

The Scots came into the Brantry district on Thursday, to be precise, burnt the houses of the Franciscan friars and killed a great number of people. That night there were four of us friars in the Brantry, Fr Tarlach Ó'Mealláin and three members of the Loughran family, Friars Eoghan, Benedict and Tadhg were their names.

Page 17

Encamped that night at Carnteel were four thousand men and six troops of cavalry from Tir Chonaill and Enniskillen under the command of Sir William Cole and Sir Robert and Sir William Stewart. They had four thousand cows to be divided among them. We four friars, unaided, managed to take three of these- two milch cows and a stripper. We killed the stripper but two bandits (*beirt chetharnach*) from the Route took the two cows from us.

17 [Saturday]
The [Irish] made a forced march into the counties of Cavan, Longford, Leitrim and Roscommon along with the General who placed a company (*campa*) of soldiers and some horsemen around the garrison of Jamestown to protect the creaghts.

29ᵗʰ [Thursday, feast of Saint Peter]
George Munroe and lieutenant General Leslie, aided by Lord Laver's son (*mac Tigherna Labhair*) and the son of Randal Stewart, mobilised a huge host. With Colonel Eoghan Connoly, the man who betrayed [the Irish] in Dublin when the Lord of Enniskillen was arrested, they crossed the Bann. They proceeded from there to Mountjoy, Killeter, Clanaghrie (*go Clainn Eachre*) and Brantry so that any of the country people who remained and who did not flee to the safety of a more distant place lost all their possessions. They encamped in Carnteel and, on the feast of Saint Peter, burned the town of Tarlach O'Neill called the Cashlan (*A'Caislén*). Thence they proceeded to Balleydonnelly where Conn O'Neill, son of Art, son of Dónall, son of Seán na Mallacht, surrendered the island of Ballydonnelly to George Munroe.
On Saturday Niall O'Neill, son of Feilim, son of Dónall, a Franciscan friar, was captured and sent to Carrickfergus where he was detained for seventeen months.

3 [Monday]
They arrived at Dungannon and demanded its surrender but were refused. The next day a party of soldiers was detailed to open fire on the town and again demand its surrender. In charge of Dungannon was vetern soldier, Captain Brian Buí Hughes (*O'hAodha*) and they had with them as chaplain (*Athair Faoisidinn*) a Franciscan friar named Pádraig O'Hamill.

July 4 Tuesday
A large force of five thousand foot and a thousand horse, led by Colonel Robert Munroe and Lords Chichester, Conway, Hamilton and Montgomery, crossed the Blackwater (*tar Abhuinn Mhóir*)

Page 18
and pitched their tents in the townland of Gortmerron, at Dungannon. At the sight of such a large force the wardens took fright; they accepted quarter and were allowed to take with them their arms and other effects. On the fifth day a Scottish garrison was placed in Dungannon.

12 [Wednesday]
The son of Brian O'Hagan, son of Denis Bradach, at considerable cost to his cause, surrendered the island of Lough Lusk *(luca)* to the Scots

It was decided that these forces should pursue the General Eoghan O'Neill and deprive him of his creaghts, accordingly, one party of them went to Truagh, Clones and Cavan; a second party went to Kinnard, Monaghan and Cavan and thence to Slieve Bruse. They sent seven hundred horsemen into the Slieve Cairbre area in pursuit of the Ulstermen and, because they did not catch up with them, they returned to base (go bun). They decided then to return to their own stations and spent the following night in Monaghan.

Let me make brief mention of Charlemont as the harvest came on and the grain crops were becoming ripe. Edward Munroe, with a great force of Scots, English and Irish, arrived at the same town and placed four field guns in Dunavalley to bombard the town. The fighting continued daily with the Scots losing men each day.

It appeared to Captain Niall O'Neill, son of Seán, son of Tarlach, son of Henry, son of Seán, that he ought to reconnoitre the roads some distance from the town. One day they came across a company of horse and foot on their way from Mountjoy to join in the siege. They attacked them, killed eight soldiers and three horses and wounded two riders. They took from them a quantity of wine, beer vinegar and whiskey, two tents, some spades and picks and two horse-cart loads of meal, butter, cheese, and linen and woollen clothes. Following this, the besieging party placed camps on all sides of the town so that the garrison had no way out. However, the besieged made a night- time raid across the river by boat and killed fourteen of the besiegers before they spoke a word.

Page 19
July

As to General Eoghan O'Neill, he placed some soldiers between the creaghts and the Jamestown garrison. The Elphin garrison arrived to take plunder and made off with horses, cows and prisoners among whom was Brian Maguire, son of Cú Connacht. Several people were killed.

2 August [Wednesday]

Colonel Richard O'Farrell of County Longford made a foray and carried off some arms, clothing, money and saddle-horses (lamhfraidh). Two young riders of the O'Quinns were killed. The general moved the creaghts across the Shannon to the summit of Slieve Bruse in Breifne and Sir Feilim arrived there from Kilkenny. The ambassador of Pope Urban V111 also came to review the army and offer his help.

14 [Monday]

Brian O'Neill, son of Art Óg, and Randal MacDonnell stayed behind the creaghts.Captain Hanly drew a party of the enemy upon them and as a result, Randal was killed and Brian was left for dead (benadh a mbaithes do Bhrian).

25 [Friday]

The nobles of Ulster consulted with the General as to whether they should go into the province of Ulster or into Meath for supplies of corn. Meath was decided upon and they proceeded from Slieve Bruse to the church of Lurgan, to Lough Ramor and the bridge of Balgeeth. The General sent a deputation to the garrison of Clonabreany to demand the surrender of the town. The garrison on seeing the strength of their enemy, surrendered and received good terms.

12 [Saturday]

The wardens of Seán O'Hagan were on the island of Loughinisholin. The enemy arrived and demanded its surrender but were refused. They then diverted another stream into the lough and dammed the outlet so that the island became submerged. The wardens of the island erected a platform (*faradh= a nest)* in the island house. One of them was killed on the platform by a cannon ball but they refused to yield on any account. One of them swam out and broke the dam and the enemy withdrew.

Page 20
August 1643

The castle of Killallon was surrendered to the General and that of Balrath to Sir Feilim. The garrisons received good terms, being allowed to retain their weapons, clothing and furniture. A messenger from the general was sent to demand the surrender of Ballybeg but it was refused. The soldiers attacked and the field guns were put in place. The town was showered by cannon fire and, after the walls of the court were broken and breached, Quarter was sought.

30 [Wednesday]

This was refused and the garrison ordered unconditionally (*tect fona mbéin).* All one hundred and eighty, cavalry and infantry, emerged and the son of Sir Henry Tichburne and Captain Cardiff were taken prisoner.

Sept 1 [Friday]

Faynstown castle was captured as was the son of Sir William Parsons of Dublin. Athboy was captured and Captain Smith and two gentlemen [taken]. Bective was captured and the castle of Balsoon on the Boyne. Trimblestown castle was captured and immediately burnt.

8 [Friday, feast of the Nativity of Mary]

On the feast of Mary, 8 September, the creaghts came with Sir Phelim from Kells to Portlester and proceeded to Ticroghan. Siege was laid to the enemy castle of Portlester and it was surrendered to the General.

Lord Moore came in pursuit of the General, his army and his creaghts so that not a living person or animal would escape his men; for he gathered a huge force of five or six thousand English and Scots by promising them big rewards.i.e. a share of the spoils. The General constructed trenches at Earl's Bridge and had his guns, large and small, placed in readiness. Our enemy came resolutely forward to the very bank of the ford (*go búr an atha*) but they were repulsed and several were killed.

11 [Monday]
Lord Moore was killed by one of Eoghan O'Neill's field guns and ninety-three of his men also fell.

12 [Tuesday]
And on the following day, after seventeen men and nine horses were killed, that great army withdrew without plunder of any kind (*gan chreich no chabbog)*

Page 21
August
Three captains, three lieutenants and six second-lieutenants claimed that, if they were given a sergeant-major and three hundred hand picked soldiers (*do nhaithibh in tsluaigh)* they would capture the town [i.e.Charlemont] within eight days. They were given all they asked and began the assault with such confidence that they believed the Irish would be unable to hold the place against them. They surrounded the bawn and, as they were unable to find a way in, they withdrew and ensconced themselves,
(*do ghlacadar sgonsa)* against the wall of an apple orchard. Those people quartered at Moy (*lucht cethroimhe an Mhadha)* came in order to view the scene of the fighting on all sides. The field guns that were within the town wre trained on them well charged with musket –shot, and terrible slaughter was wrought on those on the opposite side of the river to the north.
The captain of the castle, having consulted with his officers, decided to attack the besiegers. The soldiers under two commanding officers were sent towards them and approached them along the side of the sconce. Fire was given on both sides and then swords and lances were drawn. The enemy were wounded and stabbed and the Scots gave way. The sergeant- major, the three captains and the officers were all killed. When they took to the marshy ground, none of the *Clann Mhaoilin* was eager to be first (*nior chuma le Clann Mhaoilin cia baca bhiadh at tús)*. One of them would place his musket [on the ground} before him and would not take his foot off it till the man behind him hit him a belt on the shoulders (*bos na shinnen)* and stepped [vaulted] over him in the bog ('*sdo eirgheadh'na mhullach san churrach air)*.It is the estimate of eye-witnesses that not twenty of those three hundred escaped. The arms were brought to the castle. Dónal Mac

Veigh and Major Manus Corr, two of the best soldiers on either side, were killed that day. The Scots were permitted to bury there dead that evening.

Sir Robert Stewart, Sir William Cole and sergeant-major Waring, with an army of four and a half thousand, encamped for eight weeks at the Moy close by the castle and river. During this time they lost nine hundred and ninety-seven men (*1,000 fer ach triúr*); and the commander of the castle lost eight, between officers and soldiers.

Page 22
Sept. 1643

General Eoghan sent letters of truce to the Captain of Charlemont and to Robert Munroe suggesting that they should leave the country. The Scots taking all the corn of the country, withdrew to Trian Conghail. Monroe also left. The creaghts returned along with the General to Tyrone. The Scots left the garrisons in Dungannon, Mountjoy, Ardboe and Monymore. After the departure of the Scots, the natives returned to their land and each person did a little ploughing for himself. They remained [unmolested] in the country till summer.

1644
12 Feb. [Monday]

Robert Monroe gave Dungannon and Mountjoy to lord Chichester and [soldiers] came to garrison them. Monroe had planned to go to Scotland but, (later deciding) to remain in Ireland, regretted having handed over the two towns.

14 May. [Tuesday]

Colonel Monroe came to Belfast and sent Lord Chichester out. Both he and his son, Captain Chichester, travelled to Dublin with only their horses.

8 [Wednesday]

The creaghts were warned by the General to travel by day and night into County Armagh. The friars of Armagh came to the Fews and travelled on to Inniskeen Paul O'Neill was their Guardian.

23 [Thursday]

The General with the horse and foot arrived at Lurganboy. All the creaghts came to Farney, Clankee, and Ardmaghbreague. Sir Phelim and a large company remained to hold Charlemont.

30 [Ascension Thursday]

[...]surrendered Dungannon to Sir Phelim who placed his own garrison in it. Commissary Thomas MacKiernan with his companion Donchadh Mór O'Dálaigh came to the friars in the parish of Donacloney, from there they went to the parish of Donaghmoyne and over to Armaghbreague; thence to Kells to the creaghts, to Navan, Ardbraccan and Portlester.

2 July [Tuesday]

The Nuncio from the Pope arrived in Kilkenny and Sir Phelim received an order from the Supreme Council to leave Charlemont and join the main army. He burnt Dungannon and joined the General at Portlester.

1602-On the night proceeding Saint John's Day, O'Neill burnt Dungannon and then retired to bed.

1644 -On the night proceeding Saint John's Day, Sir Phelim burnt it and then retired to bed.

Page 23
July 1644

The earl of Castlehaven, unknown to the English, arrived from Dublin. He was a Catholic and the Irish welcomed him with open arms. The Council of Kilkenny sent two thousand infantry and six troops of horse with him to the Ulster Genaral to fight against the Scots. This force came into Meath where Eoghan O'Neill and the creaghts were. The Earl was appraised of the progress of the enemy, that all the Scots and English that were in Ulster, as well as the Irish who had been quartered by them, were combined into one huge army in order to extirpate all the Irish. They are now in Longford, which they have burned along with Granard and Ballinalee, and all nineteen thousand of them are approaching Finea.

The General and the little earl [Castlehaven] detailed three troops of horse and two hundred foot, commanded by BrianRua O'Neill, son of Conn Rua,son of Art, son of Feardorcha, to hold the bridge of Finea. The Scots reached the passages and forced their way through (*do bhenadar amach iad*)

(Aug) 8 [Thursday]

However, Captain Graham and eight of his kinsmen were killed. Brian O'Neill was wounded and two of his horsemen killed. Gerald Garbh of Meath was also wounded. Finea was the town of the earl of Meath.

These forces proceeded to Kells, Navan, Ardee and to Dundalk, where they divided – some going to Trían Conghail, some to Ó Catháin country, some to *Tír Chónaill,* some to Enniskillen, some to Drogheda and the remainder staying in Dundalk. At this time the fishermen of Carrickaness were killed at Maydown. The General and the little earl pursued the enemy and brought the creaghts with them to Port Mór in Tyrone. Their combined force numbered seven thousand foot and a thousand horse.

Page 24
August 1644
The wardens of Charlemont refused to surrender the town to the army of
the kingdom without first getting the consent of Sir Feilim who was then in
Kilkenny. Since the place was not surrendered to them they proceeded to
Tandragee where they erected their pavilions and huts. The Generals were
informed that the enemy were in Dromore in Iveagh.

12 [Monday, feast of Saint Clare]
On the feast of Saint Clare the earl and a large company proceeded against
them. More than two hundred of them, both horse and foot, fell and
Captain Blair was taken prisoner. [The earl and his party] returned the
same day. Letters came to them from the Council and Sir Feilim instructing
them to leave Charlemont to the army. They left Tandragee and, having
arrived at Dunavalley, erected pavilions, huts, and shelters.
General Eoghan caught a fever of which he suffered a relapse *(baithleagadh
é)*

15 [Thursday]
The enemy came near Armagh and sent out raiding parties to plunder
Toaghy and *Áth Feadha.* They plundered all the creaghts *(deireadh na
gcoraigheacht)* and captured Cathleen Hovenden, the wife of Tarlach O'Neill,
and took her with them, together with [her] horses and their young
attendants *(fóna malraidh)*
Some soldiers were sent to guard the ford of the Blackwater between the
creaghts and the enemy. Captain Davis, who went without orders to
reconnoitre the enemy, was wounded and captured and some of his troops
were killed.

20 August [Tuesday]
Henry O'Neill, son of Tuathall, who was sent into upper Clanboy to plunder
the area around the mouth of the Stranmilis stream, took away a large herd
of cows *(bó gabhail mhor)* and other spoils. Robert Munroe and Lieutenant-
General Earl Leslie are in Armagh with an army of fourteen thousand,
about to face the Irish of whom there were seven thousand in
Dunavalley.Colonel Tarlach Óg Ó Neill of the Fews came to assemble all the
creaghts between Dungannon and Charlemont. [He had authority] to hang
anyone who refused to co-operate with the Council [in this regard]. When
the creaghts were assembled they were, on the Generals orders, to give four
or five thousand cows to the earl of Castlehaven and his people. Because of
the scarcity of bread, the fresh meat impaired their health and brought
sickness, suffering and dysentery and a thousand of them died.

Page 25
September 1644

Sir Feilim's party, Colonel Sanford, Rory Maguire and the men of Oriel made a raid on Enniskillen and captured two hundred cows.Some of the enemy went from Srmagh into the fews where Séan Ó Conalláin, the priest of that country, was killed by them and they took some plunder.on another occasion the enemy Colonel named Mister Roden (*MaighsteirRodíín*)led five troops of horse on a night time raid across the Blackwater by *Béal Átha Cip*to Minterburn. They saw a number of Irish cavalry close by. These were retreating but, nevertheless, they attacked and Conn O'Neill, son of Niall, son of Art Óg, was wounded and captured. Art O'Neill, son of Tarlach, son of Henry na Garthann, was also captured and accepted quarter but the son of Lieutenant Graham spitefully killed him on the northern side of Knocknacloy Lough.

Alastar Hovenden was killed between the [same] lough and the Oona river. They also killed twelve men of the creaght and carried of a huge quantity of spoil Louis O'Moore, a Leinsterman, some of Castlehaven's horsemen who witnessed the killing, and Tarlach O'Neill, the son of the murdered man, pursued the raiders, killed eight of them and captured five.Upon the alarm being raised the enemy returned and took sixteen of the earl's horses from the young men who were guarding them (*ó mbalroigh coimbeada an Iarla*) They took three or four prisoners and left a certain officer stripped naked except for the boots he stood in.

Whenever Castlehaven's men were ordered to cause an uproar (*fuachas [a] bheint ann*) they only went half way and returned to their own camp through cowardice and unsoldierly behaviour, achieving nothing.

In those same days the Mountjoy garrison made a raid on Clanaghrie in search of plunder. They found some but Feilim an Chogaidh O'Neill took it from them and killed twelve of their men.

Page 26
September [1644]
13 [Friday]

When the earl of Castlehaven realised that his army was being reduced by weakness, exhaustion, cowardice and death, he decided to return with them to Leinster and Munster. Eoghan O'Neill offered him three hundred cows and seven hundred barrels of corn if he would remain a further two nights in camp but he might as well have tried to confine sand with a rope. The General sent a messenger to the chiefs of the creaghts bidding them to retire to Slieve Beagh and Truagh.

In the evening, powder and shot were distributed among the soldiers and a show was made of bringing faggots to Kishaboy as if an attack on the enemy was planned for that very night. Enemy spies noticed all this activity and warned Munroe. His people were so perturbed by the news that they decided to send the rabble (*a ndaosgar sluaigh*) to Tandragee with the supply train (*fare na gcaraiste)* and they themselves would stand firm and guard the horses and arms. Worse, however, happened; it was our own people who were fleeing.

14 [Saturday, feast of the true cross]
The general and the earl with the assistance of a moonless sky, led their forces across the bridge at Charlemont to Benburb and thence to Glaslough, through Oriel to Balleneclogh. After receiving two hundred cows from Phillip O'Reilly and the O'Reilly chiefs, they proceeded through Breifne to Ballyhaise and westward out of the province of Ulster on the feast day of the cross.
Monroe remained in camp for five weeks and, although he was assured that the armies had left the country, he sent a reconnaissance party to *Sliabh na Maol* in the Brantry area to scan the surrounding country. They assured him that the armies and all the creaghts had gone. Ballynametagh was burnt.

Oct
Monroe proceeded to Tynan where he made camp. From then to the feast of Saint Matthew the evangelist they gathered in corn from places within a twelve-mile radius of their camp. They then separated to Tir Chonaill, to the Ó'Catháin country and to the Route and Monroe's own force [went] to Armagh, on to Glanrye and then across the ridge of

Page 27
Magh Cobha. There they separated and repaired to their permanent garrisons throughout *Dál nAraithe and Dál Riada,* etc.Monroe sent a messenger to the garrison of Mountjoy with orders to burn that town and for the soldiers to come to Carrickfergus; he sent five or six hundred soldiers to Scotland to fight against the army of King Charles. The battle turned in favour of the king, seven thousand men were killed and Lord Auchinbreck and several other leaders were beheaded.

Nov.
The land was a virtual wilderness – farms, estates, whole tracts – from the Bannfoot in the north to the gates of Dundalk and from Carnmore of Slieve Beagh to Tory in the north; only eight people were left at Lough Laoghaire and eight on Loughinisholin. When the earl was leaving the country he left the son of Thomas FitzGerald as governor of Charlemont and Captain White of Limerick with one hundred and fifty soldiers along with them (*na bhfarraidh).* The earl sent five troops of horse to bring to him in Breifne the field guns and all the carriages that he had left in Charlemont. One of his horsemen said that he would sooner suffer a firing squad, (*gurab luaitií*

d'fhuileonadh bota piler do dhenamh) than come to Ulster in such a convoy. At the end of autumn, when the corn was shed, [the stubble?] burnt and trampled, some of the creaghts returned to the land, for instance Niall Mac Kenna, [and] the O'Neills of the Fews to south Armagh (*Sliocht Aodha chum an Fheadha),*

Tarlach O'Neill son of Brian to Tiranny, Pádraig Modartha O'Donnelly to Ballydonnelly and many others.The Armagh friars returned to Brantry and our Guardian, Father Henry O'Mealláin went to Multyfarnham. Daniel a Sancta Maria MacCawell, Bonaventure O'Quinn, Eoghan O'Loughran, Thomas Croalam and Edward Dowdall to other places. Our president, Pádraid Ó'Coisi, and Tadhg O'Loughran together with eleven other friars remained in Brantry (*tathaighi don Bhrentor)*

Page 28
January 1645

A rumour became current that the creaghts had turned their backs on the country, yhat those of Counties Tyrone, Armagh and Monaghan had moved westward for good. The Armagh friars fled to the Fews and from there to Clankee. A party from Lisnagarvey arrived to make a raid on all and sundry but, as they found no one in the country but those on quarter, they took one hundred and forty cows from Captain Trever. It is said, however that the good captain himself sold the cows to the English.

The chief leaders were Pope Innocent X, King Charles, the earl of Ormonde in Dublin, Eoghan O'Neill the General in Ulster, the President of the Council in Kilkenny, Lord Butler, the General of the south (*Leath Mogha),* Thomas Preston, the Primate of all Ireland, Hugh O'Reilly and the Provincial of the Franciscan Order, Brian MacIlkenny (*Mac Giolla Cainnigh),* a Connachtman.

A raiding party from Breifne, Oriel and Fermanagh went to plunder Enniskillen. They spent two nights reconnoitiring there, took the plunder but were forced to abandon it with a loss of two hundred and twenty men killed. Myles O'Reilly, who was wounded, lost his horse and five of their officers (*cuiger da ndaoinibh uaisle)* were taken prisoner. The ransom set for their release was six hundred barrels of meal, sixty barrels of seed and sixty pounds in silver.

7 March: [Friday]

The O'Hagans, because of lack of food, followed the general westward after setting fire to the island dwelling on Loughinisholin. A force from Enniskillen came to Clones to plunder Hugh and Séamus Buí O'Donnelly, Donal Gruama MacDonnell and the daughter of Cumhach Ballach Ó Catháin, son of Richard Ó'Catháin. Altogether these people lost more than two hundred cows.

26 March

The Archbishop of Fermo [Rinuccini], the Apostolic Nuncio to Ireland of Pope Innocent X, arrived with gold, silver and arms. His advice to them was that they should not make peace with the English unless liberty of conscience was guaranteed and their lands returned to the Catholic Church.

Page 29
2 May 1645 [Friday]

With the authority of the Council of Kilkenny, Sir Feilim took one hundred and fifty soldiers to place garrisons in Dungannon and Mountjoy.

27 [Tuesday]

He arrived in Charlemont about Pentecost (*aimsior na Cinncisi sin*) and three days later he went to the top of the manor house and announced that the enemy was approaching. He came to the gate and shouted loudly to those of his men who were on the outside; 'Come inside the gate and defend the town'. They did as they were ordered. However, since Captain Phillip Rua O'Reilly was not in the town, his men were given sufficient provisions and sent off to Breifne.

Seventeen of the enemy happened upon Sir Feilim's men who hanged nine of them and accepted a ransom for the remainder. They got fifteen horses the same day.

14 Aug [Thursday]

Once, while Sir Feilim was in Charlemont, one of the Lawers yeomen (*ceithiornach do mhuintir Labhraidh*) with a view to capturing the town, led five troops of horse and four companies of foot from Monroe's party to take the town. They attacked the gate by night and several volleys were fired at them. Eight of them were killed and several more wounded.

24 [Sunday]

General Monroe came with a large force from Trian Conghail to Armagh and Port Mór. He sent an emissary to Sir Feilim to demand the surrender of the town [Charlemont]. Sir Feilim's reply was that he would sooner kill himself than surrender in so dishonourable a fashion and that if [Monroe] insisted on a fight he would have one. Monroe, in fact, proceeded to Glaslough and Monaghan and consulted with the leaders of the Scots from Tir Chonaill as to what they should do; 'Let us bring succour to our garrisoned towns in Connacht'. This was done and the majority of the force returned to Tir Chonaill and Trian Conghail.We were fourteen days between the feasts of Saint Francis and Saint John Capistranus without seeing sun, moon or stars because of hoar frost for the entire period.

Page 30
Sept, 1645
15 [Monday]
A boat belonging to the governor of Masserene, and laden with two brass [?] guns *(dhá ghunna ghlasa),* ten muskets, twelve barrels of salted fish, some sailors and a company of infantry, was captured by Sir Feilim and brought [upriver] to the quay at Charlemont *(go binbhior Achadh in dá Charad)* . Some of the men were hanged and some were released.

July 15 [Tuesday]
General Monroe marched from Trian Chonghaill to Armagh, thence to *Sliabh na Maol,* Clogher and Enniskillen, burning and plundering as they went. They burnt and plundered the province of Connacht till they reached Toberbride. O'Connor surrendered Sligo to them and they left a strong garrison there.
Lismore, County Waterford, was taken by the earl of Castlehaven from the O'Brien people *(do Shíol mBrian)* Captain Manus O'Catháin, son of Cumhach Ballach, son of Richard was killed. They also captured nine garrisoned towns from Baron Inchiquin. That army included one thousand five hundred Ulstermen. Another Captain O'Catháin named Cumhach, son of Manus Galta, was also killed there.

Aug
The great garrison of Tulsk was captured by Seán Burke, Thomas Taafe and James Dillon. An Ulster captain named Hugh O'Gallagher, whose soldiers helped to take the town *(lena shaighdeoraibh do benadh an baile amach),* was killed. Elphin Castlecoote and Boyle were also taken by them, as was Jamestown.

Oct, 26 [Sunday]
The Connacht armies went to Sligo to prey on the Scots but were surprised by five or six troops from Tir Chonaill and Enniskillen who drove them back to their own camp.
Malachy Ó Caolluighe the Archbishop of Tuam, and his chaplain *(a' sagurt)* were killed. However four Scots fell at the hands of the Connachtmen in that battle. Doctor Ó Caolluighe was a man noted for his scholarship, and for a good and virtuous life. The Burkes and the Irish were taken prisoner; many of them were killed and their camp was plundered. The Scots revictualled the Sligo garrison. The burial *(leacht)* of the Bishop. General Eoghan came from Kilkenny to Carrickmacross with three thousand men from the papal nuncio. They plundered some people who were being quartered by the foreigners *(ar cheathramha ghallta)* there. They then proceeded to Ballybay where they stayed a short while before moving to Breifne.

Page 31

As for Eoghan, he sent five hundred men to to Lough Erne with Colonel Rory Maguire and Tarlach O'Neill, a vetern of Spain and an O'Neill of the Fews *do sliocht Aodh)*. Their scouts (*a lucht bratha),* who had two boats, joined them. They landed on Boa Island and burnt and plundered two islands from which they carried off more than five hundred cows, one hundred and forty laden draught horses and seventeen steeds. They brought the spoils to a place near Ballinamallard (*go fogus Béal Átha na Mallacht)* and, after the moon rose round midnight, Rory Maguire's party left, taking the spoils with them. Tarlach O'Neill, son of Brian, son of Dónal, son of Feilim Rua made the following announcement: 'Our enemy approaches,' he said, 'and will encounter this trench (*tigidh ar a'trinnsi so).* Open fire on them and let the pikemen stand firm here' This was done and eight of the enemy were killed along with a lieutenant of their horse. The pikemen fled and the enemy pressed down upon us, killing Captain MacQuillan and ten of our men. Captain Irwin Mac Sweeney of Tir Chonaill and Sergeant- Major Tarlach O'Neill were also among the slain.

1641
Nov, 29, [Sunday
Let me now make mention of Colonel Phillip O'Reilly, son of Hugh, son of Seán Rua. The O'Reillys happened to be south of the Boyne (*ós Boínn)* when they got word of a company of soldiers on their way from Dublin to Drogheda. Phillip encountered them at Julianstown and although the Irish were not well armed, they attacked and killed seven hundred of the enemy without loss of a man. Having got arms and ammunition as a result of that day, they laid siege to Drogheda till the following spring.

May (1642):
Charles Coote, that accursed scourge and merciless torturer of the Irish, fell in Trim and it is not known whether he was killed by a friend or foe.

Feb
The bloodthirsty tyrant, Simon Harcourt, knight and third commander of the company was wounded at Carrickmines and uttering blasphemy against God and his saints died the following day

24 June [Friday]
The Catholics took Limerick in the name of King Charles.

March
A party of Catholics who fought at Kilsallaghan, where Captain Rochford, some of his officers and many of his men lost their lives, forced the enemy, very much against their will, back to Dublin.

Page 32
1641

Those in the position of dispensing justice in Dublin were Sir William Parsons, Master of the Chancery Court, and Sir John Borlase, two cruel and pitiless knights.

Colonel O'Reilly rounded up all the English in Cavan, Ballyhaise, Belturbet and the hamlets of that area and had them safely conducted to Drogheda. For a period of thirteen weeks, Colonel O'Reilly besieged Croaghan and Keilagh where five hundred people had gathered and where three hundred of them died before Sir James Craig and Sir Francis Hamilton accepted quarter for the remaining two hundred who were sent to Drogheda.

9 Aug, 1643. [Wednesday]

One hundred and forty horsemen came from Trim and took much plunder. Myles [O'Reilly], son of Eamon, with thirty three riders was nearby and having observed the creaghts in flight, pursued the plunderers and attacked them at Lisnahederna. Hugh [O'Reilly], son of Myles, heard the sound of battle and made off in its direction. The enemy were put to flight and the last man of them was killed as he entered the gate of Maperath. Captain Carson was taken prisoner. [Hugh's] riders totalled eighty-one.

An army was raised in Munster by Sir Charles Vavasour to take the castle called Cloghlea. The town was surrendered to him as the wardens of the castle were short of food. They accepted quarter on condition that their lives would be spared. The condition was not fulfilled for eighty of them were put to death. When the Munstermen arrived to relieve their friends and revictual the town, they found it burnt.

They attacked Sir Charles's men so furiously that not more than two hundred of the three thousand survived. Their Colonel was taken prisoner.It was for the love of this Charles that the daughter of the earl of Cork, Sir Richard Boyle, poisoned her own husband, Lord Barrymore (*an Barrach Mór*).

Page 33
1642

The four thousand strong army of Lord Moore and Richard Grenville besieged the manor house and castle of Gerald Lacy when he was absent from home. There were only thirty wardens in the castle and over a period of five days, they killed seven hundred of the besiegers. The lady of the town accepted quarter for herself and her children. The wardens of the castle then put all of the plate, brass, iron, guns, clothing, wheat and many other valuables of that country into the manor house and set fire to it immediately. The besiegers then attacked the bawn and broke down the iron door.

First one of them entered and demanded a pistol which one of the wardens held. 'Here it is,' he said and discharged two bullets into his chest and killed him. The rest were immediately taken and bound in pairs. One young man who was badly wounded, escaped them and safely made his way to Castlerickard. Thus were twenty-nine soldiers put to death. At Babeswood in County Louth, one hundred and fifty people- men, women and children – were killed on the orders of Lord Moore.

On the word of George Garlands daughter two hundred and forty-eight people and their parish priest, Tarlach MacRory were killed by the Dundalk garrison even though they had previously been granted quarter by Lord Moore.The earl of Ormonde and a party of Catholics met in battle at the River Barrow. Both sides fought valiantly but the heretics were put to flight and one cannon was captured. Colonel Colier and Colonel Preston were taken prisoner and many were killed on both sides. That night they [the Catholic party] repaired to New Ross and were followed there by the enemy on the following day. The governor, Colonel Fox with five musketeers, so stoutly attacked their camp that they fled from us towards Dublin.Lord Moore's party swaggered across County Meath (*ar fiarlaoid na Midhe*) and burned haggards and houses, the Town of Kells and four mills on a river nearby.

More than sixty were killed in the Frenchman's mill *(Muilionn a' Fhrancaigh).* Robert Cusack received quarter but was immediately killed on the order of Sir Henry Tichburne; his son was killed without orders from anyone.

Page 34

Take note here that the chronicles of Dublin, Drogheda and Cork state that, from the first to the sixth year of the war, sixty thousand English and Scots people and soldiers died of various plagues and illnesses. The records also state that it became necessary on account of the number of horrible deaths, to find new burial places outside the towns. It is assumed that it was through the miracles of God and the sentence of Christ, the righteous judge (*tre chanaighil an Bhreithgimh Críost comhthroim),* that such a bitter fate befell them. They observed no guarantee of quarter, or promise of protection that they ever made to the Irish, but rather dishonoured them in breach of the laws of nations, being wont to kill, women, unbaptised infants, old men and those of every infirmity. Such is manifest in the events in the town of Timolin in County Kildare. Such was also manifest in the attack the English made on Preston at Lynch's Knock, a place where they killed ten or twelve hundred although they had all been given quarter and were fettered together. When questions were asked in Dublin, the explanation given was that they had fought vehemently against them and were all killed to prevent their doing the same again. Let them be challenged to cite an instance when the Irish ever failed to observe the terms of quarter when given to them.

Coote broke quarter agreement with Henry O'Neill, son of Eoghan, with Feilim O'Neill, son of Tuathal, and with other nobles at the battle of Scarriffhollis.

The above was extracted from Clo Chill Chainnigh
(*As Cló Cili Cainnigh so suas do benadh*)

Page 35
1646

The papal legate to Ireland, Joannes Baptista, Archbishop of Fermo, arrived in Kilkenny and brought with him sixty thousand pounds and a large quantity of arms. The Ulster General, in an audience with him, promised to continue service in Ulster if he received pay for his soldiers.

"You will receive pay for three thousand men for six months and add to that yourself [the cost of] a further two thousand raised at the expense of the country." The Pope was Innocent X. An announcement was made by the Ulster General that all infantry and cavalry should join him and that each would be paid three shillings and sixpence per week.

They assembled in Breifne, and seventy horses arrived at Lough Sheelin castle with arms for them from Kilkenny. They remained here till the first of June, increasing in numbers all the time (*ag cruinniughadh na slogh*).

8, May [Friday]

Seven boats were captured by Sir Feilim on Lough Neagh, fourteen men were taken prisoner and more than twenty killed. The boats were taken up to the mooring (go hinbher) at Charlemont and Sir Feilim then joined the General at his camp.

23, May. [Saturday]

The Scottish army came, to the Blackwater- foot (*go bon na hAbhanna Duibhe*) where they erected two forts on the banks of the great river, and stretched chains between them to block the access of Sir Feilim's people to the lough and it's fishing.

1, June. [Monday]

The army of the General and Sir Feilim now marched out in formation – more than five thousand foot divided among seven colonels viz the General himself, Sir Feilim, the Colonel of the Fews [Tarlach Óg O'Neill] , Alastar [MacDonnell] son of the earl [of Antrim], Manus O'Donnell son of Niall Garbh, Rory Maguire and Colonel Farrell.

There were nine troops of horse; each of the following leading a troop:- The General's son, Henry Rua O'Neill, Conn Bacach [O'Neill], Brian Rua O'Neill, Brian Rua MacMahon, Phillip O'Reilly, Hugh [O'Reilly], son of Myles, Myles [O'Reilly], son of Eamon, Hugh Maguire and Colonel Farrall.

This was the army of the people of Tyrone (*Eoghanacht Uladh*) under their own General Eoghan O'Neill. They were told that Lord Montgomery and large forces of Scots were in the valley of the Newry river (*I nGlenn Righr*) on their to Munster and Kilkenny to root out the whole Confederation. About this time [the Ulstermen] reached Benburb where they set up camp and put their horses out to pasture. They detailed a thousand men and three troops of horse to guard the camp for the enemy was approaching Armagh.

4 [Thursday]

Lord Montgomery led them in formation for he was their General. Also there were Lord Blaney, Lord Hamilton and Robert Monroe with all the men raised in Trian Conghail and the O'Catháin country. Approaching Dungannon are eighty horse and three hundred foot; and the hosting of Tir Chonaill arrived at Clossagh. Montgomery was at the head of fourteen troops of horse and nine regiments of foot. The heretics proposed attacking Benburb by the short route from Armagh. Monroe disagreed and advised that they should proceed by way of Tynan, *Áth Feadha* Caledon and then to Knocknacloy, and that they would have both wind and sun in their favour. That was done; they secluded their wagons, laden with seven weeks provision for each man, in Minterburn and left fifteen hundred men to guard them.

There were many sacks of white bandaging (*giobal geal*), sacks of biscuit, large quantities of meal, beer, wine, whiskey, flour, suger, hens, capons, and a number of tents.They unfurled their silk standards through Minterburn.

Page 37
June 1646

The General sent three troops with Brian O'Neill, son of Conn Rua, to look out for the muster that was on its way from O'Catháin country, and despatched a hundred men to Kilagevill to meet the enemy and cause confusion among them. That done, they made an honourable retreat to join their own companions.The General from the midst of his men, addressed them saying;

"Yonder approaching are the heretics, the enemies of your souls; hold valiantly against them today for it is they who have deprived you of our chiefs, your kin, your spiritual and temporal sustenance. It is they who have seized your lands and banished you, etc."

The two armies engaged at Dromflugh and the heretics withdrew after an number of them were killed beside their big guns – they had seven field-guns.

The Irish pressed down on them and fire was opened on both sides from both large and small guns. They then used their pikes and heavy-duty swords (*cloidhmhe toirt-bhuilleacha*) to pierce and disembowel one another.

Into the battle then came that honourable warrior, the magnanimous, valiant soldier and protector of the flock of Pope Innocent X, Eoghan O'Neill. About this time there arrived the three troops who had gone towards Dungannon earlier in the day. The Scots assumed that these were their party. Sir Feilim also joined the battle with a goodly company and a gap a hundred men wide (*cliathbhern céad*) made in the ranks of the enemy, threw them into turmoil. Lord Blaney was killed and Lord Montgomery was captured by Cormac O'Neill. Having been deprived of his horse and arms, he was placed in custody. The heretics now gave way and took flight. The Irish gave forth their battle-cry. The General rode before and among his well ordered army (*a dheaghshluagh*) ueging them on; the killing continued till the shades of evening and the new night descended.

A large number of them was drowned in the Blackwater and in Knocknacloy Lough.

Page 38
June 1646

The General and his army returned in the night to their camp and were cheerful and elated after the defeat of the enemy. However of the wounded [who escaped the field], few reached their own towns, but perished in the fastness. Thirteen horsemen were killed in the vicinity of Ballynametah. One of the Generals company's, on its way from Lough Sheelin to join the main force, killed twenty five of their horsemen. One of Sir Feilim's lieutenants, Tom Sanford, killed twenty-four of them beyond Armagh. A further fiftey-seven were killed by Henry O'Neill beside the glen (*cois gleanna*).

A number of others, having succumbed to exhaustion], were found dead though unwounded in the fastness. The Puritans of Tir Chonaill sent a messenger inviting the General to take the field. He sent the vanguard westward to meet them at Clossagh. He himself led the main battle and Sir Feilim brought up the rear. The enemy fled to Enniskillen and then back to Tir Chonaill. The General and his forces returned to Charlemont and thence to Loughall and Tamnamore. Manus O'Donnell, son of Niall Garbh, and Cú Uladh O'Neill, son of Feardorcha, son of Brian Carrach were killed; the casualties numbered more than three hundred, both killed and wounded. Sir Feilim arranged medical aid for the wounded in Charlemont.They had captured more than two thousand muskets, a great number of pikes, pickaxes and drums, seven field guns and thirty six standards. The General as a token of victory, sent these thirty six standards to the Nuncio and the Council of Kilkenny.The Definitor [assistant to the superior] of the Franciscan Order, Boetius Egan, and Hugh Buí MacManus, the Generals own servant, were given the task of delivering them as well as some remarkable letters found on the heretics. The heretics had determined on that day [according to those letters] to give quarter to nobody save the

General himself.The General ordered Seán and Richard Ó'Catháin, Donal Magennis, son of Lord Iveagh, and Rory Maguire to take a foraging party of fifteen hundred into Trian Conghail, Downpatrick was burnt by them, as were Saul, Bishopscourt, Ballydugan, *Baile Bocht,* Ballynewport and the mill of Kilough *(muilionnCill O'Laoch).* They took with them to Tamnamore five hundred cows, not to mention other goods. Tom Sanford, Sir Feilim's lieutenant-colonel, was sent with six hundred soldiers to Portadown and Clare and he burnt them both.

Page 39
June
The number killed between Drumflugh and *Áth Feadha* – God be praised, for He it was who performed the feat – was three thousand, five hundred and forty-eight in a battle that lasted three hours. This number is exclusive of those found dead in the fastness of Toaghy, the Fews, Orior and Iveagh who had not the bloodying of arms *(dergadh airm)* on them

19 [Friday]
The General and his forces left Tamnamore for Breifne. The dean of the apostolic nuncio and the Definitor of the Franciscan Order arrived from Limerick to meet the Ulster General. The dean paid one shilling and sixpence *(trí rialacha)* to each private soldier and a larger sum to the officers and all were billeted *(fuaradar coinnmheadh)* On the five counties of Monaghan, Cavan, Leitrim, Longford and Westmeath till crops would ripen. Sir Feilim remained in Charlemont where he attended to the wounded.
Sir Feilim sent six boats to Bunavalley. He put the boats ashore and placed soldiers between these and the garrison. He took the boats on to Trowagh Bay where he erected a fortification in which he stationed soldiers while the fishermen caught an abundance of fish. The Scots were thus beleaguered in Bunavalley and they were in great want of food *(í n-airc bhetha).*

29 [Monday]
In Breifne at Ballyheelan Brian Rua O'Neill killed Hugh O'Neill, son of Art Óg, son of Tarlach. He put a pistol shot through him. Two enemy troops came to Minterburn where they captured Hugh O'Neill, son of Brian, son of Henry Óg and carried off four horses and forty cows.
The Council of Kilkenny was making peace with the earl of Ormond without the permission of the Old Irish, and inviting him to come to meet them. This he promised to do. The court and castle were adorned for the earl's visit and a new gate, burnished with gold was erected. The earl arrived with fifteen troops of horse and two thousand foot. The Council of Kilkenny, Lord Mountgarret, Donough MacCarthy and all the country paid him homage; and having finished his business in the country, he proceeded to Cashel where the munstermen received him with delight.

About that time the nuncio convened a synod in Waterford and they got word that the earl was in the country. The nuncio called for five hundred soldiers and sent letters to the Ulster general bidding him to come with his forces from Breifne.

Page 40
1646
30 Aug, [Tuesday]
When he received the letters the General summoned the Colonels and captains with their soldiers and cavalry to meet him on a certain day (*in lá so*) on Slieve Bruse. They arrived there with Sir Feilim, Colonel of the horse. That night they were in County Longford and with the least delay reached Parksgrove. From Kilkenny there came to meet them forty horses laden with bread and beer, etc. With regard to the earl of Ormond; when he heard, in Cashel, of the Ulster General's approach he fled with his fifteen troops and two thousand foot not to his own town, Kilkenny, but to Gowran. Having been told that the General's horse were in the country, he immediately fled to Old Leighlin and fired a volley into that town.

They separated in the town and when the Earl arrived in Carlow he was accompanied by only twelve riders. He dismounted there to eat some bread and drink some wine but the riders did not dismount. All proceeded to Dublin.

As to the Ulster General; when he reached Parksgrove, his men pitched their pavilions and tents beside Deerpark. When news of this reached the two nuncios (one had come at the outbreak of the war from Pope Urban VIII, and the second from InnocentX, they came from Kilkenny to meet the General.

The General and Sir Feilim and the other nobles had audience with these holy men and received their blessing. The General asked that the castle and fortresses of the city be handed over to him: 'and let hostages of this country and town be delivered to me, viz. Donough MacCarthy, Lord Muskerry, Éamon Butler, son of Lort Mountgarret, the secretaries of the Council, [Richard] Bellings and Sir John Begneir, and four other leading men of the Council and the country'. The affairs of the hostages and of the town were well managed from then on.

The army came to be reviewed by the General and the muster of foot amounted to fourteen thousand men. Sir Feilim, colonel of cavalry, reviewed a muster of twenty two troops. All the chiefs of Ireland were present at this place, together with the two nuncios and the ambassadors of the kings of both Spain and France.

Page 41
The nuncio, archbishop of Fermo, moved from one side to the other of the ranks giving them his blessing. The soldiers discharged a simultaneous

velley of shots from six field- guns. And as he returned in the opposite direction giving them his blessing, they fired a similar volley as a token of glory and honour to God, for the Pope and the nuncio.

The nuncio then approached Sir Feilim, colonel of cavalry, and blessed his men; they fired a volley from their carbines and pistols. The muster lasted for two days. The General [and his party], having escorted the nuncios and the Spanish and French ambassadors to the city gate (*go gebhta na cathrach da n-adhlacadh*) returned to their camp. Every banquet prepared in honour of the earl of Ormond was shared with the young men of Ulster. Ten days they encamped at Kilkenny with no lack of sustenance. The gilded gate erected in honour of the earl of Ormond had been removed and hidden from the Ulstermen. The General handed back the castles, the town and the hostages to the care of the nuncio. They left everything in order and received his blessing.

28 Sept. [Monday]

On Monday the whole force marched to Castlecomer to the home of *Seán Mac Laoisigh,* where they spent four nights. From there they proceeded to Ballinakill in Laois, to the castle of Cullenagh. The General offered good terms to Captain Barrington, placed his own wardens in the town and proceeded to Port Laoise. The colonel of the horse, Sir Feilim, demanded the surrender of Port Laoise before it would be surrounded. The [governor] refused to surrender till he would see the General and the cannon. When the full force arrived the General sent a drummer to ask for the town. The governor demanded hostages in place of himself and Brian

Page 42
1642

O'Neill, son of Conn Rua, and Seán O'Neill, son of Henry, son of Tarlach of the Fews, were sent. Sir William Gilbert came [to parley] and, having completed his bisiness and seen the large force and the cannon, decided to surrender on condition that he be allowed to bring all movable goods with him.

6th Oct. [Tuesday]

The General placed Feilim O'Neill, son of Dónal, son of Henry in charge of Port Laoise and proceeded to Dysartenos. He sent a drummer to demand the town from Pigot who replied that he would go out feet first rather than surrender. The General ordered Colonels Farrell and Rory Maguire to storm the town. At first the area outside the gate was burnt. They entered by scaling the ramparts. The great hall, the stable and the huge haggard were burnt. More than eighty were killed, the Captain and Pigot included. Of Colonel Rory's men, Captain Dougal Mac Quillan and five soldiers were killed. From there they entered County Kildare and went to Reban Castle which they took. On then to Athy, which they also took. They took Grangecoor from thr enemy and likewise Jigginstown, Ballylinan, Naas, Castlemartin, Clane, the town of Sir John Hay (*Boile Sior Seon Hoii*) Ballymore Eustace, Harristown and several other towns not mentioned here. From there, within twelve miles of Dublin, they marched to Kilcullen Bridge. General Thomas Preston came with his army to join Eoghan O'Neill and they stayed thus for a long time.

Let mention be made for a while of the people of Lisnagarvey, Kilough, Newry, Rostrevor castle, and those of Carlingford, Dundalk, Drogheda and Slane. They joined together, marched on the people of Oriel and forced them to flee to the woods of Drumdoon. Their houses and haggards were burnt and plundered as far as the woods of Kilanny.

Page 43
1646

The countryside around Moybolg together with hundreds of pounds worth of goods were burnt. They returned bringing with them a large quantity of provisions from that country. They took with them the soldiers who were stationed in Carrickmacross and burnt Carrick itself. Mournful and dejected were the women and men of Breifne when they departed.

Dec

The General and his forces were still camped near Dublin, not having received from the Council of Kilkenny to proceed until December and the beginning of a spell of heavy rain which lasted three months. The armies disbanded. The General summoned his forces to advise them that they would be quartered on 'coyne' (*go bhfaghdaois ceathramha i coinmheadh*)- and that they got in Munster and Leinster.

The earl of Ormond arrived with a strong force at Trim. He was joined there by the earl of Kildare; the earl of Westmeath, Richard Nugent, the earl Burke, the earl of Roscommon, the earl of Castlehaven, who had travelled with the earl of Ormond from Kilkenny and Sir James Dillon who was a colonel of the Catholics.

They spent Saint Thomas's day in the house of Edward Bui Tuite (*go bhfuil aca so indium, la San Tomás i dtigh Edurt Buidh Tuit*) They received a contribution of two pounds per gniomh in the county of Westmeath and 'coyne' for their cavalry and infantry.

The earl of Ormond went to Breifne across farmland and collected their cows, their equipment and any of their possessions worth taking. His men repeated this work on eight occasions, collecting and binding and thirty-eight people were killed by them. They carried off from Breifne and Oriel four thousand cows.

Captain Phillip Rua O'Reilly, with the permission of his colonel, Phillip O'Reilly, son of Hugh, undertook to take a party of three hundred soldiers in pursuit of the enemy. They came to the back of the town occupied by three of them and by the end of the night they had surrounded the town;

Page 44
January, 1647
They beat the drums, fired their weapons and burnt the house over the horses and over the enemy, several of whom were killed.

18 [Monday]
The Captain [Phillip O'Reilly] and his men had ninety horses and the arms of the cavalry back with them to Bellanacargy.

21 [Thursday]
Sir Feilim launched on Lough Neagh seven boats and a bark carrying two field-guns and a strong crew. They burnt three of the enemy's fortresses in Clannaboy and a huge haggard which belonged to Major Connolly, the man who betrayed Lord Enniskillen who was executed in London in 1644. They killed people and cows and took away in the boats all they needed. They were pursued on water and land. Sir Feilim's party were erecting a fortress on Trowagh Bay in Clann Breasail when the enemy came upon them. Several of them were killed, including Robert Acheson, one of Sir Feilim's lieutenants. More than twenty were captured and some drowned. Three boats managed to escape. The big bark and five boats were captured.

26 Jan. [Tuesday
Sergeant Major General Seán Ó'Catháin and Lieutenant –colonel Feilim O'Neill, son of Tuathal, arrived in the county of Westmeath (*i gConndae a' Mhuilinn Ciorr*) with three thousand infantry and some cavalry and proceeded to Loughcrew. The following day they had a rendezvous and resolved to attack the garrison of Kells. The infantry entered by scaling the wall and the cavalry remained outside. Those who asked for quarter, about one hundred and thirty under Colonel Jones, were taken prisoner.
More than two hundred [others] were killed. The townspeople were also given quarter. The prisoners were taken to Finea, and Theophilus to the castle of Lough Sheelin.

Jan
General Monck, with a Parliamentary force of three thousand men and one hundred and twenty horse and all their cavalry equipment arrived in Trian Conghail against Ulster.

Feb.
Against Leinster there arrived in Dublin a Parliamentary force of three thousand and [? An unspecified number of ?] horse

A
True Relation
Of

The late Expedition of the right Honarable the Earl of Ormonde And Sir Charles Coote, Knight and Baronet, into the several counties of Kildare, Queens County, Kings County, and the County of Catherlagh.
Sir

I received your letter this day, being newly come from the late expedition with the Earl of Ormonde, about some occasions from my Colonell , Sir Charles Coote who is at the Naas and sent me about important business to the state, and am I to return tomorrow to him. We have banished, hanged, and killed all the Irish, and Papists in the town of Naas, and placed a new Sovereign with eight Burgesses, and all other Officers in that town, besides many tradesmen, all English Protestants; Sir Charles Coote has given them all, cattle, houses and land to relieve their present wants. He has behaved himself most gallantly, he is very charitable to the poor English. We continue about a fortnight at the Naas, to settle the poor English there, and to satisfie the town, the which being done, Lieutenant Colonell Gibson is to be Governor thereof. From thence we go to Trim to settle it with English, as we have done the Naas, the particulars of our journey with the Earl of Ormonde I send you herewith, Videlicet

(N.L.I.LOP 39 Pamphlets Irish Tracts 1641 -1690)

Castleknock Castle

Castleknock Castle was built by the Anglo Norman, Hugh Tyrrell, built on two mounds near the end of *Eiscair Riada,* which stretches from Galway to Dublin, it commanded the route from the west into Dublin. In 1642 the castle was attacked by the Earl of Ormonde.

Above, The ruin of Castleknock Castle as it stands today.

1642

"The four - thousand strong army of Lord Moore and Richard Grenville besieged the manor house and castle of Gerald Lacy when he was absent from home. There were only thirty wardens in the castle and over a period of five days, they killed seven hundred of the besiegers. The lady of the town accepted quarter for herself and her children. The wardens of the castle then put all of plate, brass, iron, guns, clothing, wheat and many other valuables of that country into the manor house and set fire to it immediately. The besiegers then attacked the bawn and broke down the iron door. First, one of them entered and demanded a pistol which one of the wardens held. 'Here it is,' he said and discharged two bullets into his chest and killed him. The rest were immediately taken and bound in pairs"[28].

Lady Lacey's speech to the defenders of Castleknock Castle in 1642

"My faithful servants, you can well judge by the action I am after performing, what hope there is of favour from our enemies, and how little clemency

---

[28] Friar O Mealláin Journal page 33.Louth Archaeological Journal

I expect at their hands.... You should not expect quarter from them, but remember the sentence which says 'let the vanquished hope for nothing from their enemies'. Take courage then, and combat to the death for the faith of your redeemer; you can never find a more glorious end, and the sooner to find it, go valiantly to attack the enemy of the cross, lest, being made prisoners, any of you should by bad treatment or the violence of torments, fail in the good resolution you have taken of dying today for the Catholic faith"[29].

In 1834 The Vincentian Fathers bought approximately forty acres of land in Castleknock on which to build a school. The fields enclosed in this land were named,Castle Field, Windmill Field, Limekiln Field, and Hops Field. Castle Field contains a mound on which stands the ruin of Castleknock Castle. Windmill Field contains a mound on which stands the remains of a tower. These mounds are near the end of The Esker known as *Eiscair Riada* and are the highest point between the rivers Liffey and Tolka.

The remains of the tower can be seen at the entrance to Castleknock College.The tower, which is built on Windmill Hill, was thought by some to have been a windmill, whilst others were of the opinion, that it was a limekiln. Today it houses a water tank. In 1834, The Dublin Penny Journal, informed its readers that,"Outside the town of Castleknock and situated in the Demesne of Mr Guinn are two steep hills, one a plain circular knoll, formally called Windmill Hill,crowned by a circular building, which was erected by Mr Guinn for an observatory, but afterwards let go to ruin".

The Dublin Penny Journal, continues to inform its readers that the owner of the castle prior to Mr Guinn attempted to excavate a chamber under the entrenchments of the Castle, "and actually found a flight of steps leading to the vaults, when panic struck his labourers that the sleeping King Morrish-tac the Dane might come upon them, and they instantly fled in the utmost confusion. The excavation was soon closed up. Money to an incre-dible amount is said to be buried in the Windmill Hill".

Castleknock was famous long before Hugh Tyrrell built his castle there, for it was here in the second century A.D. that (*Catha Cnucha*)- the battle of Cnucha was supposedly fought. Almu, the wife of Nuada of the Silver Hand, begged that her name be given to the hill. Her request was granted, and it was here she was to be buried.

Nuada had a son, named Tadg, who was a famous druid. He was married to Rairiu, daughter of Donn-Duma. When Nuada died he left his stronghold, Cnucha, to his son. Tadg was druid to Cathar. Rairiu bore a daughter to Tadg; her name was Muirne of the fair neck.This maiden grew up in great beauty, so that the sons of the kings and mighty lords of Ireland were won't to be courting her.Cumhall, son of Trenmore, king-warrior of Ireland, was then in the service of Conn, (of the Hundred Battles) and he, like every

---

[29] M.S 11657 N.L.I.

other youth, was demanding the maiden. Tadg refused Cumhal the hand of his daughter.Cumhal took Muirne by force. Tadg went to Conn, told him what Cumhall had done, and asked his help for the return of his daughter. Conn dispatched messengers to Cumall, and ordered him to leave Ireland, or to restore Muirne to Tadg. Cumall said he would not give her up; everything else he would give but not the woman. Conn sent his soldiers, and Urgriu, son of Lugaid Corr King of the Luagni, and Daire the Red son of Eochaid and his son Aed (who was afterwards called Goll) to attack Cumhall. Cumall assembled his army against them; And the battle of Cnucha was fought between them, and Cumall was slain along with many of his people. Cumhall fell by Goll son of Morna. Luchet wounded Goll in his eye, so that he destroyed it. And so it is that, the name Goll (the one eyed) was given to him.

Because of this battle at Cnucha and the slaying of Cumhall by Goll Morna that a hereditary feud existed between the sons of Goll Morna and Finn Mac Cumhaill.After the death of Cumhall, Muirne returned to her father, Tadg, the Druid, but he rejected her because she was pregnant by Cumall. Under the protection of Conns she went to Tara Mairci, where, Bodball the Druidess, a sister of Cumhall lived.Here she gave birth to a son to whom the name Demne was given. Demne stayed atTara Mairci until he became a warrior. He then declared war on Tadg, and offered Single combat unless the full *eric* (compensatory fine) for his fathers death be given to him. Tadg offered him Cnucha, this offer was accepted by Demne, and so it was that (Demne) Finn Mac Cumhaill came to live at Cnucha.

The following legend, which was published in the Dublin Penny Journal in 1834, associates Saint Patrick with Castleknock "Patrick...came to Castle-cnock, then in the possession of a Danish King, called Morrishtac, whom he endeavoured to convert, but the Dane, not wishing to be bothered by the pious saint, and unwilling to be inhospitable, after listening for some time, and giving sundry nods of approval at length fell asleep in his great armchair. St Patrick preached on for some time, until he was astounded by a most unchristian snore from the poor Dane and then his rage knew no bounds. He tore his beard and acted several ramashes, and in the height of his passion, prayed that the uncircumcised king should sleep in the same place and posture till the day of judgement".

Carraig-an-Aifrinn
Coill a' tSléibhe, Sliabh na mBán.
Co. Tipperary.

Slievenamon, which lies to the north of the town of Clonmel, is mentioned in an eight or ninth century legend of Fionn mac Cumhall, which was edited by Meyer (RC,XXX 344/347) as follows,

When the Fian were at Badamair on the brink of the Suir, Cúldub of the race of Birgge came out of Síd ar Femun (5) *ut Scotti dicunt* and carried off their cooking from them. For three nights he acted thus towards them.The third time, however, norat Finn and he went ahead to Sid ar Femun.Finn thrust successfully at him as he entered the síd and he fell on the far side.While he was drawing his hand towards him he was interfered with by a woman from the síd with a dripping vessel in her hand from which she had just been distributing drink, and she jammed the door against the síd, and Finn squeezed his finger between the door and the post.When the finger came out again he began to utter an incantation; mystic knowledge illuminated him and he said;

> Come to Femen. A Judgement!
> A happy blow from a long ever swift shaft
> Increase my dish by a pig ;
> It is Finn's ale drinking at Cúldub's tomb we chant.

(5)= Síd ar Femun (The Fairy Hill before Femen, or if we read the older al for ar, The Fairy Hill beyond Femen), is today known as Slievenamon, north of Clonmel, Co, Tipperary.

Carraig-an-Aifrinn – Coill –na-tSleibhe – Sliabh-na-mBán

The-Mass-Rock-The-Mountain-Wood –The-Mountain-of-the- Women. The rock above, where local tradition holds, mass was read during the penal times.(photo author)

There is a cairn at the top of Slievenamon which is associated with the following tale: Three strange women appear at a lonely cottage to help a young woman at her spinning, when they appear for the third night in succession she grows suspicious and goes out the front door and rushes back saying that the top of the mountain is on fire. The three women run up the hill to save their otherworld residence from destruction.

Sliabh-na-mBan

Is oth liom féinigh, bualadh 'n lae úd
Do dhul ar Ghaeil bhocht 'sna céadta slad;
Mar tá na meirligh ag déanamh game dínn,
Á rá nach aon ní leo pice nó sleá
Níor tháinig ár Magor í dtús an lae chugainn,
Is ní rabhamar féin ann í gcóir ná í gceart,
Ar thaoibh na gréine de Shliabh na mBan.
Mo lean léir ar dream gan éifeacht,
Nar fhann le héirim, is d'oiche stad,
Go mbeadh dúiche Déiseach is Iarthar Eireann,
Ag triall le chéile ón tír aneas,
Bheadh ár gcampaí déanta le fórsaí tréana,
Bheadh cúnamh Dé linn 's an saol ar fad,
Is ní dhíolfadh méirleach roimh theacht an aoire,
Ar thaobh na gréine de Shliabh na mBan.

Sé Ross do bhreoigh is do chloigh go deo sinn
Trínar fágadh mór chuid dínn sínte lag,
Na leanaí óga ;s smólaibh dóite,
's an méid d'fhan beo dínn chois claí nó scairt
Ach geallaim fós daoibh, 'té dhein an foghladh,
Go mbeam í gcóir dó le pice is sleá;
Is go gcuirfeam yeomen ag crith na mbrógaibh,
Ad díol a gcomhair le oar Shliabh na mBan

Is mó fear aosta is crobhaire gléigheal,
Ón ám go chéile do gabhadh le seal,
'na bhfuil cordaí caola 'baint lúth a ngéag diobh,
I nduinsiúin daora go domhain faoi ghlas,
Gardai taobh leo ná lámhfadh sméid orthu,

100

Go ndéanfadh plé dhóibh í dtiír thsr lear,
Dá dtabhairt soar óna namhaid gan buíochas,
In ám an tsaortha ar Shliabh na mBan

Tá 'n Francach faobhrach 's a loingeas gléasta,
Le crannaibh géara 'cú ar muir le seal,
Is é síorscéal go bhfuil a dtriall ar Eirinn,
's go gcuirfid Gaeil bhocht arís 'na gceart,
Dá mba dhóigh liom féineach go mb' fhíor an scéal úd,
Bheadh mo chroí chomh headroom le lon ar sceach,
Go mbeadh cloí ar mhéirligh, 's an adharc dá séideadh,
Ar thaobh na gréine de Shliabh na mBan

Slievenamon
Weep the great departed-the patriot hearted!
With life they parted for Irelands right;
To them give glory, while tyrants gory
Spread the false story, "they fled in fright"
O, 'twas small our terror! We fled to error,
No chiefs there were or an ordered van,
Yet when came war's rattle we fled not battle,
Though like herdless cattle on Slievenamon

May the grief each ray shuns curse their impatience,
Who did haste our nation's uprise from night,
Ere the south could gather its clans together,
And on this heather with the west unite,
Our camp had warriors-Aye freedom's barriers!
The God-sent carriers of slav'rys van!
O, no spy had found them-no fetter bound them,
We'd be freed men round them on Slievenamon.

Though at Ross defeated, few, few retreated:
Death comes-they meet it with push of pike!
Then were dragged the dying, and poor babes crying,
The flames to lic, in from ditch and dyke,
Ye who wreaked this slaughter, for the crimes you wrought there,
We swear- like water your blood shall run,
Yet- savage yeomen, of Hell an omen,
We'll meet ye, foemen, on Slievenamon!

Ah! many's the old man and star bright bold man,
Who long did hold on to free their isle,
Lie pale and markless, in deathly starkkness,

101

Bowed down in darkness of dungeon vile,
There, eve and morning, they bear all scorning,
Threats, lashes, mourning, that their tyrant's plan;
We'll pay, soon, your labours, o coward neighbours!
With our trusty sabres on Slievenamon!

For on the ocean are ships in motion,
And glad devotion on France's shore,
And rumour's telling; "they'll now be sailing
To help the Gael in the Right once more",
O! if true's that story, by my hopes of glory,
Like the glad bird o'er me I'll lilt my rann!
Were the robber routed! The Saxon flouted!
How we would shout it, old Slievenamon!

Ho! the clowns are quaking and counsel taking,
Goods times are making their firm approach,
When those who weakly still preach "bear meekly",
Will mourn all bleakly in dark reproach!
While gold and chattel, broad lands and cattle,
Pay them whose battle made freedom dawn,
And way-side dances our joy enhances,
With the gold fire-glances o'er Slievenamon.

Caoine Cill Chais

Cad a dhéanfaimíd feasta gan adhmad?
Tá deireadh na gcoillte ar lár.
Níl trácht ar Chill Chais ná a teaghlach.
's ní cluinfear a cling go brách.
An áit úd 'na gcónaíodh an dea-bhean
Fuair gradam is meidnir bidi mná
Bhíodh iarlaí ag tarraing tar toinn ann,
's an tAifreann doimhín dá rá.

Anois mar bharr ar gach mí – ghreann
Chuaigh prionsa na nGael thar sail
Anonn le hainnir na mine,
Fuair gradam sa bhFrainc 's sa Spáinn
Anois tá a cullacht dá caoineadh
Gheibheadh airgead buí agus bán;
'sí ná tógfadh seilbh na ndaoine,
'sí cara na bhfíorbhoctán.

Aicím ar Mhuire 's ar Iosa,

Go dtaga sí arís chugainn slán,
Go mbeidh rincí fada ag gabháll timpeall
Ceol fidilí 's tiinte cnámh;
Go dtógfar an bhaile seo ár sinsear,
Cill Chais bhreá, arís go hard,
's go brách nó go dtiocfaidh an díleann
Ná feicfear í 'rís ar lár!

The Lament for Kilcash

Where now is the sheltering wild wood
That we in our youth have known?
Oh gone are the groves of our childhood
And even the birds are flown.
It was there that dwelt the good lady
There the sweet bell was daily rung,
Great Earls came over the wave there,
And the deep intoned Mass was sung.

No wild goose is heard on the lake now,
No wild duck haunts the stream,
The eagles their eyrie forsake now,
No bees hum in day's bright beam.
No voices of birds now entrance us
As they once sang at evening's fall,
No cuckoo is heard in the branches
To utter his slumberous call

To Mary I pray, and the Saviour,
May our exiles return again,
With dancing and bonfires blazing,
And violin's sweetest strain
That the castle that now is so humbled
May rise with strong keep and wall,
And till earth into ashes has crumbled
In ruin no more may fall.

The Cromwellian Campaign in Ireland.

The revolt of the Irish in October 1641 opened one of the most turbulent chapters of Irish history. One of its consequences being the arrival of Oliver Cromwell eight years later in 1649. The initial rebellion was in the province of Ulster, where the Gaelic Irish held sway.The Gaelic Irish were the descendants of the ancient Celtic Race who ruled Ireland before the arrival of the Anglo-Normans in the twelfth century. Sir Phelim O' Neill and Conor,

Lord Maguire were the most prominent leaders of the revolt which was planned and led by O' Neill in Ulster. Maguire was to have initiated the capture of Dublin Castle, where arms for 10,000 men were supposedly stored. News of his intentions was leaked to the authorities, Maguire was arrested and his followers dispersed.

"On the eve of the feast (*oidhche Féil*) of Saint John Capistranus the lords of Ulster planned to seize in one night, unknown to the English and Scots, all their walled towns, castles and bawns. The date chosen was the 22nd of October, Friday to be precise, and the last day of the moon. First, to attack Dublin there went there from Ulster the lord of Enniskillen, Conor Maguire, son of Brian, son of Conor, Hugh Óg MacMahon, son of Brian, son of Hugh Óg, son of Séan Buí, and Rory O More of Upper Orior, also a party from Meath, from other parts of Leinster and from Munster, etc. Eoghan Connolly, however, made known their plan.The gates of Dublin were closed, the bells of the City were rung, houses ransacked, and the lord of Enniskillen and young MacMahon captured. The others made good their escape"[30].

Phelim O' Neill was more successful in Ulster, his forces captured many English strongholds including, Dungannon, Charlemont, the great fort at Mountjoy. Although he tried to limit military action to those against English settlements, away from Scottish enclaves in the hope that Scots would support the rebellion. As news of supposed atrocities committed against English Protestants spread, the Scots came to the defence of their coreligionists. It is claimed that as many as 154,000 Protestants were slaughtered in the first months of the uprising. This claim whether true or false created a barrier between the native Irish, and the planter population which was to last for hundreds of years. In May 1642 events in Ireland and Britain were to change the political scene. In Ireland the Catholic Hierarchy met with the Old English leaders in Kilkenny and formed the Catholic Confederation. The Gaelic Irish joined soon afterwards. For the first time in Ireland the Catholics had a central political structure under which they could air their grievance's and articulate their ambitions. At the same time in England the political situation had degenerated into civil war. consequently the supply of, money, troops, munitions, to Ireland slowed to a halt. In fact English troops in Trim, mutinied for lack of pay. As the civil war gathered momentum in England, the towns of Limerick and Waterford sided with the Confederates.In conjunction with these happenings Owen Roe O' Neill landed at Doe Castle in County Donegal in July of 1642 bringing with him weapons, money, and three hundred trained veterans of Spanish service in Flanders, who brought with them a professional military expertise which the Catholics were lacking until then. The failure of the Catholic Confederation to take advantage of their numerical superiority and

---

[30] Friar O'Meallán Journal

drive the Protestant armies out of Ireland, their failure to take advantage of Owen Roe O' Neill's victory over the Scots at Benburb in 1646 was to prove costly.The continous internecine feuding between the Gaelic Irish and the Old English which degenerated into civil war in 1648 did nothing to help their cause.

Meanwhile across the Irish Sea the Rump parliament,(so called because the Model Army had purged the House of Commons of members not in sympathy to their cause.) In December of 1648, had established a Council of State to carry out the executive Duties of the Commonwealth. The Rump Parliament gave this body the power "to order and direct all the militias and forces both by sea and land to use all good ways and means for the reducing of Ireland"

The man picked to carry out this task was Oliver Cromwell. Oliver Cromwell landed in Dublin on the 15th of August 1649 with a flotilla of thirty five ships. He was followed by Henry Ireton with between seventy and eighty ships. On the 23rd of August. They were later joined by Colonel Horton with eighteen ships. Cromwell's campaign in Ireland began when the advance guard left Dublin on August 31st led by Jones, they arrived at Drogheda on September 2nd, by the eleventh the Model Army was ready to attack Drogheda. Before attacking Cromwell summoned Sir Arthur Aston to surrender.

During the ensuing battle for Drogheda Cromwell gave the order to his troops that no quarter was to be given. It is said that Lieutenant-Colonel Axtel offered quarter to Aston and his men but when they surrendered at the Mill Mount, they were slaughtered, Aston being beaten to death with his own wooden leg.

Cromwell's Report on the Taking of Drogheda (Tredah)

"It hath pleased God to bless our endeavours at Tredah. After battery, we stormed it. The enemy were about three thousand strong in the town. They made a stout resistance, and near 1,000 of our men being entered, the enemy forced them out again. But God giving a new courage to our men, they attempted again, and entered beating the enemy from their defences. The enemy had made three entrenchments, both to the right and left of where we entered, we refused them quarter; having the day before summoned the town. I believe we put to the sword the whole number of the defendants. I do not think thirty of the whole number escaped with their lives. Those that did , are in safe custody for the Barbadoes....I wish that all honest hearts may give the glory of this to God alone, to whom indeed the praise of this mercy belongs."

Cromwells victory at Drogheda and the subsequent slaughter of its inhabitants was to be engraved upon the folk memory of the Irish Catholic. Any hope of reconciliation between Protestant and Catholic was doomed.

Ulster Protestants harboured grim memories of the massacres of 1641. Catholic memories of the slaughter at Drogheda, and Wexford would endure for centuries.

The Capture of Wexford

The following account of the massacre of some Franciscan Fathers of the convent of Wexford is taken from, 'A Brief History of the Irish Province of the Friars Minor of the Regular Observance, by Father Francis Ward.
'Brevis Synopsis Provinciae Hiberniae FF. Min. Regularis Observantiae',
auctore F Francisco Ward.
Taken from a narrative written by Francis Stafford, formerly guardian of the Franciscan Convent Wexford. M.S. in the Arundel Library, Stonyhurst. "On the 11th of October 1649, the octave of our holy father, St Francis, seven religious of the Order of St Francis, all men of great merit and natives of the town, perished by the sword of the heretics in Wexford, viz: Father Richard Synnott, professor of theology, formerly guardian of the convent; F. John Esmonde, preacher, who had singular power in relieving energumenes; F. Paulinus Synnott, who had suffered much for the faith among the Turks, and had received from Pope Urban VIII. full jurisdiction over all the Catholic captives; F. Raymond Stafford, who had left a considerable inheritance, and despising everything for Christ, had chosen to imitate the poverty of Christ under the standard of St Francis. Fifteen months before his death he had retired to an island, and led there an austere and mortified life, usindg only one each day lenten fare. F. Peter Stafford too, was much devoted to prayer. During the times of persecution, in the absence of the secular clergy, he discharged for fifteen years the duties of parish priest with great credit. Brother Didacus Chevers over seventy years of age and blind; Brother James Rochford, both men of exemplary lives, and devoted to work. Some of these men slain while kneeling before the altar, others, while hearing confession. Fr Raymond Stafford, holding in his hand a crucifix, came out of the church to encourage the citizens, and even preached with great zeal to the enemy, until he was slain by them in the market place. All these were men of exemplary life, and as they fell, the Lord deigned to show how precious their death was in his sight.

1. When they were fired at, the balls fell close to some of them without doing harm to any whatever. This I heard from a noble lady, Margaret Keating, to whom the enemy related it in presence of her children and servants.
2. Whilst they were being put to death, it happened that a little of their blood fell on the hand of one of the executioners; this he could not wash off ever or remove by any means whatever. I heard this from Mr John French of Ballolonie, who had himself seen the blood and learned the circumstances from the mouth of the wicked man after

the capture of the city; he spoke of the crime with great sorrow, saying that he bore about on his hand the token that he had slain the religious 'whose blood you see', and would carry the mark with him to his grave.

3. Mrs Margaret Keating, the wife of Captain Doran, and daughter of Mr William Keating, an Alderman of Wexford, told me she heard a soldier of the English army named Weaver say, that when the religious were mortally wounded and lay expiring in the streets, through compassion for them and wishing to put an end to their suffering, he fired at one of them twice. Though the balls touched his cowl, they did not penetrate it; they fell gently near the cowl as if they had no force. He then shot at the body, but the result was the same. Weaver was asked to fire again; he replied, 'I have done so already as well as I could; hitherto I have slain none of the Irish, nor shall I do so in future'. He left the army and became a Catholic. I was sought for to reconcile him to the Church, but as I was not found, I did not see him. But to a certainty he was reconciled by the Rev. Patrick Hampton, Chancellor of Ferns, of pious memory.

4. Some of the soldiers who put on the habits of the religious, died miserably. Mr William Hore of Harperstown told me that he warned in a friendly manner one of the English soldiers who had the habit on, to lay it aside, as it was not right to mock at St Francis or the other saints. He replied, 'that is all nonsense and superstition', 'Tell me, I beg you', said Mr Hore, 'tomorrow morning if you have had any dreams'. He agreed to do so. After he had gone to rest he was tortured by spectres all the night, thinking mad dogs were dragging him about. He was so terrified at these sights that he took sick and died.

5. Francis Whitty, a man of noble birth, told me he saw one of the English soldiers who had the habit on, die while uttering blasphemies.

6. It is commonly reported that a soldier fired at the crucifix which F. Raymond held in his hand, and that the ball turned aside and killed the captain of the company. This I heard from Sir Thomas Esmonde and from many others.

7. The Rev. John Stafford, the parish priest of Maglass, declared that, on the day when the religious and others were slain at Wexford, he saw a beautiful woman ascending towards the sky. This he saw when he was five miles from Wexford, before he heard anything whatever about its capture.

8. Divers mishaps befell those who were daring enough to dwell in the convent that formerly belonged to the religious. Many of them, soon after they came to the place, died and were buried in the convent garden. Those who survived were frequently troubled during the

night by spectres; they told their neighbours that they thought they had done wrong in killing the religious, and that they would remain no longer in the convent, even though they should find no other place to live in. This I heard from some of their neighbours who knew well of their death and burial, and who had heard from these persons that they were tormented in this way by spectres.

I the undersigned, declare, on the word of a priest, that I heard the above facts related by the aforesaid persons, and have set them down in writing exactly as they were told.

Father Francis Stafford, Of the Conception, preacher and confessor, and ex-guardian of The convent of Wexford

About Eastertide, 1654, four Franciscans were arrested in Wexford by Cromwellian officers, and hanged without formality of trial in the neighbourhood of their former convent. (Franciscan Monasteries, p 295)

There is a tradition still current in Wexford which says that three hundred women were put to death in the public square. They had flocked round the great cross which stood there, in the hope that Christian soldiers would be so far softened by the sight of the emblem of mercy as to spare the lives of unresisting women. But the victors, enraged at such superstition, and perhaps regarding their presence there as a proof that they were Catholics, and therefore fit objects for their zeal, rushed upon them and put them all to death. see History of Ireland p 574 M'Geoghegan Abbé= born 1701 sent to France at an early age, there he entered the church, was Chaplin to the Irish Brigade, during the later part of his life he was attached to the church of St Méry, in Paris, died 1764.

The following poem relates the story of the massacre.

They knelt around the cross divine,
The Matron and the maid;
Thry bowed before redemption's sign,
And fervently they prayed-
Three hundred fair and helpless ones,
Whose crime was this alone-
Their valiant husbands, sires, and sons
Had battled for their own

Had battled bravely, but in vain-
The Saxon won the fight,
And Irish corpses strewed the plain
Where Valour slept with Right,
And now that man of demon guilt,
To fated Wexford flew-

The red blood reeking on his hilt
Of hearts to Erin true!

He found them there- the young the old,
The maiden and the wife;
Their guardians brave in death were cold,
Who dared for them to strife.
They prayed for mercy-God on high!
Before *thy* cross they prayed,
And ruthless Cromwell bade them die
To glut the Saxon blade!

Three hundred fell-the stifled prayer,
Was quenched in women's blood;
Nor youth nor age would move to spare,
From slaughter's crimson flood.
But nations keep a stern account
Of deeds that tyrants do!
And guiltless blood to Heaven will mount,
And Heaven avenge it too.
Michael J Barry (Spirit of the Nation, p 252)

An Historic Relic

The figure on the enclosed crucifix in the picture below was found in the
Lady's Island, lake, in the vicinity of St Ibar's Church in the summer of
1887. When first discovered a small portion of the left arm was missing.
Acting on the instructions of the Parish Priest, the late, Venerable
Archdeacon Roche, the finder, a boy named Cogley, renewed the search and
strange to relate succeeded in finding the missing part which was
subsequently attached to the figure.

Crucifix

There is a local tradition regarding this crucifix which runs as follows,
It once belonged to the old church of St Ibars, where it was venerated by the local people. When one evening in the year 1649 the alarm was raised that the Cromwellian forces were marching from Wexford, the people made an attempt to save from destruction and abuse, the sacred vessels and ornaments from the churches of South Wexford. One young man named Duffey, rushed to St Ibar's Church, and seizing this crucifix, which rested above the Tabernacle, fled with it across the shallow part of the lake, but, alas, it was too late. He was shot down by the brutal soldiers before he could reach the other shore, and his martyred blood crimsoned the waters.
The sacred burden that he carried lay concealed in the mud of the lake for centuries, until as above recorded, it was accidently discovered in 1887.
The shrine was presented by the Rev Thomas O'Byrne C.C. Tacumshane on August 15th 1910. The dispossession of their land, the transportation and execution of their priests was to fuel a burning hatred.The common people of Ireland were the ultimate losers, especially the Catholic majority. Hundreds of thousands of men, women, and children were killed by war, famine and disease. The Catholic merchants of the major towns were driven from their homes and forced to emigrate to the continent of Europe Three thousand Catholic landowners, most of whom had relatively small

holdings, along with their servants, were forced to transplant to Connaught and to build a life on smaller and less fertile estates. Refusal to transplant was punishable by the death penalty, or transportation to slavery in Englands Carribean colonies.

In excess of eleven million acres of land was confiscated during this period. Over forty thousand men and their families emigrated to Europe serving as mercenaries in the continental armies. Thousands more became Tories and carried on a spasmodic war against the authorities.

The Incarceration of Catholic clergy on the Isle of Orkney.

From the letter written by Father Patrick of St Brigid on 26th of June 1657 "It transpired that many Irish Catholics had been deported to the Orkney Islands by command of the Protector, and that others were still being sent there; as were also numbers of English and Scotch Catholics, similarly the victims of the new persecution".[31]

On the gates of Bandon,Co Cork the following was written.
" Enter here Turk, Jew, or Atheist,
Any man except a Papist".
Underneath these lines some papist wit wrote,
"The man who wrote this wrote it well;
For the same is writ on the gates of Hell".

On a government return of March 6 1743 the Provost of Bandon reports, "By the assistance of the Burgesses and Gentlemen of this Corporation and obedient to his Graces's orders. I doe send you the names of the several popish priests of the adjacent parishes but observe to you that within the limits of this Baronye no priest or papist was ever the late King James his regine suffered to reside within the town the inhabitants are all Protestsnts and by our Corporation Laws no others are to live among us".
Ralph Clear Provost [32]

Piaras Feiritéar.

The Ferriters, (na Feiritéaraigh) were an Anglo-Norman family who had become Gaelicised. They held land in West Kerry, which included the Blasket Islands, from the Earl of Desmond. The village of Balleyferriter on the Dingle peninsula is named after them. There are also three castles said to have been built by this family. One at Baile Uachtarach in Cuan an Chaoil, near Ballyferriter, also known as Castle Sybil. They had another castle, at Rinn an Chaisleáin, on the Great Blasket Island. The Great

---

[31] (Irish Ecclesiastical Records 1917) p 488 N.L.I.
[32] Moran Patrick Francis Persecutions of the Irish Catholics

Blasket was at one time known as "Ferriters Island".Ballineanig, (*Baile an Éanaigh*) Castle Quarter (*Ceathrú an Chaisleáin*). Ballineanig Castle "castle Martin" is featured on Petty's map of Kerry in 1683, and is believed to have been built by the Ferriters. This castle stood in the old village of Ballineanig on the South side of Smerick Harbour. Piaras Feiritéar, son of Émann Feiritéar, succeeded his father and became chieftain of his people. He was a fine swordsman, and an accomplished Gaelic poet, and did not want for courage. He took the Confederate side in the Nine Years War, and forces under his command, captured Tralee Castle in 1642. He was eventually defeated at Ross Castle, Kilarney, in 1652. While "out upon his keeping", he was captured by Cromwellian soldiers and hanged at Cnocán na gCaorach, Martyrs Hill, Kilarney in 1653. Following is an example taken from his lament for the death of Maurice Fitzgerald, son of the knight of Kerry, who died in the service of Phillip II in Flanders.

"Mórbhfile nár bh'file I gcómad
I n-amhras ar fheabhas a n-eolais
D'eagla ná beadh d'eagna leo san
Marbhna nach ba mharbhna coir duit."

"The silent versifiers must refrain,
Doubting their prowess to pursue their trade,
For fear their skill but ill compass its aim,
A verity no clergy could frame."

There are many legends concerning Piaras, not least the following from the Great Blasket, which was narrated by Tomás Ó Criomhthain to Robin Flower.

"The poet it was, and, beyond being a poet, he was many other things too. He had done many deeds out of the way, things that didn't please the King and his people. So the watch was out after him, and before they caught him in the end, and hanged him, he had many a shift to keep his feet free of them. They did their best to come up with him, but he was too clever for them for a good while. He had this castle built on the brink of a cliff, and he used to live in it; but when the chase was too near to him he had another place, a cave in the hill that neither deer nor eagle could come at.

"A day of the days, on an early morning of summer, he was living lightly in his castle, and he put his head out and what should he see but the guard right over against him. Terror seized him that he should be out so early in the morning, and he had no time to think of a shift. He said to himself that the best thing he could do was to yield himself up to them and take things easily. He told their captain that, if it was he they wanted, he was well pleased to go with them, for he had been too long on his keeping, escaping from them, and he would rather go with them to suffer all they could do to him than live the life he had been living any longer. They agreed together, and Pierce said to them that maybe they had been out and about without food and drink too long, and that he would give orders for dinner to be made ready for them, if they wished. The captain said it was so and they had good need of it. Pierce told the girl to get dinner ready, and he bade them come along with him to the crest of the hill, where they might have a fine view while the dinner was preparing. He told them to throw away their guns and not to be bothered carrying them. Finding him fine and easy in the morning, they were fine and easy with him, too, and did whatever he told them. They threw aside their guns, and before they went up the hill Pierce spoke aside to the girl and told her not to spare water on the guns when they were out of sight.

This girl Pierce had was no fool, for if she had been he wouldn't have had her. "Off they went, they climbed the hill and they spent a good time walking on the hill till they thought it was time for the dinner to be ready. Then they turned back to the castle. When they were drawing near to it, Pierce said he would go in front, for the way in was rather troublesome. So he went in before them, and when he was inside there was a corner of the castle above the cliff with only room for one man at a time to go the way. The next man wouldn't know where- abouts in the castle the man in front would have stopped. When the first man came by the corner where Pierce was, Pierce thrust at him with a piece of wood and with that thrust sent him down the cliff, and the next man after him, and so with all who came in to the last man, none of them knowing where the man before had gone till there were fifty men lying in the creek, dead corpses in a heap. Pierce did well that day, but he wouldn't have been so comfortable in his castle if he had known that the pursuit was so near upon his heels."[33]

I mourn the poet Piaras Feiritéar
Whose wine and wit was rich and rare
Until the hangman strangled his elegence
In Killarnry's fairground, a ghastley dance.
Rebellion's head is high on a stake now
And warns of pillage and transportation.
No dún resounds with recitation
Nor wine, nor music, for want of a patron.
Our leaders are scattered, banished to Connaught
Our soldiers in Spain, forgotten, anonymous.
Now we have oaths witnessed by their clergy

---

[33] Flower Robin The western Isle

The meaningless drivel of landgrabbing perjury
Where can we turn, whom can we follow
Now theres no shelter in mountain or forest?
There's no relief for us from pain
But to pray to God and his holy saints.[34]

Letter from Lady Kerry to Pierce Ferriter, 1641
Directed for my loving friend, Mr Pierce Ferriter,
At Ferriter's Towne in Kerry.

These - * * *

Honest Pierce, and I hope in God, I shall never have reason to call you otherwise, this very day is one come out of Kerry unto mee yt by chance fell into the company of Florence McFiniene and the rest of that rebellious crew the very day that they robbed Haly who tells me that you promised (as he heard Florence say) to be with them the week following and to bring a piece of ordinance with you from the Dingel and join with them to take the castle of Traly, but I hope in God it is far from your thoughts for you that have ever been observed to stand upon tour reputation in smaller matters I trust will not now be tainted with so fowle and offensive a crime to God and man nor give your adversaries that cause of rejoicing and just way for them to avenge themselves upon you nor us that are your friends that cause of discontent which would make us curse the day that ever we saw you.

But I cannot believe any such thing of you and therefore will not take much pains to persuade you knowing that you want not wit and understanding enough to conceive and apprehend the danger and punishment justly due to such offenders; and therefore doubt not God's mercie in giving you grace to avoid them which none can more earnestly wish and pray for than.

Your loving friend,
Honor Kerry

Cork ye last of June, 1641

Here I am settled and do intend to stay until the times grow quieter which I hope in God will be ere long for here is news com of a mighty armie a preparing in England for to com over.[35]

The Mass-Rock and Mass-House of Tomhaggard County Wexford.
On Christmass morning in the year 1653, at a spot known locally as The Knock of Furze, Fr Nicholas Mayler was killed by Cromwellian soldiers while celebrating mass.

---

[34] O'Connell M.R Daniel O'Connell Political Pioneer institute of Public Administration
[35] An tAthair Padraig Ua Duinnín Dánta Phiarais Feiritéir 1903

114

Mass-Rock, Tomhaggard

Fr Mayler who was martyred, at the spot in the picture above, is said to be buried along with his kinsfolk within the ruin of the medieval church in Tomhaggard cemetery. He was a descendant of the Norman Maylers of Duncormick, who lost their Castle and land during the Cromwellian confiscations. Local tradition holds that a Mrs Lambert (whose family owned the farm, during this period.), who was among the faithful congregation huddled around the Mass-rock on that bleak Christmas morning, wrapped the chalice and paten in her apron and hid them in a local lake, she retrieved them later when it was safe to do so and returned them to the Mayler familily, with whom they remained for 236 years. It was later converted into a ciborium by a kinsman of Fr Mayler, Archdeacon Philip Mayler, Parish Priest of Kilmore from 1850 to 1884. He returned it to the little chapel of Tomhaggard.

On the table above the Chalice and Paten

It was fortunate that during my visit to Tomhaggard I made the acquaintance of Father Danny McDonald,C.C. Who kindly allowed me to photograph the chalice and paten above and also gave me a copy of his book,<u>Tomhaggard –A Sacred Place,</u> which I recommend to anyone looking for further information on Tomhaggard.

Tomhaggard is indeed a sacred place, its holy wells, and medieval church, its Mass-Rock and Mass-House stand today as symbols of Catholic continuity and monuments to the faith of the people, in spite of "dungeon fire and sword".

The Mass-House at Tomhaggard.
Note the segment of medieval church over the door keeping the link with the past unbroken.

Máire Rua of Leamaneh

Máire Rua was the daughter of Torlough Rua MacMahon and Mary O'Brien. She was born in 1615 or 1616. Tradition holds that she was born at Clonderlaw Castle, which was the chief seat of Torlough Rua, although an elegy composed for her claims that she was born at Bunratty Castle.

In 1634 Máire Rua married Daniel Neylon of Dysart O'Dea when he was nineteen years of age and Máire a year or so younger. Daniel had inherited extensive lands in Inchiquin, Corcomroe, and Burren. His residence was the castle of Dysart O'Dea to the south of Corofin.It was here that Máire spent the first years of her marriage, it was here that she gave birth to three sons, William [1635] followed by Daniel and Michael before her husbands death in 1639.

In October 1639, seven months after the death of Daniel Neylon, she married Conor O'Brien. He was twenty two years old and she twenty three or twenty four. They went to live in Leamaneh Castle (*Léim an Eich*- The Horse Leap), where she bore Conor O'Brien eight children, three of whom died in childhood, two little girls Mary and Slaney and a little boy by the name of Murrough.The surviving children were named, Donough, Teige, Torlough, Honora, and another girl also named Mary. Leamaneh Castle was a fifteenth century tower house and Máire and Conor spent a number of years renovating and extending it, work was ongoing until its completion in 1648. In 1641 rebellion broke out in Ulster which was soon to spread to the rest of the country, Clare included. In 1642 Máire Rua and Conor were identified as members of a raiding party by a Gregory Hickman whose land was raided and cattle seized.

Conor O'Brien was wounded in a skirmish with Cromwellian troops in 1651 according to an account given by Edmund Ludlow, a Lieutenant General of horse, who was second in command to Henry Ireton. On the death of Henry Ireton in November 1651 he assumed command of the army until October 1652. There is a tradition that when the party returned with Connor O'Brien's body to Leamaneh they were greeted from the ramparts by Máire Rua who told them, "we want no dead men here". But on hearing that he was mortally wounded she took him in and nursed him until his death.

The Legend of her Third Marriage

From an account published by Lady Chatterton (Rambles in the South of Ireland1839) She was a visitor at Dromoland Castle where she heard the story of how the O'Brien lands had been preserved; "There is a romantic traditionary story told of the manner in which the O'Brien property has been preserved amid the revolutions in Irish affairs. Connor O'Brien is said to have been the only gentleman in the County of Clare, who after the Commonwealth Party was triumphant, refused to make terms with Ireton: and Ireton is believed to have caused him to be assassinated, having detached a party of five of his best marksmen, in the disguise of sportsmen, for the purpose. Connor O'Brien's wife, Mary-ni-Mahon, informed her sons Teige and Donough of the murder of their father, and at the same time, advised them to offer no further opposition to the dominion of the English Regicides. The assassin, however, was taken and hanged; and immediately after his execution, the widow of Connor O'Brien ordered her carriage to be prepared. Dressing herself in a superb suit of blue and silver, she travelled with six horses towards Limerick, which was then the headquarters of Ireton, and where he soon after died. It so happened that on the evening of her arrival, there was a large entertainment at the General's quarters. Upon demanding at the door to see Ireton, she was refused admission by the sentinel. A discussion followed, which it would appear was of so noisey a character that it attracted the attention of Ireton, who coming to the door, enquired the cause of the sentinel's violent conduct, and why he refused admittance to lady of noble appearance; asking at the same time the name of his fair visitor. "I was" she replied, "the wife of Connor O'Brien, but I am now his widow". Ireton hesitated to believe her; but the disconsolate widow convinced him that she was free by offering to marry one of his officers. He assented to the proposal, and she was married to an officer named Cooper. By this marriage the O'Brien property was saved from forfeiture".

Little is known about Máire Rua's third husband before his arrival in Clare with the Parliamentarian forces. His rank of Cornet, was the most junior officer in a cavalry regiment and would suggest that he came to Ireland with the Cromwellian army.

In March 1656 he leased the quarter of Bunratty from Earl Barnaby O'Brien the 6th Earl of Thomond. Both Cooper and Máire Rua were opportunists, she from necessity, as the widow of an officer in a defeated army her chance of holding on to her husbands estate were slim. In the years 1654 to 1658 the Catholic landowners of Ulster, Munster and Leinster were transplanted to Connacht and Clare. To accommodate this transplantation, the existing Catholic landowners of Clare and Connacht had to be transplanted or have their estates reduced in size. Commissioners were appointed to supervise these matters. In Clare this process was initiated by the instant forfeiture of the estates of Lord Inchiquin, Sir Daniel O'Brien, and the O'Briens of Dromore. Land that was not immediately forfeited was in jeopardy. On August 18th, 1657 Donough Mac Cormac MacCarthy of Courtbrack in the Barony of Muskerry East, County Cork, agreed to convey to Cooper three hundred and fifty acres of profitable land to be laid out for him in Connacht or Clare for £51.

(see Inchiquin papers box pc 353 N.L.I.)

John Cooper went to London in the summer of 1659 bringing Donough along with him, whilst he was in London Donough changed his name to the English version Denis. He remained in London for a period of two years.

Maire Rua had a son by John Cooper whom they named Henry. Henry was Maire Rua's thirtheenth child. The Restoration of the English Monarchy in May 1660 was to change the positions of the losers and winners in the land confiscations of the early sixteen- fifties. A new regime of claim and counter claim was to begin with some parties trying to regain their Irish lands while others tried to retain what they had won by confiscation. This was a dangerous time for Maire Rua and her marriage to John Cooper which had been an advantage during the Cromwellian period failed to protect her from what was to come. John Cooper continued to prosper in County Clare. In 1661 he was appointed as a valuator to assess properties in that county for the purpose of taxation. In November 1661 both Maire Rua and John Cooper were granted a General Pardon and their names appear in the Roll of Innocents. However in the year 1662 Gregory Hickman's Deposition of 1642 was produced and Maire Rua was accused of the murder of Thomas Bacon. Hickman testified that Conor O'Brien accompanied by his wife Mary Brien, raided his property in January 1642, and that about Whitsuntide of that year Hickman's servant Thomas Bacon was murdered, he did not identify the murderer. Maire Rua's friends interceded on her behalf and appealed to the King for a pardon. On the 9th of August 1662, the King referred her petition to the Duke of Ormond who was then Lord Lieutenant, directing him to issiue a Royal Pardon if he found the facts to be as stated in her petition:

"If upon due inquiry certain allegations made in the complaint exhibited to the King by Mary Cooper (heretofore widow of Connor O'Brien of Lemineagh, in the county of Clare,Esquire, now the wife of John Cooper, Esquire), be found to be true, pardon is to pass under the Great Seal of Ireland for "words said to have been spoken by her in the year 1642, touching one Thomas Baker who was in that year murdered" Upon which words a charge of complicity in that murder has lately been founded.

Maire Rua died in 1686 but her memory lives on in the folklore of County Clare. It is probably the ferocity of that folklore which has kept it alive to the present day.

The Legends Associated with Maire Rua.

All the legends connect her with Leamaneh, all the legends characterize her as being a lustful woman, her legendry cruelty is also associated with her lust.

Maire Rua is said to have kept a wild stallion at Leamenah. In order to win her favour her suitors were expected to ride this stallion, all failed and were killed, with the exception of one hero who is identified as Torlach O'Loughlainn of Burren. He kept his seat on the stallion and turned it round with its front legs over the Cliff's of Moher and returned to Leamaneh. It is said that when Maire Rua saw the stallion return with the rider still mounted she ordered the gates of Leamaneh to be closed against them.The horse died while leaping the gate, thus giving the name, *Léam an Eich,* The Horse's Leap to Maire Rua's castle.

Leameneh Castle 2006
Note the original tower house to the right.

Nethercross

The early Christians of Finglas had a cross carved from granite and adorned with Celtic symbols. It stood seven feet high and was five feet wide. It was originally erected in the grounds of the Abbey beside Watery Lane, North of Mellows road beside the stream. The cross stood here for many centuries until the people of Finglas heard that Cromwell's army had landed at Ringsend in August 1649. They dismantled the cross and buried it in the cemetery in fear that the Cromwellians would desecrate it. Here it remained until 1806 when the Rev, Robert Walsh became curate of the parish. He was interested in antiquities and on hearing the local tradition about the burying of the cross he pursued the matter and discovered an extremely old man who related a story handed down from his grandfather, who as a boy had been present at the burial of the cross in a corner of one of the Glebe fields.

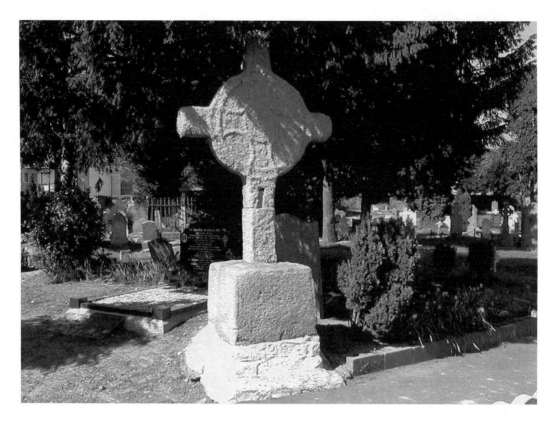

The Nethercross 2007

Rev Walsh unearthed the cross from its resting place of 160 years and had it erected in the south- east corner of the ancient grave-yard where it stands today.

Entrance to the grave-yard where the cross stands is from Barrack Lane which is at the end of Wellmount Road and runs parallel to it, the key can be had from the caretaker Mr Tommy Lynch who lives in the cottage adjoining the grave-yard.

Dudley Costello
Dubhaltach Mac Cosdealbha

The Costello clan were once a great power in County Mayo, the barony of Costello, of which Ballaghadereen is the chief town, bears testimony to this. Dudley Costello played his part in the Catholic uprising of 1641, he was one of the garrison on the island of Inishbofin, who were the last to surrender, and did so under the condition that they were free to leave Ireland and join the Spanish army. After the restoration of King Charles II to the throne of England, Dudley returned to his native country with the rank of colonel, hoping to recover some of his clan's lost lands. This hope was not realised, so in the company of an old soldier by the name of Edmund Nangle and a band of action hardened Mayomen he took to the hills and highways of North-East Connacht, there to wreak havoc and seek revenge.

It was not long before the Government proclaimed him a Tory and offered £20 for him dead or alive. Not content to confine his operations to the west he crossed the hills of Leitrim into Cavan and Fermanagh and even as far north as County Tyrone. In a letter from the officer in charge of Charlmont Fort to the Viceroy, dated June 1666.The officer reports therein how he led a troop of soldiers to Dungannon and thence to Fiontona in pursuit of Dudley Costello and his gang. The outlaws were carousing in a tavern, owned by an old Scotsman in Fiontana; but before the troops could reach the town, country people had warned them of their danger, so they all escaped.

Shane Bearna (Bearnach)
John O' The Gap.

Shane Bearnagh is alleged to have been part of Redmond O' Hanlon's band of Tories The translation of his name from the Gaelic as meaning John of the gapped mouth does not strike me as being correct. I would offer the opinion that it means John of the Gap, the gap in question being a mountain pass in the Slieve Beagh Mountains between Monaghan and Tyrone. See O.S.I. Discovery Series. Map no 28A grid Reference 527 431 - Shane Barnagh's Lough.

"Shane Bearna was one of the many Tories or Rapparee's who infected this unhappy country way back in the forties. Driven back to the mountain fastness by the greed of the Saxon invader, these men were the marrow of the midnight tribunal, that executed, flogged, and mutilated at will. Their creed was socialistic in a sense, but withal by times most charitably disposed. "Take from the rich and give to the poor "was their motto and scarcely if ever was it infringed.

Shane Bearnach, as in the Gaelic means Shane of the gapped mouth Indeed it is said that he never had teeth at all, and that his parents and immediate ancestors were similarly affected. But this want was repaired in part by his possessing remarkably hard gums. So firm had they become that he could bite through a copper or silver coin with as much ease as we could crunch a piece of griddle bread Shane, as I suggested, was a highwayman and was the terror of the old stage-coach passengers to and from Clogher.The stage road at that time came out somewhere near Connolly's corner and as far as I know took Tydarnet and Emyvale on its way. But stage robbery was not Shanes forte .Rather was he a cattle thief and a raider on the horse corrals of the lowlands. The Woodrites, Evates and Blacks, he visited in turn and woe betide the feudal lord who crossed swords with the mountain bandit. The smuggled livestock was on every occasion driven back across the Slieve Beagh hills to Shanes stables, or caves. There the horses were re-shod with shoes that pointed the wrong way in order it is said to avoid pursuit. And the brave steeds from the boddach stalls were dispersed throughout the country and sold when opportunity afforded. Similarly with the cattle. Shane Bearnach's stables are as seen at present but a deep cleft or hole in the ground. They pass back into the lowhills in the side of Minyomer Glen and reappear again on the strand of a little lake that beats against the base. To this lake edge he drove his herds to the water and after to swim them across the slender silver arm to the green knoll and heathy pastures behind. It is now the home of the badger and the wild mountain fox. For the stables bear no trace of the devil- may- care days they once knew. "Of Shane Bearnach's death we have many versions. One has it that he was betrayed by one of his henchmen and shot on the fayth of Straemuckleroigh-Strawmacelroy. Another has it that he was taken in a widow- woman's house and captured through the instrumentability of the widow herself. Be that as it may , his capture was hastened and financed by the ready English gold, and the care-free Rapparee was beheaded on his native hills and his head sent to the authorities in Monaghan Town. His body was flung into Loch Albanaigh from which it was recovered by his relatives and decently buried".[36]

"A more meritorious story is told about the notorious Sean. It is told that he pursued the priest murderer from *Leac-an-tSagairt* where he had shot Father Mc Kenna. Sean followed him to his refuge in Anketell grove near Emyvale and awaited his hour of revenge. The murderer was feeding a cow in the yard and Sean succeeded in shooting him from his little hiding place nearby".[37]

"Highwayman_Shane Barnagh was a highwayman in the slieve Beagh country, the mountainy district between Clogher, Fivemiletown and Co. Monaghan. He had his horses shoes put on backwards so that he could not be tracked. He had a safe hiding place called "Shan Bernaghs Stables "in the mountains, where he kept his stolen horses and cattle. It is somewhere near Knockatallen, across the border in Monaghan and is a cave beside a lough. He used to stay at the house of a widow woman near Ballymacann (Clogher) and in the end she gave him away. The house was surrounded he made a great fight but was killed ".[38]

[36] N.F.C. S 954 : pp 76-78 Máire Nic Cassain An Gort Mór Threemilehouse, Co Monaghan
[37] N.F.C. S 955 Collected from James McCague 68 yrs farmer Feeba Scotstown
[38] N.F.C. 1238 : p320 Collected from Miss Joan Story Corick Clogher Co Tyrone.

The O' Mahony Brothers

"In Upton long ago, there lived three brothers of the Ó Mahony clan who had a reputation for being great robbers. They only robbed the rich and helped the poor.

Two of these brothers were eventually caught and were hanged. The third brother evaded capture for some time. One day while he was travelling along the road, he met a poor widow and her children, who were after being evicted, and had their cattle seized. O Mahony told her not to worry that she would get them all back again. Continuing his journey he met the agent of the landlord whom he promptly robbed. He then retraced his steps and gave the money to the widow. Some time later this man was arrested, tried, and hanged in the town of Bandon.

At that time the law stated that if a hanging was not successful the first and second times, then the person to be hanged should be set free.

O Mahony was put on the scaffold for the first time, but the hang-mans attempt was futile. He was put up again with the same result. He was taken down and an examination was carried out and to their great surprise found a collar of iron around his neck. Written on this collar were the words "(Made by Lane of Ballinacurra). The collar was removed and the man was hanged, he was the last of the O Mahony clan".[39]

Wood-Kerne, Tories and Rapparee's
A brief history

Kerne _(ceithearn),_warrior, foot-soldier, lightly armoured freelance native mercenaries who wandered the country in search of employment from the latter part of the twelfth century. When not engaged in warfare they often intimidated the people to provide them with food and shelter. When at war they often fought without armour using swords and small spears as weapons. They were celebrated for their agility. Hugh O' Neill used them in the second half of the 16th century, where they were trained in the use of firearms.The demise of the O' Conors of Offaly and the O'Moores of Leix and the consequent plantation of the clan lands and the renaming of the territories as Queens County and Kings County in honour of Queen Mary and her Spanish husband, King Phillip, left the remnants of the broken clans living in the bogs and woods and was to coin a new name in Irish history that of "Wood-Kerne". Thomas Blenerhasset, one of the English undertakers in County Fermanagh, published a pamphlet in the year 1610 in which he equates the wood-kerne with the wolf and declares them to be the greatest danger to the English settlers in Ulster. He suggested that the planters

---

[39] N.F.C. S 347 June 1937 Collected from Helen Lernihan Langtrail Crookstown Co Cork

should engage in periodic man-hunts in order to pursue these human wolves to their lairs.

Tá gean agam féin ar Dhia is ar Mhuire
'S ar na ceithre fearaibh déag den cheithearn choille
I have love for God and for Mary
And also for the fourteen men of the wood-kerne.[40]

The land confiscations of the, Elizabethan and Cromwellian periods were to bring a new word into the realm of Irish folklore, that of the Tory, from the Irish word *Tóraidhe,* Meaning the pursued, or the attacked.

Sir William Stewart of Newtownstewart, County Tyrone, in a letter to Ormond The Viceroy, on March 17 1683 writes; "There was never such a winter for country sports as the last and I have enjoyed them in much perfection. I had very good hawks and hounds but we have not had more success in any sport than Tory hunting. The gentlemen of the country have been so hearty in that chase that of the thirteen in the county where I live in November, the last was killed two days before I left home".[41]

During the Jacobite war these Tories became known as Rapparee's, from the Irish word *rapaire-* a short pike, or sword which was their favourite weapon. These rapparees were generally land owning Catholics, who had been dispossessed of their land and went out on their keeping in pursuit of justice, or revenge. By the end of the eighteenth century they had degenerated into common thieves, robbers, and highwaymen. The authorities in Dublin Castle did not distinguish between, Wood –Kerne, Tory, Rapparee, or Highwayman they were all enemies of the establishment and were to be dealt with by sword, gun, and rope. "Story, in his *Continuation of the History of the Wars in Ireland* (published in 1693) has frequent mention of the Irish Rapparees.At page fifty" he says.

"These men knew the country, nay, all the secret corners, woods, and bogs; keeping a constant correspondance with one another, and also with the army, who furnished them with all necessaries especially ammunition. When they had any project on foot, their method was not to appear in a body, for then they would have been discovered; and not only so, but carriages and several other things had been wanting which every one knows that is acquainted with this trade; their way was, therefore, to make a private appointment to meet at such a pass or wood, precisely at such a time o' th' night or day as it stood with their conveniency; and though you could not see a man over night, yet exactly at their hour you might find three or four hundred, more or less, as they had occasion, all well armed, and ready for what design they had formerly projected; but if they happened

---

[40] From verse X of the Lament for Patrick Fleming
[41] Calendar of Ormonde Manuscripts.

to be discovered or overpowered, they presently dispersed, having beforehand appointed another place of rendezvous, ten or twelve miles (it may be) from the place they were at; by which means our men could never fix any close engagement upon them during the winter; so that if they could have held out another year, the Rapparees would have continued still very prejudicial to our army, as well by killing our men privately, as stealing our horses and intercepting our provisions. But after all, least the next age may not be of the same humour with this, and the name of a Rapparee may possibly be thought a finer thing than it really is, I do assure you that in my stile they never can be reputed other than Tories, Robbers, Thieves, and Bog-trotters."[42]

The O' Hanlon Family.

Until the plantation of Ulster in 1609, the O' Hanlon clan ruled huge tracts of land in present- day Armagh and north County Louth. The surname can be found, in the Annals of the Four Masters where it is recorded that, *Flaithbeartach O'hAnluain Lord of Uí Niallan, was murdered by the clan O' Bruascal in the year 938 A.D.* Eochy Óg O'Hanlon was involved with Sir Cahir O'Doherty in the rebellion of 1608.

1641, October
"The garrison of Liscallaghan was captured by the men of Keirigeir under the command of Conn O' Neill son of Art, son of Donal, son of Séan na Mallacht, and the English wardens who occupied it were taken".

23 (Saturday)
"The strongly fortified garrison of Tandragee in Orior was captured by Pádraig Óg O' Hanlon who was himself killed the same day.Newry and its great castle were captured by Conn Magennis son of Lord Iveagh. The town of Dundalk was captured by Lieutenant-General Brian O' Neil of the Fews, son of Hugh Buí, son of Tarlach, son of Enrí na Garthan, aided by the men of the Fews". [43]
Éamon O'Hanlon grandson of Eochy O'Hanlon commanded a company in Turlough O' Neill's regiment, as did Captain Feardorcha O'Hanlon. Both these men could be found in Clonmel in 1650 fighting on the side of the royalists against Cromwell. Éamon rose to the rank of colonel and in this capacity fought at the Battle of the Boyne.

---

[42] Story Rev Continuation of the wars in Ireland 1693
[43] Friar O'Meallain   Journal.

Redmond O' Hanlon.
The Man

The absence of documentary evidence makes it difficult to trace Redmond's date of birth. It was given as 1640 by the author of an anonymous Pamphlet which was published in 1682 entitled; "The Life and Death of the Incomparable and Indefatigable Tory Redmon O' Hanlyn, commonly called Count Hanlyn".

In an article published in the Dublin Penny Journal, 1932, by Henry M.J.O'Hanlon, It is given as 1623, while Terence O'Hanlon suggests 1632 in The Highwayman in Irish History. Local tradition holds that he was born in the townland of Aghantaraghan, south of Poyntzpass. Iveagh House Poyntzpass, in the county of Armagh, now occupies the actual site of his birthplace. It is said that Redmond was educated in England, where he became proficient in English and French. Sometime after his return to Ireland he was involved in an incident in which a young gentleman lost his life. In fear of the consequences he fled to France where he remained for a long time. Because of his refusal to come to trial he was declared an outlaw. Tradition holds that while in France he joined the French army, where his valour and prowess on the battlefield earned him the title of Count. Redmond O' Hanlon returned to Ireland during the reign of Charles II probably in hope that the O' Hanlon lands would be restored.If he did, his hopes were in vain. Count Redmond O' Hanlon is the perfect stereotype of the Outlaw Tory/ Rapparee.Dispossessed of his land and place in society, he feels honour bound to seek justice or revenge. An educated, intelligent, brave warrior hardened in battle he took to the hills and highways of his native Ulster. Redmond commenced his operations in the vicinity of Slieve Gullion around Forkhill, Jonesborough, Mullaghbawn, Slieve Gullion is in the region of south Armagh not far from the village of Jonesborough, there are three variations of the name I include all three. Sliabh Guilfhinn, Sliabh goill Fionn-The Mountain of the tears of Fionn [44] Sliabh gCuilinn - Holly Mountain Sliabh Cuilin - The Mountain of the Steep Slope.

The Hunt of Slieve Cuilinn

"Finn was one time out on the green of Almhuin, and he saw what had the appearance of a grey fawn running across the plain. He,called and whistled to his hounds then, but neither hound nor man heard him, but only Bran and Sceolon. He set them after the fawn,and near as they kept to her, he himself kept nearer to them, till at last they reached to Slieve Cuilinn in the province of Ulster.But they were no sooner at the hill than

---

[44] Gregory Lady Lady Gregory's complete Irish Mythology (Bounty Books p 208)

the fawn vanished from them, and they did not know where was she gone, and Finn went looking for her eastward, and the two hounds went towards the west.It was not long till Finn came to a lake, and there was sitting on the brink of it a young girl, the most beautiful he had ever seen, having hair the colour of gold, and skin as white as lime and eyes like the stars in time of frost; but she seemed to be some way sorrowful and downhearted. Finn asked her did she see his hounds pass that way. "I did not see them," she said," "and it is little I am thinking of your hounds or your hunting, but of the cause of my own trouble." "What is it ails you, woman of the white hands?" said Finn;" and is there any help I can give you?" he said." It is what I am fretting after," said she, "a ring of red gold I lost off my finger in the lake. And I put you under bonds, Finn of the Fianna," she said, "to bring it back to me out of the Lake".With that Finn stripped off his clothes and went into the lake at the bidding of the woman, and he went three time around the whole lake and did not leave any part of it without searching, till he brought back the ring. He handed it up to her then out of the water, and no sooner had he done that than she gave a leap into the water and vanished.And when Finn came up on the bank of The lake, he could not so much as reach to where his clothes were; For on the moment he, the head and leader of the Fianna of Ireland, was but a grey old man, weak and withered. Bran and Sceolan came up to him then, but they did not know him and they went on round the lake, searching after their master." That, now is the way Finn came by his grey hair, through thejealousy of Miluchradh of the Sidhe, because he had not given his love to her, but to her sister Aine." [45]

Sliocht as An Claibheamh Solais 18-09-1909.

"Bá gnách le Turner agus a cuid yeo a bheich ag dul thart ag loic is a dóghad na tire. Bhí de do tiobod ar na sagartaibh an tAifreann a leighead agus ata le rádh mar gheall ar an diabhlaidheacht gur marbhuig se sagart óg An Sagart Mac Aidghaille I gcarraig Clochan agus é ag briseadh Arán-an-Bheata. Tá Cloch-na-hAltórach ins an áit fós". [46]

Translation (A.Nugent)

It was usual for Turner and his yeomen to be going by, despoiling and burning the country. It was forbidden for the priests to read the mass and because of this devilment he murdered a young priest father Mac Aidghaille as he was breaking the Bread-of Life at the mass rock. The Rock-of-the-Altar is there yet.

---

[45] Lady Gregory's Complete Irish Mythology pp 208-210
[46] *An Claibheamh Solais 1919 N.L.I.* I.R 8916205 C.9

The stone on top of bleak Slieve Gullion and overlooking Cam Lough lake is, I believe, Cloch-na-hAltorach. The Altar Stone mentioned in An Claibheamh Solais. It is an impressive granite block two meters in length 66cm across and 70cm high and overlooks a natural amphitheatre on this historic mountainside. This was once reputed to be the hunting place of Fion Mac Cumhal, and also the lurking ground of Redmond O'Hanlon the displaced chieftain of the Barony of Orior, who became a renowned Tory. On the eastern slopes of Slieve Gullion overlooking the plain of Meigh, can be found Killevy Churches, Graveyard and Holy Well. This is the site of one of Ireland's early convents, founded in the sixth century by St Moninna. According to the annals, she died in 517A.D. Upon this site at present are two ruined churches, and a graveyard which is still in use, both overlooked by a holy well. St Blines Well, as it is known locally, is purported to have healing powers for ailments of the eye. To reach the well follow the path which runs along the exterior of the north wall of the graveyard and up the mountain, bearing in mind that this track can become mud after rain. An area of stone within the graveyard is said to be the foundation of a round tower which blew down in 1768.

The Legends surrounding him.

There are many legends concerning the life and career of Redmond O' Hanlon. The first is noted below and the rest will follow in alphabetical order.

Legend A
Cross on Breast

It is said that Redmond was born with a birth mark in the shape of Roman T on his breast. This was interpreted to be a headless cross and signified that he would become a martyr for the church.

Legend B
Shirt of Invulnerability.

"it is said that Réamon had a shirt made from flax which was plucked and scotched and spun and woven between sunrise and sunset and that, as a result it could not be penetrated by any other bullet except one fired from his own gun". [47]

---

[47] O'hÓgáin Dáithí Dr <u>Myth, Legend & Romance.</u>(Prentice Hall Press New York)

Legend C
Lizard and Boar

The crest of the O' Hanlon family is a shield bearing the representation of a wild boar, surmounted by a mailed hand grasping a lizard, Tradition holds that its origin lies in the following story.

"O' Hanlon, on one occasion during the period of his outlawry, lay down in the woods to rest and being very weary, fell asleep. He was awakened by a lizard crawling across his face. And not a moment too soon; for lo! As he sat up he saw a wild boar coming straight to attack him. Grasping his dagger, he faced the beast, which quickly turned tail and plunged into the depths of the forest.

Presently a fresh danger appeared in the shape of a company of troops, combing the woods in search of the highwayman, who, however, got clear away before they came up. In gratitude to the boar and lizard, whose timely arrival had thus saved him from falling into the hands of the military, Redmond honoured them with a place on his shield and crest". [48]

Legend D
Interest in the Supernatural

There is a traditional belief that Redmond O' Hanlon inherited a belief in the supernatural from his mother. It is told that he sought out fortune-tellers from an early age. The following prediction from a fortune-teller is credited with encouraging him to begin his career as a Tory.

"His enterprise would be great, his success unrivaled, his hazards numerous, his escapes miraculous, his army small, his command great, his territory small, his fortune unlimited, he would live without a house, he would die in bed, he would not be reached by the hand of justice, he would not be the victim of the law, he would lie in state, he would be buried in two different places". It is said that Redmond believed that this prediction was in his favour, in particular his protection from the gallows, in consequence he set out on his life of crime.

Legend E
Robber Overcome

One day while Redmond O' Hanlon was travelling the road between Newry and Armagh with a small band of fellow Tories, they came upon a peddler who was in a state of shock. When Redmond asked him what had befallen him, the peddler replied "that damned rogue of a Redmond O' Hanlon has

---

[48] O'Hanlon Terence <u>The Highwayman in Irish History</u> (M.H.Gill and son 1932

robbed me of more than five pounds in money along with my box of goods and because I did not comply willingly to be robbed by him, he kicked and abused me in no uncertain fashion". Redmond called the peddler a liar and a rascal and told him that it was not Redmond O' Hanlon who had robbed him but an impostor .The peddler described the robber and the route he had taken, whereupon Redmond and his men went in pursuit of him.

Eventually they overtook him on the road and brought him back to the scene of the crime, where the box and money were returned to the peddler. Redmond decided to teach the rogue a lesson for robbing in his name, without his permission. He bound the peddler under oath to prosecute him at the next assizes. He then wrote a warrant and sent the prisoner under guard to the gaol in Armagh. The warrant is reputed to have read as below. "By Redmond O' Hanlon in loco one of his Majesty's Justice's of the Peace for County Armagh, but Chief ranger of the mountains. "I herewith send you the body of ---- who was this day brought before me and examined, for robbing Mr ---- on the Kings high road, requiring of you to hold him in safe custody till the next General Assizes to be held for the said county; and for your so doing this shall be your sufficient warrant. Given under my hand this 1st day of March,1675

"Redmond O' Hanlon,

"To ---- Gaoler of Armagh". [49]

Legend F
Colleague Encountered

On hearing of the exploits of the renowned Northern Tory, Captain Power decided to take a trip North with the purpose of meeting the famous Ulster Tory. He left Charleville and set out for Slieve Gullion where O' Hanlon was reputed to have his hide-out. It is probable that it was during the course of this journey that the following story originated. Richard Power set out for the Gap of the North. Arriving in O'Hanlon country at nightfall, he sought lodgings at a way-side inn with the intention of seeking out O' Hanlon the next day. While he was at rest in the sitting-room of the inn, he noticed a distinguished looking gentleman counting his money in a corner of the room. He waited until the opportunity afforded itself, then he engaged the gentleman in friendly conversion, by which means he found out the hour of his departure the following day and the road on which he would be travelling.

The next morning Power was up at the crack of dawn and was the first person to leave the inn. Later that morning the distinguished looking gentleman left the inn and proceeded around a bend in the road, suddenly

---

[49] Kennedy Patrick. Modern Irish Anecdotes

a command rang out! "Your money or your life!" "If you are to have either," came the reply "you will have to fight for it." Both men discharged their pistols, both men missed. Then they fell upon each other with short swords, both were skilled swordsmen and could not gain advantage over each other, for many hours the duel ensued, then by mutual consent they sat down on the ditch "Tell me , my good man, who are you and what are you that you can hold me in combat for so long," said Redmond O' Hanlon. "Captain Richard Power at your service, a noted Tory from County Cork and I have come here in search of Count Redmond O' Hanlon about whom I have heard so much". "Then I must bid you welcome, for my name is Redmond O' Hanlon and in all my experience on the highways of this part of the country you have been the first to put my endurance to the test".

Power accompanied O' Hanlon to his hideout in the mountains of South Armagh and there he stayed for more than a year. A great bond of friendship developed between the two Tories and when the time came to part company, they pledged to each other that if one was in need of assistance the other would hurry to his aid.

Legend G
Colleague Rescued

After a number of years, news reached O' Hanlon in the North, that Power had been captured and imprisoned in Clonmel Gaol, and was to face trial for his crimes. O' Hanlon left for the south immediately, using the best horses at his disposal. He reached Clonmel while preparations were in hand for Powers execution at Kilnagowan the place where he had committed the crime for which he was to pay.

 There was no time to be lost. In disguise and with the aid of liberal amounts of whiskey, amongst the guards, Redmond O' Hanlon rescued his friend from the "Grim Reaper". As a result of Captain Richard Powers amazing escape from the gallows at Kilnagowan, the authorities redoubled their efforts to re-capture him. A special troop of cavalry was sent out from the City of Cork, with orders to to pursue him through hill and valley, day and night, county by county; at the same time a huge reward was offered for information leading to his capture.

Legend H
Victim Recompensed
One day while in company with some of his band near Armagh, they met with Cornet Montgomery's steward. He having collected about £500 in rents from his master's tenants, was bringing it home to his own house, near Killevan, in county Monaghan. Redmond remained at a distance while his associates robbed the steward. When the proceeds of the robbery was divided among them, Redmond made a present of his share to the Cornet's

young son, which he sent by the steward. This action impressed the cornet to such an extent, that he promised to use his influence to obtain a pardon from the King. It is said that as a result of the Cornet interceding on his behalf, Redmond was offered a protection from prosecution for three years, provided he abstained from consorting with Tories, obeyed the law, and kept the peace. This he did for a period of one year, after which, he reverted to his outlaw ways.[50]

Legend I

Soldiers Captured

One day Redmond appeared at Armagh in the garb of a country gentleman. He installed himself at the best inn, and requested, that the commanding officer there provide him with a military escort, to protect him on his journey across the Fews. He explained that as he was carrying a large some of money on his person, he was afraid of being waylaid and robbed by Redmond O' Hanlon and his outlaw band. The military commander accepted that this was a reasonable request, and agreed to comply with it, on condition that the gentleman gave the soldiers involved a gratuity.

This he agreed to do, and did so with generosity bordering on the extreme. He and his escort travelled for a distance of about seven miles, when he halted them and told them that he considered himself out of danger, and that they could return to barracks. He then presented each one of the escort with a coin, and asked them to fire a volley to celebrate his safe passage. He then requested them to repeat the volley which they did, until they ran out of ammunition, upon which he gave a whistle which brought his band from a nearby wood. They stripped the soldiers of their arms, money accoutrements, and clothes. In this sorry condition they were forced to return to Armagh.

Legend J

Outwitted by Clever Boy

To date I have come upon five versions of this legend, I include all five and offer them in numerical order from J in the main manuscript to J1-4, in an appendix, starting with J which is the version published by J. Cosgrave in 1777 and is therefore the oldest and nearest in time to the alleged event.

"A merchant in Dundalk had a draught on a merchant in Newry for a large sum, but was so much afraid of Redmond O' Hanlon, that he was afraid either to send for the money, or to go for it himself; while he was thus consulting with his wife how to get the money safely home, his apprentice, a lad about sixteen years of age overheard their discourse, and as soon as he

---

[50] Marshall John J. Irish Tories Rapparees and Robbers (Dungannon 1927)

got an opportunity, desired his master to tell him why he was so much afraid of sending to Newry? The master having answered his request, the boy asked him whether he would venture to trust him with so much money? The master said he did not doubt his honesty, but on that occasion he could not tell what to think of the matter. However by many entreaties, the boy prevailed on the master to let him go for the money, promising to forfeit his ears if he lost one halfpenny of it. The boy having obtained privilege to go for the money, immediately set about preparing himself for the journey, and by his masters assistance, being provided with about forty shillings in halfpence, he divided them into two parcels, and tied them close up in a little wallet, at each end, and then went to the field and brought home an old vicious stone mad horse, (much of the same humour with Sir Teague O'Reagan's war horse, on which he rode out to meet Duke Scomberg after the surrender of Charlemont) that when any other came up to meet him on the road, he always strove to bite or kick him, by which means he commonly kept the road to himself. With proper accoutrements the boy mounted and had the fortune to meet Redmond on the road as he was going, who as it was usual with him, demanded where he was going. The boy told him to Newry. "Pray what business have you there?" Says Redmond. "Why", says the boy, "to receive above £100 for my master."

"And when do you think you will be back?" Says Redmond. "Why", says the boy, I believe about this time tomorrow. Well, my good boy, says Redmond, you had better take care not to tell everybody what your business is, for fear you should be robbed.

"Oh" says the boy, "I'm sure such a gentleman as you would not rob me, I do not intend to tell any body else." Upon this Redmond made him a present of a ducat to drink his health, or to hire another horse, if the one he had under him should tire; and so they parted good friends for that time.

Redmond was then under some necessities for a little money; and as none of his companions were present at the dialogue, he was resolved not to let them know anything of the matter, that he might have all the booty to himself; and to make himself the more sure of the prey, he ordered his comrades to a different post the next morning, and waited himself alone on the road leading from Newry till the boy returned.

When the boy came in sight, Redmond rode up and saluted him, and after some discourse, began to ask him necessary question about the money.- The boy seemed to have no mistrust of his design, confessed to have had received it, upon which the other presently desired him to let him see it. The boy seemingly under a surprise, made several excuses, but they all availed him nothing; for after a short parley, the other began to demand with some authority, and would have taken hold of him had he not been something afraid of receiving a kick from the mad horse. Among other excuses, the boy alleged that his master would think that he had made away with the money himself, and deem him a rogue; but at length

Redmond threatening to shoot him if he refused him any longer the boy took his wallet and cast it over a slough by the road side, and told Redmond that if he must have it, he should follow it. Upon this Redmond alighted from his horse, and having tied him to a tree, with some difficulty he got over the slough and through the hedge, to the place where the wallet lay. While he was upon expedition, the boy exchanged horses, much for the better, and rode home with speed, having the money he received at Newry, safely quilted up in his waistcoat, and though Redmond called after him to stay, with all the eagerness in the world, yet he took no farther notice of him, but left him to make the best hand he could of an old garron and a bag of halfpence". [51]

Legend K
Bloodhound Slain

"Johnston seldom let him rest after his chief comrades were cut off, but hunted him over hills and dales; and more particularly once, having noticed, that he was at Narrow-water, took some men and arms with him, and pursued him hot foot all the way to Carlingford, where, for fear he might get hid, and so convey himself away by sea in the night, his passages were all intercepted, which Redmond observing, he made up to an ale-house by the riverside, at which time it happened there was no boat near hand, nor bridge within a mile and a half of the place. By some means or other old Johnston got notice of it, and hastened to the place, thinking it impossible for Redmond to escape over so broad a river while the tide was in, for he had no other way left.

When old Johnston and his men came near, they observed that Redmond had stripped off his clothes and tied them on his back, with which he took to the river, and swam mostly under water, for above two hundred yards. This prevented him from receiving the shot of his pursuers till out of danger; and what was so remarkable as this, when Mr Johnston set his dog after him to seize him, the dog snapt at the coat and at the same time Redmond turned about and took hold of him by the throat, and dragged him along with him under the water till he drowned him quite, (for Redmond was a fine swimmer), and in a little time gained the bank on the other side of the river; then dressing himself he fled directly to the island of Magee, near Belfast, where he lurked privately for a year or more, till he thought the country had forgotten him".

---

[51] Cosgrave J The Lives and actions of the Most Notorious Irish Highwaymen 1776

Legend L

Boatman Engaged

Redmond was driven by Lloyd and his men down to the shore of Carlingford Lough, "where by his wits he detected the industry of a Little Army; for perceiving a small Boat near to the shore; he rode fair and softly toward it, and abandoning his Horse and Arms; he call'd to the Boatman, and told him that he was a sickly man, and advised by his Physitian, to go two or three Leagues into the Sea, and if he would Row hin out of the harbour, to try if he could be Sea Sick for an Hour or two, he would give him ten shillings for his pains; the poor boatman was overjoy'd at the proffer, and quickly computing what an advantage it was to gain that by an Hours work, which a weeks toyl in fishing would hardly have advanced, he admitted the Count into his Boat, and rowed out from the shore, which they had not long forsaken, before the Count could perceive a multitude of men coming down from the Mountains, whom he well knew to be his Persecutors; and fearing that another Boat might be procured to follow his he spoke to the skipper to row with all haste to the other side of the Headland, which the poor man being unwilling to do (lest the wind might drive him into the main sea), the Count took out his Pocket Pistol, and with a thundering Oath assured him, that if he did not presently obey him, he should never return to land; the poor man was forced to comply, and the Count vouchsafing to put his hand to an oar, in a short time they were got quite out of sight, and then rowing to and fro under cover of the High Land all the day, they came at night into a little Creek, and the Count having Nobly paid for his passage, travelled through byways, and got safe to the house of one of his Harborers".[52]

Legend M

Steals 18 Horses

"The troops stationed in a temporary barrack near the Monaghan border of South Armagh came so close upon his trail one evening that he was forced to hide in a clump of furze to escape capture. While he lay concealed, two soldiers, the hottest of his pursuers, leapt into the furze and, prodding the undergrowth with their fixed bayonets, missed their quarry only by inches. For this chase, Redmond took swift revenge. Gathering a strong band of his trusty followers, he swooped down upon the outpost at dead of night, gagged and bound the sentry, and bore away eighteen horses from the military stables. Proceeding with their booty to Ballybay fair, the highwaymen, shortly after daybreak, were overtaken by a squad of mounted soldiers and called upon to halt. Redmond's reply was to order his men to form a half- moon and prepare for battle. After much manoeuvring for a

---

[52] Moody T.W. A Ph .D Paper 1936 on Redmond O'Hanlon

favourable position on the part of the military, and when a fight to a finish seemed certain, the officer in charge of the troops found means to convey to the raiders his willingness to call off hostilities, provided the stolen horses were restored. Redmond refused to agree unless ransom at the rate of a guinea a head were paid him for the eighteen horses.

And he got his terms in the end, together with an undertaking that he and his party should be allowed to retire a thousand yards without being molested.[53]

Legend N

Gift to Poor Man.

"'Tis said that having once overtaken a poor man who had hardly anything else left but one cow which he was driving to a fair to be sold, in order to raise the rent for his landlord, he asked him several questions, until he found certainly he was in want, and then lent him five pounds, which he was to pay him at an inn a few weeks after. The poor man proving perfectly honest, went with the money according to compact, which pleased Redmond so well, that he bestowed it on him, and five pounds more forever".[54]

Legend O

His talent for Disguise

It is said that Redmond was a natural born mimic and well practised in the art of disguise as the following narrative will show. The Duke of Ormond once ordered a small party of foot and horse to pursue him, they had information about his whereabouts and proceeded with all speed to apprehend him. To avoid capture Redmond dressed himself in the garb of an officer, and proceeded along the high road until he came upon the residence of a gentleman.

He told this gentleman that he was an officer, in charge of a party who were in pursuit of the notorious Redmond O' Hanlon. He explained that he was feeling a little fatigued, and asked if he might rest until his men caught up with him. The residents of the house willingly complied with his request, whereupon he lay down to rest requesting that they call him when his detachment of soldiers went past.

The soldiers had only gone one hundred yards past the house when Redmond rode out in pretence of meeting them, when he reached the road he galloped off in the opposite direction to his pursuers. [55]

---

[53] O'Hanlon Terence The Highwayman in Irish History (M.H.Gill and son Dublin

[54] Cosgrave J The Lives and Actions of the Most Notorious Irish Highwaymen 1776

[55] Cosgrave J The lives etc

Legend P

Horse Shod Backwards

"Redmond O Hanlon was a famous Ulster rapparee who led a band of about fifty men. Who exacted toll's and what was called a black rent from English planters. About a mile and a half from Ballyconnell is a spa of reddish water and is known to all the local people as Redmonds well. The Redmond mentioned was the famous Redmond O Hanlon the wild Rapparee. There is also beside the well the remains of Redmonds stables. These stables were mainly large pits cut out of the heathery mountains. Here he could stable his horses without any danger of being seen. He had his horse shod backwards, thus his trail was thrown in the wrong direction. It was from these stables that O Hanlon set out on many of his rides to the west of Ireland. One of Redmonds favourite pastimes was to hold up a landlord who had just lifted the rents from the peasants and to take his money and give it back to the poor."[56]

Legend Q

Escape from Four Mile House

Once Redmond was taken prisoner at four mile house, between Dundalk and Newry, by a party consisting of twelve soldiers and an officer. He submitted to their commands, and seemed ready and willing to go where they ordered. As a gesture of his thanks for their civil treatment of their prisoner, he treated them to the hospitality of the inn, and furnished them with copious quantities of whiskey, making sure to drink very little himself. When the soldiers were stupefied with the whiskey, he, with the aid of some of his band tied them up and made off with their arms and ammunition.

Legend R

Bog of Allen

After the rescue of Richard Power, Redmond and some of his band remained in the Bog of Allen for a period. They committed so many robberies during this period that the government issued a new proclamation and offered a reward of £250 for his capture. As a result of the unrelenting pursuit this proclamation brought about, he was captured, whilst in bed, at Clonbullock. However, his fellow tories rescued him as he was being taken to Nass gaol by his captors. This incident prompted a speedy return to the old haunts around Sliabh Gullion.

---

[56] N.F.C. S 968 Mrs J Gallagher Slievebrickin Bally connall Co Cavan.

Legend S

Father Edmund O'Murphy

In 1678 Father Edmund O' Murphy Parish Priest of Kileavy, denounced Redmond O'Hanlon and his band of tories from the pulpit, in answer, Redmond declared that anyone attending O'Murphy's church would be penalised by the loss of a cow for the first offence, of two cows for the second offence, if a third offence was committed the offender would pay with his life. As a consequence, one of O' Murphy's parisioners John McFulloney lost two cows and another Cully MacKavell was taken and killed. O'Murphy percieving the danger he was in hired a curate to run the parish and avoided it himself. Fr O'Murphy had a relation who used to be a member of Redmonds band. His name was Cormack Raver O' Murphy and he had been proclaimed along with Redmond in 1674, see Ormond M.S.S. He had set up his own band of tories and had fallen foul of O' Hanlon, for plundering three Scots planters who had paid black rent to Redmond, He was treated roughly by Redmond and his band, and had to pay compensation to the O'Hanlon, as a result a bitter enmity was born. Fr Edmund and Cormack hatched a plot in which Redmond was to be lured into an ambush, they took into their confidence another tory named Brien O' Neale, who passed the informationon to Redmond, who promptly ordered that Cormack be killed. This deed was carried out by O' Neale. William and Hugh O' Murphy made an attempt to avenge the death of their brother, but O' Neale became suspicious and made his escape. Fr Edmund O' Murphy continued to plot the downfall of Redmond, but the next time we come upon him, he is involved in the Popish Plot.[57]

Dunton Letters I – VII

"These letters were written by Dunton, a traveller who visited Ireland in the middle of the 17th century (1695). The copies in this volume were made at Mr Delargy's request, by Brian Gallagher who was studying at Oxford".

"After we had satisfied our eyes with staring about we steered our course towards the Bogg of Allen which tho it be the greatest in Ireland, yet never was so famous as in the last rebellion, when the Rapparees had their rendevous when they designed any mischief on the country, to the number of five or six hundred, and where they easily hid themselves when pursued; for as I am informed, this bogg is neare fifty miles long, with many woods in it, and some islands of verie good and profitable land, as the Island of Allen which they say is worth eight hundred pounds per annum.

---

[57] Moody T.W Paper 1936

140

Since I have named the Rapparees, I think it will not be improper to tell you something of them because it relates a little to the ancient warfare of the Irish.

In this warr I think they were first called Rapparees. They were some loose and undisciplined people, who were not subject to command, but like freebooters made everything that belonged to the English a prey if they could come att it. Their arms like those of the old Irish Kerne were an half pike and a skeane. They made their excursions generally in the night or by surprise, lying in ambuscade for their prey, which they had a true and constant intelligence of from the other Irish who seemed laborious people all day but at night were as great rogues as the best of them. At length they got fire arms and ammunitions, but never any courage, so that a party of the English militia of fourty or fifty men would willingly engage two hundred of them, but they could never be prevailed with to stand. You may judge by this story what martial men these untrained Rapparees are.

For a lusty fellow in the late King's reign was taken into the regiment of guards for a musketeer, and being at exercise in the field where they discharged their pieces to accustom them to firing, one mans gun did not go off at the first fire. However he charged a second time with the rest of his rank. It also mist the second time, and he put in his third bandaleer of powder, and then it went off with such a recoyle as stunned the fellow. So then he let the gun fall out of his hand.

The sergeant ran and took it up, but the soldier called out to him saying, Sherjant joy take care of will you doe, for by my shoul I put three the full of the bandleer in, and there is but wan got gon out yet.

The antient division of the Irish soldiery was into the Kernes, which were such as these Rapparees, and their Gallowglasses. These were composed of their better sort of man, who fought on horseback with poleaxes.

They were called Gallowglasses from the words, gall, white, or neate and oglagh, young men. But those who composed their armys in the late troubles were exercised and trained after the common way of other soldiers. From hence we retired to Ballimeenie after we had left Father James at home. [58]

Sloane 3323, ff. 288, 289.

Paper; XV111th cent.
A sheet of two leaves in a collection of miscellaneous papers belong to Sir Hans Sloane. Early 18th cent.
"THE RAPPAREES CHARM OR SAFETY" (so endorsed):
a prayer in Latin with Irish and English explanation, carried by Patrick, son of Edmond, son of Patrick, Murphy, a rapparee, as a charm for his protection.

---

[58] N.F.C. 448 : pp 72-73 Dunton Letters

For a similar charm carried by an Irish soldier in 1690 cf.p.32 above. The Latin charm is written continuously without punctuation and in the orthography reproduced in the transcript.

"Jesus Maria.

"Deus qui est in Celo Deducat me Pa: Murphy per viam rectam ut Revertar hue sal(v)us et sanus et angelus Domini comitetur me Deus unus et trinitus rex angelorum me Deus gubernatur Creatorarium me gubernat Deus panis angelorum me custodiat Deus Doctor Apostolorum me Docat Deus inisipirator profetarum me Inspirat Deus turis Martirum me confirmet quid plura Dieam spiritus a patre et filio procedens me repleat me custodiat me Defendat ab omni malo ab omni peccato ab omni polutione ab omnibus tentationibus tempestatibus Diabolicis Insidiis malorum omnium malorumque mulierum et Invenia(m) Necessaria ut sanus pervenire possim ad loca Desiderata sine Ullo periculo corporis et anime perveniet Spiritus patris Meum in vitam Eternam. Amen.

"Leo papa do scriobh an ortha sa thuas cum Caralus mhóir Rí Franc ^ asé Hironimus naomhta do righne í ^ is luireach dhaingen 'n aigedh na droich dhaoine ^ na droich spiorad í ^gibe iomcorus í ní bfhuighe [d]roich bhas no bhatadh farge ní haoglach do namhuid ní haoglach gan buaidh geatha ^ geomlun do bheith aige, ní bás do mnaoi torraigh iomcorus í beuraidh lenabh er basdeadh ^ ní biadh galer mor ar biadh, buaidh ttaighara [?tagra] ^ urlabhr[a] ar an tí ag mbia, deo graithiseas.
Ag sin duit ^ mo 1000 benacht a Padruig oig mic Emoinn mic Padruig ^ ma caillin tu an orthasa le hamaoil no le droich airre ní rachaidh an triubhas fan toin chena, aged uaimse go ttrasta, loir o do charuid gibe hé.

"Pope Leo wrote this Devout Prayer for Charles the great of France and it was composed By holy St. Jerome it is A strong Shield against Evil people and against Evil Spirits and whoever carryes it about him is secure from an untimely Death or Drowning in the Sea and will still be victorious in all conflicts or Battles, women in Labour who have it about them are free from Death or Danger of it their children not to Dye until Baptized and secure from Convulsions and in all Disputes and Debates by argument the advantage to be on his side in whose Custody this prayer is and this with a thousand Blessings doe I presume to present yow with young Patrick the son of Edmund the son of Patrick and if you lose this prayer by neglect you will never be fortunate afterwards and this is sufficient from your unknown friend whoever he be etc"[59]

---

[59] Sloane 3323 pp 288-289 Catalogue of Irish Manuscripts

Legend T
A Story of Redmond O' Hanlon.

"Redmond O' Hanlon lived in a cave in the Newry mountains and had14 or15 soldiers under him.He would not submit to the English. He used to go around and lift tithes and taxes from the people and anybody who did'nt give something suffered the consequences. There was an auld man called P Mac Bacach and he was always giving away on Redmond to the English.

The English were at the time round Dundalk, and near it lived a very fine looking girl called Smith. The English officer found this out and went over to her house, to try and get her to fall in love with him, but after a short conversation she took a sword from the wall and put him out with it. A short while after this MacMahon came match-making with the girl. Auld Bacach was talking about the 'cleverness' of Cap't Graves,

But MacMahon settled him. MacMahon's brother lay outside in the barn that night with 12 horsemen and brought away the girl, a prisoner through the country and into the barracks. He just arrived in time as Redmond's men were after him.

She was put in a lighted room, but still she would not submit. When MacMahon was going home, he met Redmond, and Redmond demanded his money, and MacMahon said, "let us have a test of strength first", and so they had, but O' Hanlon tossed MacMahon several times. MacMahon then handed him a purse and told Redmond that his bride had been stolen by Capt' Graves, but O' Hanlon said, "I will get her home again", and he told him to be at a certain place on a certain night. Redmond wrote a letter to Capt' Graves, in the handwriting of Cap't Lucas.

The letter stated that O' Hanlon was lying injured in the mountains around Armagh and to come and capture him. This was to get all the soldiers away from the barracks. All the soldiers went away, and O' Hanlon and his men went to the barracks. When he came to the men on guard he was asked, "who are you?" O' Hanlon: "I am Capt' Lucas" Sentinel: "You are not". O' Hanlon: "Yes I am do you not see the handwriting" presenting him with a letter.

Big Tom was behind O' Hanlon, and said, "will ye take this". O' Hanlon said to the sentry, "isin't miss Smith here? I have great influence over women, and so let me up", and he was let up.

"Sir", said Big Tom "will ye take this", pretending it was some tax or other. And O' Hanlon shouted, "come in an' put your hand to the pen" as if pretending to sign something, and while he was in O' Hanlon said,"leap in and tie that sentry".

And O' Hanlon shouted, "will you release miss Smith". The sentry said, "yes, I will", and away went O' Hanlon and Big Tom to the wedding house.

By this time Graves was in Armagh, and he went into an hotel with the rest of the 'regiment' to get provisions, but the owner of the hotel said that he had nothing good enough for them. "tip it here anyway" said Graves, and when they had hung up their carbines in another room, they began to eat and drink and make merry.

When dinner was over they rested for a while (and passed a long minute up by and several remarks were passed on him). A while after this four men came in carrying a dying woman on 'an auld dure'. Shouts were made for a Protestant minister. By the way the woman was put into the room where the carbines were, and soon the minister, who had gone up before, came in an' told the soldiers to keep quiet while he was attending her.

He now ordered a kettle of boiling water, and when he got it, he put some of it on the powder of the carbines. When this was done Graves marched off with his men, and the minister said, "I'll go with ye for I'll be catched by Redmond's men". They did not go far when they were attacked by Redmond's men and Capt' Graves was pulled down. The carbines didn't go off. He shouted to Big Tom, "have ye the cat o' nine tails with ye?" "Yes I have" said Big Tom. "Well", said the minister, "strip this man and give him forty lashes, no more no less".

This Big Tom did. Then the 13 soldiers of Redmond stripped the other soldiers of their uniforms, and tied them to trees and lashed them. Redmond and his men then marched away having the uniforms and all with them. After this a reward was to be given to anyone who would kill Redmond O'Hanlon. He was killed by his own uncle, and the uncle got £50 from the English.[60]

Legend U

Black Rent

Redmond O' Hanlon had a fine sense of humour, and drama and gave himself grandiose titles like,

> "High ranger of woods and rivers!
> Surveyor of mountains and plain!
> Examiner chief of all traitors!
> Protector of all that are true.

He imposed a Black rent or tax of half a crown per annum on any one who entered his juristiction, upon payment he promised to indemnify them from robbery. Those who made the bargain with him had their names entered into his pocket book, and every rogue in the area was warned not to interfere with them. It is said that Redmond brought the notion of imposing the 'black rent' with him from France, where the stealing of goods for

---

[60] N.F.C. S 947 : p 148 B Ó'Mordha, Currin, Co Monaghan

ransom was part of warfare, as a result of this It was sometimes called the 'French Rent'.

REPORT

ON THE

MANUSCRIPTS

OF

THE MARQUIS OF ORMONDE, K.P.,

Preserved at

THE CASTLE, KILKENNY.

VOL. 11.

Presented in Parliament by Command of her Majesty

London

Printed For Her Majesty's Stationary Office

1899

The following passages are extracted in their entirety from the manuscripts above.

Redmond O' Hanlon – Ulster Outlaws

1674, December 14, Council Chamber, Dublin.

"Essex,- Whereas Redmond O' Hanlon of Tonderegee, in the county of Armagh, yeoman, Laughlin MacRedmond O' Hanlon of Kileany, yeoman, Daniel MacMurphy Mac Thorlagh Roe O' Murphy of the same, yeoman; Cormuck Raver O' Murphy of the same, yeoman; Hugh Turr O' Murphy of the same, yeoman, Bryan Moyle O' Neale of the same, yeoman; James Roe of Ballinteggart, in the said county, yeoman; Hugh MacShane of the same, yeoman; Peter Pill of the same, yeoman; James MacNicholas O' Murphy of the same, yeoman; Thomas Wilson of Mullaghglasse of the said county, yeoman; and Thorlagh MacPatrick Goam O' Hanlon of Aghynecloghmullen in the said county, yeoman; and Owen Oge Carthy of the County of Kerry, Cnogher Reardane alias Griagh of the said county, John Howrane and Hugh Noonane of the said county, and Shane Kittagh O' Donnel, late of Prison in the county of Mayo, yeoman, James Gallagher MacEdmond Dorragh late of Kilmore in the said county, yeoman, Donnogh Boy O' Gallagher, late of Coolkearny in the said county, yeoman, Terlagh Mac Kolgeen, late of the same in the same county, yeoman, Hugh Bane Mac Brehoune, late of Carra in the County of Sligo, yeoman, Donal Oge O' Donnel MacDonnel Oge, late of Sligo in the county of Sligo aforesaid, yeoman, William O' Keavin, late of Ballyntrohan, in the said county, yeoman, Bryan MacDonnogh late of Coopany in the said county, yeoman, Donnogh Fitz John Hart, late of Knockadooe in the said county, yeoman, Owen O' Doghertie, late of Coulkearny in the county Mayo, yeoman, Tirlagh Mac Brehoune late of Carra in the county of Sligo, yeoman, and William

Gallagher late of Court in the said county, yeoman, have of late committed several burglaries, robberies and stealths in the said several counties of Armagh, Kerry, Cork, Limerick, Mayo, Sligo, and elsewhere within this Kingdom, besides divers other outrages, to the terror and annoyance of his Majesty's loyal and good Subjects, and to the disturbance of the peace of the Kingdom, upon which misdemeanours and crimes being pursued by some of his Majesty's good subjects they, the said Redmond O' Hanlon, Laughlin Mac Redmond O' Hanlon (etc as at pages 342-3), are fled to the woods and mountains, where they stand upon their keeping, so as they are not answerable or amenable to law, but wilful contemners of the same.

"And forasmuch as the actors of these disorders and offences cannot as yet be apprehended, whereby they may be punished by the ordinary course of law, whence we might justly be moved, according to the former usage and custom in the Kingdom in cases of like nature, to cause them to be forthwith proclaimed rebels and traitors, yet in mercy to them, we think fit hereby to charge and command them upon their duty and allegiance to his Majesty that they and every of them do before the first day of February next, render their persons to any of his Majesty's justices of the peace, and submit themselves to his Majesty's justice to be tried for their offences according to the laws of the land, wherein if they or any of them do fail, we do hereby publish and declare, that he or they so failing, are from and immediately after the said first of February next, to be called, reputed and taken for notorious rebels and traitors against his Majesty and accordingly to be prosecuted by all his Majesty's loving and good subjects in all hostile manner.

"And we declare further, that whatsoever person or persons shall comfort, relieve or abet them, or any of them, they are and shall be reputed, deemed and adjudged traitors in like degree with the fore-named traitors and rebels themselves, and to be proceeded against according to law.

"And we do in his Majesty's name straitly charge and command all his Majestie's loyal subjects, upon their duty of allegiance to his Majestie, not only to forbear to receive or relieve the persons aforesaid, or any of them, but also to make diligent search and enquire in what place or places the said persons shall from time to time lurk or be relieved, and by all means possible to prosecute, apprehend and take the bodies of them, and then to bring or cause to be brought under safe custody, unto the High Sheriffs of the respective counties where any of them shall be apprehended, to be by such Sheriffs kept in strict and safe custody, till we upon notice thereof, shall give further direction concerning them, or resisting or refusing to be taken, to kill them or any of them. And we do hereby declare, that whosoever shall after the said first day of February next, bring unto any Sheriff the body of the said Redmond O' Hanlon, Laughlin Mac Redmond O' Hanlon (etc as at pages 342-3), or any of them alive, or kill any of them and bring his head to the Sheriff of the county where he shall be killed, to be by such Sheriff set up in some public place in that county, shall have for his reward for each person so brought in, or his head, ten pounds, for payment whereof we will give warrant as occasion shall require.

" And whosoever of the said proclaimed persons, or any other, shall after the said first day of February next, apprehend and bring unto the High Sheriff of the county where such person shall be apprehended, or resisting, shall kill any of the said rebels and traitors particularly named as aforesaid, he shall, together with his said reward, receive his pardon.

"And towards the speedy effecting of this service, all commanders of horse and foot, and all other of his Majesty's officers and loving subjects are to be aiding and assisting, as they and every of them will answer the contrary at their perils.

"James Armachanus,-Michael Dublin,-Canc.- Clanbrasill- Conway and Kilulta.- Massereene, - Kingston.- Carey Dillon.- John Povey.- William Stewart.- Theophilus Jones.- Charles Meredith."

Members of his Tory Band.

Paul Liddy
Capt Richard Power
Manus O' Neill
Strong ¬John Mac Pherson
Shane Berragh-?-Barnagh
James Butler
John Mulhone
James Carrick
Harry Donahan "Napper "
Patrick Mc Teigue
John Reily.
Arthur O' Neill
O' Kelly from Kilkenny
Phillip Calloge
Pat Mill
Walter O' Casey
Laughlin O' Hanlon (his brother)
Edmund Bán O' Hanlon (his brother)
Séan O' Hanlon   (his brother)
Cormack O' Murphy (the raver)
Daniel MacMurphy mac Thorlagh Roe O' Murphy
Hugh Turr O' Murphy
Bryan Moyle O' Neill
James Roe of Ballinteggart
Hugh Mac Shane
Peter Pil

James MacNicholas O'Murphy
Thomas Wilson, of Mullaghglasse
Thorlagh Mac Patrick Goam O' Hanlon of Aghynecloghmullen.

Legend V

"One time a member of Redmond's band named Walter O' Casey was guilty of an outrage on a young woman named O' Rafferty. This coming to O' Hanlon's ears, he immediately ordered O' Casey to be imprisoned and bound, gave him three hours to prepare for death, and then ordered him to be shot by his comrades.[61]

Legend W

Redmond and the Popish Plot.

There is a chapter in Redmond O' Hanlon's career which speaks well of his character and is worthy of noting. At a time when a huge reward was on his head and various plans were being made in high places for his capture, while the hills of Ulster were crawling with troops searching for him, the authorities in Dublin Castle offered him their protection. What brought about this change of policy?

At that time in England, a person by the name of Titus Oates, claimed to have uncovered what became known to history as the Popish Plot. The purpose of this plot was to facilitate a French invasion of England with the purpose of overthrowing the Protestant religion in England and Ireland. Archbishop Oliver Plunkett was accused of being one of the leading instigators of this supposed plot, he was accused of raising money from the priests to maintain a French army of seventy thousand men, which was to be landed at Carlingford. Afraid that they would be unable to convict Oliver Plunket of the charges against him the Castle authorities believed that if they could produce a strong witness against him one of the calibre of Redmond 0'Hanlon whose reputation was known throughout the land, then they would be sure of gaining a conviction. Dr Henry Jones who was Protestant Bishop of Meath at that time was an ardent believer in the Titus Oates conspiracy. His daughter Deborah, was married to one of the Annesleys of Castlewellan, County Down; and it was through her that contact was made with Redmond's mother and the offer of a free pardon and the protection of the government if he would act as a witness against the Primate. To his credit Redmond refused to give false witness against the Archbishop. Oliver Plunket was arrested in 1679 and after a farcical trial at

---

[61] Dublin Penny Journal M.H O'Hanlon

Dundalk which failed to convict him, he was brought to trial in London where he was convicted in July 1681.

Legend X

The Killing of Henry St. John.

Henry St John a prominent planter and grand nephew of Sir Oliver St John, Lord Deputy of Ireland from 1615 until 1620. This family who had their residence at Ballymore Castle had planted O' Hanlon land and as a consequence were hated by the Count. This hatred was reciprocated, Henry St John's son had caught a chill and died while pursuing O'Hanlon. The father had sworn to hunt him down and anyone who aided and abetted him. On September 9 1679 Henry St John was out riding on his estate in the company of the Reverend Lawrence Power of Tandragee. Suddenly St John was seized by members of O'Hanlons band. Reverend Power was informed that if any attempt was made to rescue St John he would be shot. Almost immediately a number of St Johns men appeared and engaged the outlaws. As a result Henry St John was shot twice in the forehead. At the funeral of Henry St John the Reverend Lawrence Power delivered the following impassioned sermon.

" I must make some reflection upon this country too, concerning those skulking scoundrels that are the distributors of the best planted country of the Kingdom; no part of Ireland having so many inhabitants, yet no place so pestered with the vermin. And you know gentlemen, the obloquy you lie under, as if some of you did shelter and protect them. I confess I abhor the thought of it, that English people and Protestants should harbour such pernicious vipers in their bosom. Yet it is certain some of you do, and that of the better sort too, or else some half-a-score of ruffians could never lurk so long among you, which is such a prodigious shame that you can never wipe out the infamy of it.... Pardon me, sir's, if I express my just resentment against such dealing. I reflect upon no individual person, but this I can boldly say in front of you all, that I have heard many of you accuse one another for harbouring these infamous rebels and that they help to furnish your kitchen and tables."[62]

When informed of the murder of Henry St John, the Viceroy issued a proclamation to the effect that the crimes of the Tories would be visited upon their families, "on the wives, fathers, mothers, brothers, and sisters of such of them as shall be out upon their keeping, that is not amenable to law and committing them to close prison, until such outlaws shall be either killed or taken."

---

[62] Power Laurance, Rev,' The Righteous Man's Portion' Delivered in a sermon at the Obsequies of the Noble and renowned Gentleman Henry St John Esquire London 1680. N.L.I. Lo P14 item 12

As a result of this proclamation Redmond's family were forced to flee to County Donegal, where they purchased a house and business premises in the town of Letterkenny. Here they were safe under the protection of Sir Cahir O' Doherty who was an old friend of the family, and Sir John Conyngham, whose brother David was married to Redmond's sister Isabel. In the spring of 1681 the Viceroy ordered his subalterns to find, "an army man in the Armagh area with the credentials to carry out a dangerous task."

The man chosen for this particular task was a young officer by the name of Lieutenant William Lucas of Dromantine, near Newry. Redmond had two personal body guards, Art O'Hanlon his foster brother and William O'Shiel. Lucas sought out Art O'Hanlon and bought his treachery for £200 and a free pardon On April 25th 1681 Count Redmond O' Hanlon in the company of his foster brother Art and William Sheil set out for Hilltown, in the Mourne mountains. The purpose of this expedition was to way-lay the landowners as they returned from the fair in Banbridge and relieve them of their money, and animals. After they arrived in the early afternoon, the Rapparees decided to rest up as their prey would not appear before dusk. They found an abandoned cottage by the roadside at the rear of which they tied their horses. Art and Redmond would sleep first while William O'Sheil stood guard. At about two o clock that afternoon when Redmond had fallen asleep Art shot him dead with his own gun, thus fulfilling the prophesy that Redmond O' Hanlon could only be shot with a bullet from his own gun.

"it is said that Réamon had a shirt made from flax which was plucked and scutched and spun and woven between sunrise and sunset and that, as a result it could not be penetrated by any other bullet except one fired from his own gun."

COUNT HANLAN'S
DOWNFALL
OR
A True and Exact Account of the **Killing**
That Arch Traytor and Tory
REDMON O' HANLAN
BY
ART O' HANLAN,
One of his own Party, on the 25. day of April,
1681. near the Eight Mile Bridge, in the County of Down.
Being the copy of a **LETTER** writ by a
Country Gentleman (now in Dublin) to a Per-
Son of Quality (his friend) in the Country.
DUBLIN,
Printed for William Winter, Bookseller at the Wandring Jew
In Castle-Street 1681.
(7)

On Monday the 25th Instant, the said *Art O'Hanlan and William O'Sheel,* in company with *Redmond O' Hanlan,* were near the Eight Mile Bridge, in the County of Down, Waiting for Prize, on the force of a Fair that was held there, at which place, while they were watching for their Prey, Redmond took occasion to quarrel with Art, as they were smoking their Pipes, and in the close bid him to provide for himself, for he should not be any longer a Tory in any of the three Counties, (viz, Monaghan, Down, or, Ardmagh) whereupon Art rose up and said, I am very glad of it, and will go just now; and then taking up his arms (having his Authority and Protection about him) Immediately he shot *Redmond* in the left breast with his Carbine, and forthwith ran to The Eight Mile Bridge for a Guard, but *Art* returned with a Guard, and Mr Lucas, who soon had notice at the Newry where he was waiting *Redmonds* motions, for the same Ends, found *Redmonds* Body, but the Head was taken off by O'Sheel, who had fled with it, the Body they removed to the Newry, where it lies under a Guard till Orders be sent how it should be disposed of; and since that, Mr Lucas has sent out a Protection and Assurance to O Sheel to bring in the Head of that Arch Traytor and Tory *Redmond O Hanlan.*

This evening, *Art O Hanlan* gave in a Relation of this Adventure, to the Lord Lieutenant and Council, who ordered him to have a Sum of Money paid forthwith, for the good Service he has done. And to Mr Lucas his Grace has promised The Honour of a Command in the Army. These I mention to shew the extraordinary Care, Vigilance and Honour of the Government. If this Relation of mine may prove any way diverting to you 'twill be sufficient Reward for this trouble of Letter writing,

Which is in it self irksome to[63]

Your Obliged Humble

Servant

Dublin April 27 1681

It is said that when news of the Tory's death reached Donegal, Sir John Conynham sent an escort of troops to accompany the O' Hanlon family to Ballynabeck where Redmonds body was exhumed and brought back to Letterkenny for re-burial. In the 1930's a tombstone was discovered at Conwall Parish Church in Letterkenny The tombstone bears the O' Hanlon coat of arms and the inscription below. "The five sons of Redmond Hanlen, Mercht.in Letterkenny; John, the firstborn, Alexander, Francis, John and Redmond. Also here lieth the body of William, the Son of the aforesaid Redmond Hanlen who departed this life the 27th..........1708 Aged...........3 years...months and 14 days"

Also the remains of David Conynham, Gent, and Cath-?-, his wife, daughter to Redmond Hanlen. They were esteemed more for goodness of heart than for Affluence of fortune. Died lamented here on ...
December, 1752. 72 years old she 21st of August, 1775, aged 80." [64]

O'Hanlon Grave 2006 - *I believe, the one mentioned in the text above most of the inscriptions are no longer legible But one can recognise the inscription of a boar and lizard which form part of the O'Hanlon coat of Arms.*

---

[63] A pamphlet published in Dublin containing Art O'Hanlon's account of Redmond's death.
[64] O'Hanlon Terence

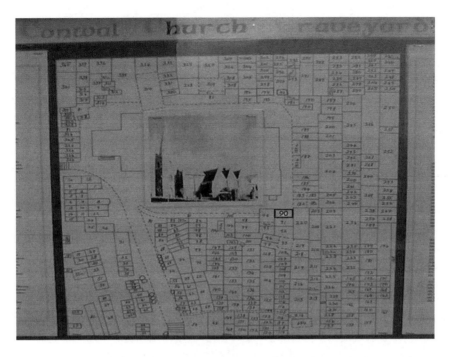

Location of Redmond's grave, plot 90 (outlined in red).

The *caoineadh* below is said to have been composed by his mother after she had seen her son's head spiked on Downpatrick Gaol.

> Dear head of my darling
> How gory and pale;
> These aged eyes see thee,
> High spiked on their jail.
> That cheek in the summer,
> No more shall grow warm;
> Nor that eye e'er catch light,
> But the flash of the storm.0 .[65]

---
[65] O'Hanlon Terence

Tory Hunters

"We have three beasts to destroy that lay burthens upon us," said a certain Major Morgan, an officer in Cromwell's army in Ireland. "The first is the wolf, on whom we lay five pounds a head if a dog, and ten pounds if a bitch. The second beast is the priest, on whose head we lay ten pounds – if he be eminent, more.

The third beast is the tory, on whose head we lay twenty pounds." As a result of this proclamation, tory- hunting became a more paying pastime in Ireland than priest-hunting. A memory of it lives still in the familiar old rhyme;

> I'll tell you a story about Johnny Magory,
> He went to the wood and shot a tory;
> I'll tell you another about his brother,
> He went to the wood and shot another.
>
> He hunted him in and he hunted him out,
> Three times through the bog, and about and about;
> Till out of the bush he spied his head,
> So he levelled his pistol and shot him dead.[66]

Later on, a law was made that any tory killing two other tories would get a free pardon for himself. This law continued in force against the rapparee's of succeeding generations, and against highway robbers down to the latter end of the eighteenth century. The planter families of the Cootes of Cootehill and the Johnstons of the Fews were very active as priest hunters and tory hunters. Especially the Johnstons of the Fews, who, were notorious priest hunters.Their tyranny is remrmbered to this day in this fire-side rhyme.

> "Jesus of Nazareth, King of the Jews!
> Save us from Johnston, King of the Fews".

---

[66] Dublin Penny Journal M.H. O'Hanlon

The Ballad of Redmond O' Hanlon.

A shepherd that lives on Slieve Gullion
Came down to the County Tyrone,
And told us how Redmond O' Hanlon
Wont let the rich Saxons alone!
He rides over moor-land and mountain,
By night till a stranger is found,
Saying "take your own choice to be lodging
Right over or under the ground".

If you whistle out Whoo! Like a native,
He leaves you the way to go clear;
If you squeeze out a Hew! Like a Scotsman.
You'll pay him a guinea a year.
But if you cry Haw! Like a Saxon,
Och, then 'tis your life or your gold!
By stages Count Redmond O' Hanlon
Gets back what they pilfered of old!

Old Coote of Cootehill is heart-broken;
And Johnson beyond in the Fews
Has wasted eight barrels of poweder
Upon him, but all to no use!
Although there's four hundred pounds sterling
If Redmond you'd put out of sight;
Mind, if the heart's dark in your body,
'Tis Redmond will let in the light!

The great Duke of Ormond is frantic-
His soldiers got up with the lark
To catch this bold Redmond by daylight!
But Redmond caught them in the dark.
Say's he when he stripped them and bound them-
"Take back my best thanks to his Grace
For all the fine pistols and powder
He sent to this desolate place!"

Then here's to you Redmond O' Hanlon
Long may your excellency reign,
High ranger of woods and of rivers!
Surveyor of mountains and plain!

155

Examiner-chief of all traitors!
Protector of all that are true-
Henceforward, King Charlie of England
May take what he gets after you!

The Ballad of Douglas Bridge
By
Francis Carlin

On Douglas Bridge I met a man
Who lived adjacent to Strabane,
Before the English hanged him high
For riding with O' Hanlon.

The eyes of him were just as fresh
As when they burned within the flesh,
And his boot-legs were wide apart
From riding with O' Hanlon.

"God save you, sir" I said with fear,
"You seem to be a stranger here".
"Not I," said he, "nor any man"
Who rides with Count O' Hanlon.

"I know each glen from North Tyrone
To Monaghan, and I've been known
By every clan and parish since
I rode with Count O' Hanlon".

"before that time," said he to me,
"My fathers owned the land you see;
But they are now among the moors
A-riding with O' Hanlon.

"Before that time," he said with pride,
"My fathers rode where now they ride
As Rapparees, before the time
Of trouble and O' Hanlon.

"Good night to you," and " God be with
The Tellers of the tale and myth,
For they are of the spirit-stuff
That rides with Count O' Hanlon".

"Good night to you," I said "and God
Be with the chargers, fairy-shod,
That bear the Ulster Heros forth
To ride with Count O' Hanlon".

On Douglas Bridge we parted, but
The gap o' Dreams is never shut
To one whose saddled soul to-night
Rides out with Count O' Hanlon.

St. Oliver Plunkett 1625-1681

Oliver Plunkett was born at Loughcrew near oldcastle, Co. Meath on November 1st 1625. His father John Plunkett, owned an estate of 680 acres until the Cromwellian confiscations. He was a kinsman to Lords, Fingal, Dunsany, and Louth, he was also second cousin to the Earls of Roscommon and Fingal. He went to the Irish College in Rome to study for the priesthood in 1647 On the first day of January 1654 he was ordained priest in the Chapel of Propaganda Fide College, off the Piazza di Spagna. *Upon the death of Dr Edmund O' Reilly, Archbishop of Armagh, in exile in Soumar in France in the year 1669, he was appointed his successor.*
On Monday the tenth of March 1670, he landed at Ringsend, Dublin. The story of St. Oliver Plunkett must be viewed against the backdrop of 17th century Ireland, when he arrived as Archbishop of Armagh and Primate of Ireland in March 1670 the Catholic church in Ireland had been brought to its knees. Almost every diocese was without a Bishop.
The strict implementation of the Penal Laws, forbidding the public celebration of Mass. The education of Catholics was forbidden. In the Archdiocese of Armagh there was not one Catholic school functioning. During this period of persecution discipline among the clergy deteriorated. Disputes and divisions between the secular clergy and the religious orders arose. One dispute between the Dominicans and the Franciscans over the right to (quest), that is the right to seek money from house to house, or before or after the various gatherings for mass. St Oliver's decision in favour of the Dominicans was said to be the reason why some priests gave evidence against him at his trial. Oliver Plunkett acted as an intermediary between the Tories and the government, and managed to persuade some of them to desist from their activities and accept the governments offer of safe conduct if they went abroad and joined a foreign army. He met with a group of Tories mainly O'Neills , Mc Donnells, and O'Hagans and persuaded fifteen of them to emigrate to the continent under a safe pass. It was widely rumoured that the government renege'd on its promise of safe passage and that this group had been transported to the Barbadoes. The murder of the "Grand Tory " Patrick Fleming, with three of his followers near Iniskeen,

Co. Monaghan in 1677 as he made his way into exile with Archbishop Plunkett's safe conduct pass in his pocket did nothing to enhance the Archbishops reputation among the common people who kept the Tory's name alive in a lament composed in his honour. (*Caoineadh Pádraig Pléimionn*).

After his arrest near the village of The Naul in north County Dublin in the year 1679 Oliver Plunkett was held For three months in Dublin Castle before anyone came forward to provide evidence against him. It was well known in Ireland that some of the Whig opponents of King Charles II in London were searching for someone who would be prepared to confirm the assertions of Titus Oates, by producing evidence of a similar plot in Ireland. Three prisoners in Dundalk gaol agreed to provide such evidence, They were, William Hetherington a Protestant from County Louth, who had served as a Tory -hunter, but had been imprisoned for being in league with Tories, and Edmond Murphy, a Catholic priest and former Parish Priest of Kileavy, Co. Armagh, who had been suspended by Archbishop Oliver Plunkett for drunkenness and consorting with Tories and Friar Hugh Duffy, who had studied at St Isidores in Rome but had been expelled in 1673. In July 1680 he was sent to Dundalk for trial. However the Dundalk trial collapsed and he was subsequently sent to Newgate Prison in London where he was brought to trial on the 8th of June 1681. He was found guilty of high treason and was sentenced to be hanged, drawn and quartered by the Lord Chief Justice Lord Pemberton.

Westmount House near Naul, North County Dublin
Where St Oliver Plunkett was arrested in the year 1679 under the guise of Mr Melready.

Lament for Patrick Fleming

Arise, ye women, from every art in Ireland
And take your share without delay
With clapping of hands, and screams of woe,
In weeping the death of Patrick Fleming
Och, ochone!

II

O Patrick Fleming, heart of generosity,
Son of James of Sydden, and heir to his patrimony,
Without sword or pistol or powder shot
You could humble and smite the Galls with a stick,
Och, ochone!

III

I'll not go to Miscash to-morrow,
To the house of Conn Fada where yon slaughter was made;
(There) guns were wetted, and shots were fired
And the hero that was brave, is the cause of my grief-
Och, ochone!

159

IV

In Miscash indeed was wrought this slaughter,
Seven heads were cast into a turf-creel,
And the bright corpses that should be put into coffins
Lay in dykes from Thursday till Sunday,
Och, ochone !

V

O Mary O'Neill heavy is your sleep,
And Patrick Fleming after being riddled [by shot]
By the un-baptised bodachs
Who came from Ardee of treachery,
Och, ochone !

VI

Behold Mary (now) going by the mountain slope,
The beads of sweat on her brow-
It would put grief on the women of Ireland-
To see her coming to Patrick Fleming's funeral-
Och, ochone!

VII

When she had climbed up the stairs
Who should confront her but Patrick Fleming;
She kissed his hands, she could not find his mouth,
For a body without a head was he- shocking the tale,
Och, ochone !

VIII

O Patrick Fleming since you are dead
'Tis I myself will make your dress (for the grave)
Silk to your feet and satin to your waist,
O kinsman of the earls who hailed from London,
Och. Ochone!

IX

Patrick Fleming of the fair flaxen hair
'Tis my bitter woe that you did not cross the water
To France with your prowess of hand,
Or to assist in war the King of Spain,
Och, ochone !

X

I have love for God and for Mary,
And also for the fourteenmen of the wood-kern,
And (particularly) for Patrick Fleming of the bright locks-
Oft was their bed in the green rushes of the wood,
Och, ochone!

XI

O Patrick Fleming, you were truly great,

I regarded you as a wondrous horse-man,
Your presence was as a golden sword in the hands of ever one (of us)
Your death will cause a great gap in the ranks of the wood-kerne,
Och, ochone !

XII

'Tis a terrible tale, and a terrible calamity,
Though you did not go to the mountain (on your keeping) for the
sake of thieving,
You kinsman of earls, Patrick Fleming,
But for writing a pardon for three Gaels,
Och, ochone !

XIII

The town of Ardee is under (the sway of) a troop of white horse,
And the murder's daughter is learning to shoot;
It is posted up on white papers that "Patrick Fleming seeks his
pardon"-
Och, ochone!

XIV

O Deceitful villain, you ignorant churl,
It seems you were not born or reared in this land,
(With) your pig's cheek sparsely covered with bristles,
And may it not be long till you are swept away-
Och, ochone!

XV

O thick lipped traitor, malicious and lying,
Where are the ribbons and pearls?
Whence disappeared the dear beautiful silk?
Or the gold rings that were on his (Fleming's) fingers?
Och, ochone!

XVI

Seven times eight times worse at the end of the year,
May Captain Colla be and Conn Fada of the hanks,
And Catherine Gearr, 'tis she did the evil deed,
Put water in the guns of the generous horsemen;
Och, ochone!

Xvii

On the scene of the slaughter may there be a heavy stream of ill
fortune
The place where heroes were cut down by treachery and injustice;
Crop or corn may it never grow there,
Nor even short grass that calves might eat:
Och, ochone!

161

Examination of Sir Wm. Tichborne relating to Papers found on Patrick Fleming 1680. Nov. 18. Who being duly sworn and examined saith that when a party of his men about the 14th of February, 1677, had killed Patrick Fleming, a Tory, there were several papers brought unto him by John Greene, one of this examinent's troopers, which he said were taken out of the pockets of the said fleming, and were only loose and inconsiderable notes, one of which said to have the shape of our Lady's foot; and a few days after Mr Samuel Banks, one of the portreeves of Ardee showed this examinant a certain letter which the said Banks told him was taken out of the pockets of the said Fleming, which letter this examinant saw delivered to Mr Serjeant Osborne and verily believeth that the copy now sworn to and subscribed by John Banks is a true copy thereof, for that he, this examinant read the said original and further saith that the general vogue of the country was that Oliver Plunkett titular Primate, sometimes assumed the name of Thomas Cox, which was the reason that the aforesaid letter subscribed by the said Thomas Cox was sent to Thomas Osborne as aforesaid and further saith not.
Will Tichborn
Taken the day aforesaid before us.
Hen Midensis. [67]

Patrick Fleming

Patrick Fleming was a gentleman from Slane and would probably have remained a good and law-abiding citizen if the following tragedy had not befallen him. Three young men, who were employed by him, retrieved some cattle belonging to a neighbour, which had been impounded by the bailiffs, during the rescue operation they were said to have ill-treated the bailiffs. Warrants were issued for their arrest and they were forced to go on their keeping and become outlaws. Patrick Fleming signed the name of an uncle, who was a Chief Justice, to a document purporting to be a free pardon for the culprits. He did this in expectation that his uncle would acknowledge it as his rather than expose his nephew to the law. He was wrong, his uncle refused to acknowledge the pardon and as a consequence Fleming himself had to take to the hills and become a tory. Here he was joined by a number of men in similar circumstance to himself and he became their leader. He levied a black-rent on the English planter families and was said to be generous to the dispossessed Irish.
While still operating as a tory he canvassed his old friends to seek a pardon for his past and present crimes. Tradition holds that was successful and had received a pardon which had been negotiated by Oliver Plunkett, Fleming was seeking a pardon for the rest of his comrades and while this

---

[67] Murrey L.P. Rev PP Louth Archaeological Journal 1933-36

was being considered by the authorities a Tory-hunter became interested in the reward money. There was a sheebeen in the Townland of Miascaish near Inniskeen, in Co Monaghan, which was kept by Conn Fada MacMahon, who was also a dealer in yarn and Connemara stockings. The Tory-hunter discovered that Patrick Fleming and his comrades were regulars at this sheebeen and he offered Conn Fada a share of the reward if he betrayed the tories.

Conn Fada agreed to betray the tories and it was decided that Conn would invite Fleming and his comrades on a particular day to partake of his hospitality.

To indicate when the tories were present in the sheebeen Conn Fada would be seen digging sods on the green hill above the house. The invitation was accepted and Patrick Fleming and his comrades came to the sheeben on the day appointed. When the tory hunter and his band saw Conn Fada digging sods on the hill they surrounded the sheebeen. While this was going on Catherine Gearr, Conn's wife was liberally plying the tories with strong drink and also pouring water down the muzzles of their guns. One of Flemings men managed to escape out the back window, but the remainder were captured after a fierce struggle. They were taken out to the back of the house and beheaded, along with an innocent boy who sold tobacco and who happened to be lodging in Conn Fada's house. The heads were placed in a turf creel and carried off and the bodies were thrown into a ditch. It is said locally that neither grass nor weeds will grow on the spot where the men were beheaded.

The Last Speech And Confession of
Mr. James Geoghan.

Priest of the Order of St Francis, who was Executed at the Common Place of Execution near Dublin, on Saturday the Tenth of this Instant February, 1693. As it was delivered by his own Hand to be Printed, before he went to Execution. Being lately called to an Account for my manifold Misdemeanors, and my Crimes having justly render'd me undeserving the Society of Men, I am now to end a Scandalous Life, by a deserved Ignominious Death. My Capital Crime, (out of which all my Iniquities have Sprung) is Disobedience; For as Obedience is the Golden Basis and Foundation of all Laws, Humane and Divine, and as 1 *Pet. 22 Ex side nascitur, sacrificiis praestantior;* Disobedience being directly opposite, is the source of all evil, and renders a Man incapable, whilst in that State, of the Protection of the Eternal Being (on which all things depend, and which can Annihilate as well as Create this World, and all things therein) as likewise of the Temporal Laws which rules us here.

Into this great Gulf I have (dear Christian) unfortunately plunged myself; and when once I relished of the Evils of a Voluptuous Life, one Mischief ushered in another,

Abysus abyssum invocat, and I no longer acted like a Loyal Subject to my Redeemer,but became an Apostate and perfect child of *Belial.*In this State and condition I continued for several years, falsely accusing the Innocent, Violating by my untrue Testimony both the Liberties and Properties of honest men, and abusing the Sacred Order of which I was an unworthy Member, and Several other Sacred Religious Orders, by pretending to be of their Confraternities whilst an Apostate, the better to attain to my wicked ends. Most dear Christians, there is nothing now left principally, but the Sacred Name of Christ, *Christus satisfactio est sincqua nemo videbit faciem Dei,*it is by him and through the Merits of his Passion I expect Salvation. He is the Balsam that Cures and Removes the Iniquities of this frail Life; *Sicut ligat Diabolus qui peccata connectit, ita solvit Christo qui debita demittit.*

I do, dear Christians, to the World acknowledge my self guilty of several grievous Crimes, as well as that whereof I have been by the Law *Convicted* , th'o not in the same manner as I have been Accused; the things alledged to be Stolen by me being Lent me, and not Stolen; yet now I freely forgive my Accuser.To repeat my manifold *Errors* might require more time than the present Circumstances of a Penitent Criminal can well afford; But in particular I humbly beg Pardon of Mr Peaton, My Lord *Bussine*, one Mr Broughil, and Garret Nugent, being severally most Unjustly Accused by me of crimes they never committed. For all which I am truly penitent and sorrowful; and do humbly implore all others which I have offended to forgive me; Acknowledging that I never knew any Mans Crime either against State or Government, of which I did accuse them. And wishing that the Infamous Death which justly I am to undergo, may be acceptable in the presence of the Lord and his People, as a Satisfaction for the Crimes I committed. And I do in the sight of God declare my self Innocent of the Blood of my Lord Primate Plunket, th'o I have been Charged to have accused him wrongfully. Now trusting to Him whose Mercy is infinite, I humbly beg the Prayers of all Faithful Christians, and especially of that Order of which I was (th'o most unworthy) a Member. Now confiding in the Mercy of God, I conclude with the Saying of St Paul, *Cupio, dissolve, et, esse cum Christo.*[68]*James Geoghan*

---

[68] Dublin, Printed by Samuel Lee in Skinner- Row, near the Tholsel.1694. N.L.I. Thorpe Pamplet no 710

Richard Power

Richard Power was born in Kilbolane, County Cork. The second son of an Irish Catholic landowner. Being the youngest of two brothers he had no rights of inheritance under English law. It is said that this is the reason that he left home and became a Tory. Richard was first proclaimed an outlaw in the year 1683, when a reward of £20 was offered for his capture. Two years later on July 17 1685 another Proclamation was issued offering £100 for his capture dead or alive.In a letter dated September 17, 1685 the duke of Ormonde revealed the reasoning behind this reward: "The Government have taken care to set a considerable price upon Power, the Tory's (head); if that be seconded by placing (some) parties of the Army in apt stations both will either apprehend him or drive him where he is not so well aquainted."

Primate Boyle in a letter to the Duke of Ormonde October 17, 1685

"Your Grace must consider that Power is an absolute ubiquitous, and tarries in no place long enough to be discovered and taken. He is sometimes in the County of Waterford, and sometimes in Kilkenny, and immediately after we hear of his pranks in the County of Limerick, and in Kerry and in Cork;
So that it is an impossible thing to pursue him from place to place."
Captain Power as the common people called him was a very audacious robber. On one occasion he decided to rob Sir John Meade, The Chief Justice of the Royalties and Liberty of Tipperary. Being late he missed his prey, but managed to rob Sir John's brother in law of £80 on the same day.His audacity knew no limits.On hearing of the forthcoming marriage of the daughter of a well known merchant from Newcastle in County Limerick, he presented himself at the house of the merchant and asked to be brought to the bride's parents, stating that he had brought a present for the bride He was brought into a reception room, where he introduced himself, using a fictitious name. After some small talk, he apologised for his bad manners in not presenting them with the gift he had brought, reaching inside his coat, he brought forth a large pistol and demanded that they give him whatever cash was in the house. After pocketing the £60 that the distraught couple had handed over he marched them at gun point to the front door, he called for his horse and when he was mounted he ordered a glass of wine, he drank to the brides health before galloping away. Power halted one evening somewhere in Leinster at a remote farm house in search of lodgings for the night. Although he was made welcome, and given sustenance he soon perceived that all was not well. On enquiry into the cause of their distress, he was informed that they had fallen into arrears in their rent to the amount of £40, and that neither they or their friends could raise such a sum.

"If someone was to be found to advance you the money would you repay the money as soon as you were able"."I would", said the farmer "and he'd have my prayers for the rest of my life"."Then allow me to be your friend", said Power as he counted out forty golden sovereigns, and handed them to the bewildered farmer. "I will take your word as bond that the money will be repaid as soon as you are able; but you must not inform the landlord that you have the money until he arrives to evict you", he said. On the appointed day the landlord, and the sheriff, and a band of bailiff's came to evict the farmer and his family from their farm. After delaying as long as he deemed safe, the tenant farmer produced the forty pounds. The landlord berated him for being a rogue and ne'er do well for trying to avoid paying his rent. The landlord mounted his horse and headed for home, he taking one road and the sheriff and his bailiff's taking another. Power way laid the landlord, and relieved him of his forty pounds, along with his watch and chain. He then returned to the farmhouse, for another nights lodgings. He revealed his identity to the family and added that they did not owe him any money as he had already taken it back from the landlord.

Strong John MacPherson.

John MacPherson came into an inheritance when he was ninteen years of age. During the next three years he squandered his inheritance. He was always the leading man at games of hurley, patrons, and all such activities. It is said that at this time he was the strongest man in Ireland. He could hold a hundred-weight at arms, length in one hand, and could twist a new horse shoe round like a gad. Eventually when John had dissipated his inheritance and was on the brink of poverty, having no skills to fall back upon and no history of, or inclination to work, he armed himself with some weapons and took to the highroads to seek his fortune. John's method of robbery was first to demand of his victims that they lend him some money. If they conceded to his demand he would only take a portion of their money. If one offered any resistance he would drag him from his horse, throw him over his shoulder and run with him into the woods and there rob him of everything. He continued to rob people in this manner for many years, generally acting alone. One evening he entered a country house alone and locked the people he came upon into one of the rooms. While he was engaged in gathering together the family valuables, some workmen who had been working upstairs, came down and released the family, when they all fell upon him with various blunt instruments.Before they could overpower him he grabbed the woman of the house, threw her over his shoulder and ran with her to a nearby wood, he placed her on the ground with his foot on her petticoats to prevent her from moving. In this position he ransomed her for twenty pieces of gold. It is said that he never murdered anybody, but that he carried out more single handed robberies than Redmond O' Hanlon, with whom he was well acquainted. He was eventually captured, tried, convicted and executed in 1678. It is said that as he was carried to the gallows he played a tune of his own composition on the bagpipes, which is called MacPherson's tune to the present day[69]

The Meehan Clan

"Some few hundred years ago there were no people living in Cornmore or surrounding districts. Parts of these districts were overgrown with brushwood or shrubbery and there were several caves in other parts. The Irish Raparee as he was called always found refuge in places like these. A local story gives an account of one of these raparees. He was named Meehan and he had six comrades of the same name and one of the name of Rooney. Probably they were some of the Meehan clan from Ballagina-Meehan which is but three miles distant. These men plundered the English settlers around the countryside during the night and rested themselves in an old house where they had an old woman taking care and cooking for them. They divided the spoils of the plunder among the poor famished peasantry around, but they were compelled to penetrate to the innermost recesss of their fastness.They had caves or dugouts made in the bog banks close to this house, which can still be seen but only a little as the bog is being cut away and consequently the caves are nearly all cut away.
The ruins of the house are not very plain to be seen, You would take it for an old house.An old man who is now dead told me that this band of men was betrayed to the Red-coats by a family by the name of Gallagher. It happened like this.One bright moonlight night they were (The Raparee's) dividing the spoils of the raid on the night, when a woman of the Gallaghers, thinking that it was daylight struck off for Ballyshannon for two stone of meal. She happened to come unawares on the band of men, and they dividing the loot. They immediately seized her and one of them produced a prayer book and made her swear that she would not speak of what she had seen on that night to any one. She was released when she had made the promise, but she did not proceed to Ballyshannon. Instead she returned home and she "hit on a plan" how to divulge the secret which was imposed on her. She asked her brother (who, by the way was a spy for the government) to go to the other side of a certain stone fence and to remain at a certain spot. He did as she told him. She went to the same spot and stopped at the opposite side to him.Then she told the stone fence what she had witnessed a short time before, but in reality the stone fence let it in one side and out the other, but not so the brother he repaired at once to the nearest military station and had the brave Raparee's in gaol before they were fully aware of how it happened.

---

[69] Cosgrave J

So ended the Bold Raparees their lives on the gallows or in some British settlement".[70]

The Kilkenny Brennans

In the year 1680, in the County of Kilkenny, a trio of Tories appeared on the scene. These were the Brennans, three cousins; Patrick from Killeshin, which is south eastern County Laois, and west of the town of Carlow and "Tall" James and "Little" James who came from Croghtenclogh.

The Brennans were dispossessed during the Cromwellian confiscations and as a consequence took to the hills in search of restitution or retribution. They were very successful and within the short span of three years had robbed an amount said to be in excess of £18,000. The Brennans are said to have been the founding members of the Kellymount Gang, who operated from Coolcullen wood near the townland of Kellymount in the Parish of Shankil.

They are mentioned in a letter dated February 5, 1683, from Thomas Otway, Protestant bishop of Ossory, to Richard Earl of Arran, (son of the Duke of Ormonde), in which he complains of the Brennans mischief and alleges that the day before they had lured, by a wile, one of the witnesses against them into a wood and there had cut out his tongue (letter from Arran to Ormonde, November 6 Ormonde M.S.S, new series, vol VII P 157)

In June 1683 they were at Balleyragget Heath to the west of Castlecomer, heavily armed with, pistols, swords and carbines, where they robbed a merchant by the name of Alexander Marshall and his two companions of goods and cash to the value of £100. In July 1683, John Keating, Lord Chief Justice of Common Pleas in Ireland, wrote to Arran complaining that the Brennans were commiting frequent robberies in County Tipperary and County Limerick in the company of a fellow tory named Munshaglin Byrne (letter from Keating to Arran July 27 1683 Ormond M.S.S new series vol vii p86)

After robbing the home of the grandson of the Lord Chancellor in Brazeel seven miles north of Dublin, they were pursued with such vigour that they fled to Ringsend on the outskirts of Dublin and took ship to England. In October 1683 they were in the city of Chester where they were confronted by one of their victims namely Alexander Marshall, who had them arrested and commited to gaol at the North Gate in Chester.

According to the deposition of Richard Wright, Keeper of the gaol, he received the three Brennans into his custody on October 19, he kept them in irons during the day and took their clothing from them at night to prevent their escape. On the evening of their second day in gaol, the Brennans, well shackled, were eating supper with Wright, his wife and Thomas Greene, a prisoner for debt, who was employed by the gaoler as his

---

[70] N.F.C. 104 : p 434 T O Babhartaigh, Cluain Uí Ruairc, Co Leitrim

assistant. During dinner, Tall James said something in Irish to the other two Brennans, wherupon Small James drew a knife and stomped upon Wright until he promised to keep still; Tall James seized Greene, while Patrick seized Mrs Wright.

Patrick then obtained arms and the necessary key to free them from their irons. They took the gaol key from Wright's pocket. While all this was happening a servant maid in Wrights employ came in only to flee to the cellar where she locked herself in.

The three Brennans made good their escape and disappeared into the night. The Brennans eventually surfaced in Ireland but kept a low profile for a number of years. On September 17 1685, James Brennan of Croghtenclogh and Patrick Brennan in the company of Donal Brennan of Crutt, Teighe Brennan of Aghamucky, Donal Brennan of Croghtenclogh, Jeffry Brennan and Loughlin Brennan broke into Kilkenny Castle, the chief residence of the Duke of Ormond, and stole a pair of andirons, a silver tankard, and the ears of a silver serving fountain (the belly being too large to fit out the window) to the value of £1,000. They also stole a box of silver plate belonging to George Mathew, Ormonde's half brother and land agent.

In January 1686, at the behest of Mathews, a petition was presented to the government in Ireland for a pardon in return for discovering a Quaker counterfeiter and a number of horse-thieves. This petition was rejected.

In February 1686 Mathew had the Brennans taken into protective custody for a period of seven months on the condition of the discovery and recovery of Ormonde's stolen silver plate. They were also to discover horse-thieves and a, "Certaine Quaker living in this kingdome who coynes vast somes of mony as six shilling peeces, 3 s peeces, English halfe crownes and shillings, etc".

In order to accomplish this, the Brennans were to be free from arrest and have the use of their firearms and horses for travelling. Taking advantage of the Lord Lieutenant's authority, the Brennans recovered the stolen plate in a nocturnal operation.

The last reference to the tory Brennans of Idough was made by William King who became Protestant Archbishop of Dublin, in 1691 he wrote,

"The famous tories, the Brennans (sic) who had been guilty of Burglary and Robbery, but of murder also, who were under sentence of death and escaped by breaking Gaol were made among the rest, officers in the Catholic army".[71]

Lilli Burlero

Ho, brother Teague, dost hear de decree,
Lilli Burlero bullen a la,
Dat we shall have a new debittie,

---

[71] William King, The state of the Protestants in Ireland under the late King Jame's Government p31

Lilli Burlero bullen a la,
Lero, lero, lero, lero, Lilli Burlero bullen a la
Lero, lero, lero, lero, Lilli Burlero bullen a la.

Ho by my soul it is a Talbot,
Lilli Burlero bullen a la,
And he will cut the English throat,
Lilli Burlero bullen a la.
Chorus
Though by me soul the English do prat,
Lilli Burlero bullen a la,
The Laws on their side, the devil knows that,
Lilli Burlero bullen a la

Chorus
But if dispence do come from the Pope,
Lilli Burlero bullen a la,
We'll hang Magna Cart and themselves in a rope,
Lilli Burlero bullen a la.

Chorus
And the good Talbot is made a lord,
Lilli Burlero bullena la,
And he with brave lads is coming aboard
Lilli Burlero bullen a la
Chorus
There was an ould prophecy found in a bog,
Lilli Burlero bullen a la,
That Ireland be ruled by an ass and a dog,
Lilli Burlero bullen a la

Chorus
And now this prophecy is come to pass,
Lilli Burlero bullen a la,
For Talbots the dog, and Tyrconnells the ass,
Lilli Burlero bullen a la

(Percy Collection)

Composed by Thomas Ist Marguess of Wharton (1648-1714)
Written in response to the appointment by James 11 of Richard Talbot Earl
of Tyrconnell (1630-1691) as Lord Deputy of Ireland, and the creation of a
Catholic army and civil service.The refrain' Lillibuléro bullen a la' is a
mocking parody of the Gaelic war-cry used in the rebellion of 1641, ("An lile

bá léir é, ba linne an lá)- 'The lily prevailed, the day was ours'.This song was sung by Williamite soldiers and it is the boast of its author, that it whistled King James II out of three kingdoms.

Richard Talbot, Earl and titular Duke of Tyrconnel 1630 – 1691.

Richard Talbot was one of the few to survive Oliver Cromwell's destruction of Drogheda. He fled to France and joined the Stuart court in exile. He was part of an un-successful plot to assassinate Oliver Cromwell, and managed to escape the night before he was due to be executed in the Tower of London. On his return to France he joined with James, Duke of York. After the Restoration of the Monarchy he returned to London where he became involved in politics. Following the death of his first wife, he married Frances Hamilton (nee Jennings) and consequently became brother-in-law to Sir John Churchill, the future Duke of Marlborough. In May 1685, he was elevated to the Peerage of Ireland as the Earl of Tyrconnel, the title by which he is generally remembered. In the same year under the authority of the Crown he began the reorganisation of the army in Ireland. He began to replace the Protestant army officer corps with one predominantly Catholic, and to disarm the Protestant militia. Following the events of 1688, he enlarged the army to a strength of 50,000, it was the strength of this army that convinced King James II of England and King Louis XIV of France that the time was ripe for a second Stuart Restoration. Following the defeat at the Boyne his influence declined, he was overshadowed by Patrick Sarsfield and other Irish leaders. He died of a stroke in Limerick on the 14th of August 1691.

John Reily and Coote of Cootehill.

The Cootes of Cootehill in County Cavan were notorious for their Tory hunting activities, and were responsible for hunting down most of the O' Hanlon band One of Redmonds compatriots John O' Reily was pursued with such fervour that he quit the country and sought refuge in France. Some time later Squire Coote while travelling in France, was engaged in a duel in which he killed a man. As duelling was against the law in France, he was brought to trial and found guilty. John Reily, hearing of Squire Cootes predicament came to his aid, rescued him from gaol, and helped him to escape back to Ireland On his return to Ireland, the Squire made some enquiries as to the whereabouts of O' Reily's family. Found his Father living on a mountainside in a small cabin with one cow and a small potato plot. He made him a freehold lease of a small farm in the County of Monaghan.[72]

---

[72] Cosgrave J

Patrick Sarsfield

Patrick Sarsfield was reared at Tully Castle near Kildare Town along with his elder brother and two sisters. Tradition holds that his mother Annie O Moore Sarsfield who, was the daughter to Rory O'Moore (Rory-of-the-Hills) taught her children the native Irish language and that at her knee they learned the ancient stories of Ireland.

The Sarsfield Family Tree

That Thomas Sarsfield was standard- bearer to Henry 11 of England in the year of Our Lord 1180. He was the father of Richard Sarsfield, who was captain general under Henry III of England, anno 1230.

This Richard had two sons, viz Sarsfield and Henry, and Sarsfield had a son named Sarsfield and Henry had a son named Henry, who came to Ireland and lived in Cork for some time, and married the daughter of Fitzgerald, by whom he had the lands from Bealogh Farrye to Kilmallock, Six miles in length in the county of Limerick, which fruitful and pleasant Estate he and his posterity enjoyed, together with the said Kilmallock for many generations.The genealogy aforesaid from Thomas, the first of all this family of the Sarsfields, to John, who lived in the reign of Henry VI. I had it out of old Irish books now in the custody of Hugh MacCurtain, alias Curtis one of the chief antiquarians of this kingdom of Ireland, and from several other relations of the family's to the year 1640; and for the rest I had out of the books of my own office (there being little or nothing in it) and out of several warrantable authors; and also from ancient of worth and credit- in witness. Thereof, nostri saluit feri 1714 The Most Noble Potent and Honourable Sir Dominick Sarsfield, Viscount Kilmallock, Lord Baron of Barret's Country and primear baronet of Ireland. Creation 'Primear Baronet of Ireland' by Patent 30 September 1619, 16 Jac 1 'Lord Baron of Barret's country, Lord Viscount Kilmallock' by Patent dated 8 May1625. 'Lord Chief Justice of Common Pleas' 'Attorney General of Munster' 4 September 42. And one of the lords of his majesty's most hon privy council of Ireland.

Family of Kilmallock

Sir Dominick was second son of Edmund, and brother to John, he was created lord baron of Ireland and Viscount Kinsale, by letters Patent granted at New Market 13 February by King JohnI of England, in the twenty second year of his reign by reason that the Lord Baron Courcey challenged the said title of Kinsale, but the title of Lord Viscount Kilmallock was continued still by Patent to Sir Dominick, from the time he was created Lord Viscount Kinsale.

The original Patent was in my custody in King James II's time. This Henry had a son named John, the father of David, who was the father of Henry, whose son John was admiral of the fleet of King Henry VI's of England; he married a daughter of – Purcells, she bore him two sons, Edmund and Roger. This Edmund had two sons, viz, John and Sir Dominick.

John had two sons, Patrick and James, Patrick married Hellin daughter to – White and by her had , John, Francis, Geoffrey, Ignatious, and Hellin; She was married to Jeffrey Galway.

John the eldest married Catherine, daughter to – Purdon, by her he had Francis now living; James second son of John and brother of aforesaid, married Hellin Rice and by her he had Paul who went to Nantz in France, in Oliver Cromwell's time and married there a French gentlewoman, and by her had Sir James Sarsfield, now living in France.The Family of Lucan Roger, second son of John, who was thirteen years admiral to King Henry V1 As above said was married to a daughter of Christopher Cusack of Kilmallock in the county of Meath and had by her John of Sarsfieldstown, in the said County, and by her he had two sons, Patrick and William.

Patrick was Mayor of Dublin anno 1554; he died sans issue. Sir William, chosen Mayor of Dublin anno 1556 and in the same year Sir Henry Sidney, being Lord Lieutenant of Ireland, and Knight of the Most Holy Garter, in the ninth year of Queen Elizabeth; he being in England and his lady in Drogheda.

John O' Neil came to surprise Drogheda with a strong party, whereupon the Lady Sidney sent to Dublin, and the said Sir William with all speed marched with a select party of horse and foot towards Drogheda, fought and routed John O' Neil and all his adherents and by that means rescued the Lady Sidney from the danger she was likely to undergo; for which service, the Lord Sidney, on his return to Ireland, knighted him in Christchurch Dublin.This Sir William married Margaret, daughter of Sir Lucas Dillon, and had by her William, Lucas, Robert, and Johanna, this William married Anne, daughter of Sir Patrick Barnwell, Knight. Patrick, second son of Sir William married Mabel Fitzgerald and by her had Peter and many other children. This Peter married Elinor, daughter of Terlogh O' Dempsey, Lord Viscount Clanmalier and had by her Patrick; he married Anne daughter of Roger Moore, and by her had Patrick, created Earl of Lucan by King James II Anno 1688. This Patrick was General to King James's army, and married Honora, daughter of the Earl of Clanricard, who bore him one son named Jacobus Franciscus Edwardus.[73] Patrick is famed for his defence of Limerick in 1691 and the terms he received in the Treaty of Limerick, a treaty which was not honoured by the English.

---

[73] Crossley Aaron *Peerage of Ireland. Dublin 1725*

Slán chum Padhraic Sáirséal

A Phadraic Sáirséal, 'slán go dtí tú,
Ó chuadhais do'n Frainac, is do champaí scaoilte
Ag déanamh do ghearáin leis na ríghibh
As dfhág tú Éire agis Gaedhil bhocht claoidhte
2
A Phádraic Sáirséal, guidhe gach nduine leat
Mo ghuidhe-se féin, a's guidhe Mhic Muire leat
Ó thóg tú an tÁth Caol ag gabháil trí Biorra dhuit
'S gur ag Cuileann O gCuanach buadhabh Luimneach
3
Geobhad-sa siar an sliabh so im aonar,
As geobhad aniar arís más féidir;
Is ann do chonnaic mé an campa Gaedhealach
An dream bocht silte nár chuir le na chéile

Translation

Farewell O Patrick Sarsfield, may luck be on your path;
Your camp is broken up. Your work is marred for years;
But you go to kindle into flame the King of France's wrath
Though you leave sick Eire in tears.
2
The Son of Mary guard you and bless you in the end!
'Tis altered is the time when your legions were astir,
When at Cullen you were hailed as conquerer and friend
And you crossed Narrow-water near Birr,
3
I'll journey to the North, over mount, moor, and wave;
'Tis there I first beheld drawn up in file and line,
The brilliant Irish hosts; they were bravest of the brave,
But alas they scorned to combine[74]

James Clarence Mangan

The Penal Laws

The Penal Laws were in operation from 1695, and were not repealed completely until the Catholic Emancipation Act was passed in 1829. Their purpose was the destruction of the Catholic faith in Ireland .They were introduced as a consequence of the Irish Catholics taking up

---

[74] Carty James <u>Ireland from the flight of the Earls to Grattan's Parliament1607 1782</u>C.J.Fallon Dublin

arms in support of King James II, whose army was defeated at the battle of the Boyne on July 1, 1690. In 1672, James, the Duke of York, who was the heir apparent to the throne of England, converted to the Catholic faith. Immediately a powerful opposition group was formed in England to deny James access to the throne. The King, Charles 11, made a very resolute stand to ensure that James would succeed hin upon his death.

In the middle of this political storm a Protestant clergyman by the name of Titus Oates, produced a forty-three article document, later enlarged to eighty one, to the effect that the King was to be ass-assinated on the orders of the Pope that the Pope had plans to take control of England. The Pope had given orders to the Director General of the Jesuit Order to nominate men to key positions in the government and the military; that the King of France had arranged with leading Irishmen the landing of the French army in Ireland, and that all protestants were to be murdered . Belief in this so called

"Popish Plot" spread rapidly throughout England bringing in its wake a wave of anti-Catholicism. The over reaction of the Irish administration leading to the arrest of many of the Catholic hierarchy including the Catholic Primate, Oliver Plunkett. He was brought to London and charged with " high treason, for endeavoring and compassing the Kings death, and to levy war in Ireland, and to alter the true religion there, and to induce a foreign power". The inevitable result of this trial was his execution, (see chapter entitled St Oliver Plunkett). Despite the fact that the terms under which Patrick Sarsfield surrendered Limerick stipulated toleration for Catholics in Ireland. "Roman Cathoilcs were to enjoy such rights of worship as are consistent with the laws of Ireland, or as they did enjoy in the reign of King Charles 11. This treaty was reneged upon by King William of Orange and there began in his reign, and continued during the reign of Queen Anne and the two Georges, a series of anti-Catholic enactments known as the penal laws. A parallel could not be found outside of hell for these infamous laws, except perhaps the decrees of Louis XIV of France against the Huguenots, or laws in Sweden against the Jesuits

"It is a memorable fact that the ferocious law of 1703 which first reduced the Irish Catholics to a condition of selfless servitude, does not allege as the reason for its provisions any political crime. It was called, 'An Act to prevent the further growth of Popery'."[75]

Under these laws, no Catholic could join the army or the navy , they were barred from commerce, the practice of law, and from all civic activity. Catholics were not allowed to vote , hold any Crown office , they could not sit in parliament, or purchase land . The law dictated that

---

[75] Lecky W.E.H. A History of Ireland in the Eighteenth Century. (The University of Chicago Press

at the death of a Catholic land owner his land was to be divided among all his sons, unless the eldest son became a Protestant, in that case he would inherit the whole. No Catholic was allowed to buy land, or inherit or receive it as a gift from Protestants, or hold life annuities or mortgages on land, or leases for more than thirty one years, or any lease of such terms that the profits of the land exceeded one third of the rent. If a Catholic leaseholder by his skill or industry, so increased his profits that they exceeded this proportion and did not immediately make a corresponding increase in his rent, his farm passed to the first Protestant who made the discovery Catholics were forbidden to attend school, they could not keep school, nor could they send their children abroad to school. Catholic worship and practice was for-bidden under law. A Catholic could not own a horse above the value of five pounds. On the death of a Catholic a Protestant Minister must be hired to officiate at the funeral. Catholic Bishops and other higher ecclesiastics were banished from Ireland, and if they returned, on capture could be hanged, drawn, and quartered. These were the main provisions of The Penal Laws, which were described by Edmund Burke the orator as "a machine as well fitted for the oppression, impover-ishment and degradation of a people, and the debasement in them of human nature itself, as ever proceeded from the perverted ingenuity of man". [76]

Lady Wilde (*Speranza)* states,
" One of the most beautiful and sublimely touching records in all human history is that of the unswerving devotion of the Irish people to their ancient faith,through persecutions and penal enactments more insulting and degrading than were ever inflicted in any other land by one Christian sect upon another."[77]

One of the Penal Statutes enacted during the reign of Queen Anne gives a synopsis for a bill for the registration of Popish priests under twelve different headings. Clause number ten states that after the first of January 1759 any person who knowingly hears the mass of an unregistered priest, or harbors him shall be liable to pay a fine of one hundred pounds, the fine payable to the person who prosecutes.
"It must be observed also that the penal code, which began under William, which assumed its worst features under Anne, and which was largely extended under George I and II, was entirely unprovoked by any active disloyalty on the part of the Catholics.It is surely absurd to describe the Irish Catholics as having manifested an incurably rebellious and ungrateful

[76] Burke Edmund
[77] Wild Lady 9Speranza) Ancient Legends, Mysric Charms and Superstitions of Ireland. London

disposition because in the contest of the revolution they took the part of the hereditary sovereign."[78]

Extract from a letter by Edmund Burke M.P. to Sir H. Langrishe 1792.
"You, who have looked deeply into the spirit of the Popery Laws, must be perfectly sensible, that a great part of the present mischief which we abhor in common, has arisen from them. Their declared object was to reduce the Catholics of Ireland to a miserable populace, without property, without estimation, without education. The professed object was to deprive the few men who in spite of these laws might hold or obtain any property amongst them, of all sort of influence or authority over the rest. They divided the nation into two distinct bodies, without a common interest, sympathy or connection; one of which bodies was to possess all the franchises, all the property, all the education; the others were to be drawers of water and cutters of turf for them. Are we to be astonished that when, by the efforts of so much violence in conquest, and so much policy in regulation, continued without intermission for near an hundred years, we have reduced them to a mob."

The French jurist, Montesquieu, said of the penal laws,
"They were conceived by demons, written in blood, and registered in Hell"

The Act of Registration 1704

"All popish priests now in Ireland shall at the next quarter sessions of the peace to be held in the several counties next after 24 June 1704 return their names and places of abode to the respective clerks of the peace in the counties where the said popish priests reside with their age, the parish of which he pretends to be popish priest, the time and place of their first receiving popish orders and from whom they received the same shall then enter into recognizance with two sureties in the sum of £50 that such popish priest shall be of peaceable behavior and not remove out of such county into any other part of the Kingdom.".

This Act of Registration was followed in 1709 by the infamous Oath of Abjuration.

---

[78] Lecky W.E.H. A History of Ireland in the 18th Century

Oath of Abjuration

I _____ abhor and abjure the authority of the Pope as well in regard of the Church in general, as in regard of myself in particular. I condemn and anathematise the tenet that any reward is due to good works. I firmly believe and avow that no reverence is due to the Virgin Mary, or any other saint in Heaven and that no petition of adoration can be addressed to them without idolatry. I assert that no worship reverence is due to the sacrament of the Lord's Supper or to the elements of bread and wine after consecration, by whomsoever that consecration may be made. I believe there is no purgatory but that it is a popish invention, so is also the tenet that only the Pope can grant indulgences. I do firmly believe that neither the Pope nor any other priest cam remit sin, as the papists rave. And all this I swear.

The Hedge-School

"And whereas it is found by experience that tolerating and conniving at papists keeping schools or instructing youths in literature is one great reason of many of the natives of this kingdom continuing ignorant of the principles of true religion and strangers to the scriptures, and of their neglecting to conform themselves to the laws and statutes of this realm, and of their not using the English habit and language, to the great prejudice of the puplic weal thereof: Be it further enacted by the authority aforesaid that no person whatsoever of the popish religion shall publicly teach school or instruct youth in learning, or in private houses teach or instruct youth in learning within this realm from henceforth, except only the children or others under the guardianship of the master or mistress of such private house or family, upon pain of twenty pounds and also being committed to prisin, with bail or mainprize, for the space of three months for every such offence".

(An act to restrain foreign education under William III 1694)

The hedge-school was another feature of the penal times in Ireland when the Irish Catholic was denied the right to own a school, or to teach school. The people ever resourceful would pay a wandering schoolmaster to teach their children in some secluded spot, hence the name hedge-school.

"In a triangular patch of ground on the margin of the first boreen south of this school and to the left of the road are still visible the remnants of the last hedge-school that flourished in the locality. Sheltered from the cold north winds by a low hill and a fringe of hazel and sally, this retreat is as sylvan and sunny as any I know. In a district cent be cent more populous at one time than it is now, that mud walled academy, no doubt flourished for a considerable number of years. In my own memory the bosses or rough sods used as seating accommodation were still visible, and rough school slates, are said to have been dug up in the North East corner.

The pedagogue who last wielded the wand of power in this seminary was one Paddy Corrigan, said to be from the Loughside in Fermanagh. Paddy was a dandy in his own way, and living as he did among the neighbouring farmers, was a great favourite with the ladies. He married while in this district, but with the dispersal of his school, himself and his wife took the road on themselves and were never seen around these parts again.

Paddy was a keen disciplinarian, and his normal mode of punishment was to hoist the delinquent on the broad of one of the high briars and while in that position to favour him with a judicious application of the birch. He was by all accounts cruelly disposed, and was hated cordially by the many bare legged urchins that hung around his dilapidated school- house. On more than one occasion these same urchins grown into stronger bodied men have had their hour of revenge by waylaying and sorely beating the tyrannical teacher.

Paddy's method of teaching was at once unique and serviceable. Of maps he had none; but a burnt stick in his hand traced on the hard bare floor of the hedge-school the outline of whatever country or locality then under study. A pupil was then sent walking on the sketch and his movements were eagerly followed by the class, who traced him to to Canada, or Brazil etc at the command of the teacher.

Dressed in his corderoy knee britches with long stockings to match, and sporting a wide brimmed hat and a tight fitting jacket Paddy was the life and soul of the party.

As a dancer his equal was hard to find, and his voice was so sweet that it was said that he had his music from the fairies. Sure enough when he first came to the county he was found on a summer's morning in the shadow of Shee Fort and he fast asleep, and although many would say that he fled there in drink, the majority hold that he was even then in communion with the fairy folk.

But now he is seen no more, and even his very name is forgotten. To us however he is a link with the dreary days of famine and persecution, and his desolate hearth a monument of a neglected people".[79]

---

[79] N.F.C. S 954 : pp 76-78 Maire nic Cassain Threemilehouse (Drumsnatt) Co Muineachain.

Carrickburn Hill, County Wexford, Hedge-School and Mass-Rock.
Situated off the N25 between Wexford and Ballynabola, Carrickburn Hill contains many monuments to our ancient past, including a grove of trees where the United Irishmen gathered before attacking New Ross in 1798.. The Mass-Rock and Hedge school can be reached by following the blue marked trail up through the forest, or by taking the next turn left off the N25 and ascending this road until you come upon the site which is marked. The picture above shows the Hedge School to the foreground with the Mass-Rock to the rear marked by a stone cross.

O.S.I. Discovery Series Map No 76 grid 833256.

Eoghan Rua O'Súilleabháin the noted poet from Sliabh Luachra in Co. Kerry was a hedge-school master in many parts of Ireland, he spent some time as a wandering labourer, and did a stint in the English navy also. During this period he composed Rodney's Glory, in honour of Admiral Rodney, one of the few poems he wrote in English and with it he hoped to gain his discharge, in this endeavour he failed.

Pure Learned Priest

Pure learned priest! Akin to Neill and Art,
Whose power protective cheer'd the poet's heart,
The first in danger's van-(so bards have sung them),
Pray tell thy flock a teacher's come among them.

Well skill'd in ancient Greek and Roman lore,
Fame-laden lays since Erin's days of yore,
And eke the foeman's tongue, upborne by Law,
Whose phrase uncouth distorts the Gaelic jaw.

Upborne by Law which exiles heroes tall,
Which dooms, by traitor's steel, the chieftains fall,
Doom's Erin's brave no refuge save their God;
And me to wield the village pedant's rod!

Mild man of God, and fair religion's glory,
Deep read in holy tomes and tuneful story,
With thy sweet tongue consign to village fame
What learned lore enwreaths thy poet.s name![80]

This poetic church notice was composed by Eoghan Rua Ó'Súilleabháin announcing the opening of his hedge school in North Cork.

In 1776 Arthur Young reported seeing schools held aback of a hedge. In 1796 the French traveller De Latocnaye tells of seeing the hedge schools. In 1714 A high Sheriff of Longford reports holding in jail "Patrick Ferrall and John Lennan, convicted of being Popish school-masters under sentence of transportation".
The High Sheriff of Dublin holds"two popish school-masters under sentence of transportion.The High Sheriff of Wicklow reports the dispersal of a "riotous assembly" at St Kevin's in Glendalough.
"We rode all night and reached the scene at 4am on June 3rd. The rioters immediately dispersed; and we pulled down their tents, threw down and demolished their superstitious crosses, destroyed their wells, and apprehended and committed one Toole, a popish schoolmaster".
William Carleton on the Hedge school

"The very name and nature of hedge schools are proof of this; for what stronger point could be made out, in illustration of my position, than the

---

[80] Reliques of Irish Jacobite Poetry, Dublin. Samuel J Mahen 1844

fact that, despite of obstacles, the very idea of which would crush ordinary enterprise – when not even a shed could be obtained in which to assemble the children of an Irish village, the worthy pedagogue selected the first green spot on the sunny side of a quickset thorn hedge which he conceived adapted for his purpose and there under the scorching rays of a summer sun, and in defiance of spies and statutes, carried on the work of instruction".[81]

Peter O'Dornin
Peadar ua Doirnin

Peter O'Dornin was born in the year 1682, near the Rock of Cashel in County Tipperary as the following quatrain written by him attests,

> *"Do bhídh árus mo chaired a g-Caisiol na ríogh,*
> *Is é dasácht na Galltacht do sgar mise dhíobh;*
> *Thug mé rása fó'n tráth sin go mullach Dhruim Críoch,*
> *Mar a bh-fuair mé fáilte gan táimhleas 's meadhair ganchíos"*

> "The lands of my fathers were at Cashel of the Kings,
> But the black English tyrant-laws drove me from thence;
> So I fled to Drumcree, as an eagle on wings,
> And I found welcome there, without grudging or expense."[82]

He showed intellectual promise at an early age which prompted his people to educate him for the priesthood. Unfortunately the imposition of the Penal Laws was to prevent him attaining this goal. A fugitive from his native Tipperary he made his way north to Drumcree, near Portadown, in the county Armagh. Here he produced an elaborate poem entitled,"The Ancient divisions of Ireland, and an Account of the different Septs that from time to time Colonised it." This work brought him to the attention of the Hon Arthur Brownlow, who took him under his patronage, to instruct his family, revise his Irish records and enhance his library. This friendship lasted for a number of years until during an election campaign Arthur Brownlow took exception to Peter O'Dornin's independent attitude and withdrew his patronage. Sometime after this he met and married a young woman by the name of Rose Turner and settled down in the vicinity of Forkhill, where he opened a school at Kilcurry. This school was shut down by the notorious Johnston of the Fews, which forced him to join with a band of Rapparees. As a teacher, he was in competition with a Maurice O'Gorman who was

---

[81] Carleton William, <u>Traits and Stories of the Irish Peasantry,</u>Dublin, James Duffy & co ltd 15 Wellington Quay
[82] James Clarence Mangan, <u>Poets and Poetry of Munster</u>

much respected in the area. .However, Peter's scholarship and teaching ability soon won over the majority of the students and O'Gorman had to leave the area and go to Dublin .O'Dornin spent the rest of his life in the vicinity of Forkhill, here he wrote a humorous poem in which he satirized O'Gorman. He died on the fifth of April 1768 at the age of eighty-six and is buried near the north-east wall of Urney churchyard in County Louth.

> Still crouching 'neath the sheltered hedge,
> Or stretched on mountain fern,
> The teacher and his pupils met
> Feloniously to learn.

Seamus MacMurphy
Seamus Mac Murchaidh
Bheirneach –na- Scéimhe, An Beirneach Mór

The earliest chiefs of the Fews were of the MacMurphy clan. They were commonly known as the Beirnigh (na Beirnig) from an ancestor named Beirn, who was son of Fearghal, a king of Ireland who died in A.D 718. He was brother to another king Nial Frasach who died in 765. Nial Frasach was ancestor to the O'Neill clan.
They are mentioned in the Annals of the Four Masters as follows,
"A.D 1172- Maolmuire Mac Murchadha, Taoiseach Mhuintire- Bhirn do marbhadh le hAodh Mac Aonghusa agus le Clann Aodha hUa nEachdhach Uladh"
(Maolmuire MacMurphy, chief of Miuntir-Beirn was killed by Hugh MacGennis and by the Clan Aodha from Iveagh.).
Seamus MacMurphy was born in Carnally around 1720 local tradition holds that he was the tallest and most handsome man in South Armagh in the 18th century. It is said that he used to introduce himself to his intended victims in the following manner,
"Mise Seamus 'A' Murchaidh is deise 'bhfuil in Éieinn."
(I am Seamus MacMurphy the most handsome man in Ireland)
Local tradition remembers him as a poet, the founder of a school of poetry, and a fearless Rapparee The following lines were penned by him while looking out from Carrickasticken Mountain over Dundalk and its bay.

> Is fuath liom an baile-cuain
> Dá nGoirtidhe Bhaile-Mhic-Buain
> Baille duairc gan chill gan chrios
> Nár théidhinn ann d'each no do chois

> I hate the harbour-town
> Which once was called Baille Mhic Buain

183

A morose town without church or cross
May God keep me out of it willing or unwilling.

When Johnston of the Fews disbanded Peader Ó'Doirnín's hedge –school at Kilcurry, Ó'Doirnín joined forces with MacMurphy and they set up a school of poetry, sometimes the sessions were held in Mullabawn, and sometimes in Dunreavey. Johnston of the Fews issued a proclamation in which he offered a reward for the arrest of Ó'Doirnín (as a person ill-disposed to the king, a favourite of the Pretender, who stirs up the people to rebel by his treasonable composition). There was a great popular meeting held on the summit of Sliabh Gullion during the summer on 1744.

MacMurphy presided at this meeting and made an impassioned speech in which he urged the people to submit no longer to foreign rule but to decide that, for the future, the Rapparees would take over the reins of Government. Rumours spread through the country that the Pretender was coming with an army. The young men joined the Rapparee bands. Johnston, fearing for his life, invited MacMurphy and Ó'Doirnín to a meeting. Fearing treachery they refused to attend. Johnston, under a safe-conduct from Ó'Doirnín came to the Rapparee camp. It is not known what inducements were offered during the negotiations that followed, but it was agreed that the two sides would not interfere with one another. Ó'Doirnín wrote a hypocritical poem entitled "Seón Johnston" in praise of the Tory-hunter, which in effect acted as a safe –conduct for Johnston. MacMurphy and Ó'Doirnín were fond of drinking and womanising and in pursuit of these habits they frequented a shebeen on the eastern side of Flagstaff, which was owned by a man named Patsy MacDacker, also known as Paitsí-na-tSléibhe, (Paddy of the Mountain). The shebeen was an excellent meeting place for the Rapparees, it was difficult to reach, it commanded a clear view of the surrounding countryside and was close to all the main roads, to Newry, to Mourne, to Dundalk, to the Cooley peninsula and the Fews .The main attraction for MacMurphy, however, was the shebeen owner's daughter Mollie MacDacker., with whom he was in love.

The lovers quarrelled, it is said that Mollie's jealousy was aroused by one of MacMurphy's comrades in arms, who was in love with Mollie himself. When the Rapparees returned to the Flagstaff after being in Dunreavey Wood, Arty Fearon used to tell Molly of the houses where MacMurphy stayed and also how he was intimate with Kate MacDonnell from Drumbally, and also with Peggy McGunshenan (Nugent) from Carnally. Peader Ó'Doirnín was also a frequent visitor to Barr-na-Fheadain. On one occasion Mollie plied him with drink and then persuaded him to compose a lampoon on Johnston of the Fews. This lampoon on Johnston was entitled Eireacach-na gCionn (The Heretic Headcutter) was scathing and vituperative. Armed with this Mollie set out for Roxborough to show the poem to Johnston and seek her revenge on MacMurphy. Mollie showed the poem to Johnston of the

Fews and told him that it had been written by Seamus MacMurphy. When Johnston read the poem he was incensed and said that the person who wrote it would suffer for it. He asked Mollie why she had brought it to him and she replied that MacMurphy had betrayed her love and she wanted revenge. Mollie advised Johnston that the following Sunday was the Patron Day of Kileavy and that MacMurphy would be spending Saturday night in their house on the Flagstaff she advised him to have the house surrounded by dawn on the Sunday and she would make sure that the Rapparee was drunk and that his powder would be watered. On Sunday morning Seamus woke from a drunken sleep to find himself in irons and under guard his anger was not directed at Mollie but at his companion in arms Arty Fearon for his part in the betrayal.

Seamus MacMurphy was put on trial before the Armagh Sessions on a charge of horse- stealing, it is more than likely that he did steal the horse but everyone knew that the real reason was the poetic lampoon on Johnston.

Peader Ó' Doirnín sent word to the court that he had written the poem and offered to give himself up, but to no avail. According to local tradition Seamus MacMurphy was sentenced on Monday and hanged on Tuesday.

After the hanging the body was left hanging for three days it was cut down and given to his friends for burial on Friday. He was waked for two nights in his mothers barn at Carnally and was buried in Creggan on Sunday.

His followers had brought home his speech and his verses from Armagh and all were incorporated by Ó'Doirnín in the official song which was ready for the wake.

Patsí-na-tSléibhe waited over in Armagh to witness the death of Seamus. As the rope was released, the sun suddenly shone out from behind the clouds, dazzled by the sun he had to keep one eye closed in order to see the hanging. It is said that he was never able to open that eye again and furthermore that all his descendants could be recognised by a squint in their eye.

It is also said that when Patsí went to collect the reward money he was given fifty pounds in copper coin which he had to carry away with him on his back from Armagh to Flagstaff, a distance of over twenty Irish miles. Coming down the Flagstaff and within sight of his own shebeen, his back gave way under the weight and he collapsed and died. Arty Fearon was killed on his way home from Armagh.

Mollie had repented the betrayal of her lover before the trial was held and was willing to testify to the truth of Ó'Doirnín's statement about the authorship of the poem. She drowned herself in the lough and is buried in the Cillín in Narrow-water Plantation.

The Lament for Seamus MacMurphy

I

On the peak of Sliabh Gullion the feast was prepared
And Seamus MacMurphy presided at the celebration
He who would refuse obedience to the English-speaking churl
But would reserve all loyalty to the wandering rapparees of Ireland

II

O Seamus MacMurphy, famed horseman
and scion of a noble race descended from kings
Why were you never told of the treachery of your own people?
Why did you not escape by night before you were sold for blood-money

III

A strong guard comes to capture the sleeping chief
Swords bared and guns at the ready
And Red Scotty from Armagh leads them
The court will be On Tuesday
And death await's at the head of the street.

IV

"Alas, that my hand had been crippled and my leg broken
Before I drank the cup of whiskey that Sunday morning
My hat was stolen, my pockets plundered
And to my eternal disgrace I let them capture me alive.

V

Alas, would that I were a blackberry on the mountain's brow
Or a fern leaf enjoying the rising sun
Or as Seamus MacMurphy, the handsomest man in Erin
I could spend another Christmas in Creggan.

VI

Were I only a rowan-berry on the Fathoms top
Or a bright little primrose in the sun's rays
Or a blackbird flying through Dunreavey's Wood
And around by Carnally where I was reared with such honour.

VII

Since the defeat of Aughrim our people have been in sorrow
Alas that I could never see my company marshalled for the battle
Alas that we are not at war with our men in camps
And Seamus MacMurphy the chief in command.

VIII

Alas that I am not on Ardaghy hill or on the high Fathom peak
Drinking from the glasses in my loved one's parlour
I would compose songs in her praise, and would drink her health with
pleasure
But, ochone, maiden of the white throat, it was you who left my mind
troubled.

IX

As the white-thorn blossoms light up the early summer
As the swaying of the white swan adds colour to the pools
Or as the rays of the bright sun dance through the ocean waves
So the memory of my love makes my mind delirious.

X

O! Molly, gentle and kind! even if it was you sent me to death
Come to my funeral and prepare my body for burial
If you still wish for our nuptials and desire all my love
Return and kiss my lifeless mouth, and my bruised heart will have rest.

XI

Dear sweetheart, you best could wash my burial shroud
Not in stagnant pools, nor even in red mountain streams
But with brandy and the crimson wine of France
And then bleach it 'neath the sun's bright rays

XII

To-morrow, St Patrick's Day, the Sessions begin
Perjury will hold sway with crowds to substantiate the lies
There will be a "strong" jury with Arty on his oath
And Tuesday will be settled for my last exit from the prison quarters.

XIII

I trusted you Arty, that had you discovered me
In the commission of a thousand murders
You would keep my secret as if it were your own
Yet now I see your breast stained with my blood.

XIV

Just a year previous to the day of my capture we were at Kileavey Patron
A year gone to-morrow we were at Dunleer Races
Today I'm lying in Armagh Gaol like hundreds before me
With my fate to be sealed at the Public Sessions

XV

In the gloomy cavern of the old dungeon I met a flat-footed hag
With about an inch of a' bob' in the centre of her bald forehead
She did not understand my dialect, and I would not speak English
But ever lonely for my heart's love the dark girl from the mountain valley

XVI

I'll rise to-morrow with the first break of day;
I'll have to walk through the street, guarded on all sides
Guns will be held high over me, without counting smaller arms
And death will await me at the end of the road

XVII

I was not aware that I had got fame from my residence in the King's
dungeon
Until I felt my shirt neck being smoothed back

My bright fancy hat being let fly with the wind
And the Beirnigh, in their crowds, gathered on every side of me
XVIII
Give my farewell to Patsy without spite
But I'm sorry that he got the chance to play the' fingers' on my knave
Give my farewell to Molly who sold me
But I forgive her for the crime of which she accused me
XIX
My heart goes out, tonight to my own loving mother
And to her five spinners who had the sweetest voices in Erin
In that residence where we used to exhibit our accomplishments
Under the guidance of a mother who had then no anxiety
XIXa) a variant)
Down in the Bog Lough are four pretty maidens
The four spinners with the sweetest voices inErin
Singing their rhymes that you could hear on the Hill of Howth
And Ally Murphy full tired trying to guide them
XX
Let me not forget Paddy and Rose MacArdle
My foster-parents from the days of my childhood
Find out if my comrades still hold out in their haunts
For I am now in Armagh without chance of escape.
XXI
Come to my funeral on Friday evening
Or, if you like follow it on the road on Sunday morning
Stretched in the coffin my ears will be searching
For the voices of Kate MacDonnell and the maidens of the district
XXII
Raise me up, and lay me down
And leave me in the barn till my mother mourns me
The keening women will each wear a yard of head-adornment
All but the dark-woman, who gave me her troth, the unfaithful dark-woman
XXIII
Raise me high and lay me low
Around to Carnally where I was reared when I had no sense
Peggy Nugent and the maidens of the country will assemble
And Beirnigh from Dunreavey's branchy Wood will gather on every side of
me.[83]

---

[83] Murrey L.P Rev PP <u>A South Armagh Outlaw Louth Archaeological Journal 1938</u>

The Legend of Mary's Well.

The following story was collected by Dr Douglas Hyde from Próinsías O'Conor, in Athlone, who heard it from an old woman who was herself from Ballintubber.

Mary's Well

[From the Irish]

"Long ago there was a blessed well in Balintubber (*i.e,town of the well*) in the county Mayo.There was once a monastery in the place where the well is now, and it was on the spot where stood the altar of the monastery that the well broke out. The monastery was on the side of a hill, but when Cromwell and his band of destroyers came to this country, they overthrew the monastery, and never left stone on top of stone in the altar that they did not throw down.

A year from the day that they threw down the altar-that was Lady Day in spring- the well broke out on the side of the altar, and it is a wonderful thing to say, but there was not one drop of water in the stream that was at the foot of the hill from the day that the well broke out.There was a poor friar going the road the same day, and he went out of his way to say a prayer upon the site of the blessed altar, and there was great wonder on him when he saw a fine well in its place. He fell on his knees and began to say his paternoster, when he heard a voice saying; "Put off your brogues, you are upon blessed ground, you are on the brink of Mary's Well, and there is the curing of thousands of blind in it; there shall be a person cured by the water of that well for every person who heard mass in front of the altar that was in the place where the well is now, if they be dipped three times in it, in the name of the Father, the Son, and the Holy Spirit.When the friar had his prayers said, he looked up and saw a large white dove upon a fir tree near him. It was the dove who was speaking. The friar was dressed in false clothes, because there was a price on his head, as great as on the head of a wild dog. [wolf] At any rate, he proclaimed the story to the people of the little village, and it was not long till it went out through the country. It was a poor place and the people in it had nothing [to live in] but huts and these filled with smoke. On that account there were many weak-eyed people amongst them. With the dawn, on the next day, there were about forty people at Mary's Well, and there was never man nor woman of them but came back with good sight.

The fame of Mary's Well went through the country, and it was not long till there was pilgrims from every county coming to it, and nobody went back without being cured; and at the end of a little time even people from other countries used to be coming to it.

There was an unbeliever living near Mary's Well. It was a gentleman he was, and he did not believe in the cure. He said there was nothing in it but pishtrogues (charms), and to make a mock of the people he brought a blind ass, that he had, to the well, and he dipped its head under the water. The ass got its sight back, but the scoffer was brought home as blind as the sole of your shoe.

At the end of a year it so happened that there was a priest working as a gardener with the gentleman who was blind. The priest was dressed like a workman, and nobody at all knew that it was a priest who was in it. One day the gentleman was sickly, and he asked his servant to take him out into the garden. When he came to the place where the priest was working he sat down. "Isn't it a great pity", says he, "that I cannot see my fine garden!"

The gardener took compassion on him, and said, "I know where there is a man who would cure you, but there is a price on his head on account of his religion." "I give my word that I'll do no spying on him, and I'll pay him well for his trouble," said the gentleman. "But perhaps you would not like to go through the mode of curing that he has," says the gardener. "I don't care what mode he has, if he gives me my sight," said the gentleman.

Now the gentleman had an evil character, because he betrayed a number of priests before that. Bingham was the name that was on him. However the priest took courage and said, "let your coach be ready on tomorrow morning, and I will drive you to the place of the cure; neither coachman nor anyone else may be present but myself, and do not tell anyone at all where you are going, or give anyone a knowledge of what is your business."

On the morning of the next day Bingham's coach was ready, and he himself got into it, with the gardener driving him. "Do you remain at home this time," Says he to the coachman, "and the gardener will drive me." The coachman was a villain and there was jealousy on him. He conceived the idea of watching the coach to see what way they were to go. His blessed vestments were on the priest, inside of his other clothes. When they came to Mary's Well the priest said to him, "I am going to get back your sight for you in the place where you lost it." Then he dipped him three times in the well, in the name of the Father, the Son, and the Holy Spirit and his sight came to him as well as ever it was.

"I'll give you a hundred pounds," said Bingham, "as soon as I go home." The coachman was watching and as soon as he saw the priest in his blessed vestments, he went to the people of the law, and betrayed the priest. He was taken and hanged, without judges, without judgement. The man who was after getting back his sight could have saved the priest, but he did not speak a word in his behalf.

About a month after this, another priest came to Bingham, and he dressed like a gardener, and he asked work of Bingham, and got it from him; but he was not long in his service until an evil thing happened to Bingham. He

190

went out one day walking through his fields, and there met him a good-looking girl, the daughter of a poor man, and he assaulted her, and left her half dead. The girl had three brothers, and they took an oath that they would kill him as soon as they could get hold of him. They had not long to wait. They caught him in the same place where he assaulted the girl, and hanged him on a tree, and left him there hanging.

On the morning of the next day millions of flies were gathered like a great hill round about the tree, and nobody could go near it on account of the foul smell that was round the place, and anyone who would go near it the midges would blind him. Bingham's wife and son offered a hundred pounds to anyone who would bring out the body. A good many people made an effort to do that, but they were not able.

They got dust to shake on the flies, and boughs of trees to beat them with, but they were not able to scatter them, nor to go as far as the tree. The foul smell was getting worse, and the neighbours were afraid that the flies and noisome corpse would bring a plague upon them.

The second priest was at this time a gardener with Bingham, but the people of the house did not know that it was a priest who was in it, for if the people of the law or the spies knew, they would take and hang him. The Catholics went to Bingham's wife and told her that they knew a man who would banish the flies.

"Bring him to me," said she, "and if he is able to banish the flies, that is not the reward he'll get, but seven times as much." "But," said they, "if the people of the law knew, they would take him and hang him, as they hung the man who got back the sight of his eyes for him before." "But," said she, "could not he banish the flies without the knowledge of the people of the law!" "We don't know," said they, "until we take counsel with him."

That night they took counsel with the priest and told him what Bingham's wife said. "I have only an earthly life to lose," said the priest, "and I shall give it up for the sake of the poor people, for there will be a plague in the country unless I banish the flies. On tomorrow morning I shall make an attempt to banish them in the name of God, and I have hope and confidence in God that he will save me from my enemies.

Go to the lady now, and tell her that I shall be near the tree at sunrise tomorrow morning, and tell her to have men ready to put the corpse in the grave."

They went to the lady and told her all the priest said. "If it succeeds with him," said she, "I shall have the reward ready for him, and I shall order seven men to be present."

The priest spent that night in prayer, and half an hour before sunrise he went to the place where his blessed vestments were hidden; he put those on, and with a cross in one hand, and with holy-water in the other, he went to the place where were the flies. He then began reading out of his book and scattering holy water on the flies, in the name of the Father, the Son, and the Holy Ghost. The hill of flies rose, and flew into the air, and made the heaven as dark as night. The people did not know where they went, but at the end of half an hour there was not one of them to be seen.

There was great joy on the people, but it was not long till they saw the spy coming, and they called to the priest to run away as quick as it was in him to run. The priest gave to the butts [took to his heels], and the spy [2] followed him, and a knife in each hand with him. When he was not able to come up with the priest he flung the knife after him. As the knife was flying out past the priests shoulder he put up his left hand and caught it, and without ever looking behind him he flung it back. It struck the man and went through his heart, so that he fell dead and the priest went free.

The people got the body of Bingham and buried it in the grave, but when they went to bury the body of the spy they found thousands of rats around about it, and there was not a morsel of flesh on his bones that they had not eaten. They would not stir from the body, and the people were not able to rout them away, so that they had to leave the bones over ground.

The priest hid away his blessed vestments and was working in the garden when Bingham's wife sent for him, and told him to take the reward that was for banishing the flies, and give it to the man that banished them, if he knew him. "I do know him, and he told me to bring him the reward tonight, because he has the intention of leaving the country before the law people hang him." "Here it is for you," said she, and she handed him a purse of gold.

On the morning of the next day the priest went to the brink of the sea, and found a ship that was going to France. He went on board, and as soon as he had left the harbour he put his priest's clothes on him, and gave thanks to God for bringing him safe. We do not know what happened to him from that out.

After that, blind and sore-eyed people used to be coming to Mary's Well, and not a person of them ever returned without being cured. But there never yet was anything good in this country that was not spoilt by somebody, and the well was spoilt in this way.

There was a girl in Ballintubber and she was about to be married, when there came a half- blind old woman to her asking alms in the honour of God and Mary. "I've nothing to give to an old blind thing of a hag, its bothered with them I am," said the girl. "That the marriage ring may never go on you until you are as blind as myself," says the old woman.

Next day, in the morning, the young girl's eyes were sore, and the morning after that she was nearly blind, and the neighbours said to her that she ought to go to Mary's Well. In the morning, early, she rose up and went to the well, but what should she see at it but the old woman who asked the alms of her, sitting on the brink, combing her head over the blessed well. "Destruction on you, you nasty hag, is it dirtying Mary's Well you are?" said the girl, "get out of that or I'll break your neck." "You have no honour nor regard for God or Mary, you refused to give alms in honour of them, and for that reason you shall not dip yourself in the well."

The girl caught a hold of the hag, trying to pull her from the well, and with the dragging that was between them, the two of them fell into the well and were drowned.

From that day to this there has been no cure in the well." [84]

Seán-na-Sagart
The Priest Hunter

Seán Ó Maoldhomhnaigh, John Mullowny was born in Béal Átha hÉan, County Mayo, he lived there, and in Ballintubber also, during the period of the Penal Laws. He had a fondness for strong drink and when he found himself penniless he took to stealing. On one occasion he stole a horse, and was caught and imprisoned but was released after converting to Protestantism and agreeing to spy on the Catholic clergy that remained in the area. Seán was responsible for the capture and death of many priests, He earned the title, Seán-na-Sagart (John of the Priest's), following the tragic events near the cavern of Pulnathacken. Here a priest by the name of Andrew Higgins was saying mass when a lookout raised the alarm, as the congeegation made their escape the Redcoats fired a volley after them. John Mullowny pursued the fleeing priest on horseback and rode into the sea and shot and killed Father Higgins as he was being pushed off in a currach.As a result of his activities the common people feared, and reviled him. Mullowny was of middle height but was reputed to be very strong and both arrogant and cunning. At the market held in Castlebar in the month of January, the sinister form of Seán-na-Sagart appeared wrapped in an old military cloak, on the fringes of a crowd that had gathered around a small stall. The priest-hunter was observing the stall- holder's assistant who was awkwardly measuring and wrapping material. He noted that the assistant made the sign of the cross over the parcel and whispered in the ear of the purchaser as he handed it over. There were so many people gathered around the stall that the priest-hunter did not dare to intervene, or attempt a capture. He was to well known in the community to escape observation for too long. Word of his presence soon reached the stall-holder's ear. While Seán's attention was distracted by a commotion at a neighbouring stall, the assistant vanished. Later that day Seán received information that the stall-holder's assistant was in fact Friar David Burke, a nephew of Father Bernard Kilger, whom Seán had arrested and deported to Portugal in 1716. He had intelligence that Friar Burke had come from Galway to meet his uncle who had already landed in Mayo, he also had heard rumours that Friar Burke would be celebrating mass on the following Sunday somewhere

---

[84] Douglas Hyde Love Songs of Connaught

in the town. On the following Sunday Seán-na-Sagart was abroad bright and early. He traversed every street and lane in the town, his eyes watching for any thing out of the ordinary. When he came by a house owned by a reputed Protestant convert, by the name of Myles Rourk, he found the owner of the house, looking on, while a group of men and boys were engaged in a game of pitch and toss. Seán noticed that every now and again one of the men or boys would slip away, he also noticed an open gateway which led to a nearby granary.

"I think I'll pitch a copper or two myself ", said Seán-na-Sagart. "Mr Mullowny" said Myles Rourke anxious to placate him.

"That kind of thing is alright for these ignorant Papists, but you and I being Churchmen should keep the Sabbath like good Protestants".

"Is that so", roared Mullowny with an oath, "I'll see what kind of service your keeping here", at the same time he made a dash through the gateway and ran towards the granary.

"Seán-na-Sagart! Seán-na-Sagart! "yelled the men by the roadside. "Seán-na-Sagart! "came in a cry of alarm from inside the granary.

Almost immediately there was a crash heard and a fearful shout of terror and suffering, for the upper floor of the granary was crowded with a congregation attending the mass which Friar Davy was celebrating. There was an instant rush for the exit, but the ancient floor collapsed beneath the feet of the panicked crowd sending them crashing to the ground below. It was a miracle that only one person was killed. When Friar Davy heard the name "Seán-na-Sagart" he quickly concealed the sacred vessels on his person, and leaped to the nearest window, jumped to the ground and made his way to the river, where a boatman awaited to take him to his hiding place.

Seán had a sister, Nancy, who was a young widow with two young children. Nancy lived in a small cabin in Ballintubber, she had a few acres of land and some cattle. Nancy had not seen her brother for more than a year, she did not condone his heavy drinking, and was deeply ashamed of his reputation as a priest-hunter. One day Seán tottered into her cabin, he was pallid as a corpse and fainting with weakness. He told her he had a terrible pain in his chest and he was afraid that he was dying. He leaned his head against the chimney breast, closed his eyes and fell into a broken slumber, groaning and moaning and exclaiming remorse and contrition and calling for a priest to hear his confession. She helped him to the bed and gave him a cup of water. Nancy was a pious woman, and even though she did not trust her brother because of his reputation, she could not bear the thought of him suffering eternal damnation. Convinced that he was dying, and that he was too weak to do any harm, she quietly left the cabin and went to find the priests in their hiding place. Nancy told the priests that she thought that her brother was dying and was calling for a priest to hear his confession. The priests were aware of Seán's reputation as a priest-hunter, and the younger priest, Father David Burke offered to go and give Seán the last rites, but the older priest Father Bernard Kilger insisted on going and told Father David to remain in hiding in case Seán proved false.

When the priest entered the little room with Nancy, Seán was still breathing heavily and muttering some broken and half distinct expressions of remorse; and beckoning Nancy aside Father Bernard softly approached the bed, and was bending close over the pretended dying man when the ruffian, started up yelling and cursing, and grasped at the priest's throat. The neck fastenings of the priest's cloak, gave way, the priest flung off the cloak and ran for the door. But he had scarcely passed through it when Seán was upon him again and dragged him to the ground. The frightened priest struggled desperately, Nancy seized her brother by the collar with both hands and pulled with all her strength, the priest broke free, Seán enraged at the intervention of his sister, flung her from him, and again attacked the priest and brought him to the ground and was trying to subdue him, when Nancy, afraid for the priest's life, struck her brother with the fire tongs, which caused him to relax his grasp, Father Bernard jumped to his feet, struck Shawn a blow with his fist and sprang for the door. Seán, by now in a murderous rage, pulled a knife from his belt and followed the priest. The poor priest had tripped as he ran for the door of the cabin and Seán was upon him in an instant and plunged the knife twice into the priest's neck shouting, "to heaven or to hell with you now, as you would not come quietly". Seán after having inflicted the fatal blow, wiped the priest's blood from the blade of the knife, and pointing it in a threatening manner at his sister, walked coolly away, swearing that if she uttered another word while he was in hearing distance from her he would bury it in her body too. When Nancy had recovered somewhat from her ordeal, she fell on her knees, and implored the Mother of God and the saints in heaven to intercede, and the Saviour to grant, that the curse of Almighty God might not pursue herself and her children for ever, for her being the instrument of the death of Father Bernard, and for having a brother whose name was to be cursed and reviled for by the people of Ireland for ever.

The following morning, before the dawn Father Davy performed a mass for the dead priest with some of the local peasants in attendance. As the grey dawn approached, this was the time arranged for the burial of the murdered priest, it being the most appropriate time for concealment. Father Davy, disguised in the cloak and head gear of a female, joined the small funeral procession of the murdered priest as it made its way to the Abbey. The funeral procession was little more than halfway from the Abbey when Seán sprang from the hedge-row and lunged at the disguised priest.

"Run Father Davy, run for your life," exclaimed two of the female mourners as they flung themselves in front of the priest-hunter. Father Davy threw off his cloak and cap and sprang forward a couple of paces – then stood for a moment with clenched fist and contracted brow, as if determined to measure strength with the murderer, and try to obtain revenge at all risks for the butchery of his uncle, Father Bernard. The priest took flight, just as Seán had shaken of the women who barred his way. Fear, and the natural desire of preserving life and liberty gave a burst of speed to the fleeing priest, who bounded over hedges, swept through fields and sprung across bog drains. The pursuing priest- hunter was more agile and used to exercise and began to gain on the priest, as they approached a small cottage the residence of the local blacksmith.

"Stop that dog of a priest – stop him," shouted the priest hunter. "That's your vile trade, ye rascal, not mine, and I have other things to be doing", replied the blacksmith.

The pursuit continued, and the priest was gaining ground, the priest hunter had lost ground while hailing the blacksmith. While running through a plantation of trees the priest tripped over the root of a tree and fell headlong to the ground. He regained his footing almost instantly but his leg had been hurt and his speed diminished, he had barely cleared the plantation, when the priest-hunter was upon him and after a brief but fierce struggle they both fell to the ground. A third party, however, had been added to the race. Johnny Higgins, a travelling salesman who was making his way to Ballinrobe had observed the chase from the small hill to the rear of the cottage, and distinguishing the parties at first glance, had darted of in pursuit at the top of his speed. He had to cross the stream, however, to be on the same side as them, as a result he was sixty yards behind when he saw pursuer and pursued grapple and fall together. Instantly he strained every nerve to reach them, before Seán could add another murder to his list he shouted to the priest, "the knife, Father Davy the knife". After an instant's struggle on the sward, Seán was on top of the priest with one hand grasping his throat and the other in the act of being uplifted to stun him with his pistol butt, when the priest heard the shout, he reached up and pulled the knife from Seán's belt and plunged it into the priest-hunter's side. The pistol dropped from Seán's hand, and Seán fell across the priests body. The priest struggled to his feet and was gazing at the bleeding priest - hunter, when Higgins ran up pulled the knife from his side and plunged it three time into the priest – hunter's body at the same time exclaiming, "murdering dog, look who's stabbing you, and know me, before your soul's in eternal perdition. It's me, Johnny Higgins, the nephew of Father Andrew, that lost his life through your means. It's me that watched you for years by day and by night, to have the delight of lending one blow to help you to hell." and so according to tradition ended the career of one, the vilest of those wretches, fashioned and fostered by the demoralising and deeply blood-stained penal statutes.[85]

---

[85] Archdeacon M. Esquire <u>Shawn na Soggarth The priest Hunter An Irish Tale of the Penal Times.</u>1844

The old people said that Seán carried a large knife wherever he went and that he could only be killed with his own knife, it was said that he was in league with the devil and that by the light of the candles of the dead he would take the wool that was growing on the sheep that day and have it clipped, spun, knitted and on his back before dawn the next day.

The manner of his death fulfilling the prophesy that he could only be killed with his own weapon.

Aill Baile Nuaid – near Partree County Mayo
Where Seàn Na Sagart was killed

The Examination of John O'Mullowny of Ballyheane taken before James Macartney and William Caulfield Esquires Lords Justices of Assize for the Connaught Circuit the sixth day of April 1715

"This Examinat being duly sworn on the Holy Evangelists and examined saith that he knows Francis Burke of the County of Galway to be reputed Vicar General and James Lynch Titular Archbishop of Tuam, and that he hath known the said Francis Burke to execute the office of Vicar General by divorcing several couples from the Bonds of Marriage particularly Thomas Paddin and Mary Mannin att Ballheane in the County of Mayo in the house of Edmond Coetello parish priest of Ballheane about five years agoe and also in the house of Teig Mally at Morisk in the Owels in the County of Mayo. He this Examinat was present when the said Francis Burke did order (ordain) Bryan Mulcroan and Peter Gibolane popish priests, who now officiate as popish priests in the County of Mayo and Peter Gibolane is popish priest of the parish of Cloghwell and the said Francis Burke now dwelleth neare Slewboghteen in the County of Galway neare Loughrea and that Patrick Duffy Registered Popish parish priest of the parish of Ballinrobe is reputed the other vicar General of the said Diocese of Tuam and that he came into the said office in the place and stead of Dominick Lynch nephew to the said Titular Arch Bishop and that the said Patrick Duffy and the said Francis Burke together with PatrickTwohill a regular, Bryan Mulcroon, Peter Gibolane, Edmund Nally, Thomas Mulkeerran all popish priests and several others of the said function not known to this Examinat met at lane neare Aghagower in the parish of Aghagower Barony of Moriske and County of Mayo and being part of the lands of Valentine Browne and on or about the twentieth day of November last, the said Francis Burke, Patrick Duffy, Patrick Twohill, Bryan Mulcroon, peter Gibolane, Edmund Nally and Thomas Mulkeeran did celebrate seven masses from Dawn of Day till twelve of the Clock. And this Examinates cause of knowing is that he saw all the said persons before named except Burke, Mulcroon, and Edmund Nally in their surplaces and saw particularly Francis Burke and Patrick Twohill elevate the wafer and the same day the said Francis Burke and Patrick Duffy ordained fifty popish priests as Patrick Twohill told this Examinat and that in or about the twentieth February last the said Francis Burke and the other persons before named were to meet on the lands aforesaid and John Nally popish priest of the parish of Barrescarney told this Examinat it would be an Act of Charity in him if knew anything of a contract between Richard Walsh and Margaret Walsh and the rest of the said persons in order to divorce the said couple. When this Examinat went to the said place the said John Nally told this Examinat that there would be no meeting that day. That Patrick Duffy aforesaid is now dwelling in Westport in the County of Mayo and that this Examinat saw the said Patrick Duffy on Sunday the 13 day of March last at Westport aforesaid in the said street and saw great numbers of people gathered about the house of Thomas Joyce, and the said Patrick Duffy came out of the said house about an hour after the Multitude of people that had been there were dispersed which gave cause to this Examinat to suppose that they had mass the said day in the house of said Thomas Joyce and further saith not.

Jurat coram nobis 7 die Aprilis 1715   Ja. Macartney
    His John x Mullowny   W. Caulfield [86]mark

---

[86] Burke William P Rev <u>The Irish Priests in the Penal Times.</u>1660-1760 (from the state papers in H.M.Record Offices Dublin and London, Waterford 1914

Grave of Seán na Sagart

Epitaph to a Priest-Hunter

God is pleased when man doth cease to sin,
The Devil is pleased when he a soul doth win,
Mankind is pleased when ever a villian dies,
Now all are pleased for here Jack Cusack lies.

Priest Hunters

Ní'l maith dham bheith d'á labhairt,
'S do ghaol le Donnchadh an tSagairt,
Le hEoghan na gcártaidh, a athair,
Le lucht na gceann do ghearradh,
Le cur í málaibh leathair,
Do bhreith leó síor do'n cathair,
'S an óir do thabhairt a bhaile,
Mar chothugadh ban a's leanbh.

Translation

There is no use in my speaking,
Seeing your kinship with Donogha-of-the Priest,

And with Owen-of-the-cards, his father,
With the people of the cutting off of the heads,
To put them into leather bags,
To bring them down with them to the city,
And to bring home the gold,
For sustenance of wives and children.

In the year 1713, The Irish House of Commons declared that the,
"prosecution and informing against Papists was an honourable service",
thus creating a new profession in Ireland, that of Priest hunting. One pract-
itioner of this new profession was a Spaniard (or Portuguese) named Garcia.
He came to Ireland in 1717, posing as a Catholic Priest. Because the clergy
was practically leaderless and widely scattered about the country he was
able to obtain considerable information to the effect that within a short
period of time, The Dominican Provincial, two Jesuits, one Franciscan and
a number of secular priests were imprisoned. For this work he was paid the
sum of £100 and given living quarters in Dublin Castle by the Dublin
Grand Jury.

Another priest hunter was an educated man by the name of Tyrell, who
discovered a Popish plot to overthrow the government. The executive was so
impressed with him that he was commissioned to write a special report for
the attention of the Queen and her Privy Council. Within a short time Tyrell
was convicted of bigamy, yet within a few months he was again working for
the Privy Council discovering new Papist plots against the government. He
made many journeys throughout the country in search of un-registered
priests. He entered into another bigamous marriage, a crime for which he
was executed in May 1713.

The following story relates to a man by the name of Ferguson, a man of
immense stature, who travelled the region of the Sperrin Mountains, armed
with a long spear. Often he could be seen walking in the direction of Derry
with the head of some unfortunate priest impaled upon his spear. On the
presentation of this horrific prize to the authorities he would receive the
sum of five pounds. One day Ferguson had come from Derry in search of a
priest, who was said to be in hiding near Carnamoney. His search for the
priest was unsuccessful and as he was returning to Derry he came upon a
small child at play beside a stream. Muttering a terrible oath, that the head
of a Papish child would be better than none at all, he cut the head off the
poor child and impaled it on the point of his spear. At the time of this
atrocity there were two brothers in hiding nearby. Their name was
MacWilliams, they were officers in the French army and were natives of
Carnamoney, they had been involved in the siege of Limerick with Patrick
Sarsfield. One of these brothers was witness to Ferguson's brutal and
wanton act, the other having gone in search of food. He shot Ferguson dead
on the spot. Being afraid of the consequences of his act, to the local

inhabitants, if Ferguson's body was discovered, he dragged the body to the nearest bog-hole and disposed of it therein. During the famine times some men working in the bog came upon the bones of what they thought at first was a horse. Investigation proved them to be human bones of unusually large dimension.The local people who knew the story had no doubt as to whose bones they were.[87]

Father Terence Craig 1652-1710

Father Terence Craig was born about 1652 in *Baile na Creige,* he was ordained a Catholic priest by Bishop Thady Keogh, Bishop of Clonfert, in 1682, in Creggan. Despite the Act of Banishment of 1697, under which all clergy were ordered to leave Ireland by May 1st 1698, Father Terence remained to preach and administer the sacraments to his congregation at Cloughaneely in County Donegal.

With the introduction of the 'Registration Act of 1704' which required all diocesan clergy to register with the civil authorities, indicating their place of ministry. On registration they were issued with a licence to conduct their religious office.

Father Terence was one of the 1,089 people that officially registered as a Parish Priest He was fifty-two years of age and resident at Bealtaine. The reason why Father Terence was hunted down and murdered in a cave on the Aghla side of Loch Altan is not known. It is probable that he refused to take the 'Oath of Abjuration' which was introduced in 1709. The taking of this oath was compulsory and refusal to take it would have made him an outlaw.

The following is a version of the story which was collected by Seán O'hEochaigh from Niall O'Dufaigh of Bealtaine in 1938.

"In the days of the persecution of the priests, there was a family of the Sweenies called Clann tSuibhne na Banríona or the Queens Sweenies. They lived in Dunlewey, and kept many soldiers. A young priest of the Craig family was on the run up at Altan, near enough to Dunlewey. The poor man was in a cave, and was trapped there.

The bloodhounds tracked him down and tore him apart, and his remains were brought back here in Tullaghobegly. A strange gravestone was erected over his grave…it shows two bloodhounds cut out in stone, and Chalice, and missals above them, and there is a lot written there in a language that is difficult to make out. But since then it seems that someone broke the tombstone and only fragments remain, to cover the grave in which it is thought Terence Craig was buried."

---

[87] *Ní Ceallaigh Eibhlín* <u>Catholic Bulletin 1912 N.L.I I.R 794105 C.I.</u>

Carraig Dubh.

This is now known as Cathal Mór's Rock, named after the infamous robber Cathal Mór Carraher, who used a cave near its summit as a hideout. During the period of the Penal Laws this rock was used as a look out post while Mass was being celebrated in a hazel glen above the Drumilly road. The rising ground over Carraig Dubh commanded a view of the highway leading from the villages of Mullaghbawn and Forkhill, which were at that time heavily garrisoned by the military. It also commanded a view of the Mass-glen, half a mile across the rocky fields in the other direction.At this time there was only one Catholic Bishop in Ulster, the Right Rev Dr. Donnelly. Bishop Donnelly's "palace" was a mud walled cabin in the rugged valley that lies between Slieve Gullion and Burren Mountain, this is in a townland which is now named Doctor's Quarters because of its association with Dr Donnelly. Bishop Donnelly was born near Cookstown, County Tyrone around the middle of the seventeenth century. He was educated by the Jesuits in Drogheda and ordained by St Oliver Plunket. After serving as a curate in Armagh and as Parish Priest in County Louth, he was elevated to the See of Dromore in 1690.There were few priests in the country at that time so that the Bishop had to travel the country in disguise ministering to the faithful in secret. A chance meeting with an itinerant harper, Fiachra MacBrady of Cavan, known far and wide as the "Bard of Stradone", gave him a novel idea to elude the priest hunters. Dressed in rags and carrying an old fiddle, he visited the local fairs and markets, playing folk-tunes and quietly ministering to his flock.When Bishop Donnelly died in 1716 the people of South Armagh, under cover of darkness, carried his coffin all the way back to his native Tyrone, and buried him among his own people at Desertcreat, near Cookstown.

Dónal na Casgadh,
Donal the Queller
Dónal Ó Caoimh, Domhnall Ó Caoimh, Donal O Keefe.

Donal O Keefe was a raparee who operated in the area of north-west Cork near the town of Cullen during the latter part of the 17th century. He was the scion of the O'Keefe clan, who had extensive lands to the west of Duhallow, Co Cork. It is said that he was forced into the hills by the victory of William of Orange and that he carried out repeated cattle – raids against the Williamites from his mountain hide-out. He also had another hiding place to the south of the county, a cave in the side of a cliff at Gortmore near Mallow, which was reached by first swimming the river Blackwater and then traversing the rock face. Donal had a lover by the name of Máiréad Ní Cheallaigh - Margaret Kelly who betrayed him to a handsome English Army officer. Arrangements were made whereby Margaret would induce Donal to a place where he could easily be captured. Donal however uncovered the plot and in a rage he killed Margaret Kelly with his knife.There are many stories told about Donal's heroic escapes one in particular has him escaping from a band of cavalrymen by having his horse leap over a huge precipice. Once when stricken with fever in a remote district to the west of Millstreet, he was betrayed by his nurse. Being confined to bed and unable to move the hut in which he was confined was surrounded by soldiers. The soldiers wrapped him in his blanket and tied him to a cart. Thinking that he was dying the soldiers were not as vigilant as they might have been and when they reached Mallow he cut the ropes which bound him with a sword which had been by his side during the course of his illness and overlooked by his captors. He jumped from the cart brandishing his sword and escaped.

One legend of his capture tells that he was finally betrayed by a close friend who invited him to a meal and then notified the authorities, who had the soldiers waiting for him. The betrayer's wife gave Donal the hint of what was going on when she remarked in Irish " *caith fuar agus teith* "which means " eat it cold and flee" but sounds exactly like *"caith fuar agus te"* which means" eat it cold and hot". At this Donal fled the house but was shot dead by the waiting soldiers.

Mairgréad Ní Chealleadh.
Margaret Kelly

(an original poem by Edward Walsh)

I

At the dance in the village thy white foot was fleetest;
Thy voice 'mid the concert of maidens was sweetest;
The swell of thy white breast made rich lovers follow;
And thy raven hair bound them young *Mairgréad Ní Chealleadh*

Ii

Thy neck was, lost maid, than the *ceanabhan* whiter,
And the glow of thy cheek than the *manadan* brighter;
But death's chain had bound thee, thine eye's glazed and hollow,
That shone like a sunburst, young *Mairgréad Ní Chealleadh.*

Iii

No more shall mine ear drink thy melody swelling ;
Nor thy beamy eye brighten the outlaw's dark dwelling ;
Or thy soft heaving bosom my destiny hallow,
When thine arms twine around me, young *Mairgréad Ní Chealleadh.*

Iv

The moss couch I brought thee today from the mountain,
Has drunk the last drop from thy young heart's red fountain-
For this good *scian* beside me struck deep an rang hollow

In thy bosom of treason, young *Mairgréad Ní Chealleadh.*
V
With strings of rich pearls thy white neck was laden,
And thy fingers with spoils of the *Sasanach maiden;*
Such rich silks enrobed not the proud dames of Mallow-
Such pure gold they wore not as *Mairgréad Ní Chealleadh*
Vi
Alas ! that my loved one her outlaw would injure-
Alas ! that he e'er proved her treason's avenger !
That this right hand should make thee a bed cold and hollow,
When in Death's sleep it laid thee, young *Mairgréad Ní Chealleadh !*
Vii

And while to this lone my deep grief I'm venting,
The Saxon's keen bandog my footsteps is scenting;
But true men await me afar in Duhallow.
Farewell, cave of slaughter, and *Mairgréad Ní Chealleadh.*

Ceanabhan a plant found in bogs, the top of which bears a substance res-
embling cotton, and as white as snow.
Sasanach is the Irish word for an English person.

*"D'eis teacht na Sasanach go h-Éirinn ghaibh treabh de chlann Uí Chaoimh
seilbh i gCuilinn agus o shoin anuas tugtar Cuilinn Uí Chaoimh air. Do réir
seanchais bhí ceannas aca o Dhun-ar-aill go Cillairne agus do b'fhialmhar
fhlaitheamhail an treabh iad ar feadh i bhfad. Do leanadar ag congbhail
greama daindin ar a nduthaigh i n-aimhdheoin a namhad go dtí aimsear an
Righ Seamas. Do chuireadar leis agus d'a chomhartha san féin bhí buidhean
o Chuilinn ag troid ar a thaobh i gcath Eachdhroma. Chum san do
dheimhniughadh innstar an scéal seo.Do bhí Ó'Caoimh lá ag caitheamh
tíonointe amach agus ar shroisint na h-áite
Dho dubhairt sé le muintir an tighe imtheacht. Leanamha mheadhon-aosta do
bhí ann agus lán an tighe de phaistibh óga aca. Do chuadar amach gan aon
achrann. Bhí an tseana-mháthair an duine deireannach tháinig amach. Nuair
chonaic sí Ó Caoimh ar an mban d'iompaigh ar a mac féin agus do chas an t-
ologon seo go fada fuidheach feargach:-*

"Gaol na ropairí groidhe
Sin é agam mo dhiol
Do théidheadh go h-Eachdhruim sios
Mac mo mhic fé'n ngaoith
Ag seasamh cirt Uí Chaoimh,
'S an luisnigh trí mhullach a thighe"

Do bhí fód teine í laimh Uí Chaoimh chun an tighe do dhoghadh, acht nuair do chuala sé rann na sean-mhná do chaith uaidh an spreidh agus dubhairt, "Thugais d'eiteach, a chailleach," Do mhaith sé dhoibh an cíos agus do chuir thar n-ais arís íad gan cíos gan cáin gan ioc gan eileamh.

Mar gheall ar ghabhail le Righ Seamas do bhaineadar na Sasanaigh an cuid ba mhó d'a ndutaigh de mhuintir Uí Chaoimh. Do chuaidh cuid aca ansan do'n Fhrainnc í gcomhluadar an tSáirsealaigh. Do gheilleadar an chuid eile í ndiaidh a chéile d'á namhaid acht amháin Domhnall Ó Caoimh.Domhnall na Casca tugadh mar leas–ainm air. D'iompuigh seisean amach na cheithearnach coille a d'iarraidh a cheart do phleidhe d'ais no d'eigean.Da bhrigh sin dubhradh agus deirtear fós,

"Da bhfuighbheadh na Gaedhil a gceart
Ba le h.O Caoimh Drom-each,"

Sé sin, an chuirt í n-ár chomhnuigh se.

File agus ceoltoir a b'eadh é agus mar sin do mhair sé í measc a dhaoine tamall: Acht scoiltean an bhreab an chloch agus de dheascaibh na breibe do dhein a bhean, Máired Ní Chealla, spíaíreacht air sa deire. I bhfraoch feirige do rop sé a scian í na croidhe agus do theith leis féin o uaimh í gCarraig an Ghuirt Mhoir i n-aice na Baintireach agus na h-allachoin I na thoir go Fáill Domhnaill na Casca, mar a raibh leabaidh eile aige, láimh le Coiscéim na Caillighe. Ní rugadar air gur léim ó'n bhfaill treasna na h-abhann t-Aireagail-cead troigh ar aoirde- agus briseadh a cos .Ar shroisint ar an dtaobh eile do bhí bean nigheachain ag an abhainn agus nuair a chonaic sí an léim uathbhásach dubhairt sí, "O! a dhuine," ar sise "is maith í do léim" "Ní h-aon tabhact an léim," arsa Domhnall agus a croidhe ag briseadh "seachas an ruthag a thugas chuichí,"

Sara r cuireadh chum báis é do fiafruigheadh dhe mar leanas car chuir sé a chuid saidhbhris í bhfolach:-

"A Dhomhnaill a dhaltha ghil, Oro!
Car ghabhais leis an airgead, Oro!
A's da h-iallaití dearga, Oro!
Do bhainis de sna Sasanaigh, Oro!"
D'fhreagair sé:-

"Treabhaigh an Mhangarta, Oro!
A's Bogach na ceannfhinne, Oro!
Taoscaigh Abhann t-Aireagail
O n-a bun go dtí n-a barra
Agus gheobhaidh an t-airgead, Oro!"

Translation (A.Nugent)

After the English came to Ireland the O'Keefe clan took posession of land in Cullen which became known as Cullen O'Keefe, they had extensive land holdings from Donerail to Killarney. History relates that their wealth and munifence was known far and wide. They continued to prosper extending their territory, despite their enemies, until the reign of James 11. They took his side in the war, and they and their neighbours fought at the battle of Aughrim. The following story bears testimony to this. One day O'Keefe was evicting tenants and despoiling the place. He told the people of the house to depart. A housefull of children and a doting old woman. They went out without any quarrell. The grandmother was the last to leave, and when she saw O'Keefe, she turned to her son and recited in a slow angry tone.

> Related to the hearty Raparrees
> That went down to Aughrim
> Standing with O'Keefe
> This is my repayment.
> My son's son out under the wind
> And the glow of the flames through the roof of his house.

O'Keefe had a lighting sod in his hand to set fire to the house, but when he heard the verses of the old woman, he threw it away from him and said. "I'll give you the benefit of the doubt old woman".

He absolved her of her rent and put her back in the house without rent or tax, or payment or tithe. Because of their stand with King James the O'Keefes were dispossesed of most of their land. Some of them went to France with Sarsfield. One by one the O'Keefes submitted to the English, except for one Donal-the-Queller by nick-name. He went out on his keeping into the woods conducting a war trying to win back his posessions. Because of this it is still said.

> If the Gaels win justice
> The O'Keefes will be on horseback.

He is rembered as a poet and a musician and lived among the people as such. But the bribe will release the stone and as a consequence of a bribe his woman Margaret Kelly sold him in the end. In a frenzy of anger he stabbed her in the heart with his knife and fled from his cave at Gortmore Rock beside the Bantry river with a posse in pursuit, to the Cave of Donal-the-Queller beside the Hags Leap. They did not catch him because he jumped across the Araglen river from the precipice one hundred feet high and broke his foot. There was a washerwoman at the river and when she saw the awesome leap she said. "That was a great leap". Donal replied with his heart breaking.

206

"The jump was nothing compared to the run I had at it". Before they put him to death they asked him where he hid his wealth.

O Donal my loyal darling, oro
Where did you hide the money, oro
And your red strapped bag, oro
That you took from the English.oro
He answered
The treasure of Mangerton, oro
And the blaze on the boggy ground, oro
Pump out the river Araglen
From the bottom to the top,oro
And you will find the money,oro.

Seán Rua an Gaorthaidh
Red John from the Gearragh.

If you follow the R584 road from Macroom to Ballingeary out through Inchigeelagh with Lake Allua lapping at the side of the road to your left , you will come upon a marshy moor-land which was once known as the " Gearragh ". This was once the retreat of a famous Rapparee who went by the name of *Seán Rua an Gaorthaidh* .
Many stories are still told of his exploits and escapades. Seán Rua a proclaimed Rapparee with a price on his head lived in a cabin in the Gearragh which was approached by a narrow boreen.
"One night Sean heard the Yeomen approaching the cabin and all seemed lost. The wheel of a cart was in the cabin, the Rapparee removed his coat, wrapped it around the wheel, opened the cabin door and sent the wheel crashing into the middle of the surprised Yeomanry. In the resulting confusion the quick thinking Rapparee made his way to safety.[88]"
"Seán was a great shot with a rifle, and one night while Hedges White, the owner of Macroom Castle and some of his friends were dining at the castle around midnight he fired a shot which quenched the candle on the dining table.
Soon after this incident a British officer, who was also a great marksman was stationed at Macroom to assist with the pursuit of Sean .It was this mans boast that if he caught one glimpse of the outlaw he would shoot him dead. It was decided to grant two day's pardon to Seán Rua in order that he and the British officer might engage in a trial of skills to see which of them was the better shot.

---

[88] N.F.C S 341 : p588 Peggy Murrey Sleaveen West Macroom Co Cork

The contest was held in Macroom before an audience of hundreds both civilian and soldiers. A crown piece was placed on the castle wall, and both contestants succeeded in hitting it. The open blade of a knife, edge forward, as a target was placed in position by Seán Rua.The British officer took first shot and narrowly missed the target. So deadly accurate was the aim of Seán Rua, that he made halves of the bullet on the edge of the knife-blade. Sean disappeared into the crowd and was on his way to Inverleary before any one had missed him. Seán Rua was never caught and it is said that he died in his bed an old man. His real name is believed to have been John O'Sullivan."[89]

O' Hare of Duhallow.
The Horse Whisperer

The Ballyhoura mountains which run from East to West through the North Cork countryside, once gave shelter to a famous rapparee named O' Hare, the following story is an account of one of his escapades with the Redcoats during the Penal Times.

O'Hare owned a magnificent grey mare which was renowned throughout the country for its speed and ability to jump any obstacle in its path. Both these skills had saved O'Hare from capture by the Redcoats on many an occasion. The authorities became so alarmed at the exploits of this rapparee that they stationed a regiment of soldiers at Buttevant with the sole intention of capturing him and his mare. One day the soldiers surrounded O'Hare in a valley in the heart of the mountains. He knew that if he tried to out run them on the mare, they would shoot the mare. He hid the mare in a thicket and made his escape on foot. During their search of the area the soldiers discovered the mare and brought her to Buttevant. The mare was very vicious and would let no one except O'Hare on her back. Eventually the mare was sent to the Curragh which was the military headquarters in Ireland and while there was claimed by one of the officers. O'Hare was very fond of the mare and missed her, he also realised that her speed and jumping prowess were skills which were most desirable to a rapparee, so he hit on a plan to get her back. On discovering that the mare had been taken to the Curragh which is in the County Kildare, he changed his appearance, dressed himself as a stable hand and set off for the Curragh. He became friendly with an Irish born officer, who succeeded in getting work for him as a stable hand.

O'Hare remained at the Curragh for the next three months working diligently as a stable hand, and waiting for an opportunity to present itself.Opportunity finally presented itself when an English based regiment issued a challenge to the Curragh based regiment to hold a horse-racing

---

[89] N.F.C . S 340 : pp53-54 Mr Denis Lane Farmer Mountmusic Foames Co Cork.

and horse-jumping competition at the Curragh. The English based regiment had at their disposal one of the finest show-jumping horses in England. The regiment at the Curragh had nothing to match the English horse, with the exception of O'Hare's mare but as no one could ride this mare all seemed lost. O'Hare in his guise as a stable hand offered to ride the mare but the officers considered it too dangerous. Eventually O'Hare persuaded one of the army officers to let him into the mares stable, in secret and alone in case he was killed by the horse no blame could be attached to the officer in question. He entered the stable alone and whispered something into the horses ear and the mare knew him instantly. The officers finally agreed to allow O' Hare to ride the mare.In the jumping competition all the horses were eliminated except the English bred mare and the Rapparee's mare. The fence was set to an exceptional height and the Irish mare with her Rapparee master on board cleared it with ease. The English mare however knocked two sods off the fence with her hind hoof. The English Officers would not agree with the judge's decision that the Irish horse had won. O'Hare spoke up, "Put another two sods on the fence and we'll jump again." He stood on his horses back an shouted. "Up Duhallow and O' Hare the race is over foul or fair I have won and have my mare." Then he jumped the fence, while still standing on her back and away with him at the gallop, to Ballyhoura and freedom. [90]

Cahir – na – gCapall
Charles of the Horses
Charles Dempsey

Charles Dempsey's father fought as an irregular, with Patrick Sarsfield, in the army of James 11. After the fall of Limerick, and the subsequent Treaty of 1691, he accepted the pardon offered, discarded his arms and returned to his small-holding in the townland of Lea, near Ballybrittas in County Laois.This was once part of the hereditary lands of the O' Dempseys and known as Glenmalier.

Charles, however, became a notorious horse- thief with an unusual method of operation. On receiving information about the location of certain live-stock in a particular pasture, Charles would notify one of his accomplices, who would remove the live-stock to another location. From there they would be brought to a distant fair, by third accomplice and sold. Sometimes the owner of missing live-stock would approach Cahir in an effort to find the missing animals, on consultation with his accomplices he would let it be known that if the missing animals were to be found in a certain location which he would suggest, a finders fee would be available to be shared among them. Although this system was not as profitable as highway

---

[90] N.F.C. S 364 : p345 1937 J Sheahan Ballygruddy Kanturk Co Cork

robbery it was less dangerous. The complicated manner in which the stolen live-stock was moved made it difficult for the authorities to gather evidence against him.

A certain William Peters, a friend and member of the same profession as Cahir was imprisoned in the gaol at Carlow for stealing a sorrel horse with a bald face and one white foot.William Peter's father sent word to Cahir and asked for his help in liberating his son. On receiving an accurate description of the horse, Cahir searched the country until he found a mare bearing the same colour marks as the stolen horse.

A confederate of Cahir brought this mare into Carlow, where the recovered stolen horse was being stabled for production at the forthcoming trial. This confederate of Cahir's made the acquaintance of the stable-hand who had charge of the sorrel and when the opportunity arose invited him to have a drink with him in the tavern where he was lodging. This invitation was accepted by the stable-hand. Meanwhile another confederate of Cahir's exchanged horses and left Carlow.

The next day at the trial enough evidence was produced to satisfy the judge that Peters was guilty as charged and as he prepared to deliver sentence, the prisoner's father asked the prosecutor by what marks could the horse be identified and whether it was a horse or a mare; The prosecutor identified the position of the coloured spots on the animal and also the gender. Peter's father requested that the animal be brought into court so that this could be ascertained. The judge acceded to his request and the animal was subsequently brought into court. The spots and colouring were found to correspond to the owners description, but to his dismay instead of a horse the was looking at a mare. William Peters was found not guilty and escaped the gallows.[91]

Ned of the Hill

Éamon Ó Riain , Éamon an Chnoic, or in English 'Ned of the Hill'.

It is said that he was born in Knockmeoll Castle in Atshanbohy, in north Tipperary. Tradition holds that he was born of noble stock, but was forced to become a 'rapparee' As a consequence, of the Williamite Wars. In 1702 a reward of £200 was offered for his capture, which resulted in his betrayal and death at the hands of a close confidant.

Eamon was probably the most famous of the 'rapparee's' made so by the popular ballad '*Éamon an Chnoic*'. Tradition holds that Eamon had studied abroad for the priesthood and that on his return home for a holiday he intervened in a dispute between a widow and a tax collector resulting in the death of the tax collector.

---

[91] Kennedy Patrick <u>The Book of Modern Irish Anecdotes</u> 1872 M.H Gill & Son Dublin

Because of this affair Eamon had to take to the hills as an outlaw. He soon attracted a strong band of men around him and fought for the Jacobite cause against William of Orange.Combining forces with another famous Raparee leader Dónal Ó hÓgáin who was known as " Galloping Hogan " they attacked and destroyed an English convoy near Dundrum in Co, Tipperary. Eamon is generally depicted alone, mounted on a fine grey horse, always gallant, robbing the rich only and helping the poor.There are many stories of Eamon giving money to tenants of greedy landlords to settle debts and then robbing the landlord and returning the money to the tenants.

It is told that Eamon met his death at the hands of a man named Dwyer, in whose house he was staying. Dwyer beheaded Eamon while he was sleeping and brought the head to Clonmel in order to clain the reward.Tradition holds that a pardon had just been granted to Eamon on the grounds of his chivalerous behavior to a lady of the Butler family, and that the traitor got nothing for his treachery.

"I heard a little from James Doherty of Ned of the Hill. According to his story Eamon was born near Dromlane a couple of fields from the place on the Thurles road known as the Metal Bridge.The following rhyme in Irish refers to his death.

"Tomás bán ó Caill a' Chluig
A bhain an ceann d'Eamon a' Cnuic".[92]

His assassin was his own first cousin, it seems he had first cousins named Ó Dwyer Bán, and also first cousins named Ryan Bán. Which of the families was responsible for his betrayal cannot be ascertained according to the rhyme above. Eamon was killed at Foilaclug near Hollyford. His head was taken to Clonmel by his assassin and his body was buried in a field near the spot known as Peg Bán's Hollow. His grave is still pointed out.

When Eamon's murderer reached Clonmel with his head, a free pardon had been granted to Eamon through the influence of a lady of the Butlers. Eamon's head was thrown into the Suir, and his assassin had to go on his keeping as a murderer. After many years Eamon's body was exhumed and re-interred in Doon. 1739 is the year given as (the year of the big frost) the date of his burial in Doon.

The Domhnall Máires a section of the Ryan Clan and inter- married with the Burkes of Faileen Milestone claim to be the direct descendants of Ned of the Hills.

---

[92] N F.C 542 : p 400 1938 P,O'Harrachtain Kilnamanagh Upper Ceapach Tiobraid Áirann

Éamon an Chnoic

Cé hé sin amuigh a bhfuil faobhar ar a ghuth
Ag réabadh mo dhorais dhúnta?
Mise Éamon an Chnoic atá báite fuar fliuch
Ó shíorshiúl sléibhte is gleanta.
A lao dhil is a cuid ,cad a dhéanfainnse duit
Mura gcuirfinn ort beinn de m' ghúna
Is go bhfuilpúdar go tiubh á shíorshéideadh leat
Is go mbeimis araon múchta.

Is fada mise amuigh faoi sneachta is faoi shioc
Is gan dánacht agam ar aon neach,
Mo sheisreach gan scor, mo bhranar gan chur
Is gan iad agam ar aon chor.
Níl caraid agam is danaid liom san
A ghlafadh mé moch ná déanach,
Is go gcaithfidh mé dul thar farraige soir
Ó is ann nach bhfuil aon de m'ghaolta.

Edward (Ned) of the Hill

"O who is that without,That with passionate shout
Keeps beating my bolted door?"
"I am Ned of the Hill, forespent , wet and chill
from long trudging marsh and moor".
"my love fond and true, what else could I do
but shield you from wind and from weather
When the shots fall like hail, They us both shall assail
And mayhap we shall die together

" Through frost and through snow tired and hunted I go
In fear both from friend and from neighbour"
My horses run wild my acres untilled
And they all of them lost to my labour
But it grieves me far more than the loss of my store
That there's none who would shield me from danger
So my fate it must be to fare eastward o'er the sea
And languish amid the stranger.

Galloping Hogan

The Hogans were descended from the Dalcassians, whose territories extended into, Clare, Tipperary and Limerick. They were driven from their land at Ardcroney during the Cromwellian plantations of 1652-53 and the land was given to Nicholas Tolar a quartermaster in the Puritan army. The following story relates how Daniel Hogan became a rapparee.

One day young Daniel Hogan was assisting his father at his forge, in the village of Goldenbridge, County Tipperery, when they were surrounded by Cromwellian troops, who were looking for evidence that John Hogan, the local blacksmith had made weapons for the rebels. On finding no such evidence, they beat the blacksmith unconscious, one of the troopers produced a rope with which they proceeded to hang Daniel, their commanding officer intervened when he saw that his horse was in need of a shoe. He ordered Daniel to replace the shoe. Daniel on completion of the new shoe, reached for the horse's hoof but the animal sensing the boy's fear kicked out at him. The officer held the reins while Daniel finished nailing on the shoe, when the task was completed he struck the officer a blow with the hammer, leaped into the saddle and away with him like the wind. Thus began the career of Galloping Hogan.

On the 24th of September 1691 the day of the capitulation of Limerick City Hogan and one hundred fellow Rapparees were engaged near the village of Cullen not far from Ballyneety. "Galloping Hogan got upwards of one hundred rapparees together to plunder and rob the settlers and people that came into his power and was now so bold as to set upon a party of wagons coming towards the camp nigh Cullen and took away with him seventy one horses." [93]

"Galloping Hogan brought word in on the following evening that all was well and they started for Cullen. There were two Hogans among the Rapparees, one true, one false. "We'll lead ", said the Galloper to Sarsfield, "don't come up with us until you hear the shot".Hogan and his kinsman started off ahead and when they got to (Pott's River?) the kinsman said, "Now is our chance to make a pot of money". "How?" said Galloping Hogan. "By betraying Sarsfield (*cad eile)*" says he. "All right", says Galloping Hogan, "but we must water our horses here, lead on".

When he got him leaning over to give his horse a drink, Hogan shot him. "Well done Hogan", said Sarsfield spurring his horse on to overtake the scout."[94]

On the day the Treaty of Limerick was signed General Ginkel moved to curb Hogan's raids. Two regiments of cavalry were ordered to hunt him and his followers down.

---

[93] Story Rev

[94] N.F.C. 407 : pp 176-177 Peadar Mac Domhnaill, Ceapach na bFaoiteach, Tiobraid Árainn

They failed in their efforts. It is said of Hogan that he was one of the last to transfer to France. Tradition holds that he finished his career as an officer in the Portuguese army.

Galloping Hogan
Old Limerick is in danger
And Ireland is not free
So Sarsfield sends a message
to a fearless Rapparee-
"come ride across the Shannon
At the sounding of the drum
And we'll blow the enemy siege-train
To the land of Kingdom come.

Galloping Hogan, Galloping Hogan,
Galloping all along
In his saddle is a sabre
On his lips there is a song
He's off across the Shannon
To destroy the enemy cannon
And he goes galloping, he goes galloping
Galloping, galloping on

The Rapparee is bearded,
Theres a twinkle in his eye,
As he rides into the city,
The Limerick ladies cry;
Mr outlaw, Mr outlaw,
Will you tarry here with me
Och I'm off to Ballyneety,
To blow up a Battery
Chorus

So tonight along the Shannon
By the pale light of the moon
There flows an eerie brightness
As of an Indian noon;
Then clippody-clop resounding
Through the lattice of the shade
The ghost of Galloping
Goes a riding down the glade.

The Rapparees

Righ Shemus he has gone to France and left his crown behind;
Bad luck be theirs, both night and day, putting running in his mind;
Lord Lucan followed after with his Slashers brave and true,
And now the doleful keen is raised- What will poor Ireland do?
What must poor Ireland do?
Our luck," they say, "has gone to France-what can poor Ireland do?"

Oh! Never fear for Ireland, for she has sojers still,
For Rory's boys are in the wood and Remy's on the hill;
And never had poor Ireland more loyal hearts than these-
May God be kind and good to them, the faithful Rapparees-
The fearless Rapparees!
The jewel were you, Rory, with your Irish Rapparees!

Oh, black's your heart, Clan Oliver, and colder than the clay!
Oh, high's your head, Clan Sassanach since Sarsfield's gone away!
It's little love you bear to us, for the sake of long ago-
But hold your hand, for Ireland still can strike a deadly blow-
Can strike a mortal blow-
Och, *dar-a-Criost,* 'tis she can still,

Can strike a deadly blow.
The Masters bawn, the Masters seat, a surly bodach fills;
The Masters son, an outlawed man, is riding on the hills,
But, God be praised, that round him throng as thick as summer bees,
The swords that guarded Limerick's wall- his faithful Rapparees!
His loving Rapparees!
Who dare say "no" to Rory Oge, with all his Rapparees!

Black Billy Grimes of Latnamard, he racked us long and sore-
God rest the faithful hearts he broke! – we'll never see them more,
But I'll go bail he'll break no more while Trugh has gallows trees;
For why? He met one lonely night, the fearless Rapparees-
The angry Rapparees!
They never sin no more, my boys, who cross the Rapparees!

Now Sassanach and Cromweller, take heed of what I say-
Keep down your black and angry looks that scorn us night and day;
For there's a just and wrathful Judge that every action sees,
And He'll make strong to right our wrong the faithful Rapparees!
The men who rode by Sarsfield's side, the roving Rapparees![95]

[95] Duffey Charles Gavin <u>Ballad Poetry of Ireland</u> pp 203-205 Forde National Library New York 1886

The Outlaw Rapparee.

1
My spurs are rusted, my coat is rent
My plume is dank with rain,
And the thistle down and the barley beard
Are thick on my horse's main.
But my rifle's as bright as my sweetheart's eye
And my arm is strong and free,
What care I for your king and law's
I'm an outlawed rapparee.
Click your glasses, friends to mine,
And give your grasp to me,
I'm England's foe, I'm Irelands friend,
I'm an outlaw rapparee.

2
The mountain cavern is my home,
High up in the crystal air,
My bed is the limestone, iron ribbed,
And the brown heath smelling fair.
Let George or William only send
His troops to burn or shoot,

We'll meet them upon equal ground
And fight them foot to foot.
Click your glasses friends to mine,
The midnight's made for glee,
Stout hearts beat fast for Ireland yet,
I'm an outlawed rapparee.

3
Hunted from our father's home,
Pursued with steel and shot,
A bloody warfare we must wage,
Or the gibbet is our lot.
Hurrah! The war is welcome work,
The hated outlaw knows,
He steps unto his country's love,
O'er the corpses of his foes,
Click your glasses, friends with mine,
In the coming days I see
Stern labours for our country's weal,
I'm an outlawed rapparee.

Wicklow Gaol.
1702 – 1924

Although opened in 1702 its first recorded inmate was a catholic priest, Father Owen Mc Fee who was convicted of saying mass in County Wicklow, in the year 1716, contrary to an Act of Parliament, he was sentenced to transportation to the British colony in America.

From this gaol, Francis Burn made his escape in 1717, he was later re-arrested and executed as a Rapparee in Blessington on Friday the 27th of December 1717.

Francis Byrne was born in Frabane in county Wicklow, at the age of twenty two he was arrested and charged with assaulting Nicolas Byrne, for which, he was confined to Wicklow Gaol.Here he met John Reily and they both escaped and joined a band of Rapparees under the command of Captain Maurice Fitzgerald. Maurice Fitzgerald, was born in County Kildare, and brought up in County Carlow, his father Garret Fitzgerald was an officer in King James's Army. After the surrender of Limerick he went to France with the Wild Geese. Maurice was left to fend for himself so he went into domestic service in Carlow and Kildare .At the age of twenty seven while in the service of Captain Sheperdson, in County Kildare, he was impeached by a proclaimed Rapparree, Hugh O'Connor, which caused him to take to the hills and become a Rapparee.

Charles Byrne was from Logduff, near Glendalough in County Wicklow. He was a merchant who operated between Dublin and Wicklow. He was impeached by a Rapparee named Hugh O'Connor, who accused him of receiving stolen silver plate from another Rapparee named John Byrne, who had been shot recently in Wicklow.

To avoid arrest he joined with Captain Maurice Fitzgerald and his band of Rapparees. These three Rapparees were betrayed by John Reily to a company of soldiers and were arrested and sentenced to be executed at Blessington on Friday the 27th of December 1717

Billy Byrne of Ballymanus was incarcerated here in 1799 before he was tried for his part in the battle of Arklow, and the defense of Slaney Bridge in Enniscorthy on June 21st 1798, where the rebels were outgunned and outnumbered, and forced to give way and disperse. He was executed by hanging, in Gallows Lane, off Abbey Street on September 26th 1799.

Billy Byrne From Ballymanus

Come all ye loyal heroes and listen to my song
It is of mournful circumstance and will not keep you long,
Concerning Billy Byrne, a man of high renown,
Who was tried and hanged in Wicklow Gaol as a traitor to the crown.

In the year of '98, my boys, we got reason to complain,
When we lost our chief commander, Billy Byrne was his name.
He was took in Dublin City and brought off to Wicklow Gaol,
And to our great misfortune, for him they'd take no bail.

When he was taken prisoner the lot against him swore,
That he a Captains title upon Mount Pleasant bore.
Before the King's grand army his men he did review,
And with a piece of cannon marched on for Carrigruadh.

When the informers they came in
There was Dixon, Doyle and Davis and likewise Bid Doolin.
They thought it little scruple his precious blood to spill
Who never robbed nor murdered nor to any man did ill.

It would melt your heart with pity how these traitors did explain,
That Byrne worked the cannon on Arklow's bloody plain.
They swore he worked the cannon and headed the pikemen,
And near the town of Gorey killed three loyal Orangemen.

They swore he had ten thousand men all ready at his command,
All ready for to back the French as soon as they would land.
They swore he was committed to support the United cause,
The Judge he cried out "Guilty," to be hanged by coercion laws.
One of those prosecutors I often heard him tell,
It was at his fathers table he was often treated well.
And in his brothers kitchen where many did he see,
The Byrnes were well rewarded for their civility.

My curse light on you Dixon, I ever will curse your soul,
It was at the Bench at Wicklow you swore without control.
The making of a false oath you thought it little sin,
To deprive the County Wicklow of the flower of all its men.

Where are you Matthew Davis, or why don't you come in,
To prosecute the prisoner who now lies in Rathdrum?
The devil has him fast chained repenting for his sins,
In lakes of fire and brimstone and sulphur to the chin.

When the devil saw him coming he sang a merry song,
Saying "Welcome Matthew Davis what kept you out so long?
Where is that traitor, Dixon, to the Crown so loyal and true?
I have a warm corner for him and, of course, Bid Doolin too".

Success to Billy Byrne! May his name forever shine,
Through Wicklow, Wexford, and Kildare, and all along the line.
May the Lord have mercy on his soul and all such souls as he,
Who stood upright for Irelands cause and died for Liberty!

The Legends of the Mac Loughlin and O'Donnell Brothers.

It is not clear whether there are two legends here or whether one has developed into two distinct legends. Both legends share common anecdotes and they both share the lament *Fil, Fil, Aroon* in which the name O'Donnell is mentioned.

This legend concerns two brothers named Mac Loughlin who boarded a ship bound for the continent of Europe in order to complete their education. The ship foundered off the coast of England and the brothers were rescued by a Protestant Minister who offered to educate the two of them for the Protestant Ministry. One of the brothers (Donal Gorm) accepted this offer while the other (Peader) refused, he made his way to the continent where he became a Catholic priest.

Donal became a Protestant minister and changed his name to Daniel. Both brothers returned to the place of their birth, one as a Protestant Minister and the other as a Catholic Priest. Daniel, the Protestant minister, had a comfortable church, a large house and all the trappings of prosperity. While his brother, Peader did not even have a church to say mass in. One day they met on the road and one greeted the other,

"Nach mór an trua go bhfuil cean again ag dul Soir agus an duine eile dul Siar!"

("is'nt it a great pity that one of us is going East and the other going West")

The other answered.

"Chan sin an rud atá cur isteach orm, ach go bhfuil duine againne dul suas agus duine eile dul sios!"

("What is bothering me is that one of us is going up and the other is going down")

Their mother was heartbroken and was forever pleading with Donal to return to the faith of his fathers. It is said that she interrupted his sermons in the Protestant Church.

He finally put a stop to these interruptions by dressing up as Satan and chasing her out of the church grounds. It is said locally that when he died there was a strange gentleman at his funeral the inference being that this strange gentleman was Satan himself.

In the first half of the 17th century a man named McLaughlin owned and lived in the townland of Claar, which was all that remained of the extensive lands owned by his forefathers. Claar skirts the river Foyle, and is situated between Moville and Redcastle. He had two sons, Domhnal and Peter, who were destined to become Catholic priests. While aboard ship en route to the continent of Europe, in order to enter a Catholic college, their vessel was shipwrecked and they were washed up on the coast of England. They were rescued by an English gentleman who brought them to his home and made them welcome there. When they had recovered from their ordeal, he proposed to them that if they conformed to the religion of the Established Church, he would have them enrolled in one of the English Universities. Domhnall accepted the proposal, but Peter refused and continued on his journey to the continent completed his education and became a Catholic priest. After a number of years he returned to Ireland where he became the Parish Priest of Clonmany. Domhnall in the meantime had become a Minister of the Established Church and returned to Ireland as rector of Clonmany. Domhnall had a large well built church under his charge and he built himself a beautiful house which he named Dresden. Peter on the other hand lived in an humble thatched cottage in the townland of Crossconnell. He had a large congregation but no church in which to worship, mass was read at small altars that stood by the sea-shore or at mass-rocks in the glens nearby. Over the years they had little communication with each other and both lived to a good old age. Domhnall died first. His death took place in 1711. It is said that Peter wept unceasingly for him and died soon after.[96]

Here is another variant of this legend from Donegal.(perhaps it is a different legend) "There is a famous story told about two brothers, dating from the eighteenth century. Both were from Carigart and both became priests. Domnic was parish priest of Clondevaddock (Fanad) in 1734 and later he was appointed parish priest of Mevagh.

However in 1739 he was received into the Church of Ireland. Why he left the priesthood is unsure. Some would say he abandoned the faith because of finance and security. It is also said that he had fallen in love with the protestant minister's daughter Susan. She was some twenty years his junior and he wanted to marry her which he did, interestingly enough, her father, the Rev. William Conygham, was rector of Raymunterdoney and Tullaghobegley in 1769 and we also find that Domnic was appointed curate here in 1773. In 1780, Domnic returned to Mevagh and spent the last thirteen years of his life there.Both Domnic and his wife are buried in the Church of Ireland graveyard in Carigart.The following inscription is now bareley legible on their tombstone.

'In memory of Rev. Dimnick O'Donnell who departed this life Nov....1793 aged 93 Also of Susan his wife...who departed this life....1813 aged 88 years' on his death bed, Domnic was visited by his brother who encouraged him, even at this late stage, to return to the church of Rome. He told his brother, *'Níl fad saoil fághta agat is atá le doigheadh ag an choinneal sin ag do thaobh'*

(you have as much life to live as is left in the candle to burn at your side)
Again the brother replied to the priest,
'A dheartháir dhóigh mé fhad le seo é agus is fiú an oral a dhoghadh comh maith'
(Brother I have burned it this far and I am as well to let it finish the inch I have left)[97]

The traditional belief in Donegal is that the following song was written by Domnic O'Donnel's mother. However in his book Danta Diadha Uladh, Enrí Ó'Muirgheasa Claims it was composed by Domnic himself.

---

[96] Inishowen its History, Traditions, and antiquities by Maghtochair (M.Harkin 1935)
[97] Aspects of our rich inheritance [Cloughaneely] ed Seosamh O'Ceallaigh

Fill, Fill a Rún Ó

Crá ort, a Dhoimnic Uí Dhomhnaill
Nach marig ariamh a chonaic thú;
Bhí tú 'do shagart Dé Domhnaig,
'S ar maidin Dé Luain 'do mhinistir!

Fill, Fill, a rún ó
Fill, a rún ó, 's ná himigh uaim;
Fill orm, a chuid den tsaol mhór,
Nó chan fheiceann tú 'n ghlóir mur bfille tú

B'fhearr duit bheith 'buachailleacht bó
Bata in do dhom, is pluideóg ort,
Ná 'd shuí faoi fhuinneógaibh móra
Ag éisteacht le glórthaí minister

A ghiolla, atá thall ar an árd,
Is tú í gceartlár duibh-aigéin
Beidh tú ar thóin leac na crón;
'S an méid atá beo den bhunadh sin.

Nuair a bhéas tú í n-ifreann go fóill,
Agus sluaite deór ag sileadh leat,
Sin an áit a bhfaigh'tú ana scéala,
Cé acu 's fearr sagart nó minister.

Thréig tú Muire agus Íosa-
A ghadaí, ní thaobhfaidh aon duine leat
Thréig tú an creideamh ar mhian tú,
Agus d'imigh tú an tslí 'do minister

Thréig tusa Peader is Pól
Thréig tú Eoin, 's an bunadh sin
Thréig tú bantiarna an domhain,
Ó, sí bhíos í gcónaí ag guí orainn.

Is cosúl nach raibh tú sa Róimh
'S nár chuala tú leabhar á dhearbhú,
Gur damnaíodh ar imigh den phór úd
'S a Mhuire chroí ó cérbh ionadh sin?

Tá mallacht an tsagairt 's a' bhráth'ra,
Leat in do mhála ag imeacht duit;
Agus nach measa dhuit mallacht do mháthara
Ná a bhfaca tú riamh den bhunadh sin.

Return, Return, O Darling

My curse on you, Domnick O'Donnell
That I ever saw you is woe to me;
For you were a priest on the Sunday,
On the morning of Monday a minister

Return, return, O darling
Return, darling, do not abandon me;
Return, O my share of the world,
Or glory will never be seen by you

It was better for you to herd cattle,
A stick in your fist, and a sack on you,
Than to sit underneath the big windows,
And listening to the voices of ministers.

O servant, that is over on the height,
And thou in the centre of Tartarus,
You shall be in the bottom of Hell,
And all those that live of that lineage.

When you are down in Hell,
And thousands of tears dropping down from you
It is there you will learn from your mistake,
Which is better, a priest or a minister.

You abandoned both Mary and Jesus,
Thief, no one will trust in you,
You abandoned the faith that you loved,
And you became a minister.

You abandoned both Peter and Paul,
You abandoned St John and that company
You abandoned the Queen of the world,
Oh, her that for us prays continuously.

It is like you were never in Rome,
And you didn't hear the book's truth,
They are damned that depart from the family,
And Mary, my heart, who would wonder, then?

The curse of the priest and the brother
Is with you in thy bag as you leave,
But worse is your mothers curse
Than all any other you might have seen.

223

William Crotty
Rathgormack Co Waterford.

William Crotty is the subject of many tales, his encounters with the Redcoats in the fastness of the Comeragh Mountains are remembered in song and story to the present day. So enduring is his memory that a lake,"Crotty's Lake", and a pinnacle of rock,"Crotty's Rock", still bear his name. **Map no 75 grid no 335 125**

Crotty was the leader of a band of rapparees, who operated in the County Waterford area. His exploits often took him into the heart of Waterford City. There is a local belief that Crotty hid his loot under a rock in the Comeraghs marked in a special manner, and because of his, betrayal, capture and execution, the location of this treasure remains a mystery. He had a hide-out in a cave,"Crotty's Hole", above the lake named after him, this cave could only be entered by lowering a rope over the cliff face. Despite the large bounty on his head, he managed to avoid capture for many years. It is said that he had his horse shod backwards in order to confuse his pursuers. (this is a recurring theme in legends of outlaws in Ireland).

"Crotty was reputed to be a cannibal and he was believed to fill these recesses with stores of human flesh on which he fed. Hence he was called the Irish,"Shawny Bean", after the highland robber of that name who is said to have had a taste for the same diet.[98]

One legend relates,that one night, William Crotty, and his companion David Norris, were passing by a cabin on the roadside, they saw a light through the window. On looking in they saw a man and his wife at their supper.The man having peeled a potato, was in the act of raising it to his mouth, "Now for my bet", said Crotty, "the ball in my pistol shall pass his lips before the potaro". He fired and the poor man fell dead, the ball having pierced his mouth, while yet the potato was at his lips.

Crotty was captured after being disabled by a shot in the mouth, and it was the belief of the local inhabitants, that it was the Judgement of Heaven on him for his act of wanton cruelty. Crotty's escapades became so intolerable that a local gentleman by the name of Hearn decided to capture him. Hearn was a man of great strength of character and indomitable resolution. He bribe David Norris's wife to give him notice when the outlaw would be found at his lair. One day she met Mr Hearn on the road, and as they passed she, quietly and without looking at him said, "the birds in the nest". Mr hearn was alone, but being well armed, he went directly to,"Crotty's Hole".

He called Crotty by his Christian name, "William", and the rapparee, caught of his guard, came up from his hiding place, the moment his head appeared, Hearn, knowing he would be well armed, and aware of his dangerous reputation, fired at him, and wounded him in the mouth.

---

[98] Walsh John Edward <u>Sketches of Ireland sixty years ago</u> 1847

Despite being wounded, Crotty, managed to make good his escape. On February 16th, 1742, acting on information he had received from David Norris's wife, that Crotty was at her house, Hearn went there well armed and effected his arrest On the 17th of March at the Waterford Assizes he was sentenced to be hanged and quartered. This sentence was duly carried out and after execution his head was cut off and spiked above the County Gaol as a warning to those who would follow in his footsteps.

The gun with which William Crotty was shot was preserved and shown as a curiosity at Shanakil House which was the residence of Mr Hearn

Lament for William Crotty

William Crotty I often told you,
That David Norris would come 'round you.
In your bed where you lay sleeping,
And leave me here in sorrow weeping.
Ochone, ochone, ochone, oh.

He wet your powder, he stole your arms,
And left you helpless in the midst of alarms.
My bitter curse on him and his,
That brought you to an end like this.
Ochone, ochone, ochone, oh.

Oh the judge but he was cruel,
Refusing a long day to my jewel.
Sure I thought that would be maybe,
See the face of your poor baby.
Ochone, ochone, ochone,oh.

But tempters gold and traitors greedy,
Have left the poor and lowly needy.
'Twas you that heard the widow sighing,
'Twas you that heard the orphan crying.
Ochone, ochone, ochone,oh.

Strong brave and true and kind to women,
Yet fierce and dread to Saxon foemen.
As thou tonight in gaol you're sleeping,
And Oh! I'm left in sorrow weeping.
Ochone, ochone, ochone,oh.

O'er Coumshingaun the dark clouds gather,
You'll sleep no more among the heather,
Through Comeraghs hills night winds are sighing,

225

Where oft you sent the Redcoats flying.
Ochone, ochone,ochone, oh.

Ahearn's gold bought Norris over,
That night the Redcoats round your cover.
May Heaven's vengeance o'er them gather,
My baby ne'er shall see its father.
Ochone, ochone, ochone,oh.

Said to have been written by Willliam Crotty's wife.

The Reynolds Clan
Clooncolry, Co. Leitrim

"In the townland of Drumard, Magyerown in which I live an old story has
been handed down from generation to generation. The incident took place
perhaps two hundred years ago, briefly, a family named Reynolds lived at
Clooncolry and seemed to be strong and powerful.Some members of this
family were Rapparee's and were much feared by the members of the
British garrison of that time at Aughamore and Foulties where lived men of
the planter breed. These Rapparees made constant war on the foreigners
and were always a source of worry and annoyance to the Nesbits and other
planters in this corner of South Leitrim.Ambushes were the order of the day
with the Reynolds clan holding their own.British inducements and threats
were used to snare, capture or seduce these bold Rapparees, but for years
without result. At last Old Nesbit of Faulties caused a feud between certain
families and the Reynolds in particular (A family was paid to entrap the
Reynolds clan).A lengthy period was spent in preparation of the plot.
Hatched and promoted by Nesbit who found willing tools to do his dirty
work. The family found to do this lived at Dromard on the border of
Renagowna town-land.So that their act of treachery should succeed, this
particular family professed great admiration and friendliness towards
Reynolds and his clan and invited them to a feast. The invitation was
accepted and on one particular day the Reynolds, the unsuspecting victims,
singly made their way towards the abode of their treacherous host. At least
twenty men crossed that doorstep, who never returned.One man and only
one escaped to tell this tale. The victims as they entered they were trapped,
inside the door was a trap door which yielded as each victim stepped there
on thus letting each down into a deep pit especially prepared for the
purpose. When they found themselves in this pit they were overpowered
and slain by English soldiers. In this way was got rid of the men who
challenged English Rule in this part two hundred years agoTradition states
that for weeks the caoin of women. The mothers, sisters, and wives could be

heard and some say that the word *Maigh Gearain* means The Plain of the Wailing Women and as a result of this incident it got its name".[99]

Shane Crossagh

Shane Crossagh, was the son of a small farmer who was evicted from his farm at Faughanvale and was forced to seek shelter on the mountains above Claudy before settling (in a place called Lingwood) among others who had been dispossessed also.

When Shane decided to go 'out on his keeping' he had no trouble recruiting a band of followers. The hills around that area were covered in woods to which the robbers could repair when they were pursued.. There are many legends associated with Shane Crossagh. The following relates how one day while travelling through the woods he was confronted by two English soldiers and arrested. "Bad luck", said he, "to be arrested and me going to meet a friend to drink a fine bottle of poteen". One of the soldiers said to him. "Let us share it with you and we won't put the shackles on you". Shane agreed and they brought him back through the woods to retrieve the poteen. However, instead of a bottle Shane retrieved a short- handled pike (*rapaire)* from a clump of bushes and disarmed the soldiers and put them to flight.

It is said that one night he came upon a poor man's cabin and found the occupants in a distressed condition. Their only cow had been seized to pay for tithes at the insistence of the local Protestant clergyman. Shane gave them four sovereigns to tend to their immediate needs. He then set out for the clergyman's house and robbed him of thirty pounds. For this robbery he was pursued night and day until he was captured and committed to Derry Gaol to await his trial. His escort of troops halted to rest at the top of Carntogher mountain Shane asked them to take off his shackles, and he would show them three leaps that would astonish them. The soldiers agreed and Shane made his three leaps on the third one he bounded off the mountain and ran in the direction of Dungiven. (There are three stone cairns which mark the length of each leap to be seen on the top of Carntogher to the present day) Shane gave his pursuers the slip in Dungiven. The following day the soldiers heard that Shane had been seen in the woods near Ballykelly. Shane spied them searching for him and headed towards Loughermore. As he was approaching Slaghtmanus the soldiers were gaining on him and Shane was confronted with the ford of the river in flood. He jumped from the precipice at the Ness to the opposite bank and thereby creating a local landmark called 'Shane's Leap'. Tradition holds that

---

[99] N F.C. S 219 : p 250, Written by Martha McGure, Dromard, Dromod, Co Leitrim told by Mrs Farrell

a farmer, seeing him leap from the precipice across the river called to him, "Bravo, Shane; that was a great leap"

"And so it should be, for I had a good run at it" answered Shane.

Tradition holds that Shane and his sons often lodged for the night at an inn halfway between Dungiven and Carntogher, where they were provided with a private room from which they could eavesdrop on travellers. One evening, while the Crossaghs were staying in the private room, General Napier along with a small detachment of cavalry rested there one evening while making the journey to Derry. At table the General heard from other guests of the exploits of Shane and his followers. The General was very loud in his condemnation of the local magistrates for their inaction in bringing the robbers to justice. Shane decided to teach the General a lesson. When darkness fell he and his two sons slipped from the inn and took the road to Derry.

At a long narrow bridge on a lonely spot on the road he placed a line of sods on each side of the road, giving the impression of the heads of armed men. When the General rode up at the head of his men, Shane shot the horse from under him. The soldiers encircled their General to defend him. A voice cried out, "Surrender to Shane Crossagh! Ready boys present arms!". With the threat of instant death to anyone who raised a musket, Shane demanded that Napier surrender his sword and order his men to stack their arms and submit to be tied in pairs. To compound the indignities heaped upon him, Shane compelled the General to exchange clothes with him, remarking, "it's the man that makes the General not the clothes". Shane Crossagh and his two sons Paudeen and Rory returned to the hills above Claudy but were betrayed by a weaver by the name of Torrens. They were captured, tried and sentenced to death by hanging. Shane was offered a pardon because of his advanced age on condition that he abandon his life of crime. When he heard that his two sons would not be offered the same conditions he refused the offer and elected to die with his sons. In the year 1725 Shane and his two sons were hanged at the Diamond in Derry. Local tradition holds that their bodies were buried in an unmarked grave in the Old Churchyard of Banagher County Derry.

The Generals Bridge

One evening fair three outlaws set upon their task.
While brave General Napier he opened up a cask
They hid 'neath a bridge with their bold fairy band
Well fixed were their weapons for here they would stand
Tonight the old redcoats would be sore and sad
At the hands of Shane Crossagh and Paudeen McFad

One flash of carbines-the General wheeled round
And the steed and his rider both rolled on the ground
His guardsmen they gaped with panic struck stare
When the voice of Shane Crossagh roared loud in the air
Surrender ye knaves to true knights of the Pad
The strong hand forever and Paudeen McFad

Now oath wildly sounded and pistols went flashing
And horses high bounding and broadswords all clashing
The demon of plunder in glory did revel
For Shane and stout Rory laid on like the devil
'Till at length fairly routed the whole scarlet squad
Were tied neck and heels by bold Paudeen McFad.

Willy Brennan

Kilworth lies two miles West of Fermoy and is surrounded by beautiful scenery.This was the home of Willy Brennan the Rapparee famous in song and story.

Brennan on the Moor

Tis of a famous highway man a story I will tell.
His name was Willy Brennan and in Ireland he did dwell.
Twas on the Kilworth mountains he commenced his wild career.
Where many a gallant gentleman before him shook with fear.
Chorus.
Bold Brennan on the Moor, Brennan on the Moor.
A brave undaunted robber was bold Brennan on the Moor.
2
A brace of loaded pistols he carried night and day.
He never robbed a poor man upon the King's highway;
For what he'd taken from the rich, like Turpin and Black Bess.
He always did divide it with the widows in distress.

229

3

One night he robbed a packman, by the name of Pedlar Bawn.
They travelled on together 'till the day began to dawn;
The Juler found his money gone, likewise his watch and chain,
He at once encountered Brennan and he robbed him back again.

4

When Willie found the packman was as good a man as he,
He took him on the highway his companion for to be;
The Juler threw away his pack without anymore delay,
And he proved a faithful comerade until his dying day.

5

It happened on a certain day, as he was riding down,
He met the Mayor of Cashel a mile outside the town;
The Mayor he knew his features; and " I think young man " said he,
" That your name is Willie Brennan, you must come along with me".

6

Now Willie's wife had gone to town provisions for to buy,
When she saw her Willie taken she began to weep and cry;
Says he " give to me a tenpenny", and even as he spoke ,
She handed him a blunderbuss from underneath her cloak.

7

So with the loaded blunderbuss, the truth I will unfold,
He made the Mayor to tremble and he robbed him of his gold;
One hundred pounds was offered for his apprehension there,
But he with horse and saddle to the mountains did repair.

8

Then Brennan being an outlaw bold upon the mountains high,
With cavalry and infantry to take him they did try;
He laughed at them and scorned them, until at length 'tis said,
By a false-hearted comerade he basely was betrayed.

9

In the County of Tipperary in a place they call Clonmore,
Brennan and his comrade were made to suffer sore;
He lay amongst the bracken that grew thick upon the field,
And nine deep wounds he did receive before that he would yield.

10

When Brennan and his comrade found that they were betrayed,
They with the mounted cavalry a gallant battle made;
He lost his foremost finger which was shot off by a ball.
So Brennan and his comrade was taken after all.

11

When they were taken prisoner, in irons they were bound,
And both conveyed to Clonmel jail strong walls did them surround;
The jury found them guilty, the judge made this reply;

"For robbing on the King's highway you're both condemned to die ".

12

Farewell unto my loving wife, and to my children three,
Likewise my aged father, that may shed tears for me;
In all the deeds that I have done I took no life away
May the Lord have mercy on my soul, against the Judgement Day.

Legend

"One day, he was met by two officers of the Fermoy garrison who recognised him and accused him of robbery and arrested him in the Queen's name. He was caught unprepared for this event, and offered no resistance merely saying " It is a poor boy like me to be the bold Brennan"? On their way to the garrison they soon reached a shebeen when Willie requested permission to "light the pipe". All three entered the shebeen in which for many a year he had been no stranger. When Willie handing his pipe to the barmaid and telling her to "put fire into that". She understood the hint implied in the request and returned with a blunderbuss hidden under her apron, with which Willie turned the tables with his captors and robbed them of their money and weapons."[100]

"Parra Glas"
Green Paddy

One of the most dangerous of the Rapparees from county Monaghan was a man who went by the name of "Parra Glas"= *Pádraig Glas*= Green Paddy. His proper name was Patrick O'Connolly of Dromsnat whose father owned a small- holding which was confiscated by the Cromwellians. It is said that his father married the daughter of a peasant and settled down on a farm in Cornaglare. There are no records to show why Patrick and his family left the farm, it is probable that he may have served in the Jacobite army and became an outlaw after its defeat.

He was described as tall and powerfully built, with a great shock of hair and an unkempt beard, both of a greenish grey colour, hence the nickname " Parra Glas ".

All his family were outlaws and made their living by robbing and plundering the settlers around Monaghan. Parra Glas lived in a cave near Tullygillen, near where the mill now stands. One of his women had a hut in the glen near Monaghan from which she was able to spy on the movements of the authorities in Monaghan and report back to Tullygillan.

At the Summer Assizes, held on August 24th 1711 the following proclamation was read in open court.

---

[100] The Shamrock vol 12 1875 p517

231

"We Present Patrick Glass O'Connolly, late of Cornaglare, Parish of Kilmore James O'Connolly late of Cornaglare aforesaid, formerly in Sligo Gaol, Married to Reggie O'Connolly daughter of Patrick Glass, O'Connolly's sister, Peter O'Connolly son of James O'Connolly's brother married to Poralone O'Connolly's daughter and Peter and Jas O'Connolly reputed sons of John O'Connolly, formerly in the Gaol of this County. To be dangerous Robbers, Tories, and Rapparees, out upon their keeping, in arms and not amenable to the laws, but robbing and plundering his Majesty's good subjects".

Alexander Montgomery, Sheriff.

"Presentment duly read in Court and confirmed. Humbly certified to Counsellor Barard in order to have said persons proclaimed as by Act of Parliament is directed.

"Jno Mullan, J"

In 1707 Bryan Roe O'Murphy was proclaimed an outlaw. In 1716 Thomas Murphy, son of Loughlin Murphy of Dernasell, Parish of Tedavnet was proclaimed an outlaw and Rapparee. In 1717 Patrick Duffy and Patrick Kerr were proclaimed for being Tories and having "Broke Gaol". Channen Rock, between Carrickmacross and Dundalk was a great hiding place for Rapparees.
Neil Mc Shane, alias Johnston, nicknamed "Forty Rags" Bryan Byrne alias Bryan-na-Poreen was proclaimed at Dundalk in 1718 and was captured in the same year. Bryen Mc Kenna was proclaimed on February 14th 1722.

Petition forwarded to the Government by the inhabitants of Carrickmacross
17th December 1717.

"To His Grace Charles Duke of Bolton, Lord Lieutenant General and General Governor of Ireland. "Sheweth".
"That there are many proclaimed Tories, Robbers and Rapparees, who do infest the above County and parts adjacent and convenient.
Many robberies and barbarous murders have been committed to the great Damage and sorrow of the country and are often harboured by the Popish inhabitants near said town, and lately are growing so insolent as to appear publicly in great numbers well armed and mounted."

Mo Thruaighe

Mo thruaighe staid nua na hÉireann
Tá a huaisle marbh sa bhFráinc 's in Éireinn
Acht fuigheall beag ar atá craidhte créachtach
Dá mocadh ó thuin go tuinn mar éan laith.

Alas the new state of Ireland
Her nobility are dead in France and in Ireland
Save a few survivors from battle, miserable and wounded
Pushed from wave to wave like birds

Penal Crosses

These are crudely carved wooden crucifixes with the christ figure carved in high relief. They are carved from a single block of wood with extremely short arms.They bear the symbols of the passion (lance, ladder, hammer, nails, three dice, pincers) and the motiff of the cock on the pot at the bottom. According to a study made in 1954 they originated in the vicinity of Lough

Derg and were sold to pilgrims making the pilgrimage to St Patricks Purgatory. There is a traditional belief that the arms of the cross are short for ease of concealment.The motif of the cock on the pot is explained by Peig Sayers, the famous story-teller from the Blasket Islands as follows,

"Nuair a bhí Iosa curtha san uaigh dúirt na Giúdaigh le chéile go ndúirt Mac an tSiúnéara, nuair a bhí sé ina bheatha, go n-éireodh Sé an treas lá.
"B'fhéidir", ar siad le cheile, "go ngoidfeadh a mhuintir leo É, is go ndéarfaidis gur aiséirigh Sé. "Imig", arsa an tUachtarán, "agus daingnig an leac le béal na huaighe; Nuair a bhí an leac feistithe go maith acú dfhilleadar thar n-ais. Bhí flea agus féasta acu ansin. Bhí pota a bhí lán de choiligh óga ag fuichaidh ar an tine. Labhair an tUachtarán,"an bhfuil bhur ngnó déanta cruinn agaibh",ar seiseann. Labhair duine acu agus d'fhreagair. "Ní éireoidh Sé anois nó go n-éireoidh an t-éan atá ag fuichaidh in iochtar an choire. Ní túisce sin ná d'éirigh an coileach ar bhruach an choire, ghread a dhá scíathán agus ghlaoigh a mhac Mhuire.
"Mac na hÓighe slán"
"Mac na hÓighe slán" ar seisean.
Sin é an bhrí atá leis an nglaoch a dhéanann an coileach ar sise".[101]

Translation (by A.Nugent)

When Jesus had been placed in the tomb the Jews spoke together saying that the Son of the Carpenter, when he was alive, had said that he would arise on the third day. "Perhaps" they said together, "that his people will steal him from there and say that he has risen". "Go," said the chief, " and secure the slab at the mouth of the tomb". When the slab was secured properly they returned and were having a celebration. There was a pot full of young cocks boiling on the fire. The chief spoke," did you complete your business properly". One of them replied. "The cock that lies boiling at the bottom of that cauldron will rise before he does"
With that the cock rose up, perched on the side of the cauldron, flapped its wings and cried out,
"The Son of the Virgin lives"
"The Son of the Virgin lives", he said.
That is the meaning of the cry that the cock makes. Said she.

The gospel of Nicodemus, Written in Greek, in the fourth century A.D. describes how, after the Crucifixion , the traitor Judas Iscariot was about to hang himself, he being fearful of the prophesy that Jesus would rise up from the dead. The wife of Judas, who was cooking a cock at the time, in an effort to reassure him, said that the cock she was cooking would crow

---

[101] Sayers Peig Storyteller from the Great Blasket Island

before that happened. With that the cock flapped its wings and crowed three times. This motif was very popular in the iconography of post-mediaeval Ireland and became a feature at the bottom of the Penal Crosses.[102]

There is a collection of penal crosses in the National Science Museum, Maynooth. There is also a collection of Penal crosses to be seen in The Wexford County Museum in Enniscorthy Castle. A collection of Penal crosses can be seen in the Hunt Museum in Limerick. The late Thomas Cardinal O'Fiaich used a penal cross as his pectoral cross.

Saint Patrick's Purgatory

Pilgrimage to Saint Patrick's Purgatory was banned under the 1704 Act to prevent the further spread of Popery. When the authorities became aware that vast numbers of people were assembling at certain seasons at a place called St Patricks Purgatory it was proclaimed that,

"All such meetings and assemblies shall be deemed and adjudged riots, and unlawful assemblies, and punishable as such, in all or any persons meeting at such places, pilgrims were to be fined ten shillings, and in default of payment publickly whipped."

Turlough O'Carolan after completing a pilgrimage to St Patrick's Purgatory was assisted out of the boat by a young lady by the name of Bridget Cruise, although he was blind he recognised her hand,

> "From his lips soft blessings came,
> He knew her hand with truest flame,
> In trembling tones he named her name,
> Although he could not see;
>
> But Oh! The touch the bard could tell,
> Of that clear hand remembered well,
> Ah! by- many a secret spell,
> Can true-love find her own."[103]

---

[102] Ó'hÓgáin Dáithí Myth, Legend & Romance
[103] Ulster Journal of Archaeology 1857 N.L.I. IR791 PP61-81.

The Kilmore Carols

In the year 1684, the Roman Catholic Bishop of Ferns, Luke Waddinge, had published in Ghent, a small book under the title,

A SMALE / GARLAND, / OF PIOUS AND / GODLY SONGS / COMPOSED BY A DEVOUT MAN, / FOR THE SOLACE OF HIS FRIENDS AND / NEIGHBOURS IN THEIR AFFLICTIONS./ THE SWEET AND THE SOWER / THE NETTLE AND THE FLOWER / THE THORN AND THE ROSE / THIS GARLAND COMPOSE.

This book contained some religious 'posies', a number of poems written for the dispossessed gentry of County Wexford and some verses relating to the Popish Plot. It also contained eleven Christmas carols, two of which are sung to the present day in the village of Kilmore in County Wexford.Luke Waddinge was a member of one of the foremost Anglo-Norman families of County Wexford. The Wexford Waddinges were the parent family of the Waddings of Waterford, who claimed among them the famous Franciscan Luke Wadding, the Jesuit theologian Michael Wadding also known as Miguel Godinez, and Peter Wadding, Chancellor of the University of Praque. During the Cromwellian confiscations and transplantations the Wexford Waddinges were banished to Connaught it is probable that at this time Bishop Waddinge was exiled, in his verses he speaks of being exiled twice. He was educated in Paris and according to tradition obtained a doctorate from the Sorbonne. In 1668 he was invited by Bishop Nicholas French to return to Ireland to represent him as Vicar General of Ferns. He appointed him parish priest of New Ross. In 1673 he was appointed Coadjutor to Bishop French with the right of succession. He built a mass-house within the walls in 1674 and from here he administered to his flock. He deferred his consecration as bishop during the life-time of Nicholas French. This saved him from banishment during the persecutions that followed the Popish Plot of 1678. In 1683 he was asked by the Congregation of Prop-aganda to explain why he had not yet been consecrated bishop of Ferns. He replied that conditions in Wexford town were deplorable, and he alone was responsible for administering to his congregation.

He was finally consecrated bishop in 1683 or early 1684 but by this time he was an old man and near death. He died a few years after his book was published, his mass-house fell into ruin and his successor was refused permission to rebuild it. His carols became very popular and were reprinted in London in 1728 and in 1731 for a Drogheda bookseller named James Connor.

Father William Devereux.

Father William Devereux, returned from the Irish college in Salamanca in 1728, he was appointed parish priest of Drinagh, Co. Wexford. He had neither chapel nor mass-house and had to read mass in the corner of a field. The Register of Popish Priests of 1731 attests to this.[104]

He built a mud hut with a thatched roof to serve as his chapel at Killiane. Father Devereux composed a garland of carols which he titled.

'A New Garland Containing Songs for Christmas'

This new garland by Father Devereux contains three of Luke Waddinge's carols,

It also contains an English carol 'Song for Jerusalem' which was first published in 1601, and is traditionally believed to have been written by a Catholic priest under sentence of death. "In an article in The People January 20th 1872 Mr James Howlin states; "it appears the song was originally written by a Father Bennett, A Franciscan martyr, while in prison in Lancashire, in the reign of Elizabeth".[105] The remainder are believed to be the composition of Father Devereux. These carols are sung to the present day, during Christmas, in the village of Kilmore, by a group of six men who divide into two groups of three to sing alternate verses. Among this group of men is a member of the Devereux family.

The following was quoted in The People, a Wexford newspaper, in January 1872,

"I have stood within many of the grandest Cathedrals of Europe and under the dome of St Peter's itself, but in none of them did I ever feel the soul-thrilling rapturous sensation that I did as a boy listening to six aged men on a frosty Christmas morning sing the carols beneath the low straw-thatched chapel of Rathangan"

The following carol which was composed by Bishop Luke Waddinge is still sung at Christmass time in the village of Kilmore.

On St. Stephen's Day

This is St. Stephen's day
His feast we solemnize
From him we learn to pardon
And love our enemies
He's the first Christian Martyr
Who passed from earth to heaven
By suffering hate and envy
And injuries of men.

More just than the just abel

---

[104] Arch Hib iv 116
[105] Ranson R The Kilmore Carols, The Past vol 5 Wexford 1949

This prince of martyrs dy'd
His blood not for revenge
But for God's pardon cry'd
For fury and for rage
He did remission crave
For malice he had mercy
And love for hate he gave.

This souldier of the Cross,
Armed not with Iron but faith
Doth not Assault but suffer
All that men doe or saith
On bended knees with hands
And eyes fix'd on the skies
With humble heart he prays
For murthering enemies.

He clos'd not up his lips
Whilst he enjoy'd his breath
To gain for them a pardon
Who did procure his death
Pardon good God thin rage
This holy saint doth pray
Lay not unto their Charge
What e're they doe or say.
This Champion of the Cross
To conquer death doth dy
Sufferings are his triumphs
Death is his victory
The stones like showers of haile,
Which Jews on him doe cast
Become pure Crownes of Pearles
And Palms which ever last.

He saw the heavens all open
His throne of glory drest
His saviour Christ prepared
To place his soul in rest
Then let us daily pray
For those who us offend
That with Saint Stephen we may
Enjoy a blessed End.

The following carol is from
A New Garland Containg Songs for Christmas (1728)
By William Devereux and is still sung at Christmass time in Kilmore village.

A CAROL FOR ST. JOHN'S DAY

1

To a good old fashion tune I will give you a new song,
In honour of the great Evangelist Saint John,
To whom our saviour dying his Mother did Commend,
And then made him her son who was his dearest friend.

2

Of John seek ye no parentage nor nobliness of birth,
Since he has got a brother, the King of heaven and Earth,
For tho he was a Fisherman taught to the Nets and Oar,
He's now the son of Mary and who can wish for more.

3

But ye that are so curious his father for to know,
He is the son of Thunder, as Christ himself doth shew,
He is the towering eagle which serves the mighty Jove,
To spread his heavenly lightning and burn all hearts with love.

4

To Christ we are all brothers in grace its plain and clear,
But John amongst the rest is Benjamin the dear,
Not one besides his brother search both earth and heaven,
Was so much belov'd by Jesus, by Angels or by Men.

5

Why then shall we compare him to any of the rest,
Who was the loved Disciple that lean'd on Jesus's breast,
Where he sucked in such Mysteries as not till then was known
To Angels or to Prophets or Man but John alone.

6

Our Church the spouse of Christ was left to Peter's charge,
Tho John had greater merit he was not come to age,
Being as yet but twenty he's fit to be a son,
But a husband to the Church you see he was too young.

7

You have seen the love of Jesus and now heres that of John,
Who still stod by his master when all the rest had gone
Tho Peter trice deny'd him before the cock did crow,
Saint John loyal and constant unto the cross did go.

8

The most afflicted mother he lovingly did hand,

239

And whilst our saviour suffered along with her did stand,
When Christ said to the virgin woman there is thy son,
He saith look to thy Mother unto his dear Saint John.

9

No heart can hear conceive nor any tongue express,
Their tears their grief their fondness their love or their distress,
All three were so united in thst one dying heart,
Tho' two were forced to live they rather die than part.

10

In short when all is over I'll not raise your grief,
In this great time of joy solrmnity and mirth,
For fifteen years he served her as the most humble slave,
Until with his own hands he laid her in the grave.

11

When John had thus discharged his chief and only care,
He then began to travel and preach both far and near,
If all his works and wonders to sing we did pretend,
A day would not suffice us our songs would never end.

12

Inflam'd with Peters glory and Pauls he goes to rome,
Hoping as well as they to die by Martyrdom,
He entered with great joy into the tub of Oil
In which the cruel tyrants intended him to boil.

13

When this nor all the rest of tortures they could invent,
Could not molest nor hurt him he doomed to banishment,
Into the Isle of Patmos with grief to end his days,
But he converts the people and lived there long in peac.

14

To see church well grounded he's left till very old,
But the glad hour at last an Angel him foretold,
His blood no hands of tyrants would God permit to stain,
But as he lived a Phoenix he died by Gods sweet flame.

15

His testament and will and constant theme before,
Was to love one another he said it o're and o're,
Thus peaceably he died but Earth could not contain,
His virgin corpse which which Angels triumphing took to Heaven.

16

And now the lov'd Disciple amidst eternal bliss
With Jesus and his mother dwels in happiness,
By Stephen we are taught to pardon by John we are taught to love,
By following their Examples you'll rest with them above.

The Historic Church of Clodiagh
County Kilkenny.

Clodiagh Catholic Church was built in the year 1700 A.D.in a deep hollow excavated in the woods on the banks of Clodiagh stream which winds its babbling way South to the River Nore. The original structure was little more than a thatched hut with a clay floor. Nearby was a small hut or cabin, which was used as a hedge school.

The people of Clodiagh, were very astute, in their choice of this hidden site.

After the rebellion of 1798, when the Yeomanry were pillaging and destroying the surrounding district they failed to discover the little thatched chapel of Clodiagh.

In the year 1800 the church was re-roofed and raised its head above the level of the rock for the first time in one hundred years.

The district of Clodiagh can claim to have had a house of worship for the Holy Mass from the sixth century to the twenty first century, with the exception of a nine year period from 1691 until 1700, when Mass was celebrated at a rock, at the foot of Brandon Hill. This rock is at present situated in the Clodiagh stream in nearby Ballygub. The ancient Parish Church of Cluanemery or Cluan continued in use as a Catholic Church until the death of Edward Fitzgerald at the battle of Aughrim on July 12, 1691.

The vestments which were used during the Penal Days were kept by the Bolger family of Ballinabarna. James Bolger of Ballinabarna House sat in the Parliament of King James 11 in Dublin in 1689. In 1930 this historic church was re-constructed under the auspices of Very Rev A Lowey P.P. Inistioge and Rev J. Guinan C.C.

The re-construction work was carried out by the late John Morrisey, son of the late Patrick Morrisey of Ballygub, who for over fifty years maintained this precious historic gem of our turbulent past.

The Historic Church of Clodiagh

The Spaniard's Church
Teach Phobail an Spáinigh

Situated on the Kilcar-Carrick road, about one mile from Kilcar, at a place called, *Bun na dTrí Sruthan* at the bottom of Gleann an Bhaile Dhuibh (known today as Cashlings) is the unusual structure in the picture below.
The following story is associated with this building. On a fine September evening in the year 1756 a Spanish cruiser was observed as it made its way round Glenhead heading for Donegal Bay. The people of Glencolmcille were aware of a storm brewing and hastened indoors. The Parish Priest accompanied by his clerk, had been on a sick call in Malinbeg. The household implored them to stay the night because of the impending storm but the priest refused to stay. As the two of them crossed *Sliabh Liag* the storm grew in intensity. The clerk entreated the priest to go back before the storm got any worse. The priest insisted they go on assuring the clerk "the angels will guard us". Halfway along the mountain they heard crying and moaning. The priest located from where the sound was coming and carefully made his way down the sea cliff marking the route as he went. Down below he came upon a fatally wounded Spanish sailor. That the priest could speak Spanish

was a great comfort to the sailor. He asked for forgiveness from God for his wasteful life, and told the priest of his lifelong habit of saying three Hail Marys for a happy death. On receiving absolution for his sins he showed his gratitude to the priest by giving him his belt which was filled with gold coins and then he died.

Local tradition holds that the priest used the Spaniards gold to build a church which became known as *Teach Phobail an Spáinigh* The Spaniards Church.

The Lament for Art Ó Laoghaire
Eibhlín Dhubh Ní Chonaill

A poem lamenting the death of her husband by Eileen O Leary (1743-1800) Arthur O leary, who was a colonel in the Austrian army, was outlawed and killed by the Sheriff of Cork at Carriginima, County Cork in 1773 for refusing to sell his horse to a Protestant by the name of Morris for the sum of five pounds. (under the penal laws Irish Catholics were forbidden to own a horse of a value more than this amount) His mortal remains are interred in the ruined abbey of Kilcrea beneath the epitaph.

Lo Arthur Leary, generous, handsome, brave.
Slain in his bloom lies in this humble grave.

This epitaph is believed to have been written by his widow Eileen O'Connell – a member of the O'Connell family from Derrynane and an aunt of Daniel O'Connell who became the champion of Catholic Emancipation and whose efforts were to bear fruit in 1829 with the passing into law of The Catholic Emancipation Act. The horse in question was later surrendered to Morris by the brother-in-law of Eileen a man named Baldwin (who was named in the poem for his pains) in order to avoid litigation. This powerful poem and it's attendant story gives the lie to the view that the Penal Laws were not enforced after 1730. I include the first verse here the complete poem can be found in various publications.

> Mo ghrá go daingean tu!
> Lá da bhfaca thu
> Ag ceann tí an mhargaidh,
> Thug mu shúil aire dhuit,
> Thug mo croí taitneamh duit,
> D'éalaíos óm charaid leat
> Í bhfad ó bhaile leat.

> My steadfast love!
> The day I saw you
> By the gable of the market- house,
> My eye took note of you
> My heart took a shine to you
> I fled from my friends
> Far from my home with you..

Seán Uí Dhuibhir a' Gleanna
Sean O'Dwyer of the Glen

This is one of those haunting, evocative poems from the 17th century, which produced some of the most heart-wrenching poetry and haunting melodies to be found in Ireland. This poem has been put to music and is sung to the present day. It is a fine example of songs of the period, the pathos, anguish, anger, and condemnation of the narrative, skilfully married to the sombre melody.

> *Ar m'éirigh dhom ar maidin,*
> *Grian a' tsamhraidh 'taithneamh,*
> *Chuala an uaill dá casadh,*
> *'Gus ceol binn na n-éin;*

Bruic is miolta gearra,
Creabhair na ngoba fada,
Fuaim ag an macalla,
'Gus lámhach gunnaí tréan.
An sionnach rua ar a' gcarraig,
Míle liú a' marcaigh,
'S beann go dúch sa 'mbealach
Ag áireamh a cuid gé.
Anois tá an triall dá gearradh,
Triallfaimíd thar caladh,
'S a Sheáin Uí Duibhir a'Ghleanna,
Chaill tú do chéim.

2

'Sé sin m'uaigneas fada,
Scáth mo chluas dá gearradh,
An ghaoth adtuaidh am leathadh,
'S bás ins an spear.
Mo ghadhairín suairc dá cheangal
Gan chead lútha ná aisdíocht,
Do bhainfeadh gruaim den leanbh
I mean ghil an lae.
'Sé rí na h-uaisle 'r an gcarraig
An ceáfrach buacach, beannach,
Do tiocfadh suas ar aiteann
Go lá deire 'n tsaoil;
'S dá bhfaghainnse suaimhneas tamall
Ó dhaoinaibh uaisle 'n baile,
Do Thriallfainn féin ar Gaillimh,
Agus d'fhágfainn an scléip.

English Translation

I would rise at morning,
When summer sun was shining-
Hear the hunters calling
And the music sweet of birds;
Badgers, too, and hare-
Woodcock striking air-
The echo everywhere
Of guns could be heard.
Across the rock the red fox-

Horsemen shout to flock-
A crone upon a tussoch
Checks her few geese.
But now they fell our woodlands,
We must fly to new lands,
Lost Sean O'Dwyer, your glens;
Gone your place of ease.

2

'Tis that's my lasting sorrow
Our refuge felled and fallow,
The north wind knocks me over
And death is in the sky.
My little hound's now tethered,
From frolicking prevented
That would have a child delighted
When the sun was riding high.
Now king of all the cragside
The antlered proud stag will bide
And on furze, alone, survive
To the last day of the world.
Oh if I could get some respite
From the townsfolk, day or night,
I'd go to Galway- there take flight
With my sporting blood all furled.

Sean O'Dwyer, was the son of Darby O'Dwyer, chief of the O'Dwyers of Kilnamanagh [Cloniharp Castle]. His cousin, Colonel Edmund O'Dwyer, was in command of a brigade of five regiments, who fought against Cromwell's army.
After the Cromwellian victory, he, with five thousand of his troops joined the Spanish army, under the command of the Prince Condé in Flanders. These troops were to become the nucleus of The Irish Brigade of Spain. Three regiments, Ultonia-El Immortal, Irlanda-El Famoso, and Hibernia-La Columna Hibernia, became famous for their defence of Naples against the Austrians in 1744.

The Abbé Mac Geoghegan to the Irish Troops in the Service of France.

Europe, towards the end of the last century, was surprised to see your fathers abandon the delights of a fertile country, renounce the advantages which an illustrious birth had given them in their native land, and tear themselves from their possessions, from kindred friends, and from all that nature and fortune had made dear to them; she was astonished to behold them deaf to the proposals of a liberal usurper, and following the fortunes of a fugitive king, to seek with him in foreign climes, fatigues, and danger content with their misfortune, as the seal of their fidelity to unhappy masters.

France... gladly opened to them a generous bosom, being persuaded that men so devoted to their princes would not be less so to their benefactors; and felt a pleasure seeing them march under her banners. Your ancestors have not disappointed her hopes. Nervinde, Marseilles, Barcelona, Cremona, Luzara, Spire, Castiglione, Almanza, Villa Viciosa, and many other places, witnesses of their immortal valour, consecrated their devotedness for the new country which had adopted them. France applauded their zeal and the greatest of monarchs raised their praise to the highest pitch by honouring them with the flattering title of "his brave Irishmen".

The example of their chiefs animated their courage; The Viscounts Mountcashel and Clare, the Count of Lucan, the Dillons Lees, Roths, O'Donnells, Fitzgeralds, Nugents, and Galmoys opened to them on the borders of the Meuse, the Rhine and the Poe, the career of glory, whilst the O'Mahonys, MacDonnells, the Lawlesses, the Laceys, the Burkes, O'Carrols, Croftons, Comerfords, Gardners, and O'Connors crowned themselves with laurels on the shores of the Tagus.

The neighbouring powers wished to have in their service the children of these great men; Spain retained some of you near her throne. Naples invited you to her fertile country; Germany called you to the defence of her eagles. The Taafes, the Hamiltons, O'Dwyers, Brownes, Wallaces and O'Neills supported the majesty of the Empire, and were entrusted with its most important posts. The ashes of Mareschal Browne are every day watered with the tears of the soldiers to whom he was so dear, whilst the O'Donnells, Maguires, Lacys and others endeavoured to form themselves after the example of that great man.

Russia, that vast and powerful empire, an empire which has passed suddenly from obscurity to so much glory, wished to learn military discipline from your corps. Peter the Great, that penetrating genius and hero, the creator of a nation which is now triumphant, thought he could do no better than to confide that essential part of the art of war to the Field Mareschal de Lacy, and the worthy daughter of that great emperor always entrusted to that warrior the principle defence of the august throne which she filled with so much glory. Finally, the Viscount Fermoy, general officer in the service of Sardinia has merited all the confidence of the crown.

But why recall those times that are so long past? Why do I seek your heroes in those distant regions? Permit me, gentlemen, to bring to your recollection that great day, forever memorable in the annals of France; let me remind you of the Plains of Fontenoy, so precious to your glory; those plains where in concert with chosen French troops, the valiant Count of Thomond being at your head, you charged , with so much valour, an enemy so formidable; animated by the presence of the august sovereign who rules over you, contributed with so much success, to the gaining of a victory, which till then, appeared doubtful. Lawfeld beheld you, two years afterwards, in concert with one of the most illustrious corps of France, force entrenchments which appeared impregnable. Menin, Ypres, Tournay saw you crown yourselves with glory under their walls, whilst your countrymen, under the standards of Spain performed prodigies of valour at Campo Sancto and at Valeti.

Fontenoy

Thrice, at the huts of Fontenoy, the English column failed,
And, twice, the lines of Saint Antoin, the Dutch in vain assailed;
For Town and slope were filled with fort and flanking battery,
And well they swept the English ranks and Dutch auxiliary.
As vainly, through De Barri's wood, the British soldiers burst,
The French artillery drove them back, diminished and dispersed.
The bloody Duke of Cumberland beheld with anxious eye,
And ordered up his last reserve, his latest chance to try,
On Fontenoy, on Fontenoy, how fast his generals ride!
And Mustering come his chosen troops, like clouds at eventide.

Six thousand English veterans in stately columns tread,
Their cannons blaze in front and flank, Lord Hay is at their head;
Steady they step adown the slope, steady they climb the hill;
Steady they load, steady they fire, moving right onwards still,
Betwixt the wood and Fontenoy, as through a furnace blast,
Through rampart, trench, and palisade, and bullets showering fast;
And on the open plain above they rose and kept their course,
Past Fontenoy, past Fontenoy, while thinner grow their ranks,
They break, as broke the Zuyder Zee through Holland's ocean banks.

More idly than the summer flies French tirailleurs rush round,
As stubble to the lava tide French squadrons strew the ground;

Bomb-shell, and grape, and round shot tore, still on they marched and
fired-
Fast from each volley grenadier and voltigeur retired
"Push on my household cavalry!" King Louis madly cried:
To death they rush, but rude their shock, not unavenged they died.
On through the camp the column trod- King Louis turns his rein:
"Not yet my liege," Saxe interposed, "the Irish troops remain";
And Fontenoy, famed Fontenoy, had been a Waterloo,
Were not these exiles ready then fresh, vehement,and true.

"Lord Clare," he says, "you have your wish: there are your Saxon foes!"
The Marshal almost smiles to see, so furiously he goes!
How fierce the look these exiles wear, who're wont to be so gay,
The treasured wrongs of fifty years are in their hearts to-day-
The treaty broken ere the ink wherewith 'twas writ could dry,
Their plundered homes, their ruined shrines, their women's parting cry,
Their priesthood hunted down like wolves, their country overthrown-
Each looks as if revenge for all were staked on him alone,
On Fontenoy, on Fontenoy, nor ever yet elsewhere,
Rushed on to fight a nobler band than these proud exiles were.

O'Brien's voice is hoarse with joy, as halting he commands,
"Fix bay'nets! Charge!" Like mountain storm, rush on these fiery bands!
Thin is the English column now, and faint their volleys grow,
Yet must'ring all the strength they have, they make a gallant show.
They dress their ranks upon the hill to face that battle- wind-
Their bayonets the breaker's foam; like rocks the men behind!
One volley crashes from there line, when, through the surging smoke,
With empty guns clutched in their hands, the headlong Irish broke.
On Fontenoy, on Fontenoy, hark to that fierce huzza!
"Revenge! Remember Limerick! Dash down the Sassanach!"

Like lions leaping at a fold, when mad with hunger's pang,
Right up against the English line the Irish exiles sprang:
Bright was their steel, 'tis bloody now, their guns are filled with gore,
Through shattered ranks and severed files the trampled flags they tore;
The English strove with desperate strength, paused, rallied, staggered, fled-
The green hillside is matted close with dying and with dead.
While cavalier and fantassin dash in upon their track,
On Fontenoy, on Fontenoy, like eagles in the sun,
With bloody plumes the Irish stand, the field is fought and won.

Thomas Davis

Bán-Chnoic Eireann Ó

Beir beannacht ó mo chroidhe go tír na hEireann,
Bán-chnoic Éireann Ó!
'S chum a mairionn de shíolrach Ir 's Eibhear,
Ar bhán-chnoic Éireann Ó!
A g-cuid meala 'gus uachtair ag gluaiseacht na flaoda,
Ar bhán-chnoic Éireann Ó!
Rachad-sa ar cuairt, no is Luach mo fhaoghal,
Do'n talamh mín suairc is dual do Ghaedhal,
'S go m'fhearr liom 'ná duais, dá uais leacht é, bheith,
Ar bhán-chnoic Éireann Ó!

Sgaipeann an drúcht ar gheamhar 's fhéar ann,
Ar bhán-chnoic Éireann Ó!
'S fásaid ábhla cúbhartha an ghéagaibh ann
Ar bhán-chnoic Éireann Ó!
Bídheann biolar 's samhadh ann a n-gleanntaibh ceóaigh,
'S na srotha san t-samhradh ag labhairt uim nedín
Uisge na Siuire ag brúcht na shlóghaidh,
Cois bán-chnoic Éireann Ó!

Ar osguilteach, fáilteach, an áit sin Eire,
Bán-chnoic Éireann Ó!
Bídheann " Toradh na Sláinte" a m'bárr na déise,
A m-bán-chnoic Éireann Ó!
Ba binne liom na méaraibh ar théadaibh ceoil,
Seinnim 's géimreadh a laugh, 's a m-bó
Taitniomh na gréine orra aorda 's óg ,
Ar bhan-chnoic Éireann Ó!.

Donnchadh (Ruaidh) Mac Con-Mara 1736

The Fair Hills of Eire O!

Take a blessing from my heart to the land of my birth,
And the fair hills of Eire, O!
And to all that yet survive of the Eibhear's tribe on earth,
On the fair hills of Eire, O!
O'er her smooth grass for ever sweet cream and honey flow,
On the fair hills of Eire, O!
O, I long am I pining, again to behold
The land that belongs to the brave Gael of old;
Far dearer to my heart than a gift of gems or gold
Are the fair hills of Eire O!

The dew- drops lie bright 'mid the grass and yellow corn
On the fair Hills of Eire O!
The sweet-scented apples blush redly in the morn
On the fair Hills of Eire O!
The water-cress and sorrel fill the vales below;
The streamlets are bushed, till the evening breezes blow;
While the waves of the Suir, noble river! Ever flow
Near the fair Hills of Eire O!

A fruitful clime is Eire's, through valley, meadow, plain,
And the fair Hills of Eire O!
The very "Bread of Life" is in the yellow grain
On the fair Hills of Eire O!
Far dearer unto me than the tones music yields,
Is the lowing of her kine and the calves in her fields
And the sunlight that shone long ago on the shields
Of the Gaels, on the fair Hills of Eire, O!

Donogh (the red) Mac Con-Mara 1736
Translation by James Clarence Mangan

An Spailpín Fánach

Go deo deo arís ní raghad go Caiseal
Ag diol ná ag reic mo shláinte,
Ná ar mhargadh na saoire im shuí cois balla,
Im scaoinse ar leataoibh sráide.
Bodairí na tire ag teach tar a gcapaill
Dá fhiafraí an bhfuilim hírálta,
Ó téanam chun siúil tá an cúrsa fáda
Seo ar siúl an Spailpín Fánach.

Im Spailpín Fánach fágadh mise,
Ag seasamh ar mo shláinte,
Ag siúl an drúchta go moch ar maidin
'S ag bailiú galair ráite.
Ní fheicfear corrán im' láimh chun bainte,
Sáiste ná feac beag ráinne,
Ach bratacha na bhFranncach o scion mo leapan
Is píce agam chun sáite.

Mo chúig céad slán chun dúiche m'athar
'Gus chun an oileáin ghrámhar,
Is chun buachaillí na Culach ós díobh nár mhiste,

251

In aimsir chasta an ghárda
Ach anois ó táimse im chadhan bhocht dhealbh
I measc na ndúichí fáin seo
'Sé mo chuma croí mar fuair mé an ghairm,
Bheith riamh im Spailpín Fánach.
Is ró bhreá is cuimhin liom mo dhaoine bheith sealad
Thiar ag droichead Gháile
Fe bhuaí, fé choraí, fé laoi bheaga gheala
Agus capaill ann le h-áireamh.
Acht b'é toil Chríost é gur cuireadh sinn asta,
'S gan deaghamhar í Leith ár sláinte,
'S gurb é bhris mo chroí í ngach tír dá rachainn
Is iad ag glaoch an Spailpín Fánach.

The Wandering Labourer
Oh, never, ever again will I go to Cashel
To sell and barter my health,
Nor to the hiring fair, to sit by the wall,
On my hunkers at the side of the road.
Lords of the land coming on their horses
To ask me am I hired,
Come, lets walk you've a long journey before you!
There goes the Wandering Labourer

I was left a wandering labourer,
Standing on my health,
Though walking the dews in the early morning
Will soon bring quartan fever,
You wont see me carry scythe to harvest,
A flail or spade handle cover,
But the French flag above my head
And a pike with me for thrusting.

Five hundred , farewell to the home of my fathers
And to our loving Island,
And the boys of Coole – who were not wanting
In the times of the troubles,
And now I am in a poor state
In the midst of foreigners slaving,
It is my heart's thought that I will never miss
The life of the Wandering Labourer.

It's well I remember my people had their day,
West at the bridge of Galway.

With cows to milk and sheep and calves,
And horses beyond counting.
But it was the will of Christ that I did them lose.
And without them my health but half recover,
And it breaks my heart, in every country I go,
To be called the Wandering Labourer

Written in 1797, this lament by one of the many young men who had been dispossessed of their land and were forced to become migratory labourers his ambition to trade his farm implements for a French pike signalled what was to come in 1798.

Wolfe Tone

Theobald Wolfe Tone was born in Dublin on the 20th of June 1763, he graduated from Trinity College and became a member of the bar in 1790. He joined the Ulster Reformers in Belfast in 1791. He was a founder member of the United Irishmen and in 1792 he helped form an alliance between the Catholic Committee and the United Irishmen. In 1794, on the summit of McArts Fort, Cave Hill, near Belfast, Theobald Wolfe Tone, S Nielson, Simms, Henry Joy McCracken, and T Russell, took a solemn obligation, "never to desist in our efforts until we had subverted the authority of England and asserted our independence".

On June 13th 1794 Wolfe Tone sailed from Belfast for America, where he stayed until he went to France in January of 1796. He communicated with the French government and established close relations with De La Croix, Carnot, General Clarke, and Hoche and he finally managed to persuade the Directory to send an expedition to Ireland.[106]

This expedition ended in failure through a combination of bad weather and incompetence and indecision the fleet returned to France without landing in Ireland or firing a shot.

On the 20th of September, 1798, another expedition set sail for Ireland from the Bay of Camaret under the command of Admiral Bompart. This consisted of nine frigates, the *Hoche, Loire, Resolue, Bellone, Coquilla, Embuscade, Immortalite, Romaine, and Semillante.* And one schooner the *Biche.* In order to avoid interception by the British fleet they took a wide sweep westwards and then to the north-east in order to bear down on the northern coast of Ireland. This expedition met with heavy winds and the flotilla was scattered. On October 10th Bompart arrived off the entry to Lough Swilly, with the *Hoche, the Loire, the Resolur, and the Biche.* On the folling day October 11th before he could enter the bay and land his troops, a British fleet, under the command of Sir John Borlase Warren, consisting

---

[106] The Autobiography of Theobald Wolfe Tone vol 1 ed R . Barry O'Brien The Phoenix Publishing Company Dublin Cork and Belfast.

of six sail of the line, one raze of 60 guns, and two frigates bore down on him. Bompart immediately gave orders to the frigates and schooner to retreat through shallow water and prepared to defend his ship.

During the ensuing battle which, lasted six hours, the *Hoche was surrounded by* four sail of the line and one frigate and subjected to sustained fire until her masts and rigging were swept away, her rudder destroyed and she was left a floating wreck.

Some days later the *Hoche* was brought into Lough Swilly, and the prisoners were landed and marched to Letterkenny. The French officers were invited to have breakfast with the Earl of Cavan, who was in command of the district. While they were at breakfast Sir George Hill accompanied by some police officers entered the room, on recognizing Wolfe Tone (they were fellow students at Trinity College), he remarked, 'Mr Tone I am very happy to see you'. In irons he was taken to Dublin, where on Saturday, November 10th 1798, he was tried before a Court Martial consisting of, General Loftus, Colonels Vandeleur, Daly, and Wolfe, Major Armstrong and Captain Curran. A Mr Patterson performed the functions of Judge Advocate. He was sentenced to death by hanging . He considered this as unacceptable to an officer of the French Army and demanded an honourable death by firing squad. When he was informed on November 11th that this was refused, he cut his throat and died eight days later. (There is a common folk belief that his throat was cut by the authorities).

Ierne United

When Rome, by dividing, had conquered the world,
And land after land into slavery hurled,
Hibernia escaped, for it was heaven's decree,
That Ierne, united, should ever be free.

Her harp then delighted the nations around,
By its music entranced, their own sufferings were drowned;
In arts and in learning the foremost was she,
And Ireland United was happy and free.

But soon-ah! too soon, did fell discord begin,
Our domestic dissensions let foreigners in,
Too well they improved the advantage we gave,
Whom they came to protect they remained to enslave.

From that fatal hour, our freedom was lost,
Peace, virtue, and learning were banished our coast,
And the island of saints might fitly be named,

The land of tormentors, the place of the damn'd.

Then let us remember our madness no more,
What we lost by dissension let union restore;
Let us firmly unite, and our covenant be,
Together to fall, or together be free.

This song was written by Theobald Wolfe Tone and was published in 1792.
It was subsequently published in Maddens *Literary Remains.* Mary Ann
McCracken informed Madden that she had heard Wolfe Tone's daughter,
Maria, sing this song to the air of *An Crúiscín Lán.*
It is recorded that this song was sung in Belfast on the 14th of July 1792 at
a dinner which was held to celebrate the anniversary of the Fall of the
Bastille, and the ending of the Belfast Harp Festival.

THE GRAVE OF WOLFE TONE

In Bodenstown Churchyard there lies a green grave,
And wildly around it the winter winds rave.
Small shelter I ween, are the ruined walls there,
When the storm cloud sweeps down on the plains of Kildare.

Once I lay on that sod- it lies over Wolfe Tone-
And thought how he perished in prison alone,
His friends unavenged and his country unfreed-
'O,bitter', I said, 'is the patriots mead!'

'For in him the heart of a woman combined
With a heroic life and a governing mind-
A martyr for Ireland-his grave has no stone-
His name seldom named, and his virtues unknown'.

I was woke from my dream by the voices and tread
Of a band who came into the home of the dead;
They carried no corpse and they carried no stone,
And they stopped when they came to the grave of Wolfe Tone.

There were students and peasants, the wise and the brave,
And an old man who knew him from cradle to grave,
And children who thought me hard hearted; for they,
On the sanctified soil were forbidden to play.

But the old man who saw I was mourning there, said,
"We come, sir, to weep where young Wolfe Tone is laid,
And were going to raise him a monument too-
A plain one yet fit for the simple and true".

My heart overflowed, and I clasped his old hand,
And I blessed him, and blessed every one of his band;
Sweet, sweet 'tis to find such faith can remain
To the cause and the man so long vanquished and slain.

\#   \#   \#   \#   \#   \#   \#

\#   \#   \#   \#   \#   \#   \#

In Bodenstown Churchyard there is a green grave,
And freely around it let winter winds rave-
Far better they suit him- the ruin and gloom
Till Ireland a Nation can build him a tomb.

Thomas Davis

Written in 1845 by Thomas Davis and published in The Nation the stars before the final verse indicate that two verses were withheld because of the political temper at the time of publication. There is no record of the missing verses.

When Thomas Davis visited the grave in 1843 he was informed by the local blacksmith, "No one walks on that grave, and even the children are taught by the grey-haired men not to harm it".

The monument to Wolfe Tone, in Bodenstown Churchyard, in the picture was erected in 1971 after the original was blown up by the U.V.F. in 1969.

Wolfe Tone's Speech From the Dock.

"I mean not to give the trouble of bringing judical proof to convict me legally of having acted in hostility to the government of his Britannic majesty in Ireland. I admit the fact. From my earliest youth I have regarded the connection between Great Britain and Ireland as the curse of the Irish nation, and felt convinced that, while it lasted, this country would never be free nor happy. My mind has been confirmed in this opinion by the experience of every succeeding year, and the conclusions which I have drawn from every fact before my eyes. In consequence, I was determined to employ all the powers which my individual efforts could move, in order to separate the two countries. That Ireland was not able to herself to throw off the yoke, I knew,

I therefore sought for aid wherever it was to be found. In honourable poverty I rejected offers which, to a man in my circumstances, might be considered highly advantageous. I remained faithful to what I thought the cause of my country, and sought in the French Republic an ally to rescue three millions of my countrymen.

Attached to no party in the French Republic- without interest, without money, without intrigue – the openness and integrity of my views raised me to a high and confidential rank in its armies. I obtained the confidence of its executive directory, the approbation of my generals, and will venture to add, the esteem and affection of my brave comrades. When I review these circumstances, I feel a secret and internal consolation, which no reverse of fortune, no sentence in the power of this court to inflict, can deprive me of, or weaken in any degree. Under the flag of the French Republic I originally engaged with a view to save and liberate my own country. For that purpose I have encountered the chances of war among strangers; for that purpose I repeatedly braved the terrors of the ocean, covered, as I knew it to be, with the triumphant fleets of that power which it was my glory and my duty to oppose. I have sacrificed all my views in life; I have courted poverty; I have left a beloved wife unprotected, and children whom I adored fatherless.

After such a sacrifice, in a cause which I have always considered–conscientiously considered – as the cause of justice and freedom, it is no great effort, at this day, to add the sacrifice of my life.

But I hear it is said that this unfortunate country has been a prey to all sorts of horrors. I sincerely lament it. I beg, however, that it may be remembered that I have been absent four years from Ireland. To me those sufferings can never be attributed. I designed by fair and open war to procure a separation of the two countries. For open war I was prepared, but instead of that a system of private assassination has taken place. I repeat, while I deplore it, that it is not chargable on me. Attrocities, it seems, have been committed on both sides. I do not less deplore them. I detest them from my heart; and to those who know my character and sentiments, I may safely appeal for the truth of this assertion; with them I need no justification. In a case like this success is everything. Success, in the eyes of the vulgar, fixes its merits. Washington succeeded, and Kosciusko failed.

After a combat nobly sustained – a combat which would have excited the respect and sympathy of a generous enemy – my fate has been to become a prisoner, to the eternal disgrace of those who gave the orders. I was brought here in irons like a felon. I mention this for the sake of others; for me, I am indifferent to it. I am aware of the fate which awaits me, and scorn equally the tone of complaint, and that of supplication. As to the connection between this country and Great Britain, I repeat it – all that has been imputed to me (words, writings, and actions), I here deliberately avow. I have spoken and acted with reflection, and on principle, and am ready to meet the consequences. Whatever be the sentence of the court, I am prepared for it. Its members will surely discharge their duty – I shall take care not to be wanting in mine.

I wish to offer a few words relative to one single point – the mode of punishment. In France our *émigrés,* who stand nearly in the same situation in which I now stand before you, are condemned to be shot. I ask that the court adjudge me the death of a soldier, and let me be shot by a platoon of grenadiers. I request this indulgence rather in consideration of the uniform I wear – the uniform of a *chef de brigade* in the French army – than from any personal regard to myself. In order to evince my claim to this favour, I beg that the court may take the trouble to peruse my commission and letters of service in the French army. It will appear from these papers that I have not received them as a mask to cover me, but that I have been long and *bona fide* an officer in the French service.

I have laboured to create a people in Ireland by raising three million of my countrymen to the rank of citizens. I have laboured to abolish the infernal spirit of religious persecution, by uniting the Catholics and Disenters. To the former I owe more than ever can be repaid. The services I was so fortunate as to render them they rewarded munificently; but they did more; when the public cry was raised against me – when the friends of my youth swarmed off and let me alone – the Catholics did not desert me; they had the virtue even to sacrifice their own interests to a rigid principle of honour; they refused, tho strongly urged, to disgrace a man who, whatever his conduct toward the government might have been, had faithfully and conscientiously discharged his duty toward them; and in so doing, tho it was in my own case, I will say they showed an instance of public virtue of which I know not whether there exists another example".[107]

TONE IS COMING BACK AGAIN

Cheer up, brave hearts, to-morrow's dawn wll see us march again
   Beneath old Erin's flag of green that ne'er has known a stain.
And ere our hands the sword shall yield or furled that banner be-
We swear to make our native land from the tyrant's thralldom free!

Chorus
For Tone is coming back again, with legions o'er the wave,
The scions of Lord Clare's Brigade, the dear old land to save.
For Tone is coming back again, with legions o'er the wave,
The dear old land, the loved old land, the brave old land to save!

Though crouching minions preach to us to be the Saxon's slave,

---

[107] The Worlds Famous Orations, William James Bryan editor in chief Vol VI 1906 Funk &Wagnals co New York

We'll teach them all what pikes can do when hearts are true and brave.
Fling freedom's banner to the breeze, let it float o'er land and sea-
We swear to make our native land from the tyrant's thralldom free!
Chorus

Young Dwyer among the heath-clad hills of Wicklow leads his men;
And Russell's voice stirs kindred hearts in many an Ulster glen.
Brave Father Murphy's men march on from the Barrow to the sea-
We swear to make our native land from the tyrant's thralldom free!
Chorus
Too long we've borne with smouldering wrath the cursed alien laws,
That wreck our shrines and burn our homes and crush our country's
cause;
But now the day has come at last; revenge our watchword be!
We swear to make our native land from the tyrant's thralldom free"

anon

Wolfe Tone's Grave, Bodenstown

Miles Byrne

Miles Byrne was born in Ballylusk in County Wexford in the year 1780. In 1798 he led the rebels of the Monaseed district at the battles of Tubberneering, Arklow, and Vinegar Hill above Enniscorthy. After the collapse of the rebellion in Wexford he led a contingent of rebels into Glenmalure in the heart of the Wicklow Mountains, where they waged a guerrilla campaign against the English until November of 1798. He then went into hiding in Dublin where he remained until the failure of the Robert Emmet inspired rebellion forced him to flee to France in 1803. In France he joined the French Army and served with distinction until he retired in 1830 with the rank of *Chef de Bataillon* of the 56th Regiment. He died in 1862

"Here I first saw the brave, intrepid Michael Dwyer. He had already acquired a great reputation in this mountainous district. Every time the cavalry tried to reconnoiter the position near the entrance to the Glen, he was sure to be on their flank or in ambuscade, before daylight awaiting their arrival. Both he and his followers were from this country, and were very good marksmen. They took delight in terrifying the cavalry, who wheeled about and fled the moment a shot was fired at them. So, by reason of Dwyer's bravery, we were perfectly safe at night, to rest and recover from the fatigues of our Wexford campaign.The famous Holt had just arrived in the Glen. Worth special mention is a night expedition which we made under his command, and during which we encountered, suddenly, near the bridge of Greenan, an enemy army marching from Rathdrum to reconnoiter our position in the Glen. Hearing the noise of our column's advance, the enemy delivered a fierce discharge from their pistols, and then awaited in silence our approach. I shall never forget Holt's presence of mind in this danger. He cried out with the voice of a Stentor, ordering our pikemen to march in a body across the bridge. In the same loud voice he ordered the gunmen to wade across the river and attack the enemy's flanks. The enemy apparently terrified, retreated in disorder to Rathdrum, while we, on our side, had the greatest trouble in rallying our men and keeping them from disbanding. However after some time panic subsided and we rallied again on the road and returned to the glen.

Glenmalure is nearly three miles long. The little river, Avonbeg, coming down from the high mountains, runs through it. There were several houses on each side of the river, and in those houses our men could cook the mutton which they got in abundance. They found timber for pike handles in the rafters of the smelting house belonging to the lead mines. Soon we were fairly well armed with pikes, though still badly provided with firearms and ammunition.

Sad tidings now reached us of the defeat and complete dispersal of our main army, which had marched into the counties of Meath, Louth and Dublin. The chiefs of the Glen held a meeting and resolved in consequence to defend the Glen more carefully than ever.Among those who escaped to Glenmalure from the Boyne were Esmond Kyne and my brother Hugh. The former would not stay with us. He insisted on returning to Wexford, where he expected to get a safe hiding place. Alas! He was hanged and gibbeted like the other patriots whose heads already decorated the public buildings in the town of Wexford.

Had Father Kearns and Anthony Perry reached Glenmalure, they would have been able to make use of the great advantages these Wicklow Mountains offered against the enemy. But they were doomed not to die the death of soldiers. They were both captured and hanged at Edenderry."

Michael Dwyer

Michael Dwyer was the son of a respectable farmer, who lived on the borders of the Glen of Imaal, in County Wicklow. He attained the rank of Captain during the rebellion of 1798, under the command of Billy Byrne of Ballymanus. He took to the mountains and glens of Wicklow after the suppression of that rebellion. From the Glen of Imaal and Glenmalure he and his comrades carried out a guerrilla war against the English.

In February 1799 a heavy fall of snow forced Michael Dwyer and his men to leave their mountain caves on Lugnaquilla and seek shelter in the Glen of Imaal. Michael and three of his men, Sam McAllister, John Savage, and Costeleo found shelter in a house in the townland of Dairenamuck, they were spotted by an informer, who reported their whereabouts to the military at Hacketstown. The following dawn the house was surrounded by soldiers. The officer in charge called upon Dwyer to surrender. He refused to answer until the civilians present in the house were given safe passage from the house. The English allowed the civilians safe passage. Dwyer refused to surrender. In the battle which ensued, Savage and Costoloe were killed and McAllister was wounded in the right arm. The English then set the house on fire. In order that his leader might have a chance Sam McAllister unbolted the door and darted out in front of the waiting soldiers, and took the full impact of the rifle volley. Dwyer ran out of the house, turned at the gable, and ran six miles across the snow covered mountain in his underwear, and crossed a tributary of the river Slaney to freedom.

The cottage from which Michael Dwyer made his escape 2006

The following narrative was recorded on an Ediphone machine in July 1934 by Mrs O Toole of Ballycumber, Ballyglen, Co. Wicklow. The recording was transcribed by Mr Pádraig Ó' Tuathail, O.S. Hackettstown, Co. Carlow.

Mrs O Toole, who, died on the 30th of April 1935, at the age of eighty-six was the grand-daughter of Larry Byrne who played an important role the insurrection of 1798 and was a companion of Michael Dwyer's.

"On one occasion Dwyer and my grandfather and Hugh Byrrne of Monaseed and poor McAllister – I am troubled to the heart when I think of poor McAllister; he was a true man, well the four of them were in a cave on Lugnaquilla when the daylight came by and the sun shone in through the heather which hung over the hole they crept in. They were as comfortable as the day is long lying in a big bundle of clean straw and good bedclothes that was brought from a farmers house; and the farmer's house was my great grandfather's. They were brought from a farmer's house near to the mountain and placed there designedly for the boys. So the four awoke, and they began to talk, and they got up and struck their flints and steel 'cause there were no matches. Then they lit their pipes each of them, and they commenced to smoke and to talk as happy as the day is long, when a robin came in – and a robin is unusual so high up in the mountain, you know – a robin flew in and she jumped around the quilt over them, and one grabbed

262

at her, and another, and she flew out from the whole of them, and it wasn't two minutes till she came in again, and when she came in she bustled and set herself just as if she was going to jump at them, and she got wicked looking and;

"O", says they, "there is something in this". The four jumped to their feet and one of them put his head through the hole and he pulled back excited. "O!" he says, "the hillsides is red with soldiers," "Which will we lie in," says another, "or will we get out? If they have bloodhounds were found out". "That's right," says they, and they all jumped to their feet, and the blood hounds came into the bed, but they dragged on their breeches and put their hats on them, and out they went with their guns. Dwyer whipped his sea-whistle and he whistled, and he could be heard, I suppose in Arklow, and they fired off their three shots, and the soldiers turned around and they ran for their lives, and they never got time to look back till they fell over Lugnaquilla, and they told when they got below that the hills was full of rebels.

Sam McAllister's Grave

The Walking Magazine

There was a woman who used to deal in carrying bread around to the farmers herself and selling it to the women and children and otherwise, and when '98 broke out she was a valiant heroine woman and should be good, should have been of good blood or she wouldn't have been so sound as she was, for she never divulged it, and she carried scores and maybe hundreds of back loads of powder to the boys and a dozen penny buns put in over the pack, and no one ever detected it that she carried back loads of powder to the boys during the whole of '98 and was never detected. Her name was never made known afraid they might find out what she was at, and she would have got a horrid death, but, thanks to God! She didn't – she was never known by anything but the "Walking Magazine".

Escape from Knockananna

One Sunday morning Dwyer and McAllister were at mass in Knockananna Chapel, and they brought their guns with them and left them by the wall. The priest remonstrated with them and said that the House of God was no place to bring guns, but McAlliater who was a Presbyterian but used to go to mass with Dwyer said; "It is not always we have a rebellion, Father. Go on with the mass!" And the priest did so.

During the mass a neighbour came to Dwyer and said that he had been at the window and that the chapel yard was full of soldiers, and Dwyer picked out two clever young fellows and he told them to go away to a field a distance from the chapel-yard but in sight of it and says he; "take off your coats." He told them to run along the field in their shirts as fast as they could, and he picked out two or three more young chaps of boys that were clever enough to understand him, and he told them to go down beside the soldiers and stand looking down at this field and to cry out each one in surprise and wonder; "There they go! There they go!" And they did so, and the soldiers asked them who did they mean by there they go, and they told them- all cried out; "Dwyer and McAllister! Dwyer and McAllister!" The soldiers started out for to overtake Dwyer and McAllister, and they failed on it for Dwyer and McAllister was hid in the chapel and when the soldiers cleared out they cleared out and went their way in peace and quietness. The soldiers went out across the fence and they came upon the two boys that ran and they sitting with their coats on, and they smoking their pipes and they asked them did they see two men running through the fields, and they said no and they said "no", that they were not long there. So Dwyer and McAllister walked off in safety.

264

Almost Captured

Dwyer was near being captured in Imaal after that when the soldiers came to a house where he was, but he got out and into a piggery behind a big old sow, and when the soldiers came in the sow sat up on her hind legs and made battle with them, and Dwyer gave her a little stab now and then behind her back and they prodded at her with their bayonets, and she groaned at them fearful wicked, and by and by they got tired and said he wasn't there after all.

Escape from Glendalough.

Dwyer and my grandfather and the boys went on to a friend's place in the Churches and there was a born cripple lodging at the house, and no one mistrusted anything about him. He was at one side of the kitchen and they were at the other talking over their plans, and Dwyer said that he would get into St Kevin's Bed and let the soldiers surround him, and the boys would surround him and he would fire off a shot as a signal. So the cripple gathered up the whole story, and when he got up the next morning and got in his box where there were four dogs drawing him, it was a strange sight to see, he got on to the camp, and he informed on the poor fellows, and told every word he heard the night before. He informed on them, and when he mentioned St Kevin's Bed the English Officer said he knew nothing about St Kevin's Bed, and the cripple brought the soldiers on to show them where St Kevin's Bed was, and when he came there he pointed it out to them. But Dwyer rose up on his elbow when he saw him and he let fly at him and he blew him out of the old box. The soldiers took flight then, and got away with their lives. So when Dwyer expected they'd be surrounding him backwards he jumped into the lake which was never done since or before by any man.

Moonlight by the Slaney

When Dwyer was after being married to his wife, a beautiful woman, Doyle, an officer came from Humewood camp where they were staying , several of them and a lord – an English Lord, Lord Huntley and this old officer came to Mrs Dwyer in the absence of Dwyer, and he asked her to come out on the road that he wanted to speak to her. He was very nice to her, and made her great promises. He told her that there was as good men in England as Dwyer – she should have been cool – it wasn't I was in it! – I suppose he meant to give her the pick of an Englishman, and as well that she'd never want, that she'd have money at her command every place she'd go, and he told her that there was as good men in England as Dwyer. If she'd just let him know where was Dwyer every thing would be right, and then he looked around him and he said; "Maybe, Mrs Dwyer, you wouldn't like to be seen speaking to me here on the road? If you'd come down to yonder grove beside the Slaney at the dusk of night, such an evening as there was moonlight, we would have a private conversation where there'd be no one to see us." Mrs Dwyer agreed with him and said she would go, and when Dwyer came home she told him the whole story. Dwyer told her that they'd save her the journey, that he'd go and have a loving chat with this old officer, and he said to her to dress him in her grey cloak, as there was cloaks with a big hood at the back worn by girls in them days. So she dressed Dwyer in the grey cloak which covered him down to the feet, and he started to have a loving conversation with the old officer. He went down to the bank of the Slaney, and he made himself as small as he could, and he sat down concealed in his grey cloak. The old officer stepped out of the grove and gently tipped him on the shoulder to have the loving chat with Mrs Dwyer, and to his great surprise Dwyer jumped to his feet and whipped hold of him by the throat, and threw him into the Slaney, and hammered him against the stones there till he had him boneless and senseless and lifeless, and he laid him down there beside the Slaney. He was brought off by the soldiers and buried and they made no fuss about him at all.

Surrender and Deportation

Two neighbours of Dwyer's went to the glen of Imaal and advised him to surrender and not to give the English Government the pleasure of arresting him and hanging him as a dog, after all his bravery and good acts he had done. He told them he'd never go into Humewood to lay down his arms to a British subject, that he'd suffer death a thousand times before he'd do it, and he'd stay where he was and give them more of it. So the two men importuned him not to venture his life altogether, and that they'd go into Humewood and propose to Hume that he'd have to come out to meet Dwyer, to come to some settlement, that he wouldn't go into Humewood, that he'd never do it. Hume agreed to come out, and that he'd bring no guard of soldiers with him, nor to come by day, and he done neither, but he brought two farming men like what they were along with him and they put on Imaal Gap after nightfall, and when they were drawing near Hume got a bit shaky about Dwyer and he cried out; "Was that Dwyer?" and Dwyer said it was and he asked him; "Dwyer have you got arms on you?" "I have", says Dwyer, "but they wont affect you tonight."

So they drew near to each other and Hume mentioned a number of the transports abroad, but Dwyer told him if he made up his mind to go anywhere he'd go where he liked, and if not he'd stay at home and give them more of it. Hume, delighted to hear of a chance of getting shut of him at all, to get him out of Ireland, threw up arms and he said; "All right, Dwyer, all right. Go where you please we'll send you anywhere".

So Dwyer said he'd go to Sydney in Australia, and if they did not send him there he'd go nowhere at all but would stay home and give them more of it. So they sent him to Sydney in Australia, and he brought his pike along with him".[108]

The terms of Michael Dwyer's surrender on the 14th of December 1803 included the right of Michael Dwyer and his family to emigrate to America. Upon his surrender he was incarcerated for eighteen months before being transported to Australia in August 1805. In Australia he became a land-owner and for a period of time he was the Chief Constable of the town of Liverpool in New South Wales. He died on the 23rd of August 1825 at the age of fifty-three.

The Outlaw's Bridal

1
As the torrent bounds down from the mountain
Of cloud-helmed, stormy Kaigeen,
And tosses, all tawny and foaming,
Through the still glen of lone Carrageen,
So dashed a bold rider of Wicklow,
With forty stout men in his train,
From the heart of the hills, where the spirit
Of freedom has dared to remain!

2
Of grey frieze their caps and their surcoats,
Their carbines were close to their knee,
And their belts were well furnished with pistols,
Like men who knew how to be free!

3
Oh ! grass-green the sash on their shoulders,
Their caps crested green with cockades;
And their leader he wore a long dagger-
The brightest and keenest of blades.

4
To the right ran Imale's lovely valley,
And before them was meadow and mound,
And the gallop of freemen was music
The echoes sprang out to resound!

5
Thou leader of horsemen! why hasten
So fleetly to Brusselstown Hill?
What foeman, what yeoman await thee,

---

[108] For further details see, Pádraig Ó' Tuathail , Wicklow Traditions of 1798, *Béaloideas*, vol 5 no 2 (Nollaig 1935) pp174 - 178.

To question, in Wicklow, thy will!
6
No foemen or yeomen they're seeking,
Though furiously onward they ride;
But their leader, he loves a young maiden,
And he's speeding to make her his bride,
7
"Halt" Bridles were drawn, and they halted;
Theres a farmstead looming ahead,
And the door of the dwelling is open;
Now the leader rode forward and said.
8
"There's somebody seeking thee Mary;
A boy who came down from Kaigeen,
With forty brave bridesmen from Laragh,
With cochades and crosses of green."
9
Oh ! Mary came out in her beauty,
The loveliest maid of Imale,
The loveliest flower that blossomed
In all the wild haunts of the vale.
10
Arrayed in an emerald habit,
And the green and the white in her hat,
The leader he sprang from his courser,
As light as a hawk from the air-
He pressed her fair hand to his bosom;
She felt the big throb of his heart-
" My Mary! I'll love thee forever,
Till God on this earth will us part!"
11
They led out a horse on the heather;
She patted his neck with her hand,
Then sprang on his back like a feather,
And stood in the midst of the band!
12
The leader was soon in his saddle;
"Castle Buddery's ruins" he cried;
"The priest's house is near to Green's River
And here is the ring for my bride".
13
Away dashed the cavalcade fleetly,
By beauty and chivalry led,
With their carbines aflash in the sunlight,

And the saucy cockades on their head,
14
The priest he demurred and he pleaded,
The maiden she blushed and she frowned,
And the Leader of Forty felt nervous,
And tapped with his gun on the ground,
And thus went the parley, till even
Began to fall down on the glen,
And the priest thought a matron were better
To be mid such wild, bearded men.
15
They were wedded; "To horse!" cried the leader
And the bridal pair led the hot flight;
And away rode Dwyer, the Outlaw,
To his mountain- cave, back in the night.

Campion

Captain Dwyer

Draw nigh, ye sons of liberty,
Come listen to my story,
The truth to you I will relate,
It's of Hibernia's glory.

All in the chains of slavery,
Since Cromwell and his damned decree
Has robbed us of our liberty,
But now the time is over.

Now the time is drawing nigh
When we shall be delighted,
Those heroes brave on Wicklow's plains,
So bold and firmly united.

No Orange tyrants of the land,
No cavalry can them withstand,
They fly like chaff before the wind,
With dread in heart sincerely.

There is Captain Dwyer from Imail,
A true stout-hearted member,
The bloody twenty-fourth of May

He can very well remember.

Then the cavalry like birds of prey,
Exulting in their tyranny.
And many a bleeding victim lay
Along the streets of Stratford.

This hero brave oft did declare
That he'd have full satisfaction,
As soon as he could well prepare
To join in warlike action.

But soon the boys they did him join,
And Hacketstown surrounded,
With pike and gun they made them run,
Their schemes were soon confounded.

Captain Byrne was there that day
As stout as Alexander,
That Hardy and his troops knew well,
For shortly they were conquered.

To hear them bawl, to shout and run,
Crying out that they were now undone,
At every corner of the town,
They were driven to destruction.

Those heroes brave, with loud huzzas,
Maintained the fight with valour;
The soldiers, to protect their lives,
Retired within their barrack.

But soon did Dwyer, with Holt and Neal,
And Reynolds too that man of fame,
Set the town and barrack in a flame,
Which caused a deal of ruin.

The next attack was in Keadun bog,
When they met with Captain Dwyer,
One hundred cavalry and more
On him began to fire.

He and six more behaved so well,
The cavalry to their grief may tell,

You would laugh to see how many fell,
And wallowed in the mire.

Out of six he lost but one,
Yet there was something hasty,
Of soldiers more than half a score,
He gave them such vexation.

To think how he had so much odds,
And they were hampered in the bogs,
Which made them curse and blame their Gods
That they had them forsaken.

There is a curse o'er Baltinglass,
And likewise o'er Dunlavin,
For spilling innocent blood thereon
Which is for vengeance calling.

Those vicious hearts that took delight
In deeds of blood both day and night,
But our heroes brave gave them a fright,
That their wits have them forsaken.
Now to conclude and make an end,
Let us fill up our glasses,
And drink to every daring man,
While time and season passes.
And steady in themselves, prepare
The green cockade once more to wear,
Drive tyrant villains to despair,
And that's our only glory.

R.R.Madden

This ballad above differs from the others in that it celebrates Michael Dwyer's exploits as a Captain of a company during the rebellion of 1798, whilst the others extol his exploits as a guerrilla fighter in the aftermath of the rebellion.

Michael Dwyer

At length brave Michael Dwyer and his undaunted men
Were scented o'er the mountain and tracked into the glen;
The stealthy soldiers followed, with ready blade and ball,
And swore to trap the outlaw that night in wild Imaal.

They prowled around the valley, and towards the dawn of day

Discovered where the faithful and fearless heroes lay,
Around the little cottage they formed in a ring,
And called out; 'Michael Dwyer! Surrender to the King!".

Thus answered Michael Dwyer – 'into this house we came
Unasked by those who own it; they cannot be to blame,
Then let those guiltless people, unquestioned pass you through
And when they've passed in safety, I'll tell you what we'll do'.

T'was done, 'and now', said Dwyer, 'your dirty work begin';
You are a hundred outside – were only four within;
We've heard your haughty summons, and this is our reply-
We're true United Irishmen, we'll fight until we die'.

Then burst the war's red lightening, then poured the leaden rain,
The hills around re-echoed the thunder peals again;
The soldiers falling round him brave Dwyer sees with pride,
But, ah! One gallant comrade is wounded by his side.

Yet there are three remaining, good battle still to do;
There hands are strong and steady, there aim is quick and true-
But hark that furious shouting the savage soldiers raise!
The house is fired around them! The roof is all ablaze.

And brighter every moment the lurid flame arose,
And louder swelled the laughter and cheering of their foes;
Then spoke the brave McAllister, the weak and wounded man-
You can escape, my comrades, and this shall be your plan;

'Place in my hands a musket, then lie upon the floor-
I'll stand before the soldiers and open wide the door;
They'll pour into my heart, boys, the fire of their array,
Then while their guns are empty, dash through them and away'.

He stood before the foemen, revealed amidst the flame;
From out their levelled pieces the wished for volley came.
Up sprang the three survivors for whom the hero died
But only Michael Dwyer burst through the ranks outside.

He baffled his pursuers, who followed like the wind.
He swam the river Slaney, and left them far behind,
But many a scarlet soldier he promised soon would fall
Foe those, his gallant comrades, who died in wild Imaal.

T.D.Sullivan (1827-1914)

Michael Dwyer

Have you heard of Michael Dwyer and his mountain men?
Burns your blood like molten fire when you hear again
How he dashed like mountain torrent on his country's bitter foes
Like a thundering towering torrent on the craven Yeos?

Here's the chorus, chant it loudly on the still night air,
As the war- cry proudly rises o'er the trumpets blare.
Chant it, peal it till it echoes over every hill and glen,
Here's to gallant Michael Dwyer and his mountain men.

When the star of freedom vanished and our flag went down
And the nations hope was banished from each vale and town,
Borne intact through flood and fire, Irelands banner waved again,
Held aloft by Michael Dwyer and his mountain men.

But the nations hearts are burning as they burned of yore
And the young and strong are yearning for the battles roar.
But the blessed star of liberty shall never blaze again,
Till we strike like Michael Dwyer and his mountain men.
                    Peadar Kearney.

Mountain Men

Did you mark e'er a smoke drift go sailing
  A while ago down by yon wood?
Did you hear in the glen the wind wailing
  Where a barrack a week ago stood?
Did you hear the Yeos boasting to trap us,
  And hang us like dogs on a tree?
Why, then, were not strangers, and maybe
  You'll join in this chorus with me.

Sing ho! for the boys of the mountain;
  And hey! For the boys of the glen!
Who never showed heel to the soldiers-
  Here's *Sláinte* to Dwyer and his men!

We're not given much to parading;
  There's not many guns in the throng;
But he that comes spying our quarters
  Wont bother the world for a-long,
The troopers come seeking us daily,
  To drive us to hell, so they say,
But the road's a bit long, so we send them
  Before us to show us the way.

There's many a white- livered villain
  That dreads to awaken our ire,
And tries to be civil for treason
  We visit with steel, lead and fire.
The people all bless us, for many
  A cabin's left safe and secure
For fear of the men of the mountain
  Whose guns are the guard of the poor.

We laugh at their offers of money
  And scorn their power, if we fail
It wont be the soldiers or traitors
  Who'll bring us to grief, I'll go bail.
We're only a few, but the valleys
  And mountains are ours- every hill
And while God leaves the strength in our sinews
  We'll keep the old cause living still.

William Rooney 1898

Commemorative stone in Glenmalure

Twenty men from Dublin Town

Twenty men from Dublin town,
Riding on the mountain dide,
Fearless of the Saxon Frown,
Twenty brothers true and tried.
Blood flows in the city streets,
There the green is lying low,
Here the emerald standard greets
Eyes alike of friend and foe.

Fly the city, brothers tried,
Join us on the mountain side;
Where we've England's power defied
Twenty men from Dublin Town.

Twenty men from Dublin Town
Full of love and full of hate,
Oh! Our chief, our Tone, is down,
Hand of God avenge his fate.

Joy it is where ere we meet
Redcoats on the mountain track,
Ah! As deer they must be fleet
If they get to Dublin back.

Twenty men from Dublin Town,
Every night around the fire
Brimming methers toss we down
To our captain Michael Dwyer.
Sláinte, Michael, brave and true,
Then there rings the wild hurrah!
Health we drink, dear land, to you,
Éire, sláinte geal go brách.

Arthur Griffith 1890s

The Walking Gallows

Edward Lambert Hepenstal was born in Upper Newcastle, County Wicklow around 1776. Through the influence of his brother, a clerk with the Dublin police, he received a commission with the Wicklow Militia in 1796. He is described in the Irish Magazine in January 1810 as follows,
"Amongst the monsters which the Insurrection Act, passed in 1796, called into loyal activity, none have surpassed 'The Walking Gallows', for atrocity, nor more distinguished for moral depravity".
"The loyal giant Lieutenant Hepenstal, who towering almost to seven feet, with chest and muscles in proportion, and that he dispensed with the formalities of assembling juries and erecting gibbets and on encountering a supposed criminal threw a rope round his neck, and swung him over his own shoulders, as he would have a young deer or rabbit there to dangle till he was dead."[109]
In 1796 he was in command of a column in Moyvore in Co Westmeath, which had been declared under martial law, he ordered the alarm drum to be sounded and then proceeded to murder the inhabitants. He ordered a man named Smyth and his two sons to be dragged into the street. He ordered that the cord of a drum be taken off, and with his own hand's he simultaneously hanged the two brothers from his shoulders. He then ordered that the father be shot. The next morning the three bodies were drawn through the town behind a cart.
It is said that he killed six men in cold blood in Gardenstown and Moyvore in 1797. In 1796, Hepenstal half hanged a prosecution witness named

---

[109] Bernard Bayle The life of Samuel Lover 1874 vol 1 p6

Hyland to encourage him to give false evidence against a man for an armed attack. Hyland retracted his statement in court and was arrested, indicted, convicted, sentenced and hanged on the same day.

During a trial in 1796 Hepenstal admitted that he had not only,"used some threats and pricked him with a bayonet", to obtain testimony from a prosecution witness, but that the prisoner himself had also "been pricked with a bayonet to induce him to confess: a rope had been put around his neck, which was thrown over his (Hepenstal's) shoulder he then pulled the rope, and drew the prisoner up, and he was hung in this way for a short time, but continued sulkly, and confessed nothing".

The defence attorney put it to Hepenstal:

"Then you acted the executioner, and played the part of the gallows?" "Yes please your honour", was the reply of Lieutenant Hepenstal. The Solicitor-General, Mr Toler, (destined to become Lord Norbury the infamous 'hanging judge') who tried the case, in his charge to the jury regretted the treatment of the prisoner, "but it was an error such as a young and gallant officer might fall into warmed by resentment". The prisoner was found guilty.

Epigram on Lord Norbury
In former times the murder's tongue,
Denied the deed, or silent hung,
Appalled with fear and dolor,
But now the villain boasts his guilt,
The murderer is the Tolor.[110]

According to the Irish Magazine, Hepenstal died at his brother's house, in Andrews Street, in Dublin, in 1804, and was buried secretly in the church yard there Mrs O'Toole say's that he was killed, in 1798, along with two companions in an engagement with rebels, and was buried opposite the barracks, in Aughavanagh, with a slab at his head and feet, to denote his immense build.[111] Mr Keogh of Aughavanagh, who worked for Charles Stewart Parnell, and the Redmond family, claims that Hepenstal's body was removed from Aughavanagh Rath and re-buried in Arklow.[112] Fitzpatrick in his book (Ireland before the Union 6th edition p 247) offers the opinion that he is buried in Rathfarnham cemetery where tombs to his family may be found dating from 1710. Local tradition holds that he hanged his last victim at the gates of Aughavanagh Barracks, which later became a youth hostel, and that various hostellers have seen his huge ghost even though they were not aware of the story.

---

[110] Madden R.R. Litery Reamains of the United Irishmen p 171
[111] For further details see, O'Tuathail Padraig , Wicklow Traditions of 1798, *Béaloideas,* Vol 5 no 2 (Nollaig 1935) pp 174 - 178
[112] N.F.C 265 Mr Keogh Aughavanagh, : p 555

The following epithet was proposed by Rev Dr Barratt [113]

Here lie the bones of Hepenstal,
Judge, jury, gallows, rope, and all.

Hepenstal – The Walking Gallows

Father Manus Sweeney

Some say that Father Manus Sweeney was born in the village of Keel, on Achill Island in the year 1763. A local historian Padraic Ó'Morain claims that he was born in his grand-mother's house in Rossmore near Newport. He received his primary education at a hedge–school in Achill, and his classical education at a school run by his brother at Dookenella, also in Achill. He was noted for his piety and as a consequence was sent to France to study for the priesthood at the Irish College in Paris. Following his ordination to the priesthood he returned to Ireland and in 1798 he was curate in Newport.

Following General Humbert's success in Castlebar he sent a detachment of troops to secure Newport. Father Manus recognised one of the French

---

[113] Madden R.R. <u>The United Irishmen Their Lives and Times</u>

278

officers, Captain Boudet, and invited him to dine with him. After the defeat of the French, and Irish, at Ballinamuck, Fr Manus was arrested and taken to Castlebar Gaol. He was later taken to Newport for trial by military tribunal. He was lodged in the house of the local Protestant rector the Reverand Mr Heron. Reverend Heron was sympathetic to the priest's condition and helped him to escape to the mountainous region of Glenlara where he spent some time. He then made his way back to Keel, where he spent some time. He also stayed in the village at the base of Slievemore which was the largest village on Achill at that time this village was deserted at the time of the Famine and can be seen to the present day. He finally went to stay in Valley and here he was captured in 1799. There is a local tradition that he was captured by accident.

"The soldiers were searching a house for a man by the name of Maguire unable to find him they were about to leave the house when one of them began thrusting his bayonet up into the loft, the old woman of the house cried out in alarm,

(*Ná maraigh an sagart*) – Don't kill the priest.

One of the soldiers understood Irish and so the priest was discovered hiding in the loft. On the 22nd of May 1799 at the court in Castlebar he was sentenced to death by hanging. On the 9th of June he was brought to Newport where he was hanged.

There is a local legend that a man named Lyghtal, observing the priest hanging in agony from the crane in Newport remarked, "That the priest's bacon was hanging high today". The priest's sister, overhearing this insulting remark, prayed that the scoffer might meet his death on top of a mountain.Some years later Lyghtal while travelling in Achill disappeared and nothing was heard of him until dogs found his remains on Cortoon Mountain and dragged his bones down to the villages of Owenduff and Tonragee.

According to tradition the parish priest of Newport, Canon Waldron, was unhappy with Fr Sweeney's radical opinions. While the priest's body was being prepared for burial the Canon insisted that he be buried in Achill and this was agreed upon. However when the hearse bearing the coffin of the priest reached the road leading to the Abbey at Burrishoole, the horses stopped and refused to go any further. The mourners then decided to bury the remains of the priest within the walls of the Abbey.

The Abbey of Burrishoole

Law has sent them from the Abbey and the pure and holy spring,
Yet to these spots, with childlike love, the faithful fathers cling.
Close by they've raised a shealing, hidden from the prowler's gaze,
There, unknown, with simple clansmen, do they pass away their days.
'Tis the grey dawn of the morning, in the shade of ruins rude,
The priest is at the altar – kneels around a multitude –

Birds make music in the foliage, in each rift the angels guard,
And the pale light of the candles glimmer oer the dewy sward.
Grim graves are all around them, holding dust of sainted dead;
Books, sculpture, blood-stained floor flags through the tall rank weeds are
spread,
And the hush is only broken by the whispering of prayers –
So await the dawn of freedom, hunted flock and outlawed Friars.

The Abbey of Burrishoole

Robert Emmet

Robert Emmet was born in 1778, became a leader of the United Irishmen, led an unsuccessful uprising in Dublin in 1803 for which he was hanged in front of St Catherine's Church in Thomas Street.He was a brilliant student, winning, five academic honours from Trinity College Dublin, before being expelled for his radical republican opinions. He was a linguist, who spoke five languages fluently and had negotiated with some of the most powerful political figures of his day, such as Talleyrand and Napoleon. His speech from the dock is said to have inspired young Abraham Lincoln to study for a career in law and politics.

Robert Emmet's Speech from the Dock.

An impromptu address delivered at the Session House in Dublin, before the court which had found him guilty of treason and sentenced him to death.
"My Lords:- What have I to say why sentence of death should not be pronounced on me according to the law? I have nothing to say that can alter your predetermination, nor that it will become me to say with any view to the mitigation of that sentence which you are here to pronounce, and I must abide by. But I have that to say which interests me more than life, and which you have laboured (as was necessarily your office in the present circumstances of this oppressed country) to destroy. I have much to say why my reputation should be rescued from the load of false accusation and calumny which has been heaped upon it. I do not imagine that, seated where you are your minds can be so free from impurity as to receive the least impression from what I am going to utter- I have no hopes that I can anchor my character in the breasts of a court constituted and trammelled as this is - I only wish, and it is the utmost I expect, that your lordships may suffer it to float down your memories untainted by the foul breath of prejudice, until it finds some more hospitable harbour to shelter it from the storm by which it is at present buffeted.
Was I only to suffer death after being adjudged guilty by your tribunal, I should bow in silence, and meet the fate that awaits me without a murmur; but the sentence of law which delivers my body to the executioner, will, through the ministry of that law, labour in its own vindication to consign my character to obloquy- for there must be guilt somewhere; whether in the sentence of the court or in the catastrophe, posterity must determine. A man in my situation my lords, has not only to encounter the difficulties of fortune, and the force of power over minds which it has corrupted or subjugated, but the difficulties of established prejudice: the man dies, but his memory lives. That mine may not perish, that it may live on in the respect of my countrymen, I seize upon this opportunity to vindicate myself from some of the charges laid against me. When my spirit shall be wafted to

281

a more friendly port; when my shade will have joined the bands of those martyred heroes who have shed their blood on the scaffold and in the field, in defence of their country and of virtue, this is my hope: I wish that my memory and name may animate those who survive me, while I look down with complacency on the destruction of that perfidious government which upholds its domination by blasphemy of the Most High- which displays its power over man as over the beasts of the forest- which sets man upon his brother, and lifts his hand in the name of God against the throat of his fellow who believes or doubts a little more or a little less than the government standard- a government which is steeled to barbarity by the cries of the orphans and the tears of the widows which it has made.#

#=Emmet was interrupted by the judge-Lord Norbury, who said, "that the mean and wicked enthusiasts who felt as he did were not equal to the accomplishment of their wild designs." – W.J.B.

I appeal to the immaculate God-I swear by the throne of Heaven, before which I must shortly appear-by the blood of the murdered patriots who have gone before me-that my conduct has been through this peril and all my purposes, governed only by the convictions which I have uttered, and by no other view, than that of their cure, and the emancipation of my country from the superinhuman oppression under which she has so long and too patiently travailed; and that I confidently and assuredly hope that, wild and chimerical as it may appear, there is still union and strength in Ireland to accomplish this noble enterprise. Of this I speak with the confidence of intimate knowledge, and with the consolation that appertains to that confidence. Think not, my lords, I say this for the petty gratification of giving you a transitory uneasiness; a man who never yet raised his voice to assert a lie, will not hazard his character with posterity by asserting a falsehood on a subject so important to his country, and on an occasion like this. Yes my lords, a man who does not wish to have his epitaph written until his country is liberated, will not leave a weapon in the power of envy; nor a pretense to impeach the probity which he means to preserve even in the grave to which tyranny consigns him.#
Here he was again interrupted by the court.
Again I say, that what I have spoken, was not intended for your lordship, whose situation I commiserate rather than envy-my expressions were for my countrymen; if there is a true Irishman present, let my last words cheer him in the hour of his affliction. #
Lord Norbury once more interrupted Emmet, saying he did not sit there to hear treason.
I have always understood it to be the duty of a judge when a prisoner has been convicted, to pronounce the sentence of the law; I have also understood that judges sometimes think it their duty to hear with patience,

and to speak with humanity; to exhort the victims of the laws, and to offer with tender benignity his opinions of the motives by which he was actuated in the crime, of which he had been adjudged guilty; that a judge has thought it his duty so to have done, I have no doubt-but where is the boasted freedom of your institutions, where is the vaunted impartiality, clemency, and mildness of your courts of justice, if an unfortunate prisoner, whom your policy, and not pure justice, is about to deliver into the hands of the executioner, is not suffered to explain his motives sincerely and truly, and to vindicate the principles by which he was actuated?

My lords, it may be a part of the system of angry justice, to bow a man's mind by humiliation to the purposed ignominy of the scaffold; but worse to me than the purposed shame, or the scaffold's terrors, would be the shame of such unfounded imputations as have been laid against me in this court: you my lord {Lord Norbury}, are a judge, I am the supposed culprit; I am a man, you are a man also; by a revolution of power, we might change places, tho we never could change characters; if I stand at the bar of this court, and dare not vindicate my character, what a farce is your justice? If I stand at this bar and dare not vindicate my character, how dare you calumniate it? Does the sentence of death which your unhallowed policy inflicts on my body, also condemn my tongue to silence and my reputation to reproach? Your executioner may abridge the period of my existence, but while I exist I shall not forbear to vindicate my character and motives from your aspersions; and as a man to whom fame is dearer than life, I will make the last use of that life in doing justice to that reputation which is to live after me, and which is the only legacy I can leave to those I honour and love, and for whom I am proud to perish. As men my lord, we must appear at the great day at one common tribunal, and it will then remain for the searcher of all hearts to show a collective universe who was engaged in the most virtuous actions, or actuated by the purest motives- my country's oppressors or # (here Emmet was told to listen to the sentence of the law) W.J.B

My lord, will a dying man be denied the legal privilege of exculpating himself, in the eyes of the community, of an undeserved reproach thrown upon him during his trial, by charging him with ambition, and attempting to cast away, for a paltry consideration, the liberties of his country? Why did your lordship insult me? Or rather why insult justice, in demanding of me why sentence of death should not be pronounced? I know, my lord, that form proscribes that you should ask the question; the form also presumes a right of answering. This no doubt may be dispensed with-and so might the whole ceremony of trial, since sentence was already pronounced at the castle, before your jury was impaneled; your lordships are but the priests of the oracle, and I submit; but I insist on the whole of the forms.

I am charged with being an emissary of France! An emissary of France! And for what end? It is alleged that I wished to sell the independence of my country! And for what end? Was this the object of my ambition? And is this the mode by which a tribunal of justice reconciles contradictions? No, I am no emissary; and my ambition was to hold a place among the deliverers of my country-not in power, nor in profit, but in the glory of the achievement! Sell my country's independence to France! And for what? Was it for a change of masters? No! But for ambition! O my country, was it personal ambition that could influence me? Had it been the soul of my actions, could I not by my education and fortune, by the rank and consideration of my family, have placed myself among the proudest of my oppressors? My country was my idol; to it I sacrificed every selfish, every endearing sentiment; and for it, I now offer up my life. O God! No, my lord; I acted as an Irishman, determined on delivering my country from the yoke of a foreign and unrelenting tyranny, and from the more galling yoke of a domestic faction, which is its joint partner and perpetrator in the patricide, for the ignominy of existing with an exterior of splendour and of conscious depravity. It was the wish of my heart to extricate my country from this doubly riveted despotism.

I wished to place her independence beyond the reach of any power on earth; I wished to exalt you to that proud station in the world.

*   *   *

Be yet patient! I have but a few words more to say. I am going to my cold and silent grave: my lamp of life is nearly extinguished: my race is run: the grave opens to receive me, and I sink into its bosom! I have but one request to ask at my departure from this world- it is the charity of its silence! Let no man write my epitaph: for as no man who knows my motives dare now vindicate them, let not prejudice or ignorance asperse them. Let them and me repose in obscurity and peace, and my tomb remain uninscribed, until other times, and other men, can do justice to my character; when my country takes her place among the nations of the earth, then, and not till then, let my epitaph be written. I have done.

OH! BREATHE NOT HIS NAME

Oh! Breathe not his name-let it sleep in the shade
Where cold and un-honoured his relics are laid!
Sad, silent, and dark, be the tears that we shed
As the night-dew that falls on the grass o'er his head!

Night dew that falls, though in silence it weeps,
Shall brighten with verdure the grave where he sleeps,
And the tear that we shed, though in secret it rolls,

Shall long keep his memory green in our souls.

Thomas Moore

The Bastille-A Fragment

And must I then part with these objects so far?
In the pain of my spirit I said:
But, subduing the thought, I made haste to repair
To the cell where the victim is laid.

The battlement walls that overshadow this gate
Resound-and the dungeon unfold,
I pause; and at length through the glimmering grate
That outcast of pity behold.

His thick matted hair on his bosom is burst.
And deep is the sigh of his breath;
While with innocent conscience his eye is intent
On the fetters that link him to death.

When from the dark senate of blood-reeking field
To his chamber the Monarch is lead,
All soothings of sense, this soft virtue shall yield
And silent attention shall pillow his head.

Should the suffering patriot a moment but pause-
And oblivion his torturers appease.
On the iron that galls him....
In the dark dripping vaults of disease.

When fall fair he would sleep, and has patiently tried,
No longer his body to turn,
And the irons that enters so deep in his sides
Has entered to deep to be borne:

While the Jail Master's howl at the dull clanking chain,
From the roots of his hair then shall start
A thousand sharp punctures of cold sweeping pain,
And terror shall leap to his heart.

But now! He half raises his duly sunken eye

And the motion unsettles a tear!
It seems the low voices of full pain to supply
And asks of me "Why am I here?"

Poor victim! No idle intruder has stood
With o'rwhelming complacence, our status to compare
But one whose first wish, is the wish to do good,
Is care as a brother thy sorrow to share.

And that faith should compassion to nature resign
Then in Tyrants mouth thy report be a stain,
If the arm of the mighty were mine
I'd plant thee where yet, thee might blossom again.
Deem not that vainly I grieve
That her grasp on her fame
L...d wife shall reprieve
Round the dwelling of shame.

Robert Emmet 1803

Arbour Hill

No rising column marks the spot
Where many a victim lies;
But Oh! The blood which here has streamed
To Heaven for justice cries.
It claims it on th'oppressor's head
Who joys in human woe,
Who drinks the tears by misery shed
And mocks them as they flow.

It claims it on the callous judge,
Whose hands in blood are dyed,
Who arms injustice with the sword,
The balance throws aside.
It claims it for his ruined isle,
Her wretched children's grave;
Where withered freedom droops her head,
And man exists-a slave.

O Sacred justice! Free, this land
From Tyranny abhorred;
Resume thy balance and thy seat-
Resume-but sheath thy sword.
No retribution should we seek-
Too long has horror reigned;
But mercy marked may freedom rise,
By cruelty unstained.

Nor shall a tyrant's ashes mix
With those our martyred dead;
This is the place where Erin's sons
In Erin's cause have bled.
And those who here are laid to rest,
Oh! Hallowed be each name;
Their memories are forever blest-
Consigned to endless fame.

Unconsecrated is this ground,
Unblest by holy hands;
No bell here tolls its solemn sound.
No monument here stands.
But here the patriot's tears are shed

The poor man's blessing given;
These consecrate the virtuous dead,
These waft their fame to heaven.

Robert Emmet

This poem was written by Robert Emmet after he had visited the site of the Croppy Graves near Arbour hill in Dublin. (see picture below) The "callous judge" mentioned in verse two is none other than Lord Norbury who presided at Emmet's trial and was known as the 'Hanging Judge'.

Croppies Acre

Bold Robert Emmet

The struggle is over, the boys are defeated,
Old Irelands surrounded with sadness and gloom,
We were defeated and shamefully treated
And I, Robert Emmet, a-waiting my doom.

Bold Robert Emmet, the darling of Erin,
Bold Robert Emmet will die with a smile,
Farewell companions both loyal and daring,
I'll lay down my life for the Emerald Isle.

Hung, drawn and quartered, sure that was my sentence,
But soon I will show them no coward am I,
My crime is the love of the land I was born in,
A hero I lived and a hero I'll die.

The barque lay at anchor awaiting to bring me
Over the billows to the land of the free;
But I must see my sweetheart for I know she will cheer me,
And with her I will sail far over the see.

But I was arrested and cast into prison,
Tried as a traitor, a rebel, a spy;
But no one can call me a knave or a coward,
A hero I lived and a hero I'll die.

Repeat Chorus

Hark! the bells tolling, I well know its meaning,
My poor heart tells me it is my death knell;
In come the clergy, the warder is leading,
I have no friends here to bid me farewell.

Good-bye, old Ireland, my parents and sweetheart,
Companions in arms to forget you must try;
I am proud of the honour, it was only my duty-
A hero I lived and a hero I'll die.

Repeat Chorus

Tom Maguire

MY EMMET'S NO MORE

Despair in her wild eye, a daughter of Erin
Appeared on the cliff of a bleak rocky shore,
Loose in the winds flowed her dark streaming ringlets
And heedless she gazed on the dread surge's roar,
Loud rang her harp in wild tones of despairing,
And in soul-thrilling strains deeper sorrow declaring,
She sang Erin's woes and her Emmet's no more.

Oh, Erin, my country! Your glory's departed,
For tyrants and traitors have stabbed thy heart's core,
Thy daughters have laid in the streams of affliction,
Thy patriots have fled or lie stretched in their gore!
Ruthless ruffians now prowl through thy hamlets forsaken,
From pale hungry orphans their last morsel have taken,
The screams of thy females no pity awaken,
Alas! My poor country, your Emmet's no more!

Brave was his spirit, yet mild as the Brahmin,
His heart bled in anguish at the wrongs of the poor;
To relieve their hard suffering he braved every danger,
The vengeance of tyrants undauntedly bore,
Even before him the proud villains in power
Were seen, though in ermine, in terror to cower,
But, alas! He is gone, he has fallen a young flower,
They have murdered my Emmet-my Emmet's no more.

Written in the early nineteenth century this song was sung to the air of
Savourneen Deelish

EMMET'S FAREWELL

Farewell love, farewell love, I'm now going to leave you,
The pale moon is shining its last beams on me.
The truth I declare that I ne'er will deceive thee;
For next to my heart, sure, was Erin and thee.

Draw near to my bosom, my first and fond true love
And cherish the heart that beats only for thee.
And let my cold grave with green laurel be strewed, love
I die for my country, green Erin, and thee.

Oh, never again in the moonlight we'll roam, love,
When birds are at rest and the stars they do shine.
Never again will I kiss your sweet lips, love,
Or wander by streamlet with hands pressed on thine.

But should another love, oh, make you forget me,
Will you give me one promise before that I'll die?
That you'll come to my grave when all others forget me,
And there with the soft winds breath sigh for sigh.

My hour is approaching, let me take one fond look, love
And watch thy pure beauty till my soul does depart;
Let thy ringlets fall on my face and my brow , love,
Draw near till I press thee to my fond and true heart.

Farewell love, farewell, the words are now spoken,
The pale is shining its last beams on me.
Farewell love, farewell love, I hear the death token,
Never more in this world young Emmet you'll see.

From The Mount Callan Garland, Tom Munnelly's edition of Tom Lenihans
song repertoire

WHEN HE WHO ADORES THEE

When he who adores thee has left but the name
Of his fault and his sorrow behind,
Oh! Say, wilt thou weep when they darken the fame
Of a life that for thee was resigned?
Yes, weep! And, however my foes may condemn,
Thy tears shall efface their decree;
For Heaven can witness, though guilty to them,
I have been but too faithful to thee!

With thee were the dreams of my earliest love
Every thought of my reason was thine;
In my last humble prayer to the spirit above
Thy name shall be mingled with mine!
Oh! Blessed are the lovers and friends who shall live
The days of thy glory to see.
But the next dearest blessing that Heaven can give,
Is the pride of thus dying for thee.

SHE IS FAR FROM THE LAND

She is far from the land where her young hero sleeps,
And lovers around her are sighing;
But coldly she turns from their gaze and weeps,
For her heart in his grave is lying.

She sings the wild songs of her dear native plains,
Every note which he loved a-waking;
Ah! Little they think, who delights in her strains,
That the heart of the minstrel is breaking.

He had lived for his love, for his country he died,
They were all that to life had entwined him;
Nor soon shall the tears of his country be dried,
Nor long will his love stay behind him.

Oh! Make her a grave where the sunbeams rest,
When they promise a glorious morrow;
They'll shine o'er her sleep, like a smile from the West
From her own loved island of sorrow.

Thomas Moore

Thomas Moore was a friend and fellow student of Robert Emmet at Trinity College Dublin. The subject of this song (She is far from the Land) is Sarah Curran who was Robert Emmet's fiancée.

Her father the lawyer, John Philpot Curran, defended Theobald Wolfe Tone at his trial.

Young Emmet

In Green Street courthouse in eighteen and three.
Stood young Emmet the hero true and brave.
For fighting the tyrant, his country to free.
And to tear from her brow the name of slave.

There are still men in Ireland both loyal and true.
Who remember her patriots with pride.
And with God's help, young Emmet,
We'll give to you, the epitaph unwritten, since you died.

The verdict was 'Guilty', the sentence was death
And in Thomas Street the tyrant's work was done
But young Emmet smiled as he drew his last breath
For he knew that the fight for freedom would be won.

Alone and defiant he stood in the dock
While Lord Norbury, the hanging judge, looked down.
Against his false charges he stood firm as a rock
Yet another Irish martyr to the crown.

Paidí Bán O'Broin

Green Street Courthouse

Daniel O'Connell

Daniel O'Connell was born near Cahersiveen County Kerry in 1775, he was educated at Saint-Omar, Douai, and London. He studied law and became a successful barrister.

In his early thirties he became involved in politics and in 1823 he was involved in the founding of the Catholic Association and became the chief spokesman for that organisation. Daniel's suggestion that the association open its ranks to anyone prepared to pay a subscription of one penny a month transformed the Catholic Association into a major political organisation without parallel in Europe. His election to Parliament in 1828 brought about the passing of the Catholic Emancipation Act, which earned him the title of 'The Liberator'.

Daniel O'Connell is recognised as one of Ireland's foremost political figures. His skills as an orator are unsurpassed, his prowess as a lawyer are legendry and his parliamentary activities earned him the admiration of the majority of the people.

Although O'Connell was a native Irish speaker, as were the vast crowds he addressed, he never spoke Irish in public, and let it be known that he would welcome the demise of the Irish Language. O'Connell was against the use of physical force, he had been appalled at the excesses of the French Revolution and the repression which followed the Irish Rebellion of 1798. In 1815 Daniel O'Connell was challenged to a duel by Norcot d'Esterre a member of Dublin Corporation. During the duel O'Connell shot d'Esterre, who, died two days later. From that day on O'Connell wore a black glove on the hand that fired the pistol. He provided a pension for the family of the deceased.

Popular belief at the time was that d'Esterre was a marksman hired by the authorities to kill Daniel O'Connell.

There are many anecdotes concerning Daniel O'Connell in Irish folklore tradition.

It is said that his birth was a reward for a good deed done by his parents and that the mountains of his native Kerry echoed a thunderous welcome at his birth. It is said that his parents sought shelter from the elements at an old church which was very much in need of repair. They subsequently made a donation to the parish priest to have the repairs carried out. The priest is said, to have told the couple that they would give birth to a son who would be the champion of Ireland.

His cloak is said to have contained a cure and many people are said to have been cured of different ailments by touching it.

It is said that when he was a child a very difficult law- case was in progress in Cahersiveen. This case concerned one man who was suing another man for the loss of an eye. The eye was lost in the following manner, the plaintiff in the case was drowning, when the accused threw him a fishing line, the fishing line contained a fish-hook which impaled the plaintiff's eye causing its loss. The judge was at his wits end trying to come to a judgement. While he was out walking he overheard some children playing out the court-room drama. One little boy, by the name of Daniel, was acting the part of the judge and he gave the following judgement. He ruled that the plaintiff should be put back into the water and if he could save himself without the aid of the fishing line, then he should be awarded damages against the accused. The judge realised that this was the correct verdict and ruled accordingly.

Another story relates how a poor man was emigrating to America and before he boarded the ship a certain woman gave him a meal of fried eggs. Many years later the man returns after becoming very wealthy in America. The woman sues him for a large sum of money, claiming that if she had kept the eggs they would have multiplied and she would now be the owner of a large chicken farm. The man engaged Daniel to plead his case, which he does by producing peas in the court-room and endeavouring to sow them on the wooden floor. The judge demanded that Daniel explain his behaviour, to which Daniel replied, 'that the peas would have the same chance of sprouting from the wooden floor as the fried eggs had of hatching chickens', thereby winning the case.

The Legend of how Daniel O'Connell won Catholic Emancipation.
This is a folk account of how Daniel O'Connell won Catholic Emancipation by a ruse. It is said that, having failed for a long time to gain support for his Bill, he finally decided on a ruse. He wrote the terms of his Bill on a parchment and hid it inside a walking cane which had detachable silver top. While he was in his seat in Parliament he nudged the Member beside him and handed him the cane. The Member admired the skill of the silversmith and Daniel whispered to him to pass it on to the next Member. In this manner the cane was passed around the House of Parliament with everyone admiring its fine craftsmanship. When the cane returned to Daniel, he stood up and asked, did all present approve of his handiwork, to which all answered 'aye'.
With that he screwed off the top of the cane and said "Gentlemen I congratulate you-we have Emancipation".

Daniel and the Woman who sold the same cow three times.
It is said that a woman once sold the same cow to three different buyers at a market. When she was brought to trial for this offence she engaged Daniel O'Connell as counsel for her defence. Daniel advised her to pretend to be mad and to answer 'moo' to every question she was asked. This she did and was acquitted by the judge on the grounds of insanity. When Daniel approached her for his fee she answered him 'moo'.

The Plot to Poison Daniel O'Connell

In this legend it is said that a group of English politicians attempted to poison Daniel. He was invited to dinner and they had laced his drink with poison. Before he could drink an Irish servant girl spoke to him in Irish and warned him that there was poison in his drink.

"A Dhónaill UíChonaill, a' dtuigeann tú Gaelainn?
Tuigim, a chailín, is a mhaireann dem' ghaolta.
Tá an iomarca salainn sa glaoinne san taobh leat,
Mas fíor san, a chailín, is maith í do Spré-se."

Translation
"Daniel O'Connell, do you understand Irish?
I do girl, and so do all my relations.
Theres too much salt in that glass in front of you.
If that's true, girl, you'll get a good dowry."

In mock surprise he stood up and said that he had seen a royal carriage pass by the window. Thinking that some member of the royal family was coming to visit them they all got up from the table and gathered around the window. While they were preoccupied Daniel quietly switched the glasses. When they returned Daniel proposed a toast which proved to be fatal for one of his would be assassins.

In another court-room story Daniel is engaged to defend a will against a set of dishonest relatives of the deceased. These relatives claimed that a later will had been prepared by the deceased before his death. Daniel asked one of the relatives was the will prepared while the deceased was still alive. The relative replied that the will was written 'while there was life in him'. Daniel perceiving a trick, asked, 'was it the life that God put in him'. The relative then admitted that it was not, that a fly had been placed in the dead man's mouth while his hand was guided to sign the will.

There are many accounts of ruses he used to win hopeless cases. One such, has him going in disguise, to the chief witness for the prosecution and getting this witness to lay a bet on the outcome of the trial. Then at the trial, he makes the witness disclose that he stands to gain from a conviction at the trial, and is therefore disqualified and the case for the prosecution collapses.

In another anecdote it is said that while Daniel was defending a client on a capital charge, he discovered that the judge, a notorious hanging judge, had in the past taken bribes, namely a white horse and a barrel of red wine. While the court was in session Daniel pretended to fall asleep and then cried out loudly causing consternation in the court. The judge demanded that he explain his behaviour. He told the judge that he had a nightmare in which a white horse was drowning in red wine. Fearing that Daniel was about to expose him the judge dismisses the case.

The Doneraile Conspiracy

An unpopular Irish magistrate was murdered and while this murder was being investigated it was discovered that a conspiracy existed to kill a number of oppressive landlords. One hundred and fifty people were indicted and were to be tried in three batches of fifty. The first batch of fifty was tried and convicted and sentenced to death. The remaining prisoners in desperation sent a messenger in great haste to Derrynane in County Kerry pleading with Daniel O'Connell to come to their defence.

O'Connell made the ninety mile journey from Derrynane to Doneraile in a light gig with relays of horses without food or rest and finally arrived at the court-house whipping his exhausted horse, which dropped dead between the shafts on stopping.

There was a huge crowd in the square waiting to catch a glimpse of the Liberator and the cry went up 'he's come!' he's come!'.

In the court-room the solicitor general turned white. O'Connell bowed to the judges and apologised for not wearing a wig and gown. He asked for permission to receive refreshments in court. The judges agreed to his request, and a bowl of milk and some bread was brought, and as he refreshed himself a junior barrister gave him an account of the trial to date. The prosecution continued to try the case but O'Connell kept up a barrage of contradiction which the judges upheld. When it came time to cross-examine the witnesses, he tore their evidence apart and reduced them to a helpless babble to such an extent that one of them is said to have said.

"God knows 'tis little I thought I'd meet you here this day, Counsellor O'Connell! May the lord save me from you!"

The jury sat for a day and a half but could reach no agreement so the remaining two batches were acquitted. The sentence of those already condemned to death was commuted to transportation.

The following legend has Daniel O'Connell fighting a duel against the great-est swordsmsn in England.

'One time Daniel O'Connell had to fight a duel in London. The greatest swordsmsn in England was against him. He was no match for Dan. Time and time again the Counsellor got through the Englishman's guard only to find that his sword buckled on the Englishman's chest. The Englishman was wearing a vest of armour, unknown to Dan. He'd be there yet getting nowhere only for that an Irish boy in the crowd, knowing the secret, called out to him: "*A Dhónaill, conas a mharófá muc age baile*".

(Daniel, how would you kill a pig at home?)

Dan saw what was meant. He lunged at the Englishman's throat and killed him.

Bua Uí Chonaill
Atá Turcaigh is Gréagaigh ag gabháil dá chéile
Agus caillfear na céadtha í bhfus agus thall;
Aimseoidh Sasanach agus Franncaigh a chéile
Agus lasfaidh Éire le faobhar lann;
M'impí ar Iosa, Dia hAoine a cEasafh
Nár théigh mé in éag go dtige an t-am
A mbeidh gach cuid acu ag planncadh a chéile
Agus go bhfághmaoid pléisiúr ar "Orangemen".

Gunnaí is lámhach is tinte cnámha
Beidh again amárach, agus tá sé in ám,
Ó fuair Ó'Connail buaidh ar a námhad
Aipeochaidh bláith is beidh meas ar chrainn;
I gCondae an Chláir tá uaisle is ard-fhlatha
Ag crathadh lámh is ag déanamh grin

Acht bog faoi an gcárta go n-ólam sláinte
Na bhfear ó Árainn go hinse Chuinn.

O'Connell's Victory

The Turks and Greeks are attacking one another
And hundreds will be lost near and far;
The English and the French will meet,
And Ireland will light with the edge of blades;
I implore Jesus who was crucified on Friday
Not to let me die until the time comes
For the lot of them to be beating one another,
And until we take revenge on Orangemen.

We'll have guns and shooting ,
And bonfires tomorrow, And it is time,
Since O'Connell gained victory over his enemies
Flowers will bloom and trees will blossom;
In County Clare the nobility
Are shaking hands and celebrating,
So send round the measure and we'll drink the health
Of the men from Aran to Inchiquin.

Anthony Raftery

O'Connell Monument

Conclusion.

When King Henry VIII of England, who was proclaimed King of Ireland in 1542, introduced his policy of surrender and re-grant, which was devised by Henry and his ministers to separate the Gaelic chiefs from their ancient customs, laws, and language, to undermine the legal system under which they held their power. The poet to the O'Carroll's was prompted to pen the following, (from the Irish)

> "Shame on ye, Gaelic ones,
> Not one of ye lives;
> Foreigners are dividing your lands
> Ye are like a fairy host"...

The assassination of Rory Óg Ó'Moore of Laois, on June the 30th 1578, by his one time friend Mac Giolla Phaidraig inspired the composition of the following lament,

The Green Woods of Slew

> In the heart of the forest a thrush 'gan to sing
> Of losses the sorest, the death of a king!
> Soon to his bough leafless, my sympathy flew;
> For I, too, roamed chiefless in the Green woods of Slew!

> He, high 'bove the heather, I, low 'mong the fern,
> Mourned sadly together – a bird and a kerne!
> Cried he, the sky-winger: "A Hawking cuckoo
> Has slain the chief singer of the Green Woods of Slew!"

> Like his, was my story: "Our glory is o'er,
> For dead lies young Rory – the valiant O'Moore.
> The scourge of the stranger, he chased the false crew,
> Like a wolfhound of danger, in the Green Woods of Slew!

> My curse chill your castle, *Giolla Pháidraig* the base!
> No Saxon Queen's vassal was Rory of Leix!
> The Palesmen he vanquished: they parleyed with you;
> And I am left anguished in the Green Woods of Slew.

> Smile Sydney and Perrot! – the gold that oft failed –
> Wise weasel, fierce ferret – on the Gaeilge prevailed;
> The friend of his bosom proved faint and untrue,
> and left me heart – woesome in the Green Woods of Slew.

To joy turned our singing; for free from its nest,
A fledgling came winging with many a rest:
The gold its crest tins'ling, like dawn o'er the blue,
Another plumed princeling for the Green woods of Slew!

Away, sorrow blinding! – leave to women the dead –
Far better be grinding the grey axe instead:
For soon, brave and bonny, from the hand of Mac Hugh,
Shall fly little Owny, to the Green Woods of Slew.

Most of the major events of Irish history are commemorated in poetry, song
and story and the period of the dispossession of the Irish from their land,
their language, and their religion is no different. In fact the traumatic,
events of that, period enlarged and enhanced the body of Irish folklore to
such an extent that it can be easily recognised under the following
headings, *Carraig-an Aifrinn.* The Mass Rock -The Priest Hunters - Hunted
Priests, Tories and Rapparees, The Penal Laws, Penal Crosses, The
Hedge-School, The 1798 Rebellion and Catholic Emancipation.
The Elizabethan period is remembered for its cruelty and treachery
culminating in the massacres at Smerwick, Rathlin Island and
Mullaghmast. Prominent people of that period, Queen Elizabeth I of
England, Walter Devereux first Earl of Essex. Sir Francis Drake, Sir Walter
Raleigh, Sir Francis Cosby, who are remembered in England as heroes are
reviled in Irish folklore as lustful treacherous and merciless.
The president of Munster in a tour of the province in 1577 was responsible
for the execution of four hundred people in eight months.
The destruction of the native woodlands for the threefold purpose of
producing timber for the building of ships for the English fleet, the
production of charcoal for iron production, and the deprivation of shelter
and sanctuary for the rebellious Irish wood-kerne and Tory was the
inspiration for the haunting lament, *Caoine Chill Chais,* with its opening
line posing the question,

> *Cad do dhéanfamaoid feasta gan adhmad?*
> What will we do in the future without wood?

The decline of the ancient Irish order is marked in particular by the
Munster poets of the 17th century, *Séathrún Céitinn, Brian Mac Giolla
Phádraig, Pádraigín Haicéad, Piaras Feiritéar,*(still a folk hero in his native
Kerry), *Dáibhí Ó Bruadair,* who in verse describes the decline of the poets
with the passing of the old order thus, (from, Woe to that man who leaves
on his vagaries) from the Irish.

It's a thirsty task. Ploughing this lonely furrow,
With a weapon I never employed when I was rich:
This sword-play into the earth has swelled my ankles
And the shaft has martyred my fingers totally.

During this period the Annals of the Four Masters was undertaken on 22nd of January 1630 and was finished in a cottage adjacent to the ruined Abbey of Donegal on the 10th of August 1636, under the direction of Brother Michael O'Clery.

The Cromwellian dispossessions and the transplanting of thousands of Irish Catholics above the rank of tradesman or labourer inspired the writing of poems of the calibre of *An Dibirt go Connachta* –The Exodus to Connaght, by *Fear Dorcha Ó'Mealláin* in which he equates the situation of the Irish Catholics with that of the Israelites in Egypt for example,

> People of my heart, stand steady,
> Don't complain of your distress,
> Moses got what he requested,
> religious freedom- and from Pharaoh.

> Identical their God and ours,
> One God there was and still remains,
> Here or Westward God is one
> One God ever and shall be.

The three icons that can easily be identified with that period are the Mass-Rock, the Penal Cross and the Tory – Rapparee. There are many legends concerning the Mass Rock , the arrest and execution of priests for saying mass, for example Father Nicholas Mayler P.P of Tomhaggard who was killed on Christmass morning 1653 while celebrating mass. There are stories concerning the killing of priests on the spot almost all relating that the killing was carried out at the time of the consecration.

Sliocht as An Claibheamh Solais 18-09-1909.

"Ba gnách le Turner agus a cuid yeo a bheich ag dul thart ag loic is a doghad na tire. Bhí de do tiobad ar na sagartaibh an tAifreann a leighead agus atá le rádh mar gheall ar an diabhlaidheacht gur marbhuig sé sagart óg An Sagart MacAidghaille í gcarraig Clochán agus é ag briseadh Arán-an-Bheata. Tá Cloch-na- hAltórach ins a áit fós.

Translation of above.
"It was usual for Turner and his yeomen to be going about lighting and burning the country. There was a prohibition on the priests to be reading

and saying the mass and on account of this devilishness he killed a young priest Father MacAidghaille at Clochan rock while he was breaking the Bread of Life. The Altar Stone is there still".

(This stone can be seen to the present day on Slieve Gullion in South Armagh)

There are stories relating to the hunting down and killing of priests with dogs. There are stories of miracles happening at mass rocks for example the following from Kerry,

Cactra na Baintrige,

In which the mother of a poor widow distracted by the children crying for food brings them to the local mass rock which was called Leac-an- tSagairt (The –Priest's- Slab), a common name for a mass rock) and while she was cleaning moss from the mass rock a batch of bread appeared from no-where. There is another mass –rock in the Knockmealdown mountains in Co Tipperary which is associated with a miracle. There are many legends relating the deeds of the notorious priest-hunter *Sean-na-Sagairt*= Sean of the Priests. The area which is most prolific in the production of legends is the area of the Tory or Rapparee. These, young men for the most part, deprived of there inheritance, their homes and their income, "went out upon their keeping" into what remained of the woods and up into the mountain glens and valleys and from these retreats they attacked and burned and plundered the settlers who had taken their land.

There are a number of individuals who stand out above the rest in song and story, one in particular, Redmond O'Hanlon looms large on the landscape of Irish folklore. The stories about him are legion and one particular legend has no fewer than six variants which are contained in an index to this work. This is the legend of Redmond being overcome by a clever boy. This story can be recognised as an international folktale.

It is said of him that he robbed the rich and helped the poor. This is said of most Tories and Rapparees. It is also said that he was a great horseman, an attribute also claimed by many others such as Cahir-na-gCapall, O'Hare of Duhallow, and Donal na Casgadh. In the end like many of his calling he was betrayed by one whom he trusted and even his betrayal and death fulfil a prophesy. The death of Arthur O'Leary, a colonel in the Austrian army, who was shot by the Sheriff of Cork in 1773 for refusing to sell his horse to a Protestant for the sum of five pounds was the inspiration of one of the most evocative of Irish poems, *Caoineadh Airt Uí Laoghaire* The Lament for Art Ó'Leary which was written by his wife Eileen O Leary, *Eibhlín Dhubh Ní Chonaill,* who was an aunt of Daniel O'Connell the champion of Catholic Emancipation who was himself the inspiration for many legends.

The same Penal Laws were to be the cause of the peoples Rebellion of 1798 which was to bring its own brand of legend and song into the realm of Irish folklore. Theobald Wolfe Tone who became the hero of the nation and his tragic death was the inspiration for many poems and ballads. The heroes of Wexford are celebrated in many ballads, such as Father Murphy, The Croppy Boy, Kelly from Killann and Boolavogue. "Bold Robert Emmett the darling of Ireland" is best remembered for his speech from the dock which is still recited. There are many stories told about the exploits of Michael Dwyer and his compatriots in Glenmalure who held out in the mountains until after the failure of Robert Emmett's rebellion, when he surrendered in 1805 and was deported to Australia.

Last but not least are the legends concerning Daniel O'Connell whose wit and perseverance won Emancipation for the Irish Catholics, although the legends concerning him celebrate his prowess as a lawyer and generally ignore his political achievements. There are many monuments around the country dedicated to his honour. The main street in the Dublin bears his name as does the main bridge over the River Liffey. His last resting place is marked by a magnificent round tower. There are many legends, poems and ballads omitted from this work. Those contained in this work form a broad sample of the material of that period and are presented in a somewhat chronological order except where people, venues and events overshadow one another.

Apendix of Redmond O'Hanlon and the Clever Boy legends
Legend J;1

Outwitted by Clever Boy

"A merchant in Dundalk was to receive a large sum from a correspondent in Newry, if he could find sufficient courage to go for it, or if he could induce any friend to make the venture. He made no secret of his trouble to his family and people.

So one of his apprentices said to him one day, "Mr---, if you are satisfied to lose about thirty shillings I engage to bring you the debt in spite of O' Hanlon and all his men".

He thought the trial worth making, and handed over the sum demanded.

The adventurer then mounting a horse, the own brother of Sir Teague O' Regan's steed for ill conduct in the management of teeth and hooves, began his journey.

He did not expect to escape a for-gathering with Redmond, and his guess was a correct one. He was overtaken by a well-dressed and well-mounted gentleman, and they entered into conversation. The boy was all simplicity, and made no secret of the end and the object of his journey, and his fears of coming under the notice of the great road-surveyor. "I wouldn't let you know all this, sir", said he, "only I see you are a finished gentleman." "You are quite right in saying nothing to any one about your business, and I advise you not to mention it to any other person, gentle or simple, except the Newry merchant. When will you be on the road back?"

"This time tomorrow I expect to be about here". "Well, well, mind what I said to you. That is a bitter tempered beast under you – good morning".Just as he said, the boy was jogging back the next day, and at the same place and same hour the gentleman was coming out from a by-lane on the high road. "Well isn't this curious?" said he, that we should meet again the same as yesterday? You have the money safe I suppose?" "Oh, faith I have; there it is safe in the two ends of that canvas bag, and no sign of O' Hanlon thank God". "You are grateful too soon; I am the man; hand over the purse".—"Oh, sir, honey, you wouldn't do a poor boy such harm.

My employer will kill me or put me in jail. Maybe he'll say I kept the money myself".

All this time the boy's steed kept prancing, and wheeling round, and lashing out. "Keep your beast quiet, and hand over the bag, or I'll put a bullet through you". "Oh, vuya, vuya! What'll become of me? "Well, if the money is to be yours you must take the trouble of crossing the ditch for it".By *ditch* the speaker meant the fence, a thick one headed with bushes and shrubs which happened to border the road at that part, and was divided from it by a real ditch full of muddy water. Across the fence went the heavy little wallet and O' Hanlon was obliged, nolens volens, to scramble through water and brake to recover it. The boy improved the occasion. Slipping down from his ill tempered charger, he mounted the robber's docile steed, and was several perches on the road to Dundalk before O' Hanlon could attain the solid road again. Vain were his shouts after the simple youth, vain his attempts to bestride Rosinante, or even seize the bridle, and the heap of halfpence (many of them raps), provided by the lad in Newry, poorly repaid him for the loss of his trained horse. Perhaps his defeat by the clever boy went nearer his heart than all. That lucky apprentice reached his home in triumph with the money well quilted in his waistcoat". [114]

Raps? A rap is an Irish counterfeit coin—The Concise Oxford Dictionary

Legend J-2

Outwitted by Clever Boy

A merchant in Dundalk had a draught on a merchant in Newry for a large sum of money, he was so much afraid of being robbed by Redmond O' Hanlon that he would neither go for it himself, or send anyone else to collect it. One evening while discussing this matter with his wife his apprentice, a young lad of sixteen overheard their conversation and offered to go to Newry and collect the said money.

After much debate and deep consideration, the merchant agreed that the apprentice should collect the money. The young lad made preparation for his journey and he asked his master to provide him with forty shillings in half-penny coins, on receipt of which he divided into two lots and placed them into a leather wallet. He then went to the field and brought home an old vicious war horse, which he saddled and set out on his errand. He was not to far along the road to Newry when he was accosted by Redmond, who enquired of him where he was going. The young boy informed him that he was bound for Newry. What is the purpose of your trip to Newry? Asked Redmond .To collect a large some of money for my master answered the boy innocently. When do you think you will be back?, asked the tory slyly. About this time tomorrow replied the apprentice. Well, my lad, said Redmond, do not tell everybody you meet the purpose of your travels lest you be robbed by some rascal of a highwayman. I have no fear of being robbed by a fine gentleman such as yourself, and I have no intention to tell anybody else. Redmond presented the lad with a ducat with which to purchase refreshments.

Whilst on the road and with that bade him safe journey. At that time Redmond was strapped for cash, and as none of his companions were with him he decided to operate alone and keep all the booty for himself.

---

[114] Kennedy Patrick <u>Modern Irish Anecdotes.</u> 1872

To make sure of this he sent his band to a different location whilst he awaited his prey on the Newry Armagh road the next day. When the boy eventually came into sight Redmond rode up and greeted him, and after some small talk he asked the boy if he had collected the money for his master. On being told that he had indeed collected the money, Redmond asked him if he could see it. The boy refused this request at which Redmond demanded that he hand over the money, whilst at the same time keeping his distance from the wicked horse upon which the boy was mounted. The boy took out the leather wallet and threw it over the hedge into the bog telling Redmond that if he wanted it then he would have to follow it. Redmond dismounted from his horse and tied him to a nearby tree, with great difficulty he scrambled through the hedge and across the bog to where the wallet lay. Whilst the Tory was engaged in this precarious labour, the boy swapped horses and galloped away in the direction of Dundalk with the £100 quilted into his waistcoat, leaving the disgruntled Redmond with a mad horse and a wallet full of half-pennies. [115]

Legend J-3

The man that outwitted Redmond O' Hanlon

"There was a fellow the name of Murphy, an' he lived in the Isle o' Cale (Lecale) beyont Dundrum. His master had a lump o' money in the bank in Dublin, this money in the bank, it was very hard to get it out of it for fear of being robbed. The man said he'd give the best horse he had an' a hundred poun's to the wan was to bring it back. None of them would go, but there was one fella they called a him soft O' Murphy, and in the end he said he would go.
He said "I'll not take the best horse, but I'll take that oul Joch".
So he saddled him and started for the road. He was the best whistler that ever curled a lip. So he came out and still he was whistling, and he came to Ned Grant's Cross Roads. It was nothing but a trail then. Redmon was on his way an' the whistling attracted his attention. He had a fine grey horse, an' he came till him, an' he says,
"what is your name?"
"My name is John Murphy", says he.
"And what part of Ireland are you from?".
"I'm from Lecale beyont Dundrum", says he
"An' if it's a fair question where are you going?"
"I'm goin' to Dublin for a gentleman's money, he has two thousan' Poun' in gold in the bank in Dublin, an' I have to lift it".

---

[115] O'Hanlon Terence The Highwayman in Irish History (M.H.Gill and son 1932)

"Would you not" says he "be afraid of being robbed?".

"No I would not"

"Would you not be afraid of Redmon' O' Hanlon?".

"No I would not for who'd think of a *naked* boy like me with such a bad horse havin' money". So they talked on through Hilltown till they came to the yellow road.

"Now", he says, "I'll have to go this road over the mountains, what time" says he

"Murphy, will you be back?"

"I'll stay" says he, "in Newry the night, and I'll start for Dublin in the morning,

an' I'll reach it, plaze God, the morrow night, I'll get my money the next morning an' I'll remain in Newry that night, so it'll be about twelve or one on the following day".

In Dublin he got a poun' in copper an' he put it in a little bag.

"Now", he says, "would you be so kind to put another poun' in copper in the other one". He tied it in the middle and he threw it on the weathercloth of his horse.

He rode on from Newry to Hilltown, an' according to_plan he met his noble Redmon O' Hanlon at the very same place he parted from him.

"Murphy", he says "you got on well, did ye get yer money?" "Yes", says he "I did" so they rode on to a place they call the Red Bank an' Redmon says—

"Did you know that I'm Redmon O' Hanlon an' hand me up that money". "I will not", he says, I'll never give it to you nor any other man".

An' he pitched it out across the Bann, "ye'll get near as much bother lookin' for it", Says he, "as I did". So smart Hanlon crossed the fence till he got the booty.

And Murphy got on the grey and away he went. So he landed home.

"What did you do" says the boss, "did you get everything right?"

"I got everything right only for two poun'". "Well you must be forgiven for that" says he. And Murphy handed him up the money. "An' where did you get the horse, such a beautiful grey horse?"

"Well I took him off a man", says he, "that was goin' to rob me, an' I left him oul Joch". "Very good you'll have to go back with the horse, for I'll get my place wrecked if this horse is seen about it". He thought he could get out of giving the hundred pounds.

"Very good", he mounted his grey again and rode on until Grants Cross Roads, an' met his man in the same place again. He was whistling like a nightingale.

"Well Murphy are you on the road again". "Well Redmon I came back with the horse to ye, an' I wanted to charge", says he, "when I was going home, but I don't care for the one I've goy now".

"Well" he says "Murphy, you're the smartest man that ever encountered me" And he opened his saddle bags, an' he filled his cap o' sovereigns, an' he says. "No matter where you live I'll call with ye for you're the smartest man I ever met in my runnin' about, but I'll call with ye only in disguise.

This man that he lived with had a brother an' he died an' the farm was a selling. There was a hundred acres of lan' in it. So the auctioneer says, "whose for the farm?" An' some of the neighbours says that who would be first but Murphy, who has the money. Redmon had a solicitor there. Murphy bid three hundred poun' for it an'the auctioneer says, "is there any offers on Murphy for the farm", nobody spoke. "Well then, we'll give it to him, he can pay the fees anyway".

Redmon had him properly trained at this time. There was so much deposit an' the fees to be paid, so Murphy went in and paid for the farm, an he says "what is the fees" "Oh ", says he, "I would'nt sell it at all".

"Are'nt ye a licensed auctioneer? Was'nt I the highest bidder?, did'nt ye read the terms of sale". "Oh but that would'nt do", he says "for such a farm as this". "Here's me solicitor", says Murphy.

So the solicitor came forward, an he turned about an' he bought all the stock was on the farm, horses, sheep, cattle, hens, hay, straw, harnesses, plough. An he paid for them all then an' there. The boy that Murphy lived with had one daughter an' he married her an' got all.[116]

Legend J-4

Outwitted by Clever Boy

This is another variant of the clever boy outwitting the outlaw motif, with the addition of an introductory story in which the boy meets a priest and gains employment. He then proceeds to outwit the local Protestant Minister. He then outwits Redmond O' Hanlon and steals his horse. He joins with Redmond and wins back his horse. A fifth legend is added in which Redmond robs the Mayor of Derry before setting sail for America. His adventures in America constitute a sixth legend.

A

"There was a young fellow one day, a bright sunny day, an' he got a horse's shoe on the road. He went in under the shade of a tree, an' there was a priest comin' along riding, an' he came out before the priest, an' he asked the priest,
"what is that?" "That is a horse's shoe".
"Well it is a nice thing to have the learning", he says.
"I don't know between a horse's shoe an' a mare's shoe".
"You should hire with me", says the priest.

---

[116] N.F.C. 925 : p 278 Mrs Taggart, Mulloch Cearnchan, Mochaire Geal Co Aon Truim.

"I don't mind", he says.

B

So he was hired with the priest, and the priest used to send a salmon to the minister every Christmas, an' someone told the young fella that the minister use'nt give them anything. He went over to the minister with the salmon, an' he opened the hall door and went in. He threw the salmon onto (the plate) that he was eating out of.
"That is not the way to come to a gentleman with a salmon", but he says, "sit you here an' I'll go out, an' I'll come to the door, an' I'll tell you how to do it".
The minister went out with the salmon, an' he rapped on the hall door.
"Who is there?" "It's the priest's boy with a salmon".
"Well there is a gentleman at his dinner, an' wait until he is finished with his dinner". So when he was finished with his dinner he went to the hall door. "There's a salmon his reverence sent over to you". "Oh thanks very much", an' he was putting his hand in his pocket an' giving the minister a half crown. He wouldn't take it.
"Oh that's what I always do", says the minister.

C

He travelled on then till he came to Tyrone. He hired with a man in Tyrone, an' what? Was this man but a landlord. He had a big estate in Connaught. Every year he used to go across to collect the rent. So they were digging potatoes an' the young fellow was gathering. Says he, "I have an estate in Connaught, and I'm going away every year an' I'm robbed" "You should let me away in your stead". "Oh don't you know you would be robbed anyway". "Well sure I can't be robbed but the same as yourself".
"Well" he says "I'll think over it". A couple of days after that he says, "Well I'll give you my own black horse".
"No I'll take the oul white one", he says.
He got his boots an' went away an' started for Connaught. He met Réamon O' Hanlon on the way. "Where are you going?" says Réamon. "I'm going to collect my masters rent, he is robbed every year an' I'm going instead of him". "Be damn but you're a manly young fella, an' when will you be back?" "I'll be back on such a day". "Well God bless you".
The last days he was there he gave a warrant for twelve shillings in copper. He had all the coppers that was in Connaught with him in front an' an odd pound an' an odd shilling in through them. And he had all the gold, and five pound notes, an' ten pound notes, all around him in a belt. He came on ahead an' when he came to where Réamon was. "Well did you get back?" "I got back". "How did you get on?"
"Oh I got on far better than the landlord, because", says the young fella.

310

"They gave me all the arrears an' I got far more money than what the landlord got". "You're a manly young fella, come an' give me all your money".

"Oh surely to God you wouldn't go to rob the likes of me". "I robbed your master an' why wouldn't I rob you". Well he went to cry, an' he caught the bag an' threw it into the drain on the roadside. "Well, says the outlaw, only for your a young fella I would kill you, houl this horse until I gather up the money". He held the horse an' when he got Réamon stooped in the mud, he jumped on Réamon's horse an' away. Réamon got on the old white steed, but he didn't go very far. When he landed at the landlord's place the landlord was very glad to see him, an' Réamon's horse with him.There was three hundred guineas lined in the saddle.

There was three horse pistols hanging from the saddle. Every year then for five or six years he used to collect the masters rent, an' Réamon couldn't get up to him at all.

D

So him an' the landlord fell out at last. Réamon came in one night an' he was sitting at the fire. He closed the door, an' he reached for a sword that was hanging on the wall.

"Oh! you rascal you", he says, "after robbing me now for six or seven years, coming into my house now, and my wife died of hardship".

"Oh, I'll try to get back your horse, Réamon", he says, "so don't touch me".

He stayed there for a fortnight. "Oh we'll go for the road the day". Him an' Réamonn went for the road and when they were near the landlords house, he tied a rope around Réamonn's body and was dragging him about two or three yards after him. The landlord came out, "my oh", he catched his two hands, he was that glad to see him.

"I was sorry", he says, "an'I did not sleep a wink, but thinking on you, an' what kind of a job have you know".

"Well I done a lot of bad in my time", he says "an' I met this oul fella, an' I took it for penance on myself to stay with him as long as he would live, an' I'm asking only a night in every home, an' I'm asking a night off you".

"A fortnight, a month, two months, an' I don't like to see you leaving me at all".

After the young fella went away, there was a watch on Réamon's house, an'd there was a back kitchen in it, an' a fine fire, an' they out watchin the horses in their turn.

The young fella an' Réamon went in, an' he left Réamon lying on the turf at the lower end. And the landlord came in to have crack with him, the two was cracking away about Connaught, an' one place, an' another, about Réamon robbing them, an' he said he was too smart for Réamon.

"Do you know me?"

"Why wouldn't I know a man that was seven years on my floor"

"Do you know that man there?"

"That man is with me for seven years, an' you don't know", he says, "the man that robbed you for ten years is down there, for seven years".

Oh! When Réamon heard this, Réamon ran out, he made for the gun to shoot him,

So be God when he got the place clear, loosed the horse an' away another road with Réamon's horse. He was sitting at the fire when Réamon came in.

"Your trying to kill me the night, an' your sitting here now".

"An' what could I do?" he says"I couldn't do nothing else" he says.

"I have the horse in the stable". "Well have you", he says. He kissed the young fella then. Every year for six or seven years they robbed the landlord. The young fella went out to hunt with his two hounds, and the horse, and there came a mist on them, and the horse fell with a spink, an' the horse was killed an' the young fella was killed,

The hounds came home that night, an' Réamon could not go out because it was too dark. He waited for day clear in the morning, an' when he went out, the young fella was killed, an, the horse was killed.

E

It was too heavy a burden on Réamon to live in Ireland after that. He thought he would take shipping to America. He went down to Derry an' bought a ticket.

It was sailing boats was going at the time. He bought a ticket for New York.

He thought then he wouldn't have enough money, an' he went up to the Mayor of Derry, an' he knocked at the door, an' the girl came out. He asked her was the Mayor of Derry in, an she said he was, did he want to see him?

So the Mayor told him to come in, an' he said he wanted to speak to him in private for a few moments. He took him into a private room, an' he made him go on his two knees, an swear the book that he wasn't to speak about this for two hours, an' that he would give him five hundred pounds. The Mayor of Derry shook on his knees, an' he went on his two knees an' he trembled, an' the revolver was at his nose, an' he went to the safe, an' he counted out five hundred pounds for him.

When he went down the boat was ready to go as he put his foot aboard the boat an' away he went. When he gave the report, the boat was too far away, an' there was no wire or nothing going out at the time, an' Réamon went across an took a cottage outside Phill.adelphia. He lived there happy and well for a year an' a half.

F

So one day he was coming in at the wood, an' he met three young fellas, an' the three crying. He asked them what was with,

"Oh we were robbed out there in the wood, our three purses was taken from us, an our tickets were in the purses, an' what are we going to do".

"An' who are you". "I'm the son of the Mayor of Derry".

"Who do you belong to?" "I'm a son of Bigges (ers)"

"Who do you belong to ", he says.

"I'm a son of Leckey's".

He put his hand in his pocket, an' gave every one of them three sovereigns, an' told them stay in a hotel until he would call on them next day. He went in through the wood, an' the three robbers came out before him.

"Your money or your life!" "Oh" he says "I have no money, I'm out in that position myself".

"Who are you". "Réamon Ó Hanlon from Ireland".

"Oh I heard our father talking about you, an' our grandfathers, an' our father would like to see you".

"You must go to see my father, many is the time he told us about your robbery, that you were the greatest robber in the wirld". They catched him an' trailed him into the woods , an' they came to a nice stairway, an' they went down into a cave, an upstairs an' all in the cave.

"Father do you know who have we withus?". "Who?" "Réamon Ó Hanlon the highway robber from Ireland".

"Ah the rascal, the rascal !, the robbery failed on him in Ireland, an' he came now to destroy the robbery on you ones; he'll not leave youse worth one three-halfpence". "Cut the head off him, on that block opposite me; get the hatchet an' get up the block".

"Oh", he says, I've done a lot of badness in my time", he says, an' give me a quarter of an hour, to do penance in a private room". "Oh I think it is too long to give you a quarter of an hour, you oul rascal you, coming to take the living off us here in America".He put him up to a place that was in it, in a back room upstairs, an' it is not praying Réamon was, but loading his revolver with gun powder.

The oul fella was watching the clock, an' he told the young fella to take him down.

"Don't listen to nothing from him, take him down, for I would like to see the head off him". Begorra, when the fella went up he lowered him and trailed in behind him.

He told the next fella to go up , an' not listen to any of his blarney at all.

He done the same with him.

He told the young fella to go up, he done the same with the young fella.

He looked around, an' who did he see comin' down the stairs but Réamon.

"Hey you oul rascal !", he says, "you wanted to see my head cut off on the block", he says, "but your head will soon be cut".

"Oh" he says, "don't kill me".

"Ha ! you oul rascal, I will", he got his sword , an' he cut the head off him, an' he took with him a bunch of keys, an' he went down to the room, an' didin't he see the three purses on the mantelpiece with their names an' surnames on them. He put the three purses into his pocket, an' he opened the chest an' it was all full of gold.

He filled his pockets with the gold, an' he locked up the place, an' he stayed in his own we shanty that night, an' at twelve o clock next day he went down to see the three young fellas. He threw the three purses out, an' each reached for his own, this is mine, this is mine, this is mine.

"Well", he says, "I put myself in danger of my life for you three boys, an' I wouldn't", he says, "but the time I was leaving Derry, I was scarce of money, an' I went up to your fathers house", he says, "an' demanded five hundred pounds off him". "Only for that", he says, "I wouldn't do what I done".

He counted out five hundred pounds, for the mayors son, and told him , "give it to your father when you go home". So when the boys went home, the Mayor of Derry came back for Réamon. Him an' the wife, an' the son went over an' took Réamon over, an' he had all the gold with him. They put up a big monument over Réamon, an' his name an' his surname is on that headstone yet, and will as long as anybody is alive.[117]

There are two versions of this story written in Irish

An Buachail Cloiste = The Clever Boy

An Fear Bocht agus Réamon Ó' Hanlaigh an tÁrd Rubailligh,

The Poor man and Reamon O'Hanlon the High Robber.

These can be found in the archives of the National Folklore Collection at U.C.D.

---

[117] N.F.C. 336 : pp 195-209 A scríomh le Seán Ó'hEochaidh ó béal- aithrís,Donaí Ó'Brisleán, feirmeoir ó gCor- Leitir Mhic a'Bhaird Conntae- Tirconaill.

References

1. Cambrensis Geraldus, <u>Expugnatio Hibernica, The Conquest of Ireland</u> 1189
2. May 5 1487 Lambert Simnel who claimed to be the Earl of Warwick, lands in Ireland, with 2000 merceneries. He was crowned King Edward VI in Christchurch Cathedral Dublin on May 24th. He was defeated by Henry VII at Stoke on June 16.
3. Pamphlet, by the late Eamon Chandler available at Whitefriar Street
4. Ronan Myles V. <u>The Reformation in Ireland under Elizabeth I</u> Dublin 1930.
5. <u>Calender of State Papers Ireland – Elizabeth 1574-1585</u> Vol IX N.L.I. RR941
6. <u>Calender of State Papers Ireland – Elizabeth</u> Vol LVIII 1577 April – July.
7. O'Donovan John <u>Annals of the Kingdom of Ireland</u>, by the Four Masters.
8. O'Grady Standish, <u>The Bog of Stars and other storiesand sketches of Elizabethan Ireland.</u>
9. O.S.I. Discovery Series Map no 50 grid ref 181232
10. O'Donovan John <u>Annals of the Kingdom of Ireland.</u> By The Four Masters
11. Ó'hÓgain Daithi Dr <u>Myth Legend & Romance</u> Prentice Hall Press. New York, London.
12. *Ó Cléirigh Lughaidh <u>Beatha Aodh Rua O'Domhnaill</u>* Irish Texts Society London 1948.
13. Sir William Drury, Letter to the Privy Council 1577
14. *Ó'hÓgain Daithí Dr* <u>Myths,Legend and Romance.</u>
15. Calender of State Papers vol clxxii p 184
16. Annals of the Kingdom of Ireland by the Four Masters National Library of Ireland <u>I.R. 941 A5</u>
17. Annals of the Kingdom of Ireland 1595
18. *O'Siocfhradha M.A Sean-Stais na hÉireann 1930*
19. O'Curry Eugene <u>Manuscript Materisl from Irish History 1861</u> N.L.I.
20. O'Curry Eugene <u>Manuscript Materisl from Irish History 1861</u> N.L.I.
21. Burke William P <u>The Irish Priests in the Penal Times</u> 1914
22. O'Connor Dermod Esq, <u>Keating's General History of Ireland,</u> 1865 N.L.I.
23. Clanricards Memoirs, Prifoa, London 1722
24. *Dánta Amhrán is Caointe,Sheathrúin Céitinn Eoin Cathmhaolach Mac Giolla Eáin Connradh na Gaedhlige, Baile Átha Cliath 1900*
25. *Waterford Archaeological Journal April 1895*
26. Treasury Warrants 352
27. <u>Annals of the Kingdom of Ireland</u>

28. Murray Laurence P Rev (ed) <u>An Irish Diary of the Confederate Wars</u> County Louth Archaeological Journal 1923-1930 (Cin Lae Uí Mhealláin) Friar Meallan Journal.
29. <u>M.S 11657 N.L.I.</u>
30. <u>Friar O'Meallan Journal</u>
31. <u>Irish Ecclesiastical Records 1917</u>
32. Moran Patrick Francis <u>Persecutions of the Irish Catholics</u>
33. Flowers Robin <u>The western Isle</u> National Library of Ireland.
34. O'Connell M.R. <u>Daniel O'Connell Political Pioneer</u> (Institute of Puplic Administration)
35. *An tAthair Pádraig Ua Duinnín <u>Dánta Phiarais Feitéir</u> 1903*
36. N.F.C. Vol S 954 An Gort Mór Co Muineacháin 24-11-37=06-12038
37. N.F.C. Vol 955 James MacCague Feeba Scotstown
38. N. F. C. Vol 1238 p 320 Miss Joan Story Carrick Cligher Co Tyrone
39. N.F.C. Vol S 347 June 1937 Helen Lernihan Longstrail Crookstown Co Cork.
40. Verse X Lament for Patrick Fleming
41. Calendar of Ormonde Manuscripts N.L.I.
42. Story Rev <u>Continuation of the History of the Wars in Ireland</u> 1693
43. Friar O'Meallain Journal LP. Murrey PP Louth Archaeological Journal 1923-30.
44. Gregory Lady <u>Lady Gregory's Complete Irish Mythology</u> (Bounty Books p208
45. As above
46. An Claibheamh Solais 1919 N.L.I. IR 8916205 C 9
47. Ó'hÓgáin Daithí Dr <u>Myth, Legend and Romance</u>
48. O'Hanlon Terence <u>The Highwayman in Irish History</u>
49. Kennedy Patrick Modern Irish Ancedotes National Library of Ireland
50. Marshall John <u>Irish Tories Rapparees and Robbers</u> (Dungannon 1927)
51. Cosgrave J. <u>The Lives and Actions of the most Notorious Irish Highwaymen 1776</u>
52. Moody T.W.E. A PhD Paper on Redmond O'Hanlon 1936
53. O'Hanlon Terence <u>The Highwayman in Irish History</u> (M.H.Gill and son 1932
54. Cosgrave J. <u>The Lives and Actions of the Most Notorious Irish Highwaymen 1776</u>
55. Cosgrave J as above
56. N.F.C Vol S 968 Miss J Gallagher Slievebricken Co Cavan 10-38=11-39
57. Moody T.W.E. PhD Paper on Redmond O'Hanlon 1936
58. N.F.C. Vol 448 pp72-73 Dunton Letters
59. Sloane 3323 ff 288-289 Catalogue of Irish Manuscripts
60. N.F.C. Vol S 947 Mrs Taggart, Mochaire Geal, Co Antrim

61. Dublin Penny Journal, M.H. O'Hanlon
62. Power Laurence Rev The righteous Man's Portion Delivered at a sermon at the Obseques of the Noble and Renowned Gentleman Henry St John London 1680 N.L.I. LO P14 item 12
63. Pamphlet, Downfall of Redmond O'Hanlon
64. O'Hanlon Terence The Highwayman in Irish History
65. O'Hanlon Terence The Highwayman in Irish History
66. Dublin Penny Journal M.H O'Hanlon
67. Murrey L.P. Rev Louth Archaeological Journal 1933-36
68. Dublin Printed by Samuel Lee in Skinners Row
69. Cosgrave J
70. N.F.C. Vol 104 p434 T O'Babhartaigh, Cluain Ui Ruairc, Co Liathroma
71. King William The State of the Protestants in Ireland under the late King James's Government
72. Cosgrave J
73. Crossely Aaron Peerage of Ireland 1725
74. Carty James Ireland From the Flight of the Earls to Grattan's Parliament 1607-1782 (J Fallon Dublin)
75. Lecky W.E.H. a History of Ireland in the Eighteenth Century (The University of Chicago Press).
76. Burke Edmund
77. Lady Wilde (Esperanza) Ancient Legends Mystic Charms and Superstitions (London)
78. Lecky W.E.H. a History of Ireland in the Eighteenth Century (The University of Chicago Press).
79. N.F.C. Vol s954 Maire Nic Cassain, Threemilehouse (Drumsnatt) Co Monaghan 24-11-37=06-12 -38
80. Mahen Samuel J, Reliques of Irish Jacobite Poetry Dublin 1844
81. Carleton William Traits and Customs of the Irish Peasntry
82. Mangan James Clarence Poets and Poetry of Munster
83. Murrey L.P. Rev PP A SouthArmagh Outlaw Louth Archaeological Journal 1938
84. Douglas Hyde. Love Songs of Connaught.
85. Archdeacon M Esquire Shawn na Soggarth The Priest Hunter An Irish Tale of the Penal Times.
86. Burke William P. Rev The Irish Priests in the Penal Times 1660-1760 Waterford 1914
87. Ní Ceallaigh Eibhlín Catholic Bulletin 1912 N.L.I. IR 794105C1
88. N.F.C. S341 Peggy Murrey Sleaveen West Macroom Co. Cork
89. N.F.C. S340 PP53-54 Mr Denis Lane-farmer Mount music Co Cork.
90. N.F.C. Vol S 364 1937
91. Kennedy Patrick Modern Irish Anecdotes

92. N.F.C. Vol 542 p400 P. Ó 'Hanrachtáin Killnamanagh Upper Ceapagh Tiobrid Áirann
93. Story Rev Continuation of the Wars in Ireland 1693
94. N.F.C. Vol 407
95. Duffey Charles Gavin.Ballad Poetry of Ireland pp 203-205 Forde National Library New York 1886
96. O'Ceallaigh Seosamh Aspects of our Inheritance(Cloughneely)
97. Harkin C.M. Inishowen its History Traditions and Inheritance 1935
98. Walsh John Edward Sketches of Ireland Sixty Years ago 1847
99. N.F.C. Vol S 219 p250 Martha McGure Dromard Dromod Co. Liathroma
100. The Shamrock Vol 12 1875 p517
101. Sayers Peig Storyteller from the great Blasket Island
102. O'Hógáin Daithí Dr Myth, Legend and Romance
103. Ulster Journal of Archaeology 1857 N.L.I. IR 791p 61-80
104. Archiveum Hibernia 1V 116
105. Ranson R The Kilmore Carols The Past Vol V Wexford 1949
106. Wolfe Tone Biography ed R.Barry O'Brien Phoenix Publishing Company
107. Bryan William James Editor in Chief The World's Famous Orations Vol VI 1906 Funk & Wagnalls co New York.
108. Béaloideas Journal of the Folklore of Ireland Society 1935
109. Bernard, Bayle. The Life of Samuel Lover 1874
110. Madden R.R. Literary Remains of the United Irishmen p171
111. O Tuathail Padraig, Wicklow Traditions of 1798 Béaloideas 1935
112. N.F.C. Keogh Vol 265
113. Madden R.R. The United Irishmen their Lives and Times
114. Kennedy Patrick The Book of Modern Irish Anecdotes1872 M.H Gill & Son Dublin
115. Hanlon Terence The Highwayman in Irish History M.H.Gill and son 1932
116. NF.C. Vol 925 Mrs Taggart Mulloch Ceanchan Aon Truim
117. NF.C. Vol 1336 pp195-209 a scríobh le Seán Ó hEochaidh, ó béal aithrís Donaí Ó'Brisleáin ó Gort Leilin Mhic a' Bhaird Co Tirconaill.

Bibliography.

1   Annals of the Kingdom of Ireland by the Four Masters I.R. 941 A5
2   An Claibheamh Solais 1919 N.L.I. IR 8916205 C 9
3   Archiveum Hibernia 1v 116
4   Archdeacon M Esquire, Shawn na Soggarth The Priesthunter an Irish Tale of the Penal Times
5   Bernard Bayle The Life of Samuel Lover 1874
6   Béaloideas .Journal of the Irish Folklore Society
7   Bryan William James, Editor in Chief, The Worlds Famous Orations
8   Burke Edmund
9   Burke William P The Irish Priests in the Penal Times 1914.
10 Carty James Ireland From the Flight of the Earls to Grattan's Parliament 1607-1782 (J Fallon Dublin)
11 Calender of State Papers vol clxxii p 184
12 Calender of Ormonde Manuscripts
13 Cambrensis Geraldus Expugnatio Hibernica The Conquest of Ireland 1189
14 Carelton William Traits and Customs of the Irish Peasantry
15 Cearnach Conaill Trí bior- chaoite an Bháis. Goeffrey Keating N.L.I. IR 89162 K12
16 Chandler Eamon Pamphlet Available at Whitefriars Street
17 Clanricards Memoirs, Prifoa, London
18 Cosgrave J. The Lives and actions of the most Notorious Irish Highwaymen
19 Crossley Aaron Peerage of Ireland Dublin 1725
20 Dánta Amhrán is Caointe,Sheathrúin Céitinn Eoin Cathmhaolach Mac Giolla Eáin Connradh na Gaedhlige, Baile Átha Cliath 1900
21 Downfall of Redmond O'Hanlon Pamphlet 1681
22 Dublin Penny Journal
23 Duffy Charles Gavin Ballad Poetry of Ireland 203-205 Forde National Library New York 1886
24 An tAthair Pádraig Ua Duinnín.Dánta Phiarais Feitéir 1903
25 Drury, William Sir, Letter to the Privy Council 1577
26 Flowers Robin The western Isle National Library of Ireland
27 Gregory Lady Lady Gregory's Complete Irish Mythology (Bounty Books p208
28 Harkin C.M. Inishowen its History Traditions and Inheritance 1935
29 Hyde Douglas
30 Hogan Edmond Ibernia Ignatiana 1880 p 12-24 also Ronan Myles V. The Reformation in Ireland under Elizabeth 1558-1580 London 1930
31 Irish Ecclesiastical Records 1917
32 Kennedy Patrick Modern Irish Ancedotes

33 King William, <u>The state of the Protestants in Ireland under the late King James's Government</u>

34 Lecky W.E.H. <u>a History of Ireland in the Eighteenth Century</u> (The University of Chicago Press).

35 Marshall John <u>Irish Tories Rapparees and Robbers</u> (Dungannon 1927)

36 Moody T.W.E. PhD Paper on Redmond O'Hanlon1936

37 Moran Patrick Francis <u>Persecutions of the Irish Catholics</u>

38 Murrey l.P.Rev <u>Louth Archaeological Journal.</u>

39 Mahen Samuel J <u>Reliques of Irish Jacobite Poetry</u> Dublin 1844

40 Mangan James Clarence <u>Poets and poetry of Munster</u>

41 Madden R.R <u>Literary Remains of the United Irishmen</u>

42 M.S. 11657 National Library of Ireland

43 N.F.C. National Folklore Collection U.C.D.

44 *Ní Ceallaigh Eibhlín* <u>Catholic Bulletin 1912</u> N.L.I. IR 794105C1

45 *Ó Cabhla Séan Cuailin Uí Chaomh Millstreet Co Cork 05/ 12/38*

46 *O'Ceallaigh Seosamh* Aspects of our Inheritance(Cloughneely)

47 *Ó Cléirigh Lughaidh* <u>Beatha Aodh Rua O'Domhnaill</u> Irish Texts Society London 1949

48 O'Connor Dermod Esq <u>Keating's General History of Ireland 1865</u> <u>N.L.I. IR941OI</u>

49 O'Connell M.R. <u>Daniel O'Connell Political Pioneer</u> (Institute of Puplic Administrati

50 O'Donovan John <u>Annals of the Kingdom of Ireland,</u>By the Four Masters

51 O'Grady Standish. <u>The Gael Feb 1901 New York</u>

52 O'Hanlon Terence <u>The Highwayman in Irish History</u> (M.H.Gill and son1932

53 *O'hÓgain Daithí Dr* <u>Myth Legend & Romance</u> Prentice Hall Press New York, London.

54 *O'Siocfhradha M.A Sean-Stais na hÉireann 1930*

55 O.S.I. Discovery Series Map no 50 grid ref 181232

56 Pamphlet

57 Power Laurence Rev The righteous Man's Portion Delivered at a sermon at the Obseques of the Noble and Renowned Gentleman Henry St John London 1680 N.L.I. LO P14 item 12

58 Prendergast John P. <u>The Cromwellian Settlement in Ireland</u> (Constable London 1

59 Ranson R <u>The Kilmore Carols The Past Vol v Wexford 1949</u>

60 Ronan Myles V. <u>The Reformation in Ireland under Elizabeth</u> (Dublin 1930 p 484)

61 Sayers Peig Storyteller from the great Blasket Island

62 Shamrock The Vol 12 1875

63 <u>Sloane 3323 ff 288-289 Catalogue of Irish manuscripts</u>

64 Story Rev <u>Continuation of the Wars in Ireland</u> 1693

65 *Waterford Archaeological Journal April 1895*

66 Wheeler James Scott <u>Cromwell in Ireland</u> (Gill &McMillan

67 Wilde Lady (Esperanza) <u>Ancient Legends Mystic Charms and Superstitions</u> (London)

68 Wolfe Tone Authobiography.

National Folklore Collection Archive
University College Dublin
Belfield
Dublin 4
Ireland
Material collected from oral sources.
N.F.C. Vol. S 954 pp 76-78 Máire Nic Cassain, Threemilehouse An Gort Mór Co. Monaghan
N.F.C. Vol. S 955 p259, Collected from James McCague Tydavnet Co. Monaghan
N.F.C. Vol. 1238 p320 Mrs Joan Story Corrick, Clogher, Co. Tyrone
N.F.C. Vol. S 347 June 1937, Helen Lernihan, Langtrail, Crookstown,Co. Cork
N.F.C. Vol. S. 968. Mrs J Gallagher, Slievebrickin, Ballyconnell Co.Cavan
N.F.C. Vol. 448 PP 72-73. DUNTON LETTERS.
N.F.C. Vol. S 947.p 148 B Ó'Mórdha,Currin, Co. Monaghan
N.F.C. Vol. 104 p434 T O Babhartaigh, Cluain Uí Ruairc, Co. Leitrim
N.F.C. Vol. S 954 pp 76-78 Maire Nic Cassain, Threemilehouse, Drumsnatt Co,Monaghan
N.F.C. Vol. S 341 p 588 oide Pádraig Ó'Hanlúin from Peggy Morris, Sleaveen West Macroom Co. Cork
N.F.C. Vol. S 340 pp 53-54 Mr Denis Lane,farmer, Mountmusic Foumes Co. Cork
N.F.C. Vol. S.364 1937,J Sheahan, Ballygruddy, Kanturk Co. Cork.
N.F.C. Vol. 542 p 400 P O Harracháin, Kilnamanagh Upper, Cearnagh Toibrid Arainn
N.F.C. Vol. 407 pp 176-177 Peadar Mac Domhnaill, Ceapach na bFaoiteach, Tiobraid Árainn
N.F.C. Vol. S 219 p250 01-11-37=30-06-38 written by Martha McGure Dromard, Dromod, Co Leitrim told by Mrs Farrell
N.F.C. Vol 27 pp 86-91 Tadg O Murchadha M.G. An Coirréan, Co. Kerry
N.F.C. Vol. 925 Mrs Taggart p 278, Mochaire Gheal Co Antrim
N.F.C. Vol. 336 pp 195-209 A scriomh le Seán Ó hEochaidh, o béal Dónaí Ó'Brisláin, Leitir Mhic a'Bhaird, Co. Tirconnail
N.F.C. Vol 265 Keogh Mr Aughavanagh

Material from Béaloideas
Béaloideas Vol 5 no 2 (Nollaig 1935) pp 174-178, Wicklow Traditions of 1798, Michael Dwyer, Pádraig O'Tuathail